THE LOWER MANHATTAN PLAN

To New York City: past, present, future

THE LOWER MANHATTAN PLAN:

The 1966 Vision for Downtown New York

A reprint of the 1966 report by
the New York City Planning Commission

Carol Willis, Editor
Essays by Ann Buttenwieser,
Paul Willen and James Rossant

PRINCETON ARCHITECTURAL PRESS, NEW YORK
THE SKYSCRAPER MUSEUM, NEW YORK

Published by
Princeton Architectural Press
37 East Seventh Street
New York, New York 10003

For a free catalog of books, call 1.800.722.6657.
Visit our web site at www.papress.com.

Editor: Jennifer N. Thompson
Designer: Jan Haux

Special thanks to: Nettie Aljian, Ann Alter, Nicola Bednarek, Janet Behning,
Megan Carey, Penny Chu, Russell Fernandez, Clare Jacobson, Mark
Lamster, Nancy Eklund Later, Linda Lee, Jane Sheinman, Katharine
Smalley, Scott Tennent, and Deb Wood of Princeton Architectural Press
—Kevin C. Lippert, publisher

Library of Congress Cataloging-in-Publication Data
Buttenwieser, Ann L., 1935-
   The lower Manhattan plan : the 1966 vision for downtown New York /
introduction by Carol Willis ; essays by Ann Buttenwieser, Paul Willen,
and James Rossant.— 1st ed.
      p. cm.
   ISBN 1-56898-380-8 (pbk. : alk. paper)
   1. City planning—New York (State)—New York—History—20th century.
2. Manhattan (New York, N.Y.) I. Willen, Paul. II. Rossant, James S.,
1928- III. Lower Manhattan plan. IV. Title.
   NA9127.N5 B88 2002
   711'.4'097471—dc21
                              2002010899

TABLE OF CONTENTS

ACKNOWLEDGMENTS   6

INTRODUCTION   10
by Carol Willis

'FORE AND AFT: THE WATERFRONT
AND DOWNTOWN'S FUTURE   20
by Ann Buttenwieser

IN RETROSPECT   28
by Paul Willen and James Rossant

THE LOWER MANHATTAN PLAN

ACKNOWLEDGMENTS

The destruction of the World Trade Center forever marks "before and after" in the history of New York City and especially of Lower Manhattan. As we confront questions of how to memorialize the lost and of what kind of city life should return to the site, *The Lower Manhattan Plan* of 1966, an ambitious past projection of downtown's future, has great resonance.

The Skyscraper Museum, which since 1997 has mounted exhibitions in temporary venues in the financial district, was displaced from its gallery space on Maiden Lane by the events of 9/11. Shortly thereafter, we began to plan an exhibition that would pay tribute to the towers and explain their conception and construction in the context of New York of the 1960s. "WTC: Monument" was shown at The New-York Historical Society from February 5, to May 5, 2002, and we are grateful to the Society for offering us that space and opportunity. The idea to reprint *The Lower Manhattan Plan* arose from the exhibit and programs that accompanied it.

Research for the exhibition led to a number of people who helped me understand the dynamic that propelled the *Plan*. In particular, I am grateful to Paul Willen, one of the then-young architects who worked on the *Plan*. He and James Rossant, another member of the original team, have contributed their reflections here in the essay "In Retrospect." Donald Elliott and Elinor Guggenheimer also shared their thoughts on the New York City Planning Commission in those years.

My colleague Ann Buttenwieser has long studied Manhattan's waterfront and her experience as both historian and planner brings an invaluable perspective to her essay. Exhibitions and books require time and concentration, and I could not have accomplished them without the staff of The Skyscraper Museum who soldiered on through the sad fall of 2001: Laura Lee Pedersen, Lily Pollans, Mari Sakamoto-Nakahara, and Sueyoung Park, as well as our summer interns Ned Dodington and Alison Fraser. As always, Mark Willis paid the price in patience of a devoted spouse. At Princeton Architectural Press, Jennifer Thompson balanced patience and pressure to get things done, and Kevin Lippert earned my gratitude for agreeing that the effort was important.

The original format of *The Lower Manhattan Plan* was 11 3/8 inches square, a dimension that we have reduced slightly here, we think without losing legibility. The two-inch-thick report was plastic spiral-bound with a beige cardboard cover and contained one fold-out map, 22 3/4 inches square, that is not reproduced here: the image is a line drawing that is the basis for the color plate used as the cover of this book and is reproduced in black and white as the plate facing p. vii. According to the cover letter from the consultants, also printed here, only one hundred copies were prepared, which has made the document exceedingly rare. We hope that now it will be much better known. The copy we used for this reprint belongs to Paul Willen.

Carol Willis, Director
The Skyscraper Museum

View of Lower Manhattan from New York Harbor, August 3, 1956,
by Thomas Airviews. Courtesy The New-York Historical Society.
© Collection of The New-York Historical Society

View of Lower Manhattan from New York Harbor, May 5, 1976,
by Thomas Airviews. Courtesy The New-York Historical Society.
© Collection of The New-York Historical Society

INTRODUCTION
Carol Willis

Lower Manhattan through its history has been a site of both gradual, continuous change and of cataclysm. About a third of the city's buildings burned to the ground in the Great Fire of 1776 and again in 1835 and 1845, but in general, the process of destruction in New York has been intentional and creative—to replace the old with the new, the small with the large.

In the past, at least through the 1960s, this sort of change was most often considered progress. If this view is no longer widely held, the most likely reason is the reaction against the form of urban renewal practiced in the sixties and exemplified by the World Trade Center. The vast scale of the Twin Towers and of their sixteen-acre superblock site erased twelve blocks of old New York and drove the vibrant life of the street underground into an ordinary (though extraordinarily profitable) shopping mall. Other projects of the era such as the behemoth highrises at the southern end of Water Street exhibited the same "bigger is better" architectural sensibilities. Today, in the hometown of Jane Jacobs's civic activism— indeed, within sight of her sixties stoop—many consider the bulldozer urbanism that razed districts such as Radio Row and the Washington Market to have been a cataclysm by planners.

An alternate view of the era, advanced here, focuses not on what was destroyed, but on what was created. In the 1960s and 1970s, planners, politicians, architects, and engineers achieved no less than a reinvention of Lower Manhattan for the needs of the late twentieth century. Through an aggressive policy of urban renewal, they transformed an obsolete port and aging office district into a new financial center. They spurred a vast increase in office space—more than thirty million square feet—and added, eventually, ninety-two acres of new land at Battery Park City, placing residential development, parks, and recreational space at the river's edge.

This modernization answered an urgent need, for as the statistics and analysis of the 1966 *Lower Manhattan Plan* demonstrate, downtown was in danger of complete eclipse. A major problem was the exodus of corporate headquarters and jobs to midtown and beyond. Lower Manhattan held its status as the nation's largest central business district through the mid-1940s, but in the fifties and sixties, an array of signature glass towers on Park Avenue and Avenue of the Americas established the International Style as the image of modernity and success. The linear order of midtown's new corporate corridors presented a striking contrast to the irregular jumble of downtown's narrow streets and limestone canyons. Choked by traffic and challenged in every way by its congested physical conditions, downtown was in jeopardy.

Another overwhelming obstacle was the decaying waterfront, where a corset of finger piers bound the island's edge, constraining growth. Shipping in Lower Manhattan had been rendered obsolete, first by larger boats with deeper drafts, and from the late 1950s on, by the technological revolution of containerization, which required vast vacant spaces like the New Jersey lowlands to unload and store trailer-sized units. In

1966 only about a third of Lower Manhattan's piers were active. Still, the remnants of the working waterfront continued to exaggerate congestion, as cargo was unloaded onto the street. Elevated highways intended to improve flow further segregated the public from the rivers.

The extraordinary physical transformation of Lower Manhattan within just two decades is apparent in two Thomas Airviews photographs of 1956 and 1976. The earlier view shows a district that differed in no significant detail from the skyline of 1932, the year when the Cities Service Building (70 Pine Street), the last and the tallest of the cluster of great art deco towers, was completed. The oversupply of office space created in the 1920s and the stagnant or shrinking demand through the Great Depression and war years meant there was no market for new construction downtown through the 1940s. The first exemplar of International Style modernism would be 1 Chase Manhattan Plaza, commissioned in 1955, but not completed until 1961. The most antiquated aspect of the 1956 photo is the waterfront, distinguishable from early twentieth-century views only because there are fewer ships. Dozens of finger piers, close as teeth of a comb, created a zone between the river and shore that cut the city off from the water. At street level, imposing architectural portals secured the storage areas and prevented public access, while inland along West Street or on the east side along South Street, shabby low-rise structures of the nineteenth-century waterfront economy stretched for long blocks.

Flash forward twenty years: the Airviews photograph of 1976 shows an entirely new scale of construction overlaid on the district. The extreme examples were the Trade Center twins, which at 110 stories and more than 1360 feet were the tallest buildings in the world until Chicago's Sears Tower in 1974. Multiplying floor plates of nearly an acre, they each contained more than four million square feet of space, comprising the largest office complex anywhere. On the East River along Water Street, there was another range of new giants, high-rise containers of more than two and three million square feet, including 1 and 2 New York Plaza and 55 Water Street, which was heralded as the largest privately developed office building in the world. Another crop of major towers at the center of the district stands out in the 1976 photograph as black prisms of dark metal and tinted glass. These speculative buildings, stimulated by economic incentives from the city, added more than twenty million square feet of new space to the ten million created by the Port Authority at the World Trade Center.

The overpowering scale and volume of the new buildings was matched in boldness by the big blank slate of landfill in the Hudson destined to become Battery Park City and the World Financial Center. The piers were swallowed in the sands of an experiment in urban design that would take many iterations over the next decades, but was consistently conceived as a new neighborhood, planned to integrate business, residential, and recreational space. Already realized in 1976 were parts of the urban renewal projects north of the World Trade Center, for which more than twenty blocks of old warehouses and lofts had been razed; Independence Plaza North provided middle-income housing in a line-up of forty-story towers.

Like the results or not, one can see clearly in the photographs that Lower Manhattan changed dramatically in the 1960s and 1970s. Midtown changed, too—but it simply *grew*, driven by private investment and channeled and shaped by the new 1961 zoning code. Lower Manhattan did not just get taller, or larger, or more dense, as it had in past cycles: it was transformed and reinvented. How was this accomplished? Through the usual city-building dynamics of power and politics, to be sure, but within that, by planning and public policy.

The successful implementation of plans of the 1960s can be credited in large measure to an extraordinary confluence of power in the persons of the brothers Rockefeller, David and Nelson. As president of The Chase Manhattan Bank and the leader of the influential business organization, the Downtown-Lower Manhattan Association (DLMA), David Rockefeller was the key figure in the revival of downtown. By deciding to maintain the bank's headquarters in the financial district and erecting a signature sixty-story skyscraper, he stanched the out-migration of the banking and brokerage industry to midtown and anchored the future of the financial district for the rest of the twentieth century. The DLMA became active in many important initiatives, including the first schemes for a "World Trade Center," and they worked closely with the City Planning Commission, which officially embraced and advanced many of their proposals.

As governor of New York from 1958 to 1973, Nelson Rockefeller was able to deliver state support for large-scale projects. He represented the better half of the political muscle overseeing the bi-state agency, the Port Authority of New York and New Jersey (the developer of the World Trade Center), and he made the decision that the state of New York would become the anchor tenant, leasing 1.9 million square feet in the south tower. His pet plan downtown was Battery Park City, which was created in its first stage of landfill from the excavations for the Trade Center. In 1966 he worked directly with his favorite architect, Wallace K. Harrison, to propose a design for a new community of more than 60,000 residents and workers. (Fortunately, their austere *siedlung* slabs, marching in identical rows, soon gave way to other ideas.)

The instrumental role of the Rockefellers in the re-invention of Lower Manhattan should not be under-estimated, nor should it be overvalued. While the brothers could produce an impressive synergy of private-sector initiatives and public funding, the problems they sought to solve were far broader than their self-interest in protecting the family's real estate investments downtown, as some have contended. The sons of Standard Oil were certainly not the only players on the chessboard of Lower Manhattan.

The Port Authority itself was a considerable power that envisioned its mission of improving and modernizing the port and transportation facilities in increasingly ambitious terms. Established in 1921 to coordinate rail-freight planning, the Port of New York

Authority (the name was changed in 1972 to the Port Authority of New York and New Jersey) expanded its activities in the 1930s to include building and operating bridges and tunnels. With the toll revenues from the Holland and Lincoln tunnels and the George Washington Bridge, the Port Authority grew through "entrepreneurial vision and political power," to quote from the aptly titled history by Jameson Doig, *Empire on the Hudson*. In the 1940s, led by Executive Director Austin J. Tobin, the agency added the metropolitan airports and Newark harbor and piers to its base and built two regional truck terminals, as well as the world's largest bus terminal in midtown Manhattan. With a lucrative revenue stream and the power to issue bonds, the Port Authority had financial independence and the capacity to operate on the scale of a regional government—albeit with fewer checks and balances.

With its relative autonomy and willingness to act boldly, and for its deep, deep pockets, the Port Authority seemed a perfect partner for the plans for a World Trade Center advanced by the DLMA. In 1960 the DLMA promoted a design for a complex comprised of a large, low-rise trade mart, a securities exchange, and an office tower-*cum*-hotel of sixty or more stories to be built on thirteen and a half acres along the East River on a stretch of Water Street from Old Slip, north to Fulton Street. The Port Authority had tentatively agreed to develop that complex, but in 1961 the site shifted to the Hudson River waterfront in a political accommodation with New Jersey interests that required the agency to take over the bankrupt

Hudson and Manhattan Railroad and tubes and to operate them as the PATH commuter rail system. On those sixteen acres, the Port Authority began to design a building program that grew to ten million, and later to twelve million square feet, a volume that exceeded at that time the total downtown office space of Philadelphia, Los Angeles, or Boston. Such a venture into real estate conformed only obliquely to the agency's charter and was the subject of considerable criticism, especially by those with interests in "competitive buildings" (as privately financed commercial highrises were called by the industry). The Port Authority justified its ambitions with statements about strengthening and solidifying New York's position as the nation's largest port and the center for global commerce. Recognizing the unique capacity of the agency to build and finance a major new office district, the city reluctantly agreed to cede both control over the land and the annual property-tax revenues and to allow the Port Authority to erect the World Trade Center.

The other master planner and builder with both a regional reach and interests downtown was Robert Moses. In a career in public service that spanned the mid-1920s through the late 1960s, Moses was responsible for an unprecedented number of public works—parks and parkways, playgrounds, public housing, civic and cultural centers, hospitals, highways, world's fairs, and more—that will doubtlessly never be equalled. His empire was fashioned from twelve separate state and municipal offices, but especially from the tolls of the Triborough Bridge and Tunnel Authority, which, like its parallel at the Port Authority, provided an income stream and the capacity to issue bonds for the construction of new projects. An even greater source of funds was the mostly federal dollars accessed through highway and urban renewal projects. According to Robert Caro, counting "only those public works that he personally conceived and completed, from the first vision to ribbon cutting," Moses was responsible for projects costing $27 billion in 1968 dollars, the equivalent of $139 billion today. (*The Power Broker*, p. 9) His activities in Lower Manhattan were fairly limited: the Brooklyn-Battery Tunnel and public housing near the Brooklyn Bridge and along the East River. In 1966 he was still trying to plow the Lower Manhattan Expressway across Broome Street and the West Village, but was thwarted by community activists including Jane Jacobs. In 1968 his power was further undercut when Governor Rockefeller forced the Triborough Bridge and Tunnel Authority to merge with the Metropolitan Transit Authority, effectively ending his forty-year career as a master builder.

Moses and the Port Authority demonstrated that planning and construction on a vastly ambitious scale were possible. Through the mid-1960s, though, the City of New York had no master plan to coordinate its many large-scale urban renewal projects. Robert A. M. Stern has argued that this absence was largely due to the dominance of Moses, who "combined his official powers with the financial clout of federal funds to rebuild whole areas of the city, usurping the commission's role and planning the city with what was in effect no plan at all." (*New York 1960*, p. 40) What the City Planning Commission did accomplish in 1961 was a radical revision of the zoning code that among other provisions encouraged the modernist "tower in the plaza" formula and set a "floor-area ratio" (FAR) that substantially reduced the volume of space previously permitted on a given lot, limiting overall space in dense districts. This provision was not planning per se, but land-use regulation with an added dose of architectural aesthetics, aiming to create open space. It was, in fact, a potent tool for reshaping buildings, the skyline, and the streetscape of commercial districts, especially in Lower Manhattan's dense historic core.

As established by charter in 1936, the City Planning Commission was required to prepare a comprehensive plan, though none had ever been published. In 1959 the impetus for a master plan became greater when the federal government required one to maintain its urban renewal subsidies. *The Lower Manhattan Plan* of 1966 can be seen as a partial step toward an official master plan, which eventually was issued in 1969 as the *Plan for New York City*. That great, oversized six-volume set was produced during the Lindsay administration by the Department of City Planning, which had been enlarged and reorganized by Chairman Donald H. Elliott. He also formed the Urban Design Group and employed a stable of talented young architects and planners that has been admired since as an unparalleled moment of enlightened urban design.

Initiated under the previous administration of Mayor Robert F. Wagner and Commission Chairman William Ballard, the 1966 *Plan* was a worthy predecessor of the

Urban Design Group's standards. The project was not done in-house at the Department of City Planning, but was prepared as a report of outside consultants. As Paul Willen and James Rossant, two members of the architectural team, describe here in their essay, the three teams of consultants representing land use, architecture, and traffic studies collaborated with the staff of the Department of City Planning and representatives of the DLMA. They began work in March 1965 and in June 1966 delivered a 368-page spiral-bound document. Only a hundred copies were printed, so the report was clearly not intended for public distribution; however, it did garner the attention of professionals and the press. An admiring review in the *American Institute of Planners Journal* in July 1967 called the *Plan* "comprehensive, long-range, and exciting."

There was a burst of energy that erupted in the planning process, as Willen and Rossant describe in their reflections on the work, and this excitement seems apparent in the document. It is conveyed in the cover letter that delivered the *Plan* to Chairman Ballard when they refer to "the massive renaissance of Lower Manhattan," and it can be sensed in the maps and graphics, repeated in many variations, that outline the acres of interventions then underway or planned across the district. One sees this, for example, in Plates 19, 20, and 24 in the lines that inscribe the long swaths of projected new land on the water, shaded and labeled East and West Side "Opportunity Areas," in the arrows that indicate the "Expansion of the Core," or the circular lines radiating from the new office magnets showing desired waves of growth.

The year 1966 stands halfway between our pair of Thomas Airviews photographs of 1956 and 1976, and in many ways the *Plan* is a snapshot of sixties attitudes. There was great value given to modern design and little attention to potential landmark structures or existing context other than in the historic core of the financial district. Large scale and bold gestures were embraced, even while some skepticism was expressed about the oversized superblock of the World Trade Center complex. Urban renewal was seen as positive action.

There is little need to recount the points of this lucid study here, as they are clearly presented throughout and well worth reading. On page v there is a summary of nine goals, most of which are still relevant today. These include: strengthen the downtown business core, diversify its business life, and reduce its vulnerability to the decisions of a single institution; provide a powerful new magnet for housing in the core area; take maximum advantage of the great beauty of downtown's waterfront for residence and recreation; improve the working environment and public amenities; and improve mass-transit access to the region.

Of these perennially important issues, the idea for waterfront residential communities was the one most enthusiastically developed. The authors conceived a series of linked enclaves that could house 80,000 to 100,000 residents. The vision of a necklace of neighborhoods was presented in a number of bold maps and graphics, including the *Plan*'s only color drawing, which appears on the cover of this reprint. Six new neighborhoods centered on spacious plazas, great pie-shaped wedges that opened up to the water and connected to the older core by streets reserved for pedestrian use. (Plate 44) In the most striking architectural rendering, a scheme for the foot of Wall Street, they envisioned both low terraced structures and tall apartment towers surrounding a plaza and marina. (Part 1, Land Use) Each of these enclaves could contain a community of 10,000 to 15,000.

Another of the goals of the *Plan* was "to rationalize downtown transportation through maximum feasible separation of pedestrian, arterial, and service traffic." (p. v) A pedestrian zone was envisioned for Nassau Street (this has since been largely accomplished) and for Broad Street. One rendering imagined the area in front of the New York Stock Exchange and Federal Hall as an "open-sky subway station" and pedestrian mall—an idea one hopes might still be realized. (Plate 2–17) In 1966 there was serious discussion about moving the Stock Exchange to a modern facility on the East River, one of a variety of proposals for relocating the Exchange that never came to fruition and remain active issues today.

Many other images prepared for the *Plan* are of interest to students of New York history. The "Cross-Island Section," cut at Wall Street, compared the skyline in 1950 with the scale of the projected World Trade Center and new towers imagined for 1980. (Plate 28) Other drawings showed how landfill enlarged the island over four centuries. (Plates 26, 27) A map of the topography of Lower Manhattan showed the high

points near the city's first seat of government on the site of Federal Hall at Wall and Nassau streets and at the present-day City Hall. (Plate 25) Dozens of maps of Lower Manhattan gathered in the *Plan* presented information and analysis in categories that included: Pier Use and Condition; Building Age and Condition; Building Life Expectancy; an Employment Inventory; and Volumes of Traffic Flow. (Plates 19, 20, 22, 16, and 2-2, respectively) Printed mostly at the same scale (1:1,000), the maps make Lower Manhattan look manageable. Significantly, they also emphasize that it is one place that needs to be considered altogether in any planning agenda.

One place. In the wake of 9/11, that idea seems the primary relevance of the 1966 *Plan* for discussions of the future of Lower Manhattan. The boundaries of downtown's problems today stretch well beyond the sixteen acres of the World Trade Center site, and the solutions should be considered while assessing the strengths of the district and working to protect them. Downtown's assets include a dense, coherent office district that is both the nation's third-largest central business district (after midtown and Chicago) and a place of rich cultural heritage. It also embraces the distinctive communities of Chinatown, Tribeca, Battery Park City, among others. The historic core focuses on the Dutch street plan of New Amsterdam and preserves major nineteenth-century monuments including Trinity Church, Federal Hall, and the Merchants' Exchange at 55 Wall Street, but it is better known worldwide as the home of the New York Stock Exchange and the district's skyscraper canyons. Further north up Broadway, pre-Revolutionary St. Paul's Chapel, the glorious 1812 City Hall and its park, and the Woolworth Building record a history that is even older and more varied. As places to work, to live, and to visit, these landmarks and neighborhoods represent fundamental strengths of Lower Manhattan that should be protected and celebrated.

A second, not inconsistent lesson of the *Plan* is the need to adjust to new realities and to think boldly about change. This is what the 1960s planners did when they envisioned gracious new waterfront communities encircling the tip of the island where there were currently decaying piers. The obsolescence of Manhattan's shipping industry was their opportunity for the reinvention of the waterfront for residential and recreational uses, and that transformation would in turn create amenities for the white-collar workforce at the district's core. Before September 11—indeed, for nearly a decade before—technological and structural changes in the financial services industry, especially electronic trading, threatened to loose the New York Stock Exchange from its Wall Street moorings and to allow the district to drift elsewhere. How, or if, the city secures the markets somewhere in Lower Manhattan will be critical to its future. As part of this problem, the current paralysis of free movement in the Wall Street high-security zone will have to be ameliorated.

In a last, rather ironic parallel, the *Plan's* recommendation to sequence development and distinguish sources of funding seems relevant to the problem of rebuild-

ing at Ground Zero. The 1960s planners outlined priority zones for immediate and secondary actions and recommended three different sources of funding: public-private (which meant an authority such as Battery Park City), public, and private. The latter was referred to as "unassisted urban renewal" (p. xi), an odd term that underscores the dominant role of government money, especially federal dollars, in the development efforts at that time. (Plates 58, 59) Today, for the first time in more than twenty years, New York City is again receiving a huge infusion of federal dollars for urban renewal of a different sort. How these funds are spent will be critical. A model for what was, on the whole, a remarkable cooperation of state and municipal politicians, state and bi-state authorities, and public-private partnerships might well be found in the 1960s when many of the same parties came together to accomplish a transformation of much of Lower Manhattan.

Cities, especially great capitalist cities like New York, do not often grow by plans: they grow by market forces during periods when the economy is strong. During boom times, city government can generally only regulate or channel growth. When markets are weak or declining, planning can play a more important role. In the 1950s and 1960s, Lower Manhattan was a weak market in a strong economy because it was hobbled by the weight of its old technology. The obsolete waterfront and aging office stock of the historic core was a problem that could be remedied, or at least positively affected, by planning and public policy, and it was.

Many did not like the results, especially at the World Trade Center or along the East River, and that interpretation of failure is one reason the term "master plan" has not been used much in recent decades. Consensus-building is the goal to which planning aspires today, not mastery. Certainly, this process is seen in the efforts of "visioning" sessions, community meetings, and endless discussion and interest in Ground Zero in the press and media. To this end, a prediction of the 1966 *Plan* (p. 55) seems worth noting: "The future of Lower Manhattan will be determined more by what people want and take collective action to get, than by the unseen market forces whose cumulative impact is beyond the community's capacity to influence. This conclusion points up the critical role that planning can play and the importance of spelling out in the *Plan* the possible and appropriate goals."

'FORE AND AFT: THE WATERFRONT AND DOWNTOWN'S FUTURE

by Ann Buttenwieser

New York City was born of its harbor and its port, which, from its colonial foundations through the early twentieth century, was the basis of most of its jobs and wealth. The Dutch settled around the Battery in the early seventeenth century, eventually displacing the native inhabitants and by 1647 had built the first dock into the East River at Schreyer's Hook. As trading expanded under British rule, East River docks were filled with ships' ballast and excavation debris to create new ground space for homes and industry. With the invention and proliferation of steamboats and the opening of the Erie Canal in the early 1800s, the man-made profile of the lower West Side began to alter the natural meandering shoreline. A traditional English grid with blocks of residences, warehouses, and markets developed on landfill from which finger piers extended out into the Hudson River. By the Civil War, Lower Manhattan had been enlarged by a third, with West Street and South Street demarcating the outer limits. (Plate 27)

As shipping and its associated services expanded the edge of the island and began to dominate its space and activity, the owners of gracious homes on the rivers moved northward, first to the area of Union Square, then to the areas of Twenty-third Street, Thirty-fourth Street, and midtown. This migration left downtown almost totally to business and commerce. By the 1890s, tall office buildings on lower Broadway housed shipping and insurance companies and other captains of industry, while bankers, brokers, accountants, and lawyers clustered in high-rise buildings in the heart of the financial district at Wall and Broad streets. In the

early 1910s, Lower Manhattan boasted a skyline of towers such as the Singer and Woolworth buildings that symbolized the rise of American corporate capitalism and ranked as new wonders of the world.

By the end of the First World War, the competing sectors of finance at the core, and shipping and industry at the edges made downtown a very challenging place to do business. Narrow, winding, interior streets were clogged with office workers, vendors, curb traders, and those attempting to deliver supplies. Near the water, commerce caused congestion and interfered with the overall flow of traffic. Cargo was stored in the streets, awaiting pick-up. Carts and trucks often waited for days along the West Street and South Street docks to load and unload their merchandise.

Lower Manhattan's piers were already in decline in the 1920s, with many of the Hudson and East River docks ill-suited or too small to handle modern vessels. Ninety percent of docking facilities were located in New York City, while most rail lines ended, or began, in New Jersey. When the major market was the city itself, this arrangement made sense, but as Kenneth T. Jackson has observed, for New York City as the entrepôt to a national market, "The irony bordered on the incredible: The world's busiest harbor was not designed for direct rail-water shipment." (in Doig, *Empire on the Hudson*, introduction, p. xvi) To address this problem, in 1921 a compact between New York State and New Jersey created the Port of New York Authority whose mission was to keep the harbor competitive by coordinating and modernizing terminals and transportation. Over the next decades the Port Authority built and managed its portfolio of bridges, tunnels, and terminal facilities so successfully that the City of New York agreed in the 1940s to cede its airports to the agency and the jurisdiction over some shipping and passenger docks in the 1970s. Throughout this period, the New York City agency, the Department of Docks (so called until a name change in 1942 to the Department of Marine and Aviation, and in 1969 to the Department of Ports and Terminals), had pursued a policy of modernization of facilities, especially in the outer boroughs, but most of the ambitious plans remained unbuilt. (Betts, p. 79 in Kevin Bone, ed., *The New York Waterfront*)

In the 1920s the growth in the downtown economy was concentrated in the financial district where in a boom of construction at the end of the decade, nearly a quarter of all the properties around Wall and Broad streets were demolished and replaced by bigger buildings. A new crop of skyscrapers, slender fifty- to seventy-story spires punctuated a skyline also transformed by new setback, ziggurat-like structures that conformed to the regulations of the 1916 zoning code. From 1925 to 1932 downtown added an astonishing ten million square feet of new office space. Most of that came onto the market as the economy spiralled into the Great Depression, with the result that many of the new buildings suffered a decade of high vacancies and did not see black ink until the 1940s.

Lower Manhattan's spiky skyline remained unaltered and iconic until the late 1950s, while midtown began a dramatic change, adding a series of gleaming glass towers on Park Avenue that set the style of postwar modernity. The exodus of big banks and corporate headquarters to midtown was a major concern. The action that stemmed that flow was the construction of 1 Chase Manhattan Plaza, the flagship of The Chase Manhattan Bank and downtown's first stylistically and technologically modern skyscraper. Designed by Gordon Bunshaft of Skidmore, Owings & Merrill, the sixty-story slab was clad in glass and white aluminum and rose in the center of an open plaza that covered what had been a four-block parcel of densely built blocks between Liberty, Nassau, Pine, and William streets. Completed in 1961, 1 CMP added nearly two million square feet of first-class office space, using only about sixty percent for its own purposes and renting the remainder.

The key figure in Chase's decision to invest in a new downtown headquarters was David Rockefeller, president of the bank and also the leader of the Downtown-Lower Manhattan Association (DLMA), a powerful alliance of the business leaders of the major banks and brokerage houses. As described in the Introduction and the Willen and Rossant essay, the DLMA initiated many of the proposals to revitalize downtown, and its power was buttressed and multiplied by Nelson Rockefeller, who as governor could deliver state funds.

Even the confluence of Rockefeller power, though, could not turn back the tide of technology in the harbor. Containerization, a 1950s technological revolution, spelled the end of Manhattan's maritime waterfront. This new method of shipping used huge, deep-draft ships to move cargo that was piled high on decks in metal containers that were the size of, or actually were, railroad cars and truck trailers. Such vessels required wide berths, not finger piers, as well as acres of open land to stack and store containers (as in New Jersey). With giant cranes to move the tonnage rather than an army of stevedores breaking up batches, a container ship could be unloaded in under twenty-four hours instead of the old standard, twelve days.

By 1965 Lower Manhattan's working waterfront had largely disappeared. Of fifty-one piers, all but seven had been built at the turn of the century, and only about a third (eighteen) were active. Parking often had become the highest and best use. The Staten Island and Governor's Island ferries were all that remained of a once-vibrant waterborne passenger transport system. Industry, too, was on the wane. Textile manufacturers, once situated around Hudson and Canal streets, had relocated to the West Thirties. In a project initiated in the late 1950s, the city demolished the former Washington Market wholesale produce facilities (on the site of the future World Trade Center) and relocated the market to modern facilities at Hunt's Point in the Bronx. Even the status of the historic Fulton Fish Market, located at Fulton Street since 1825, was in doubt—it, too, was likely to move to the Bronx.

But there were also signs of regeneration. Sparked by the financial-center lead, civic center and waterfront rejuvenation were announced. A federal office building and plaza would be built three blocks north of City Hall, and, not least, the World Trade Center, the city's and world's tallest towers, would rise along West Street. To the west of the towers lay the Hudson River and a mile of unused piers. Here was an area ripe for the landfill from Trade Center excavations. In response to the opportunity to once again widen Manhattan, a study commissioned in 1962 by the Department of Marine and Aviation recommended adding a new appendage to the city. A hotel, thirteen "executive" apartment towers of twenty stories, offices, a yacht basin, and public open space were to rise on sixty-five acres of landfill between Battery Park and Chambers Street.

The Department of City Planning published its *Lower Manhattan Plan* in June 1966. On the one hand, this was a codification of much of the prior thinking and recognition of the totality of projects on the drawing boards, planned in an ad hoc manner and as yet unbuilt. In others ways, it was downtown's first coherent blueprint for the future.

The original intention was to prepare a traffic study to alleviate the intolerable congestion. A new circulation plan envisioned three systems separating cars, delivery vehicles, and pedestrians. Led by transportation experts Alan M. Voorhees & Associates, the team was augmented with the expertise of the planning firm of Wallace, McHarg, Roberts, and Todd and architects Whittlesey, Conklin, and Rossant, and the traffic planning quickly gave way to broader interests. Seizing on the opportunity presented by the hundred-foot-deep excavations for the World Trade Center and the models already recommended by the 1966 Stock Exchange plans, as well as by the Marine and Aviation Battery Park City proposals, the planners switched the focus away from traffic alone to an expansion of Lower Manhattan at its waterfront. Between the bulkhead and pierhead lines on the Hudson and East rivers, south of Canal Street on the west and the Brooklyn Bridge on the east, the planners envisioned a whole new territory to resolve transportation problems and to address other needs.

Planners tackled the shrinking job market and the lack of residential choice by recommending the creation of six riverside development areas containing housing, commercial, and office space for eighty-five thousand residents and half a million workers. They hoped to improve the quality of life for transients and residents alike with waterfront plazas, each at the termination of an east-west street, and they envisioned abundant public open space, including three large riverfront parks connected by a continuous esplanade encircling the tip of the island.

There would even be traffic relief. The elevated Miller Highway on the west and East River Drive would both be demolished, and the cars would disappear underground on new expressways under the landfill. The enormous costs of depressed highways was to be partly financed from the sale of air rights. New pedestrian zones included a continuous esplanade along the riverfront, as well as the closing of many upland streets to traffic.

At its release the *Plan* was hailed as "the most important in the city's history since the original gridiron streets were laid out in 1811." Ada Louise Huxtable of The New York Times reviewed it as a "powerful, imaginative stimulant." Commenting on the comprehensive approach and redevelopment strategy, another critic claimed the *Plan* was "just what New York so desperately needs." The image that captured the reviewers' imaginations was of "windows on the waterfront," a term that had been used in the 1930s to justify clearing slums on the Lower East Side.

Such lavish praise seems surprising today when many of the assumptions of the *Plan* have become alien to standard planning principles. There was no question, for example, about the viability of landfill. This, after all, was how Lower Manhattan had been built over three hundred years. Historic preservation and the idea of the rehabilitation of old buildings, or "adaptive reuse," was still in its infancy in New York. It was only at the last minute, through the efforts of South Street Seaport Museum founder Peter Stanford, that the Schemerhorn Row buildings, standing alone among the renewed waterfront blocks, were included on the *Plan*. No remorse was expressed, however, for the loss of the landmarks of the city's early skyscraper history such as the Richard Morris Hunt's pioneering Tribune Building or Joseph Pulitzer's World Building on "Newspaper Row," demolished for the urban renewal district south of the Brooklyn Bridge.

The street patterns and building scale that were called for by the *Plan* were out of context with the existing area fabric. The grid was ignored save for six Lower Manhattan streets that were to continue into the newly designed waterfront plazas. Once inside the new neighborhoods, the geometry and building volumes had little to do with the character of old Manhattan; rather, the model was more in keeping with the scale of the World Trade Center. The planners imagined an interconnected megastructure of sorts, a "town-within-a-town" where workers, tourists, and residents would be able to move from highway to underground garage to office, shop, park, or home, barely knowing they were in Lower Manhattan.

The *Plan* was embraced by the Lindsay administration, which established the Mayor's Office of Lower Manhattan Development to implement it. One area of focus was the Water Street Access Corridor where the city encouraged the construction of jumbo highrises that would provide acres of affordable back office space for large corporations. By 1970, 1 and 2 New York Plaza and 55 Water Street were completed or under construction, creating more than six million square feet of new space, and others followed. Without landfill, Water Street was the outermost thoroughfare unencumbered by an elevated highway. Plans were also progressing for the reuse and renewal of the South Street Seaport buildings and Pier 17.

There was also considerable interest in Manhattan Landing, as the proposed East River landfill between the Manhattan Bridge and the Staten Island Ferry terminal was called. The Tishmans, a New York realty and construction family, were working on a plan for new

housing, shops, and offices in the river immediately south of the Seaport. De Matteis, another construction firm, eyed Pier 6 at Coenties Slip, and the Stock Exchange continued to discuss using the river at the foot of Wall Street for its new establishment.

The planners considered it important to connect the new designs on the landfill with the historic street pattern. To this end, they set up special zoning districts for Battery Park City, the Seaport, and Manhattan Landing that required view corridors to the water. On the west side, elevated pedestrian cross streets were outlined to connect the old and new city without interference from north-south traffic. They also created a system of open space to tie the developments together, mapping public rights-of-way within each special district to assure connections among the new projects.

The Office of Lower Manhattan Development worked with the architectural firm of Venturi, Rauch, and Scott Brown to design the first piece of an esplanade system for an area where they felt private development was unlikely. A widened bulkhead on landfill would connect existing Lower East Side neighborhoods at the northern end of Manhattan Landing with the to-be-filled land south of the Brooklyn Bridge. A fish-shaped platform would be built in the river and would hold much-needed ballfields and seating; a floating playground and swimming pool would be attached to form its tail.

With several public and private designs for East River developments proposed, a major concern arose over how best to extend the shoreline without narrowing the East River or affecting its currents and salinity. Using an ingenious simulation of the New York estuary created by the U.S. Army Corps of Engineers, the designers constructed scale models of landfills and platforms. They then injected dye into sewer outfall replicas to test which of the land changes had the least effect on the waterway. Platforms on pilings won hands down.

With that issue theoretically out of the way, the planners debated the type of housing for the new neighborhoods. All agreed with the recommendation for a mixed community; the question was which group should come first? Federal and state subsidies were available for low- and middle-income housing, and studies revealed that demand was high for such apartments in Lower Manhattan. Yet the attraction of "windows on the water" and walk-to-work convenience for Wall Street executives was obvious, and creating market-rate housing and a self-supporting community, some argued, would not deplete the limited funds available for other neighborhoods totally dependent on housing subsidies. Such an upper-income strategy could also have economic benefits if convenience for Wall Street decision-makers might mean keeping thousands of jobs in the city. Underlying these justifications was an unspoken dilemma: if the pioneer tenants in these new neighborhoods were poor, wealthier residents might never move in.

The point was made moot by the fiscal crisis of the mid-1970s when all plans were on hold. Resurgence in the 1980s put much of the *Plan* back on track. Development on the west side began in earnest under the public-development entity the Battery Park City Authority, which brought together state and federal assistance and extensive private investment. The first residential neighborhood at the southern end of the area created apartment towers erected by private developers according to urban design guidelines by Alexander Cooper and Stanton Ekstut. In the mid-1980s the suite of four major towers of the World Financial Center, designed by Cesar Pelli and developed by Olympia and York, rose at the center of the Battery Park City site and directly west of the World Trade Center, extending and strengthening that office core along the lines envisioned in the 1966 *Plan*. The elevated Miller Highway was demolished downtown and replaced—not by Westway, the long-discussed, but aborted plan of the 1970s for a depressed highway covered by a park, but, at grade, by the intimidating expanse of the multi-lane West Street.

On the east side, the South Street Seaport opened and more office towers lined Water Street. Another potential icon, South Ferry Plaza, was designed to finish off the southern tip of the island. Without developer interest and the administrative structure to guide them, though, plans for the East River appendages never materialized. South Ferry Plaza along with the rest of Manhattan Landing (scaled back and renamed East River Landing) became the victims of the next recession. The Wall Street tennis bubbles replaced the often-discussed financial exchange. This waterfront, now without landfill, failed to be woven into the fabric of Lower Manhattan. The Water Street towers pushed out the commercial downtown to the edge in a great wall, but did keep open the view corridors to the old city. Unfortunately, the elevated East River Drive, with blocks of parking lots and lines of tour buses underneath, continues to separate the core activities from the river.

The real estate lull caused by another recession that began after the stock market crash in 1987 provided an opportunity to reevaluate the *Lower Manhattan Plan* and to devise an updated blueprint for the future. In 1993, under the administration of Mayor David Dinkins, the Department of City Planning published another *Plan for Lower Manhattan*. What is most striking about this document is its recognition that, in fact, the 1966 *Plan* had succeeded. Wall Street—despite ups and downs—was flourishing; foreign banking and service jobs had replaced maritime and blue-collar industries. The residential population had grown from 833 in 1970, to about 14,000 people, and tourism had become a major source of economic activity. Since then, the northern residential section of Battery Park City has been steadily adding apartment towers. Its park area is almost fully developed, and it is linked to the state-funded Hudson River Park that continues up the west side to Fifty-ninth Street. New esplanades and bikeways have been built piecemeal along the East River, and there are plans for further consolidation. Battery Park City and the World Financial Center had transformed what the 1960s planners had described as "obsolete and often dilapidated piers, the blight of the elevated expressways, sprawling

parking lots" into a vibrant community. From the North Cove marina, yachts, tour boats, ferries, water taxis, and recreational sailboats define a new image of the waterfront.

The near-idyll of Battery Park City with its verdant parks, active playgrounds, and varied population of residents, office workers, recreationists, and tourists was jolted to reality on September 11, 2001 and is still recovering its senses. Oddly, only the offices in the east-facing sides of the World Financial Center remain constant eyewitnesses to the void of the World Trade Center site, although the emptiness is visible from all over the city and the region. A landmark of loss now lies at the heart of downtown, and one hopes it will not inhibit its future.

An earlier version of this essay appeared in the Fall 1991 issue of Seaport, *the magazine of the South Street Seaport Museum in New York City. Thanks to Carol Willis for her contributions to this essay. For further history on New York City's waterfront, see Ann Buttenwieser,* Manhattan Water-Bound: Manhattan's Waterfront from the Seventeenth Century to the Present *(New York, 1987; 1999).*

IN RETROSPECT

by Paul Willen and James Rossant

I.

It is now nearly forty years since Lower Manhattan, the cradle of the city, was given the opportunity to reinvent itself. The first move, in the early 1960s, came from the confluence of extraordinary political and financial power that generated the World Trade Center.

The second move, in the mid-1960s, was the transformation, by a group of design consultants hired by the city, of a modest traffic study into a breathtaking glimpse of a vast new waterfront development that would stem from, and rejuvenate, the historic core of towers whose jagged pyramidal silhouette had become the very definition of modern business. This conversion of the downtown waterfront into a twenty-four-hour residential and business community was the first of many such projects in cities across America.

We were among the multi-disciplinary consultants who, by some stroke of fortune, were given the opportunity to initiate this plan—a chance that, in scale and significance, would not occur again in our lifetimes. Plates 26–28 (after page 30) in our report dramatically illustrate the growth of Lower Manhattan, beginning in the seventeenth century as the island's shoreline was pushed, century by century, steadily into the two great rivers.

But this was the first attempt to control this outward expansion with an urban plan. This bold initiative from city planning was an event in itself. It came in late 1964, one year prior to the John Lindsay administration, when urban design truly came to the fore. In this sense, the *Plan* foreshadowed much of what was to come.

The work was presided over by then-Chairman of the Planning Commission William Ballard, a distinguished architect, tall and handsome, with an imperious old New York manner. At that time the department was not yet the glamorous agency it was to become under Lindsay, but a strong and respectable one, armed with the power of Mayor Robert Wagner's own considerable authority. The fee for our work was $150,000—more than $850,000 in today's currency—which was thought to be a good sum in those days.

Nevertheless, considering this a unique opportunity, we substantially overran the budget.

At the kickoff meeting in March 1965, held in Ballard's spacious office, we recall the following people: Ballard and his aides Jack Smith and Art Wrubel, and from our side, besides ourselves, Bill Conklin, Alan Voorhees, and David Wallace. John Goodman of the Downtown-Lower Manhattan Association, a key player, was there also. Ballard was in good form, sensing that we were on the verge of something significant, and letting us know that he expected an independent report representing our own true findings.

II.

The original impetus for the *Plan* was a "reinvention" that rivaled the World Trade Center in ambition and sweep, but was thwarted almost from the start: a civic center encompassing a gigantic new half-mile park—

stretching from Park Row northward all the way to Worth Street—focused on a monumental tower, designed by Ed Stone, in which the entire city government was to be consolidated. An eminent transportation engineer, Alan Voorhees, was hired to solve the horrendous traffic problems that would be created by this superblock. A well-known planning firm based in Philadephia, Wallace, McHarg, Roberts, and Todd was retained to make land-use sense of the new superblock. And finally, as the idea grew in scope to take in the waterfront as well, an urban design team, Conklin Rossant, fresh from designing the Reston newtown, was brought on to give the whole thing clarity and visual scope.

The superblock and Ed Stone's supertower, lacking powerful supporters outside the city itself, never went anywhere and died a fairly quick death.

Notwithstanding, a whole section of our report was devoted to the examination of a series of underground vehicular tunnels penetrating the civic superblock. But by that time this lofty vision—serene in its vast green setting—was transferred to the planners of an even more ambitious superblock and an even more powerful vertical mission.

Thus, by the time our planning team was assembled and set up, it was clear that our major challenge was not the city's dying superblock but the waterfront and its immense opportunities. The piers on both rivers had been abandoned, affecting much of the upland area as well. The entire swath of land cried out for a plan that would reuse the pier area and its upland, and thereby revitalize the historic core.

In the early phases of our work, David Wallace's partner, Ian McHarg, the author of the epochal work *Design With the Land*, joined us. He was appalled by the broad scope of our urban vision, and particularly by our readiness to reshape the Hudson River itself. He felt that, if anything had to be built at all, it should be a naturalistic park around the tip of Manhattan. Failing to deter us, he dropped out of our discussions. In time, he and David Wallace would go their separate ways.

The work of our team was done in a large loft rented for the joint venture, above a luncheonette at Seventeenth Street and Broadway. Many disciplines were involved, including an economist, Chuck Laidlaw, who evaluated the viability of each of Lower Manhattan's economic components—many of which no longer exist as coherent neighborhoods, such as the Butter, Eggs, and Cheese wholesale district, now Tribeca, and the Insurance district centered on Pine and John streets, now largely relocated.

The question of the peripheral highway system was heavily debated. The City Planning Department liaison continually cautioned us against what he considered extreme solutions. Nevertheless, we drew up a plan for depressing the highways on both rivers, with linkages at the surface at limited but key points. Studying the alternative locations, it soon became obvious that the depressed road should be inboard at the inner side of the landfill.

III.

The role of the *Plan* itself was complex. We said that we were providing a "framework for decisions," not an explicit plan, and indeed, it was the framework that proved useful in the decades to come and not so much the formal design proposals. This framework provided a new vision of a continuous edge of waterfront buildings broken by tower clusters, forming tight little communities connected to the historic core. This diagram has been criticized as a megaform solution, but in fact it was meant to match, in its linear strength, the boldness and power of Lower Manhattan. In time, this would evolve into the more conventional reworking of Manhattan's historic residential grain, with its nostalgic recall of Park Avenue of the 1920s. While the goal was to duplicate the land-use diversity of midtown, we believed that, architecturally, Lower Manhattan deserved its own characteristic style.

The framework—so far mostly applied along the Hudson River—was realized to a large extent, unlike many visionary plans. It consisted of a series of plazas and coves at well-defined intervals corresponding to key existing streets, which defined the several waterfront communities and tied them back into the historic core (and its subway intervals). Indeed, these spaces sprang from the historic core itself with its teeming canyons.

These "openings to the waterfront" occurred at the World Trade Center, Rector Street, and the Battery, and represented a strong response to the river as a rediscovered element in urban life, creating a structure for our ambitious transportation plan. A similar series of openings was staked out on the east side at Wall, Fulton, and Broad streets—but these remain to be realized. (Indeed, the vast Gehry Guggenheim Museum plan would close off the very interior connections to the water to which we attached such importance.) We proposed Hudson-to-East River pedestrian connections at Rector, Wall, and Fulton streets, which are now under study again as part of the AIA "New Visions" project following the collapse of the World Trade Center.

The key transportation improvement recommended by the *Plan* was the depressing of today's surface and elevated peripheral roads from Canal Street on the Hudson around the Battery to the Brooklyn Bridge on the East River; thereby allowing easy access from the canyons of Lower Manhattan to the east and west promenades, and the plazas, shops, restaurants, museums, and theaters closely linked to the waterfront communities. This important idea in our plan remains a high priority in thinking about downtown's future.

We recommended a special governmental official, David Wallace, to implement the plan. He provided a strong case for the economics of our complex proposals, adding a "decision tree" to guide us in our endeavors. The Lindsay administration, which came to power in 1965, established the Office of Lower Manhattan Development, whose initial charge was simply to build this very plan! Dick Buford was the first director, and in time, as conditions changed, this office became part of the larger urban design effort then underway. The development organization we had envisaged came later in the mid-1970s.

IV.

The World Trade Center was a conundrum for us. On the one hand, we were highly critical of its inhuman scale, its sharp break with the historic core and the downtown street pattern, its turning away from the waterfront (still dominated by grim, crumbling piers when the twin towers were planned), and its barren plaza sitting over a dense internal shopping center. On the other hand, we recognized its potential as a welcome engine of growth for downtown—successful enough, as it turned out, to cause the relocation of the proposed new office center from the southern tip of Battery Park City (as originally pushed by Nelson Rockefeller) to a position in the new landfill directly west of the World Trade Center.

We tried (in vain) to show the towers as a harbinger of a new scale that might mediate between the historic core and the towering structure. We did not foresee the iconic vision and authority these giant buildings came, in time, to assume. The sheer size and audacity of the entire undertaking—unprecedented anywhere in the world—created its own value system, making its many great failings seem almost trivial.

Indeed, the impact of the World Trade Center was positive from the very start. The original plan for the disposal of the enormous excavation of the seventy-foot-deep "bathtub" was to haul it by barge well out into the Atlantic. In a meeting with the Port Authority, we suggested instead using it as the initial landfill for Phase I of our proposed waterfront development. To save costs, the Port Authority agreed to our proposal to simply truck it across West Street, providing the basis for Battery Park City. Thus the two moves came together.

Among the current studies of the rebuilding of Lower Manhattan, some have recalled the 1966 *Plan* itself, especially the improved transit and the depressing of the highways, starting with the area adjacent to the devastated blocks. Four decades later, there may yet be a second chance for *The Lower Manhattan Plan*.

THE LOWER MANHATTAN PLAN

The Lower Manhattan Plan

NEW YORK CITY CAPITAL PROJECT ES-1

Wallace-McHarg Associates
Whittlesey & Conklin
ARCHITECTS AND PLANNERS

Alan M. Voorhees & Associates, Inc.
TRANSPORTATION AND PLANNING CONSULTANTS

23 East 17th Street, New York, New York 10003
Telephones: 212 / 675-1816, 675-1780

June 1, 1966

William F. R. Ballard
Chairman
City Planning Commission
2 Lafayette Street
New York, New York

Dear Chairman Ballard:

In fulfillment of the Contract with the City of New York, dated February 23, 1965, herewith is the Technical Report in 100 copies called for.

Our Report has addressed itself to the two major themes outlined in the original Contract: the land use and circulation problems raised by the massive renaissance in Lower Manhattan, and the new development opportunities, especially the proper reuse of the waterfront.

The purpose of the study was to develop a framework of policies "to enable the City to respond creatively to private initiative and to guide public activities so that this area reaches its great potential."

With your assistance, and the participation of your staff, we have, we believe, developed such a framework -- ambitious enough in scope to match the past achievements of Lower Manhattan, but practical enough to be translated into immediate realizable action.

DAVID A. WALLACE
Wallace, McHarg, Todd and Roberts

WILLIAM J CONKLIN
Whittlesey Conklin & Rossant

ALAN M. VOORHEES
Alan M. Voorhees & Associates, Inc.

THE LOWER MANHATTAN PLAN

CAPITAL PROJECT ES-1

Wallace, McHarg, Roberts, and Todd
ARCHITECTS AND PLANNERS, PHILADELPHIA

Whittlesey, Conklin and Rossant
ARCHITECTS AND PLANNERS, NEW YORK

Alan M. Voorhees & Associates, Inc.
TRANSPORTATION AND PLANNING CON-
SULTANTS, WASHINGTON, D.C.

PREPARED FOR

THE NEW YORK CITY PLANNING COMMISSION

William F. R. Ballard, Chairman

Francis J. Bloustein, Vice Chairman
Harmon H. Goldstone
Elinor C. Guggenheimer
Lawrence M. Orton
Beverly M. Spatt
James G. Sweeney

Richard K. Bernstein, Executive Director

TABLE OF CONTENTS

Summary of Findings and Proposals   iii

CHAPTER I
Introduction and Summary --------------------- 1

PART I - LAND USE

CHAPTER II
Background and Setting ------------------------ 5

CHAPTER III
Structures and Building Sites -------------------- 25

CHAPTER IV
Current and Committed Projects ----------------- 35

CHAPTER V
Goals for Lower Manhattan --------------------- 55

CHAPTER VI
Development of Land Use and Circulation Plans ---- 65

CHAPTER VII
The East Side Case Study ----------------------- 91

CHAPTER VIII
Optimum Development and Next Steps ----------- 101

PART II - TRANSPORTATION

CHAPTER IX
Introduction -------------------------------- 1

CHAPTER X
Street Traffic -------------------------------- 5

CHAPTER XI
Functional Classification of Streets -------------- 11

CHAPTER XII
Recommendations ------------------------- 17

CHAPTER XIII
Subways ------------------------------------ 23

PART III - APPENDICES

a) LAND USE

APPENDIX I
Structures of Permanent Value ----------------- 1

APPENDIX II
Composite Block Evaluation ------------------- 7

APPENDIX III
Neighborhood Development Areas -------------- 17

APPENDIX IV
Depressed Highway: Construction Problem
and Costs -------------------------------- 21

b) TRANSPORTATION

APPENDIX A

APPENDIX B

APPENDIX C

c) REPORT ORGANIZATION

Interview Sources

List of Graphics

List of Tables

Organization of Report

SUMMARY OF REPORT

This is a Plan for Lower Manhattan: for its business core, its transportation facilities, its waterfront and its land, for its place in the Manhattan Central Business District and in the metropolitan region as a whole.

It is thus not merely a project, or even a series of projects, but a system of development, on an area-wide scale, in which every phase of downtown life is related in an overall process of planning and change.

The Plan begins with an analysis of the inner city: historic downtown, the financial district, with its great canyons, its dense network of subway lines, its position in the national economy. Long-term goals are outlined for this Core, as well as for the surrounding areas. Areas of growth and change are demarked and formed into a coordinated pattern in which each improvement has a related and multiplying effect.

Proposals for the new waterfront are set within the context of this analysis: each link in the conceptual plan - pedestrian routes, waterfront plazas, the peripheral highway, the housing and office groupings - are all related to the Core, as well as to each other.

The result then is not simply another project, which can be accepted or rejected, depending on time and circumstance, but rather a general strategy for the redevelopment and growth of an area; an approach, a process and an organizing concept. Development can occur, within the framework of guiding principles, in a number of different ways, at different times in different places.

New York has not, in recent generations, developed such area-wide plans. But increasing positive achievement and hence competition from other urban areas, and the ever more turbulent needs of this City, make the establishment of higher goals and coordinated planning achievement mandatory.

Lower Manhattan was chosen for such a study because it is an area undergoing rapid change, and an area of unique strengths immediately adjacent to great opportunities. This Report confirms that judgement and points out a way of realization. The great strengths of the area make possible a plan that can be achieved largely without public assistance. The opportunities clearly point to an incomparable working and living environment.

THE PROBLEMS

Today Lower Manhattan is undergoing a series of massive changes which may alter many of its functions and revamp its patterns of circulation.

Sparked by such projects as the Chase Manhattan Bank, the Civic Center, the World Trade Center, downtown is in the midst of a significant enlargement of its office capacity. Two urban renewal projects -- Brooklyn Bridge Southwest and the Washington Street Renewal -- represent "beachheads" of new institutional and residential functions hitherto largely unknown in the area.

But in spite of these signs of strength, Lower Manhattan's position remains vulnerable in many respects, and its potential value to the City still not fully realized.

Its problems can be summarized in three categories: Problems of 1) function, 2) environment and 3) access and movement.

Problems of Function:

Although office expansion has been substantial in recent years, downtown's rate of growth has by no means matched midtown's. As a working environment, Lower Manhattan cannot today successfully compete with Midtown, with its rich diversity of facilities. Furthermore, in spite of the office expansion, downtown's employment seems to be declining -- from about 400,000 in 1960 to about 375,000 in 1965. As a business community composed of a handful of functions, it is exceedingly vulnerable to the decisions of a few powerful institutions and businesses.

Downtown's peripheral areas (mostly goods-handling in character) are in continued and sharp decline. Of the 51 piers on the two rivers, only 18 are in fairly regular use, and all but seven over 50 years old. Of downtown's three waterfront markets, one is moving out (fruit and vegetables) and another is scheduled for future relocation (fish). Other historic downtown functions (textiles, butter and eggs) are contracting, and the number of blue-collar jobs has declined by perhaps 35,000 in the last ten years.

Problems of Environment:

At the periphery, the remnants of once-thriving goods-handling

industries, produce an uncongenial atmosphere: obsolete and often dilapidated piers, the blight of the elevated expressways, sprawling parking lots, heavy truck traffic. In the Core, an absence of noontime amenities, attractive open space, employee diversions: a reasonably good subway system made un comfortable by grim, poorly organized stations and poor connections.

Problems of Access and Movement:

The complex of narrow canyon-streets (a natural pedestrian precinct) must also handle the servicing of a gigantic business activity, generating a serious conflict between the pedestrian and the vehicle. The intrusion of heavy volumes of traffic on and off the Brooklyn Bridge dominates traffic movement in the entire Civic Center area, posing serious problems, especially for the proposed new superblock.

The transit system is designed primarily to serve the older areas of the city, and operates poorly in relation to the areas to the north and east, where the growing professional and managerial class is increasingly concentrated.

SUMMARY OF GOALS

Lower Manhattan has a complex role to fulfill in the future. It has played a critical role in the history of both the City and the nation, but its past will not wholly predict its future. The City, and especially the region, have new needs and aspirations. To meet these needs, the following list of goals for Lower Manhattan was formulated.

(1) To strengthen the downtown business Core, with its important regional and national roles, by providing for prime office expansion, improving its working environment, diversifying its business life, reducing its vulnerability to the decisions of a single institution, improving internal transportation, and enhancing the City's economic and tax base.

(2) To provide a powerful new magnet for housing in the City's core area; to broaden its share of that part of the region's new housing market composed largely of younger households amenable to central city living; to contribute thereby to the reduction of the regional journey-to-work by providing walk-to-work housing, and by taking advantage of underutilized capacity in many existing subway lines.

(3) To broaden the regional choice of work opportunities by diversifying downtown's range of employment; and to broaden the regional choice of residence by introducing new housing in the vicinity of major existing employment centers.

(4) To take maximum advantage of the great beauty of downtown's waterfront and its striking physical plant -- thereby best serving the downtown business community, the new residential population, and providing regional recreation as well. To do this, the waterfront development must be designed as an integral part of the Plan for the future of the business Core.

(5) To rationalize downtown transportation through maximum feasible separation of pedestrian, arterial and service traffic. This will facilitate traffic moving through Lower Manhattan and minimize the severe conflicts between vehicles and pedestrians in an area of heavy pedestrian movement, the central business Core.

(6) To improve the working environment in Lower Manhattan by providing daily amenities, services and attractions found elsewhere in the City, and by improving the quality and character of public space and internal circulation: its pedestrian routes, subway access, intra-area mass transit.

(7) To protect existing blue collar jobs in the goods handling area by defensive actions where necessary, industrial rehabilitation where feasible.

(8) To assist in the incorporation of current major downtown projects (Civic Center, World Trade Center, Battery Park Site) into the existing and future fabric of Lower Manhattan, to minimize disruptions due to street closings, and to provide for connections to future adjacent developments.

(9) To improve Lower Manhattan's mass-transit access to those portions of the region -- particularly to the north and east -- where residential growth has been greatest and where the higher skilled workers now in greatest demand are increasingly concentrated.

DESCRIPTION OF THE PROPOSALS

The Plan is conceived as a framework for decisions, an organizing concept to guide present and future growth. The physical expression of that framework is a newly rationalized circulation system, extending from the streets and subway stations of the inner city to the complex movement systems required by new developments proposed at the water's edge. The major deterrents to change are now the remnants of old movement systems, with their concomitant small irregular lots, and the elevated highways with their inhibiting influence.

The Movement System

Beginning in the old Core, the Plan designates and treats the old streets as either arterial, pedestrian or service.

Arterial vehicular streets are Church, Broadway and Water-Pearl (in a north-south direction) and Worth, Warren-Murray (or Chambers-Warren), Barclay-Vesey and Maiden Lane-Liberty (in an east-west direction).

Between these arterial vehicular streets will be the pedestrian streets, located to follow the major concentrations of downtown subway stations and the major lines of movement: Wall, Chambers, Broad, Fulton.

Out of the irregular old street pattern a rational and efficient system of movement thus can be organized, providing the basis for important links to future development at the Core's periphery.

Transit station improvements designed integrally with the pedestrian system will bring passengers out of stations to street level with great speed and less congestion at the stairways. At certain locations the streets above the station mezzanines can be opened to provide daylight, enhancing both utility and appearance.

Intra-Bus

To serve the unique needs of Lower Manhattan, particularly as the Core expands and distances between major concentrations of workers and residents become greater, a small, low, moderate-speed vehicle is proposed for selected routes of the pedestrian system. This conveyance will provide frequent service for people moving distances too short for subway, too long for easy walking.

The new vehicle, called Intra-Bus, should be designed expressly for this purpose, with a low floor and relatively open sides so that it would be easily boarded, even in motion. Stopping time would thus be kept to a minimum.

Depressed Peripheral Expressways

To achieve direct pedestrian access from the Core to the waterfront, and a truly integrated waterfront development producing the highest land values, the Plan calls for the construction of depressed expressways, on new fill just outside of the existing bulkhead, and the eventual demolition of the existing elevated highways.

The cost of this new construction, including fill, bulkhead and highway, will be around $ 22 a square foot, and can be included in the price to developers of the newly-created land. It was found that, with City subsidy allocations already committed to more critical areas elsewhere, the entire development will be completely self-financing.

Altogether, the total investment in the waterfront development will be in the neighborhood of two billion dollars.

A Residential Community

The Plan calls for a downtown waterfront residential community of 80,000 to 100,000 people, to be constructed on some 450 acres of land at the periphery of the downtown business Core. Of this 450 acres some 190 will consist of new fill (replacing the largely unused and obsolete piers) and 260 will be inland area now available for redevelopment. In terms of phasing, this development could be carried out in 20 years.

The new residential community is to be composed of six interconnected development areas ("neighborhoods") of 10,000-15,000 people, each centering around waterfront plazas at the ends of the major downtown pedestrian streets and axes: Wall,

Broad, Chambers, Fulton, the World Trade Center.

These plazas will form "windows on the waterfront", broad openings into the very heart of the City. They will serve as the focal points of retail and community services for both the new residents and office workers.

Altogether some 40,000 dwelling units are planned -- ultimately serving a wide range of income and family types. A complete development of new retail and community services, including cinemas, schools and supermarkets, will be constructed to service the new community.

Each development district (or "neighborhood") will contain a mixture of housing at the water's edge and offices next to the existing business Core -- some structures will combine both offices and housing. The anticipated offshore expansion is designed to reinforce the cohesiveness of the Core, rather than to diffuse it.

Preliminary calculations indicate that the introduction of 40,000 new dwelling units in Lower Manhattan will not overload the existing transit network. By providing walk-to-work housing, it should in fact reduce the incoming subway volumes. Workers going to the midtown area will be using the excess capacity made available by the exodus of workers at downtown stations.

Waterfront Parks

The plazas will be connected together along the water's edge by a waterfront esplanade, providing public pedestrian access around the entire tip of the island and especially to the three major waterfront parks: Battery Park at the island's tip, and two new proposed parks, one between Catherine and Peck Slips on the East River (directly under the Brooklyn Bridge), and one between Canal and Hubert Streets on the Hudson.

Neighborhood Parks

Above the service cores will be located recreation facilities, for the joint use of residents and office workers in that district.

Servicing and Parking

Parking and service facilities are shown at the center of each development district, separated from pedestrian movement and linked to the new below-grade expressway.

The new highway will provide for both express by-pass traffic and local movement to service the new waterfront districts. Parallel service roads will connect to inland streets and to parking garages constructed over or adjacent to the depressed highway. As a matter of policy, new downtown parking facilities will be confined to this peripheral system -- within easy walking distance of the inner Core, out of the way of local service traffic. Some 20,000 new spaces will be required, 15,000 for the new residential population, and 5,000 to replace and to augment downtown's current supply.

Administration of Development

It is recommended that, after review by appropriate City and civic agencies, the implementation of these proposals be delegated by the City to an area development agency, with broad powers to carry out the major elements of the Plan, subject to periodic review by the City. Such an agency should be a joint enterprise between the City, its relevant agencies, and private interests.

This agency will determine the detailed development of the sequence of projects, establish basic form, function and economic controls, undertake the development of the substructure of landfill, highways and utilities, and lease out parcels to private developers who, under the guidance of the Plan, will actually build the vast majority of structures along Lower Manhattan's new waterfront.

Strengthening the Core

The working Core of Lower Manhattan has shown many signs of growth and strength in recent years, particularly in the field of banking, securities and government. But in spite of this impressive building program in the last decade, it would appear that Lower Manhattan's employed population (south of the Chambers-Worth line) has dropped since 1960.

As a working environment, downtown has few of the attractions

and conveniences which make midtown the preferred choice of
many office workers. A major goal of the Plan is to alter this
condition. Current estimates indicate a downtown employment of
perhaps 435,000 by 1980 -- if no substantial change occurs in the
structure of downtown life. On the other hand, if the major
recommendations of the Plan are instituted, this figure could be
as high as 500,000. The Plan shows a new ring of office buildings, concentric to the existing core, to contain this increased
working population.

But perhaps more important than this quantitative expansion of
office space will be the enhanced working environment, the improved transportation, economic diversification, a change in the
whole quality of working in Lower Manhattan, a change which
will result in a more intense and valuable business community.
These changes point to the importance of close business participation in, and commitment to, the realization of these far-reach-
ing proposals.

MAJOR RECOMMENDED IMMEDIATE ACTIONS

The Report contains a detailed list of immediate actions related
to the movement system, the committed projects, and land use and
renewal activities. The major recommendations are summarized
here with the movement system considered first as the most immediate.

The Movement System

   A. Adopt the street classification system (of arterial
streets for major traffic, service streets for deliveries, and pedestrian streets, the latter to be closed part   all of the day to all
but necessary service traffic).

   1. Arterial Streets

         North-South: Water (2-way), Broadway-Church,
                       West (2-way), Park Row (2-way).

         East-West: Canal (2-way), Worth (2-way),
                     Warren-Murray (or Chambers-Warren),
                     Barclay-Vesey, Liberty-Maiden Lane
                     (part 2-way).

         Through Traffic: The peripheral expressways.

   2. Service Streets
       All other except pedestrian streets.

   3. Pedestrian Streets

         North-South: Broad-Nassau(part), Broadway (com-
                       bined).

         East-West: Chambers, Fulton-John-Dey (part),
                     Wall. Improve.Fulton Street for com-
                     bined pedestrian and vehicular service.

   B. Street Modifications

1. Tunnel from Brooklyn Bridge Approach under City
    Hall Park to connect the Bridge with the Warren-
    Murray (or Warren-Chambers) arterials.

2. Complete the widening of Worth Street.

3. Widen portions of Liberty Street and Maiden Lane.

4. Extend the widening of Water Street.

5. Provide short sections of new street at Baxter and
    Madison.

6. Complete Brooklyn Bridge approaches.

C. Transit System

1. Station Improvements
    Institute station improvements and entrance redes-
    ign at the Chambers, Fulton, Wall-Broad, Foley
    Square station complexes. Connect stations at
    Bowling Green.

2. Subway Facilities
    Proceed with modernization of existing subway
    facilities into the downtown area and improve tran-
    sit access between Midtown and Downtown by means
    now being studied by the Queens-Long Island Mass
    Transportation Demonstration Program. The findings
    of the Water Street Subway study now underway by
    the Downtown-Lower Manhattan Association should
    be evaluated as part of this program.

3. Local Transit
    In cooperation with Transit Authority, begin deve-
    lopment of a new transit vehicle for intra-bus ser-
    vice on the pedestrian streets.

D. Peripheral Highways
Undertake engineering studies of relocation of existing
elevated highways in cooperation with relevant agencies.

CURRENT PROJECTS

World Trade Center

Analysis indicates that the long-term impact of the World Trade Center on Lower Manhattan will be a positive one, and that its traffic and transit impact will not produce undue disturbances. The Center should become the focus for a broad regenerative development on the west side of the island.

Efforts must be made, however, for closer coordination of the current design with downtown's existing fabric and future adjacent projects.

1. Re-examine role and relationships of central plaza and concourse level below, particularly as they relate to elevator entrances, retail shopping, and adjacent pedestrian levels.

2. Consider extension of the main pedestrian plaza to the east, along Dey Street, to Broadway, to provide a strong visual and functional connection to the heart of the island. Investigate possible use of an overpass at Church Street.

3. Plan for grade separated pedestrian crossings at Fulton Dey and Liberty.

4. Plan for extension of the plaza over West Street, anticipating the waterfront development.

5. Study alignment of underground ramps at Barclay Street for better relationship to surrounding street alignment.

Battery Park Site

A development of comparable size to the New York Stock Exchange has been assumed at the Battery Park Site. These recommendations are made for this site.

1. Broad Street at this point should remain physically open, although perhaps for pedestrian traffic only.

2. The Water Street widening should be extended to Whitehall Street.

3. Future pedestrian connections to the waterfront should be planned.

Brooklyn Bridge Southwest

This middle -income housing project will help establish the feasibility of residential family living in Lower Manhattan. Two recommendations are made for its detailed design.

1. As Fulton Street is improved, it should be designed in conformity with its recommended use as a pedestrian -service street.

2. A future pedestrian connection to waterfront housing in the Fulton Fish Market area.

Washington Street Market Urban Renewal Area

This project, whose land and buildings the City has already acquired, can have a major and positive long range effect on Lower Manhattan. Although it is hemmed in by blighting neighbors and economically difficult to develop for industrial purposes, it can serve as the nucleus for west side development.

Recommendations are:

1. If current Board of Higher Education Study proves the feasibility of this site for an educational complex -- as proposed in this Report -- it should be conceived as the first step in an integrated waterfront development.

2. Promote development of the northern end of the project for use by the graphic arts industry or for

research and development related to the educational use.

3. Reserve the southern portion of the project area for future intensive office use related to the World Trade Center. An interim use is off-street parking and as a construction material site.

4. Include a study of the preservation and development of the Duane Street Park as part of the Washington Street redevelopment.

The Civic Center

At this writing the Civic Center is under detailed study by the City Planning Commission. In this reexamination, the following principles should be considered:

1. If a Civic Center superblock is desired, the most direct and economical traffic solution would be an underpass through City Hall Park.

2. Even without the superblock, the underpass solution should be considered as a long-range solution of the heavy conflicts caused by the intrusion of Brooklyn Bridge traffic into a pedestrian area.

3. The preservation of as much as possible of the City Hall Park, as an open green area, should be a major goal.

4. Service functions for both federal and municipal complexes in the area of the present Duane Street should be consolidated in such a way that the heavy pedestrian movements generated by these complexes can easily move through this critical area.

5. In consideration of the designation of the Hall of Records as an historical building, consider the relocation of the planned Municipal Tower to the west, along Broadway.

6. As a principle, the bulk of proposed parking should be located to the east of the old Municipal Building, where it will be closer to highways and away from the congested core.

7. Examine carefully the feasibility and finances of the extensive retail facilities proposed for the underground concourse.

8. Two basic pedestrian routes should be considered as central design elements. First, Chambers Street, running across the Civic Center, through the Municipal Building, and then by overpass to the expanded site of the Police Headquarters. Second, an extension of the Broad-Nassau pedestrian route, across Park Row, and into the heart of the Civic Center, joining there with the pedestrian path of the Brooklyn Bridge.

WATERFRONT DEVELOPMENT

A. Organizational Procedure

Establish together with civic leaders and the business community, an appropriate quasi-public organization to prepare detailed plans for the proposed waterfront communities, to manage, promote and carry out the actual development, including the relocation of the peripheral highway, and to explore the various mechanisms of development including unassisted urban renewal.

B. First-Stage of Development

To undertake, as the first priority, the development of the area between Fulton and Wall Streets, from Water Street to the Pierhead Line; and, as second priority, the proposed waterfront development unit west of the World Trade Center.

C. Clear Unutilized Piers

In cooperation with the Department of Marine and Aviation, work out schedule for removal of piers, beginning with those presently unused, and relocating tenants of those in only partial or occasional use, and undertaking negotiations with owners of several piers in private ownership.

D. Waterfront Park

Adopt the Brooklyn Bridge Park proposed for the offshore area between Catherine and Peck Slips as part of the public park system, as the first step in the park system proposed for the perimeter of the entire peninsula.

When funds are available, fill the area and develop it for general park and waterfront use as well as for relocation for the nearby residents.

Industrial Rehabilitation

The area bounded by Canal Street, the Holland Tunnel approach, North Moore Street and West Street is considered suitable for its present industrial and warehousing use. Special study of its problems -- conflicts between through and local traffic, need for off-street parking, some deteriorated and obsolete structures -- be made in conjunction with owners and occupants of the area.

Residential Rehabilitation

Urge local leadership in Chinatown to undertake planning study, with City guidance, of means of alleviating problems associated with age and condition of buildings, parking, etc. to make possible maximum benefits to region and Chinese community itself. Principle of self-rehabilitation should be followed throughout.

NEXT STEPS IN THE IMPLEMENTATION OF THE PLAN

Since the Plan is not merely a set of specifications for a "project" or a map with proposed land use changes, but rather a guide for long-range decision-making, it is not appropriate to conceive of its "adoption" as a single legislative or administrative act.

Rather, an organization should be created capable of continuing the process of consensus begun by this Report. This agency (a development committee), presided over by civic, business and governmental organizations, will be the focus for the many refinements required before the plan can be transformed into legislative reality, new ordinances, etc.

The refinement of methods of plan implementation should be carried out with the assistance of the relevant departments of the City Government, as well as civic groups, particularly those most concerned with Lower Manhattan.

This development committee could become the nucleous for the area development agency proposed in this report.

When the major elements of the Plan are thus consolidated, they will be presented to the appropriate agencies and legislative groups for implementation and adoption.

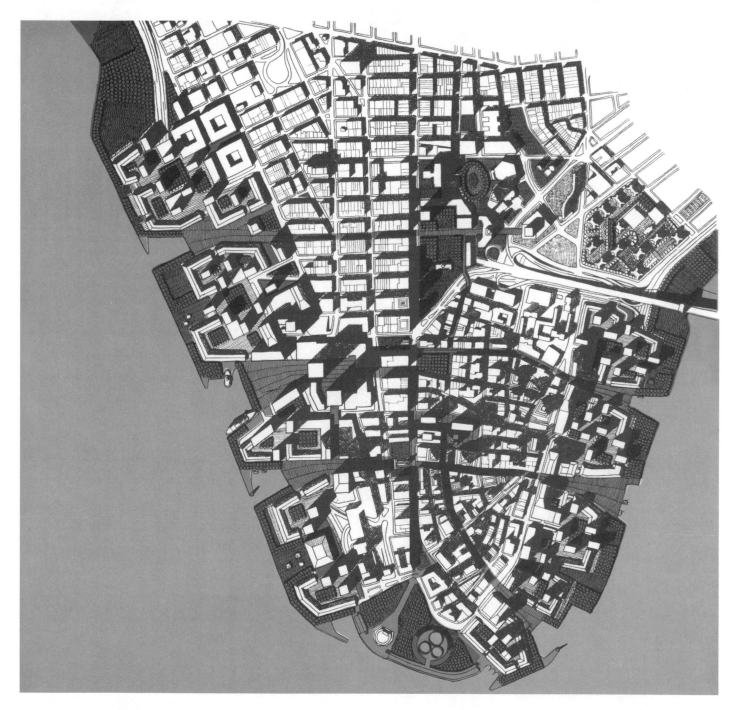

0'   500'   1000'   2000'

LOWER MANHATTAN PLAN

CHAPTER I

INTRODUCTION AND SUMMARY

Planning for one of the world's most important pieces of real estate, and for the heartland of a number of its most important activities, poses a unique challenge.

The problem here is not the usual one of fostering a renaissance in a dying and formless city, but rather of preserving and enlarging one of the boldest urban complexes ever built: a solid core of towers grafted onto a 17th century street pattern, framed by two great rivers, set on a strong spine (Broadway); a sharply defined mass of buildings and activity by which the very image of the modern city was fixed in the boom years of the 1920's.

IMMINENT CHANGES

Today Lower Manhattan is undergoing a series of massive changes which, in a short time, may drastically alter many of its activity and circulation patterns -- posing both problems and opportunities.

The first of these changes is already well underway. It is the revival in office construction sparked by such recent projects as the Chase Manhattan Building and others. Since 1955 some sixteen million square feet of office space have been added to downtown's stock. Another sixteen million are now projected.

On the west side of the island, a small "city within the city" is in formation -- the World Trade Center. This project, housing some 50,000 people in a great superblock, will establish new traffic patterns, recast the downtown skyline, introduce new business functions into the area, and eventually provide a new impetus to growth in a declining area.

To the north of City Hall, a new governmental Civic Center is under construction. This enlarged concentration of municipal and federal employees, centered on the biggest superblock in Manhattan, will form a strong new anchor of office activity. It also creates an altogether new pattern of pedestrian flow, contricts and reorganized vehicular traffic, and requires complex solutions and a high degree of planning coordination.

In the financial area to the south, the New York Stock Exchange has considered a move down Broad Street to the water's edge, a move which would influence the center of gravity of the financial district, enlarge the traditionally tight Core, and open up the waterfront for new growth.

In addition to these major new office concentrations, two urban renewal projects are planned: the Washington Market Redevelopment Area (31 acres) along the Hudson River, and Brooklyn Bridge Southwest (15 acres), introducing institutional and residential functions hitherto unknown in the area.

THE PROBLEMS AND OPPORTUNITIES

These projects call for widespread street closings and major traffic changes. In many cases, street widenings will have to precede the creation of the new superblocks. In others, new arteries must be pieced together to replace old ones that have been disrupted. The complex and awkward system by which heavy volumes of traffic converge on the Brooklyn Bridge must be completely revamped.

For downtown as a whole, an overall circulation plan is clearly needed, a plan classifying streets by predominant function and designing them accordingly.

In the financial Core itself -- a natural pedestrian island -- steps must be taken to separate people from trucks and autos, sidewalks from service area, to remove as many of the conflicts as possible. The expansion of the Core may also require the development of a new intra-area transit device.

To the north, where major east-west and north-south traffic is in constant conflict, a lower Manhattan expressway is looked to for relief of downtown congestion.

In spite of the broad scope of the projects outlined, they

only begin to tap Lower Manhattan's broad potential. Future growth possibilities, beyond these projects and generated in part by them, suggest even more drastic changes. These long-range changes will be concentrated in the areas surrounding the central office Core.

Although office expansion has been substantial in recent years, downtown's growth has by no means matched midtown's, where some 4 million square feet of office space are added annually (compared with a current downtown rate of around one million). As a working environment, Lower Manhattan cannot today successfully compete with Midtown, with its rich diversity of facilities.

In spite of physical office expansion, Lower Manhattan's employment seems to be declining -- from about 400,000 in 1960 to about 375,000 in 1965. Within Lower Manhattan's office stock, a wide range of condition prevails. In the financial district seventy-five per cent of the office area is postwar or modernized, but to the north the comparable figure is only forty per cent.

Although downtown's office Core is growing, the areas surrounding it (mostly goods-handling in character) are in general and sustained decline. Of the 51 piers on the two rivers, only 13 are in use and only 7 are of post-1916 construction and in good condition. Of downtown's three major waterfront food markets, one is in the process of moving out (fruit and vegetables) and another is scheduled for early relocation (fish).

In the last fifteen years some 4.5 million square feet of loft space has been demolished in the area; and another four million are scheduled to go in the next few year, to be replaced by renewal projects, office buildings or parking lots. Employment in goods-handling activities has declined from 75,000 to about 40,000 in this period. Roughly 20,000 of this drop was in the "northwest" portion of the area alone, where textiles, hardware, machinery, graphic arts, and warehousing are the predominant industries. Since this loss has been largely in critical unskilled and semi-skilled jobs, it is a matter of deep concern to the City.

To the south, along both waterfronts and adjacent to the office Core cargo-handling has been greatly reduced with no new major leases or construction in recent years. Little likelihood exists of a revival in maritime activity in this area, due to the inherent superiority of shipping facilities, upland conditions and transportation connections elsewhere in the region. This opens the opportunity for new uses to be considered here.

Altogether a 515 acre-area of land (and water), within a half mile of the Core will soon be available for new functions. Many parts of this land are already under development. Interest has been indicated by developers in much of the rest of it. A great opportunity down both riverfronts for further growth, new functions and new ideas is available.

For the City and the region, the challenge is to make available this underutilized regional resource: its dramatic waterfront, the imposing physical plant and employment center, with its key location and excellent transit facilities. This seems the ideal place to begin a program of maximum utilization of New York's waterfront as a means of increasing the attractiveness of the central city as a place to live and work.

Purpose of the Study

This summary of problems and opportunities is the background against which the Study was made. The purpose of the Study undertaken in February 1965 was two-fold.

(1) To assess the impact of the currently planned projects, both in land use and circulation and to recommend to the City those actions which were deemed appropriate and necessary to resolve problems raised, and to take advantage of opportunities created. Most of the projects were planned in relative isolation from one another. Coordinated decisions were generally beyond the scope or authority of the agencies involved in each individual effort.

(2) To prepare a long-range plan to be used as a guide for optimum future development of Lower Manhattan as a prt of Manhattan's Central Business District.

---

† See New York City Planning Commission, The Port Of New York, Proposals for Development, September, 1964, p.21. The report advocates that "Lower Manhattan Waterfront from Battery to Chambers Street should be redeveloped to complement the renewal of the Downtown Financial District."

Study Definition Area

The terms "Lower Manhattan" and "downtown", as used in this Report, are virtually synonymous in meaning, although each has a slightly different connotation.

In general usage, "downtown" refers to the office core centering around Wall Street. It includes City Hall and the government buildings to the north at Foley Square. Its effective boundary follows a line formed by Chambers and Worth Streets.

For the Study, this was the zone of special concentration. Much of the report's demographic work following this definition, both because it defines a coherent functional area (primarily office in character) and because it was consistent with data from earlier studies of the Downtown-Lower Manhattan Association.[1]

Lower Manhattan embraces a somewhat larger area north to Canal Street. It includes two adjacent zones: the goods-handling area to the east of the Civic Center, and Chinatown. These were included because many of downtown's problems and opportunities depend on the ultimate stability or redevelopment of these neighboring areas.

Lower Manhattan was accepted as the Study Area. It is bounded on the north by a line from the Hudson River along Canal Street to the termination of the Manhattan Bridge, south on the Bowery, and then southeast on Catherine Street, to the East River. It includes all the area south of this line to the Battery, from river to river.

The northern boundary slices a number of functional areas such as "Chinatown", and the warehousing area to the west. However, it defines an area large enough to provide an adequate planning setting for the major concentration of the Core to the South.

NATURE OF THE REPORT

This report summarizes the findings and proposals of the year-long Study of Lower Manhattan conducted by consultants for the City Planning Commission.

In Part I, the first four chapters of the Report describe Lower Manhattan, its problems, component parts, potential growth elements and current projects.

Chapter V sets forth a series of principles and goals for future development. Chapter VI outlines circulation and land use plans to fulfill these goals.

Chapter VII describes the mechanisms, staging sequence and costs of development of a case study area. Chapter VIII shows a long-term view of future alternatives, and the immediate steps to be taken.

Part 2 deals in more specific detail with Lower Manhattan's transportation system, summarizing field surveys, the computerized traffic network models, and detailed recommendations.

The Appendix is a series of papers dealing in depth with major land use and planning problems raised by the plan, and the investigation that led to it.

The plan and the process which produced it have occurred in a context of contribution and cooperation with the City Planning Commission and Department, its chairman and staff, as well as its technical resources.

---

[1] Downtown Lower Manhattan Association - 1958, 1963.

CHAPTER II

BACKGROUND AND SETTING

As a physical unit, Lower Manhattan seems like a separate city. Its 375,000 employees are clustered together in a tight mass and share a special heritage. Many of its firms are old, its ties to past tradition strong, and its sense of identity in striking contrast to the more amorphous Midtown image.

This sense of partial isolation from the rest of the City is to a degree justified. Lower Manhattan's greatest industry, finance, is not tied to a local or regional market, but to a national one. The volume of business on the Stock Exchange rises and falls with the Gross National Product. It reflects the fortunes of national business activity, and sets the tone for much of downtown business life.

The relative purity of the functions of the area is at once its elegance and its weakness. No business area of comparable size is so specialized. Lower Manhattan has many characteristics in common with a "one-industry" town. When prices are good, the economy soars; when they slip, retrenchment is generally necessary.

In recent years, prices have been very good. The area has experienced a substantial boom in new construction, led by the banking and securities industries. This reflected a national trend. Between 1945 and 1965 financial employment in the United States jumped from roughly one to three per cent of the working population.

Lower Manhattan's apparent self-sufficiency is nevertheless not the whole story. The area is also a part of the larger Manhattan Central Business District extending from the Battery to 60th Street, with nearly two million workers. Lower Manhattan is the lesser of the two poles of activity -- the other being the East Midtown area which, with its 500,000 office workers, its great shops and showrooms, constitutes the current center of New York's business, cultural, and social life.

In this larger context, Lower Manhattan's boom is less imperative, its position less secure, its future more problematical.

HISTORY OF CHANGE

The split in the Manhattan CBD dates from the middle of the 19th century. Little by little, the City's business center moved northward out of Lower Manhattan: first to Union Square, then to 23rd Street and 34th Street, and finally today to the East Midtown area north of Grand Central Station. The shift in offices was paralleled by a movement in fashionable living, until almost no residents are left downtown.

This northward movement out of Lower Manhattan continues today. Within the last decade several of the remaining corporate headquarters, along with a few major banks, have relocated uptown. Some large law firms have also moved, or shifted substantial segments of their operations. Of the insurance business, only marine and casualty is left. The flow has been almost always out, virtually never in.

The decline in downtown manufacturing and wholesaling has been even more dramatic, reflecting a condition common to the entire CBD. The relocation of the textile district represented a substantial loss -- leaving behind only a specialized remnant in elegant cast-iron buildings north of Leonard Street that once housed the entire industry in New York.

In recent years coffee, diamonds and leather goods have been displaced. The fruit and vegetable market is on its way to Hunt's Point in the Bronx and the City has a policy of the eventual relocation of the Fulton Fish Market. The World Trade Center will cause the removal of an entire district of "electronics" wholesalers. Activity on the downtown piers has declined so sharply that altogether new waterfront uses can seriously be considered.

As has been cited, in the "northwest" part of the Study Area -- north of Chambers Street and west of Broadway -- employment has dropped an estimated 20,000 in the last eight years, from 90,000 to 70,000. Further declines are anticipated, and some wholesaling groups will probably be phased out of the area altogether.

The decline of goods-handling is, of course, common to the entire Central Business District. And as in the rest of the CBD, it is office functions that have shown the greatest strength. New York's role as a national administrative center has been continuously growing.[1]

THE COMPONENT PARTS OF LOWER MANHATTAN

The Office Core

The downtown office Core is composed of four distinct elements: 1) financial community 2) insurance 3) corporate headquarters 4) shipping. Altogether, some 200,000 people are employed in these four groupings, tightly packed into an area from Beekman street south to Beaver Street, between Church and Water Streets. They occupy 35,000,000 square feet of office space.

The Financial Community: Of the four, the most dynamic by far is the financial community. At its heart are the ten thousand specialists who establish the day-to-day operating terms of the nation's money market. Some 100,000 workers are clustered around them for supporting activities.

This community is composed of two divisions: the securities market, involving about 50,000 people, and the banks, who employ some 60,000 people in this area.

The Securities Market includes the two exchanges (the New York and the American Stock Exchanges) handling 90% of the nation's trading, the commodity markets (Coffee and Sugar, Produce, Cocoa and Cotton), headquarters of the 400 odd brokerage houses that conduct 91% of the nation's securities business, and the market-related functions of the commercial banks. It is this grouping that has created the popular concept of "Wall Street," the place of interplay of ideas, men, and rumor that enters into maintaining the active market in financial instruments.

Here physical proximity is essential. No office is more than eight minutes' walking distance from another. Compactness is the key element. Fraternity is important too. The men of Wall Street and the money market know each other. They see each other often enough to have confidence and understanding about the deals they make.

Centrality is important. A vast national communications network focuses on the financial district. Orders, quotes, confirmations, queries, responses pour in and out by wire and mail. Wall Street serves a highly specialized central place function.

Address, name and reputation count very heavily in the tradition of Wall Street. These reinforce the sense of fraternity so critical to confidence in money dealing.

These ingredients are held together by paper work. The great mass of workers are not money specialists, but information processers: billing, accounting, quoting, confirming, clearing, counting, transferring, mailing. These are the activities around which today's computer revolution revolves. What the computer does to these activities spells much of the future of the financial district.

In the financial district are major central offices of five of the six largest banks in the United States.[2]

---

[1] The New York Metropolitan Region, with 11 per cent of the nation's employment, has 20 per cent of the nation's central office employment, including the headquarters of roughly one third of the nation's 500 top industrial firms. The Manhattan CBD itself contains the headquarters of one quarter to these 500 firms. (Regional Plan Association, Memorandum, "Forecast and Analysis of Past Trends," May 3, 1966.)

[2]   SIX LARGEST COMMERCIAL BANKS (Dec. 31, 1964)
1. Bank of America (S.F.) $ 15,498,892,000
2. The Chase Manhattan Bank (N.Y.)   13,018,151,000
3. First Nat'l City Bank (N.Y.)   12,452,369,000
4. Manufacturers Hanover Trust Co. (N.Y.) 6,970,520,000
5. Chem. Bank New York Trust Co. (N.Y.) 6,231,244,000
6. Morgan Guaranty Trust Co. (N.Y.)   6,109,015,000

PART I

Land Use

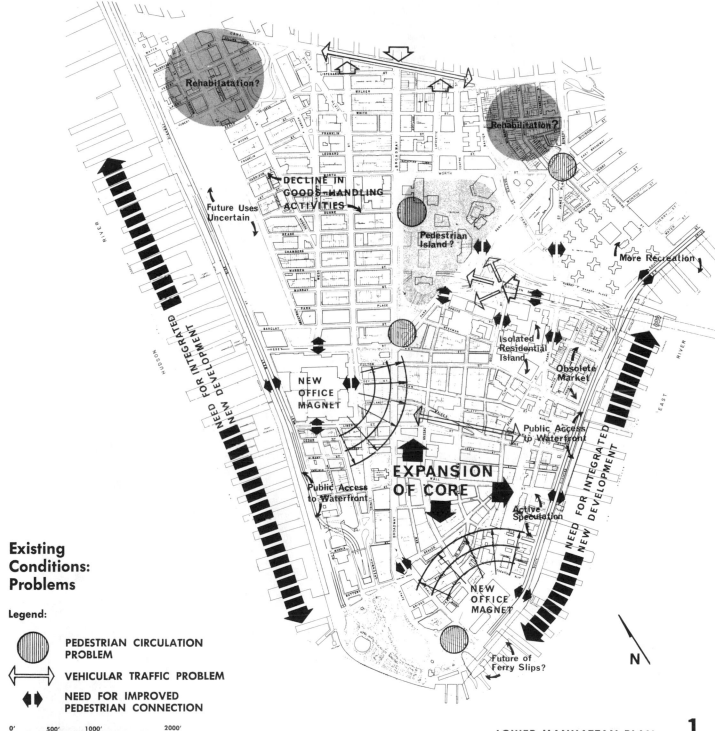

Existing Conditions: Problems

Legend:

⊘ PEDESTRIAN CIRCULATION PROBLEM

⟷ VEHICULAR TRAFFIC PROBLEM

◄► NEED FOR IMPROVED PEDESTRIAN CONNECTION

0'   500'   1000'   2000'

LOWER MANHATTAN PLAN   **1**

Rehabilatation?

Rehabilation?

DECLINE IN GOODS-HANDLING ACTIVITIES

Future Uses Uncertain

Pedestrian Island?

More Recreation

Isolated Residential Island

Obsolete Market

NEW OFFICE MAGNET

Public Access to Waterfront

EXPANSION OF CORE

Public Access to Waterfront

Active Speculation

NEW OFFICE MAGNET

Future of Ferry Slips?

NEED FOR INTEGRATED NEW DEVELOPMENT

NEED FOR INTEGRATED NEW DEVELOPMENT

HUDSON RIVER

EAST RIVER

N

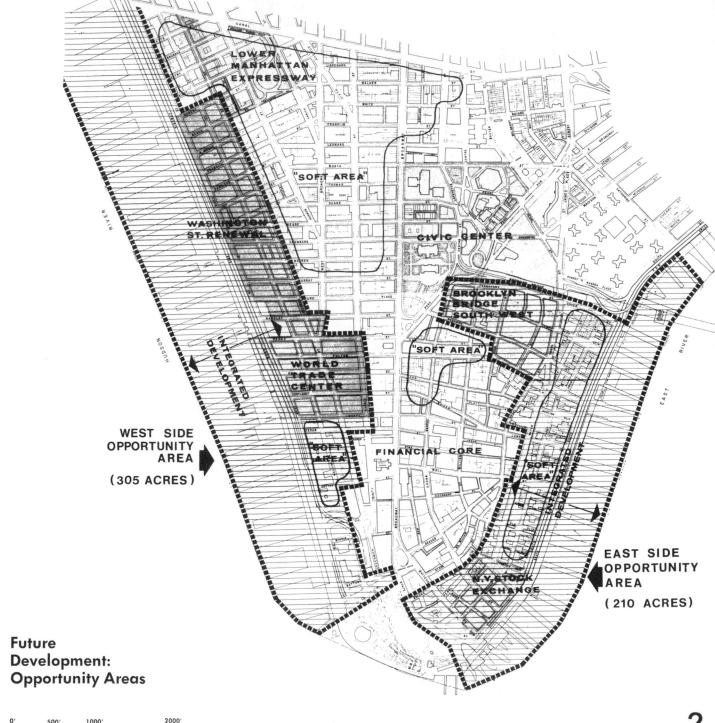

LOWER
MANHATTAN
EXPRESSWAY

"SOFT AREA"

WASHINGTON
ST. RENEWAL

CIVIC CENTER

BROOKLYN
BRIDGE
SOUTH WEST

"SOFT AREA"

INTEGRATED DEVELOPMENT

WORLD
TRADE
CENTER

FINANCIAL CORE

"SOFT AREA"

INTEGRATED DEVELOPMENT

WEST SIDE
OPPORTUNITY
AREA

(305 ACRES)

"SOFT
AREA"

EAST SIDE
OPPORTUNITY
AREA

(210 ACRES)

N.Y. STOCK
EXCHANGE

HUDSON RIVER

EAST RIVER

**Future
Development:
Opportunity Areas**

0'   500'   1000'   2000'

LOWER MANHATTAN PLAN **2**

Manhattan CBD:
Functional Areas — 1850

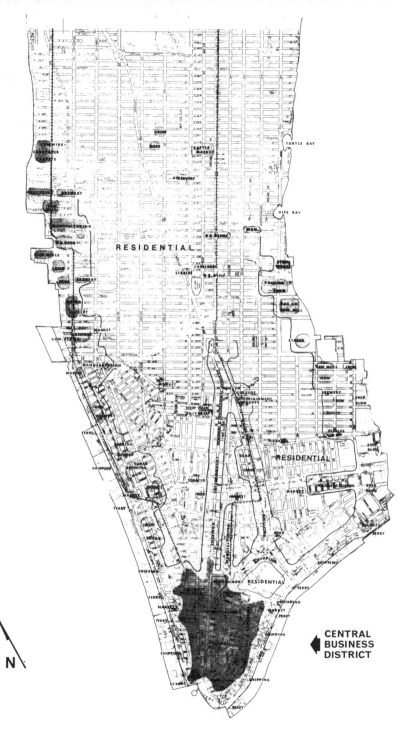

RESIDENTIAL

RESIDENTIAL

TURTLE BAY

KIPS BAY

CENTRAL
BUSINESS
DISTRICT

N

Source:
LMP

0   ½ mi.   1 mi.   2 mi.

Manhattan CBD:
Functional Areas—1965

MIDTOWN
OFFICE
DISTRICT

DOWNTOWN
OFFICE
DISTRICT

N

Source:
LMP FIELD SURVEYS

0   ½ mi.   1 mi.   2 mi.

LOWER MANHATTAN PLAN 4

60,000 employees work in these downtown banks, administering hundreds of branches in New York State and around the world, and participating in investment decisions affecting long-term national and international interests. Also located downtown are the Federal Reserve Bank, the Check Clearing House, and other critical auxiliary institutions of the financial system.

Only a small portion of the banking business is directly related to the securities exchanges, and must therefore be physically located in the Wall Street area. Nevertheless, these remaining functions constitute an important and substantial activity. The stock transfer departments of the major banks operate a $100-million a year business that is considered "as essential to the search operation of the financial market place as the broker on the floor of the exchanges." [1] This function is bound to Stock Exchange not only by tradition but by law.

Other similar activities include divided payments. The Morgan Guarantee Trust Company alone sends out some $1.8-billion a year as agent for corporations.

In recent years, several major banks have relocated their administrative components to the Midtown area, leaving only the market-related activities downtown. In one case, this has meant a relocation of about 80 per cent of its employees. In two others, it has meant the transfer of administrative headquarters. However, most of the others have kept the two components together downtown, while increasing branch services in the growing Midtown area.

Like insurance and shipping, (discussed later) banking has strong ties to the downtown area, quite aside from the linkages cited. Since it has become quite apparent that major banks can operate successfully from Midtown headquarters, the decision to remain downtown reflects the tenacity of these traditional ties.

Insurance: Adjacent to the financial district, sixteen out of twenty five of the nation's largest fire marine and casualty insurance companies are located in a cluster of buildings along Maiden Lane, Williams and John Streets along with the three remaining life insurance companies.

These companies are part of the financial district only in the special sense that they are involved in a financial business. In fact, they represent a wholly separate enclave of business activity whose relations to the money market and banking are of no more significance than any other New York business grouping.

Although they share certain common problems with the Wall Street community to the south, they lead a separate existence, with their own clubs, associations and linkages. The atmosphere is discernably different from Wall Street, lacking its obvious bustle.

This grouping of insurance firms is not the primary insurance center for the United States, or even for New York for that matter. There is probably more insurance employment in the remainder of the Manhattan CBD than in the downtown area. The casualty and fire firms are not consumer oriented and have historically found it advantageous to be together -- although the element of risk pooling which brought them together has lessened over the years.

Employment in insurance here has increased very little, if at all, and is stabilized around 45,000. Its rate of growth in behind the national average, true generally of insurance in New York. In 1947, the region held 38% of the nation's insurance employment; today, it is around 30%.

Corporate Headquarters: Along with banking, securities and insurance, headquarters of a number of major corporations make up a large part of the employment. These latter are in two distinct groups. Several major utilities, (AT&T, Western Electric, Western Union, N.Y. Telephone) are strung out in the northern part of the Study area. A small group of corporations, mostly in metals, is in the financial district itself.

---

[1] H. Erich Heineman, "Stock Transfer Business: Center of a Battle," The New York Times, Thursday, March 31, 1966, p. 56.

Here,too, no special linkages are involved, but rather historical factors with no current relevance hold the corporations to downtown.

Altogether, some 30,000 employees are involved. The AT&T complex at Fulton and Broadway shows signs of a small expansion in the near future and has moved many times in Lower Manhattan. The trend among the other corporate groups is towards a further reduction in downtown facilities. No new corporate headquarters have been established downtown in many years; barring a major change in downtown's character and environment, none is expected.

Shipping: This category is composed of the headquarters of several of the nation's largest shipping companies as well as a group of freight forwarders, agents, the Custom's House and supporting activities.

Employment is stable, perhaps declining slightly. The industry itself is not growing. It has no significant functional connection to the day-to-day money market but still looks symbolically to the Narrows as the source of trade. The World Trade Center should be a stimulant, but this remains largely unquantifiable.

Along the East River, on Front and Water Streets, are the remnants of a once-thriving group of shipping service stores. This is where the great port of New York began. Today port activity has moved elsewhere, and the East River piers are largely inactive or abandoned. The Seaman's Church Institute, a remnant of busier days, is moving from its present large building on Coenties Slip to a new,smaller location on State Street. One by one, the marine supply houses also are moving out.

Government

The second major component of Lower Manhattan is government. Lower Manhattan houses the region's great governmental center operating at municipal, state and federal levels. Included are several major courts, City Hall, and administrative headquarters for the City, state and federal operations. Some 45,000 employees are now working in the area

involved.

Next to securities and banking, government is downtown's major growth industry. This expansion is simultaneously occuring at all levels, and a coordinated plan for a "Civic Center" to accommodate the growth has been under discussion for some time.

The additions now planned or in execution are as follows: the Federal Building on Foley Square; the Municipal Tower on Chambers Street; the Family Court on Lafayette Street; the Police Headquarters east of the Civic Center; and that portion of the World Trade Center to be occupied by the offices of New York State and the Port of New York Authority.

There are no significant connections between the government center and the downtown office core described earlier. It is even rare that the two groups occupy space in the same buildings. However, in many instances they share the same business services that occupy the older office space along Broadway, from Worth to Dey Street.

The Northeast Residential Area

The third major component of Lower Manhattan is the residential area north of the Brooklyn Bridge and east of the Civic Center. It consists of four distinct parts 1) "Chinatown", the historic core of Chinese-American population, and a popular tourist attraction; 2) the Governor Alfred E. Smith Houses, a low-income public housing development; 3) Chatham Green and Chatham Towers, middle-income housing developed under the Mitchell-Lama program, and 4) the area to the northeast below the Manhattan Bridge.

Chinatown: The Chinese-American population lives in an area of mixed housing and commercial uses, running from the Governor Alfred E. Smith Houses north across Canal Street to Hester Street at the edge of "Little Italy", and east from Chatham Square to the Manhattan Bridge.

This historic nine blocks attracts some half-million tourists annually. It is the area originally settled by Chinese in the 1850's (along Mott Street) and then in rapidly increasing

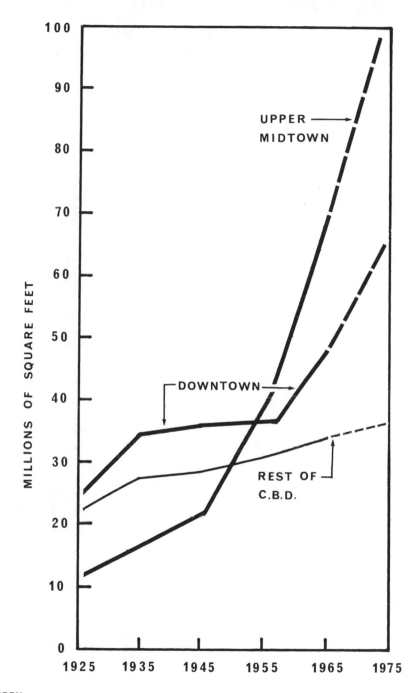

**Growth of
Office Space in
Manhattan CBD**

LOWER MANHATTAN: Battery Pk. to
Chambers Street

UPPER MIDTOWN: 38th-60th Street

Source:
   CPD, REAL ESTATE BOARD OF NEW YORK

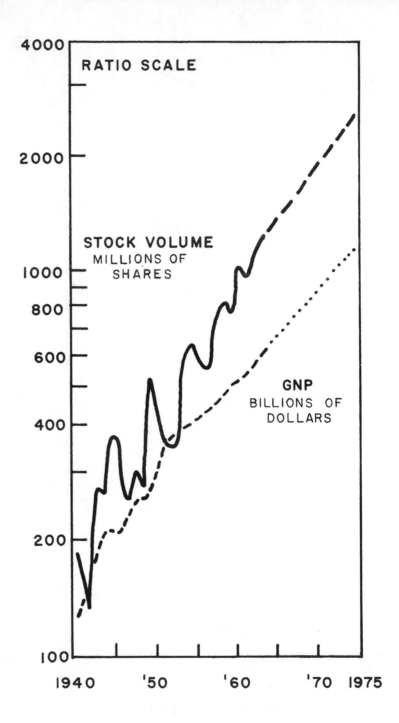

**Gross
National Product
and
N.Y. Stock Exchange
Volume
(Projected to 1975)**

Source:
N.Y. STOCK EXCHANGE

RATIO SCALE

STOCK VOLUME
MILLIONS OF
SHARES

GNP
BILLIONS OF
DOLLARS

4000

2000

1000

800

600

400

200

100

1940   '50   '60   '70   1975

numbers in the 1890's. It is the home of the greatest single concentration of Chinese-American population in the East. It is also the center of Chinese-American educational institutions, family associations, and shops and restaurants for the approximately 33,000 Chinese-Americans in the metropolitan region.

Estimates of the residential population of "Chinatown" vary and are not considered reliable. The 1960 Census indicates a non-white (predominantly Chinese) population of approximately 4,000 persons. Other estimates range between seven and ten thousand persons. About 1,000 Chinese-Americans live in the Governor Alfred E. Smith Houses.

The neighborhood is served by more than 200 shops and 60 restaurants. There are several theatres featuring live and filmed productions in Chinese, five daily Chinese language newspapers and over 65 family and trade associations.

It is believed that an increasing number of Chinese-Americans are moving from this area and that it is functioning increasingly to provide services to the tourist population and other Chinese-American residents of the region. Almost a third of its employed population work in local eating and drinking places.

The Chinatown population is predominantly low-income. Its housing is in poor condition and most dwellings are old-law tenements. Only one new residential building has been constructed since 1939, though several have been remodeled.

A rehousing plan was put forth in 1952 by the New York State Housing Commissioner to demolish the existing buildings in the center and replace them with a public housing project to be called "China Village", with a fringe area devoted to shops, restaurants and a museum. The proposal was successfully opposed by the community.

The area is notably deficient in off-street parking spaces. During peak tourist hours, streets are highly congested. This deficiency can only worsen as the area becomes still more tourist-oriented unless steps are taken to correct it.

The Governor Alfred E. Smith Houses: This New York City Housing Authority Project was completed in two stages in 1949 and 1952. It provides housing for approximately 7,600 people. They are located in 1,900 apartments in twelve 17-story buildings on an 18.5 acre superblock.

Sixty percent of the residents are Negro or Puerto Rican; another fifteen percent are Chinese-American. The demographic characteristics of these residents are typical of a 15-year-old public housing project. There are a high percentage of parents in the 35-45 year old age bracket who moved in when the project was new. A large percentage of residents are children between 6-16 years of age.

Playground space is inadequate to serve these children. The site of P.S. 126 now under construction at one end of the project area was formerly used as a playground and housed a gym. A parking lot for 95 cars occupies another potential playground site. Heavy truck traffic to the Journal-American plant nearby on South Street makes access hazardous to the Tahney Playground located across Catherine Street. No off-street parking spaces are available for an estimated 200-300 tenant-owned automobiles.

The Hamilton-Madison House, a social work center specializing in group work, is located in the lower floors of one building. There is a critical need to expand its facilities to take care of its increasingly heavy workload.

Chatham Green and Chatham Towers: These two middle-income, cooperative apartment developments were proposed by the New York City Housing and Redevelopment Board as a reuse for land made available under Title I of the Federal Housing Act in the Park Row Urban Renewal Area.

Chatham Green, located on a site east of Park Row, was completed in 1962. It was subsidized under a limited divided program by the City and sponsored by the Association for Middle-Income Housing, Inc. Its 1,200 residents occupy 420 dwelling units. A playground and some commercial space also occupy the site. It has been estimated that from 50 to 60 percent of the employed residents of Chatham

Green work south of Worth Street in Lower Manhattan.

Chatham Towers was completed in 1965 on a 2.6 acre site west of Park Row. It too was also sponsored by the Association for Middle-Income Housing, Inc. and is subsidized by the State under the limited-dividend program. When fully occupied, approximately 550 persons will live in 240 dwelling units. Below-grade parking will be provided for 125 cars. Playgrounds and plazas will occupy the 85 percent of the site not covered by buildings.

The apartments are cooperative and require an equity investment ranging from $ 3,980 for a studio to $ 8,930 for three bedrooms with a terrace. Monthly carrying charges range from $ 105 to $ 270.

Nearby Residential: Another major residential area adjoins the Lower East Side of Lower Manhattan to the north near the Manhattan Bridge. It is a vigorous neighborhood which historically has been the port of entry of new immigrants to New York City.

Most residents of this area are in service occupations. A substantial number of white collar workers has always lived in Knickerbocker Village, an early middle-income project immediately north of Catherine Street. The increasing number of cooperatives and subsidized housing in the area promises a gain in middle-class professional and white-collar workers.

The housing pattern nearby has been characterized in recent years by the growing blight in the remaining privately-owned housing, and by the growth of large public and middle-income housing units. The Two Bridges Neighborhood Council serves this area and is working to help meet the areas' housing and community needs.

The Fulton Fish Market

The Fulton Fish Market has been operating continuously at its present location on the East River at the foot of Fulton Street for over 140 years. The more than 90 wholesale dealers of fresh and frozen fish, processors and purveyors are housed in old, run-down buildings. Two City-owned market buildings on South Street are occupied by dealers in salt-water varieties of fish. Wholesalers handling fresh water species are concentrated on Peck Slip, a City-owned pier.

Truck transportation accounts for 93% of the annual total receipts of fresh and frozen fish. Nevertheless, water-borne delivery is still important to the Market. During some months, these landings represent 15% of the total volume in terms of receipts.

Annual receipts at the Market have been steadily declining. This decline is attributed to the increased consumption of packaged frozen fish shipped directly from points of production; to the awkward location of the Market which makes it difficult for buyers to come and go freely; and to the unattractiveness of the run-down, unkempt and functionally inadequate market buildings.

According to a recent survey of conditions at the Fulton Fish Market,[1] little if anything can be done to improve conditions at its present location. It was concluded to be in the best interests of the City and market users to relocate rather than attempt to rehabilitate.

Four potential new sites were recommended for the relocated market: Brunswick Inlet in Brooklyn; Hunts Point in the Bronx; Newtown-Creek, Brooklyn; Newtown Creek, Queens. They were selected on the basis of (1) accessibility, (2) location relative to receipts and shipments, (3) land area, (4) cost of land, (5) site development, (6) zoning requirements and (7) potential acceptability of site by Market users. Hunts Point is the most likely, and a move by 1970 is possible.

The Northwest Goods Handling Area

This area is part of the great "valley" of manufacturing-wholesaling that stretches from Lower Manhattan well into Midtown. Here it is characterized by small businesses in older buildings, declining employment, and an increasingly

---

[1] Edwards and Kelcey, Wholesale Fish Market for New York City, Department of Public Works, October 4, 1962.

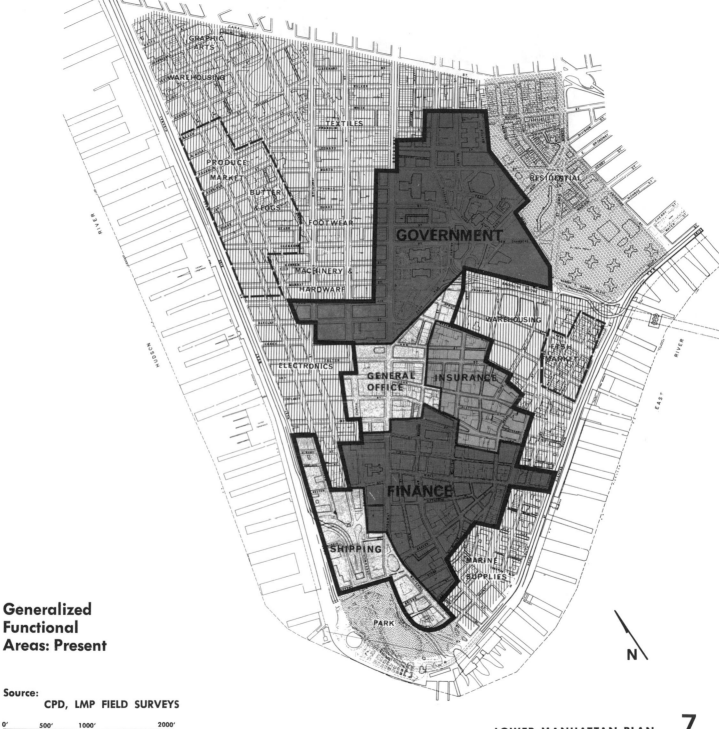

**Generalized
Functional
Areas: Present**

Source:
CPD, LMP FIELD SURVEYS

0'   500'   1000'   2000'

LOWER MANHATTAN PLAN   7

RESIDENTIAL

WHOLESALE AND INDUSTRIAL

Functional Areas:

Source:
CPD, LMP FIELD SURVEYS

FINANCIAL MARKET

MARITIME

INSURANCE

MARKETS

GOVERNMENT

LOWER MANHATTAN PLAN 8

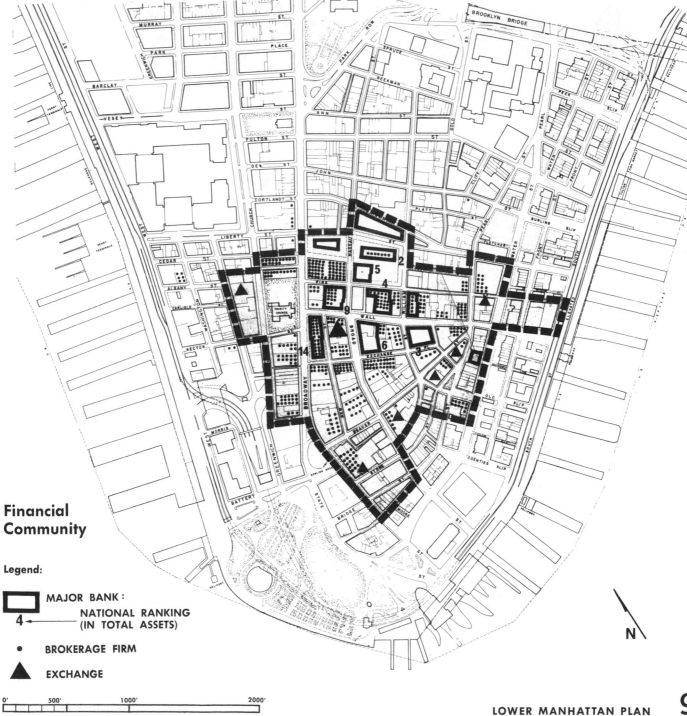

**Financial
Community**

Legend:

☐ MAJOR BANK :
         NATIONAL RANKING
4 ←   (IN TOTAL ASSETS)

● BROKERAGE FIRM

▲ EXCHANGE

0'   500'   1000'   2000'

LOWER MANHATTAN PLAN **9**

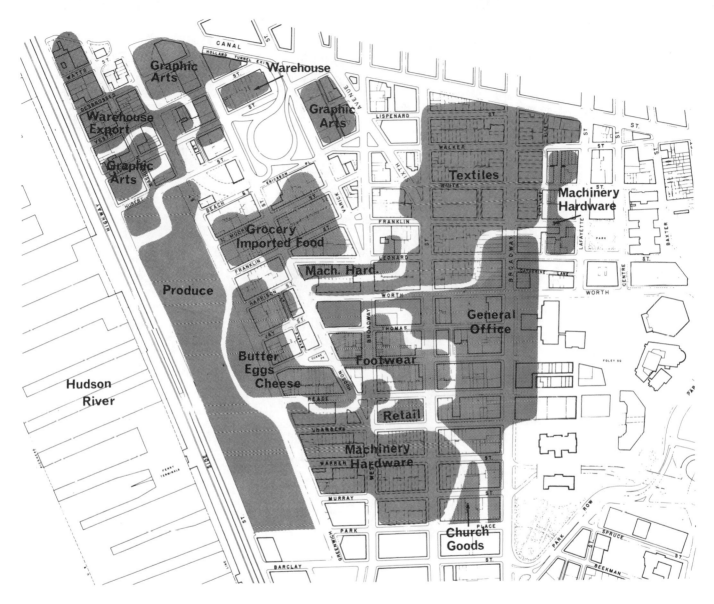

Graphic Arts
Warehouse
Graphic Arts
Warehouse Export
Graphic Arts
CANAL
HOLLAND TUNNEL EXIT
LISPENARD
WALKER
Textiles
Machinery Hardware
Grocery Imported Food
FRANKLIN
Mach. Hard.
LEONARD
General Office
Produce
WORTH
WORTH
THOMAS
Butter Eggs Cheese
Footwear
Hudson River
Retail
Machinery Hardware
WARREN
MURRAY
Church Goods
PARK
BARCLAY
FOLEY SQ
BEEKMAN
SPRUCE

**Functional
Areas:
"Northwest" Goods Handling**

N

Source:
CPD, LMP FIELD SURVEYS

0'   500'   1000'

LOWER MANHATTAN PLAN **10**

TABLE I

NORTHWEST LOWER MANHATTAN

SUMMARY TABULATION OF ESTIMATED EMPLOYMENT BY FUNCTION

FUNCTIONAL AREA	GROSS ACRES	ESTIMATED TOTAL	EMPLOYMENT IN FUNCTION	IN OTHER ACTIVITIES
Butter-Cheese Eggs	14	3,000	2,000	1,000
Dry Groceries & Import Food	12	3,100	2,000	1,100
Warehousing & Export Packing	11	900	800	100
Wholesale Shoes	7	1,500	500	1,000
Textiles	30	12,000	8,500	3,500
Graphic Arts & Paper	18	5,300	4,000	1,300
Hard Goods-Wholesale	18	4,500	2,500	2,000
Hard Goods Manufacture	4	1,700	1,500	200
Retail	4	800	400	400
General Office	25	25,000	20,000	5,000
Government	4	5,100	4,500	600
Miscellaneous	23	9,300		9,300
NORTHWEST AREA TOTALS	170	72,000	46,700	25,500

ESTIMATED EMPLOYMENT BY ACTIVITY CHARACTERISTICS		
	GOODS HANDLING	30,000 – 35,000
	TRANSACTIONS	30,000 – 35,000
	RETAIL-SERVICE	10,000 – 12,000
	GRAND TOTAL	70,000 – 82,000

Source: Field Survey checked against estimates derived from Bromley Map measurements of floor space and assumed employment per square foot.

TABLE II

ESTIMATES OF EMPLOYMENT IN THE LOWER MANHATTAN FINANCIAL DISTRICT: 1965-1985

FINANCIAL EMPLOYMENT	1 1965	2 1985 LOW	3 1985 HIGH	4 1985 LIKELY
Banking	50,000	30,000	70,000	60,000
Securities	55,000	40,000	85,000	75,000
Insurance	45,000	30,000	50,000	50,000
	150,000	100,000	205,000	185,000
SERVICES	50,000	30,000	65,000	60,000
TOTAL	200,000	130,000	270,000	245,000
FLOOR SPACE	30,000,000	20,000,000 [5]	45,000,000 [6]	38,000,000 [7]

Sources: [1] LMP

[2] Yavitz, op. cit.

[3] Vernon, op. cit.

[4] LMP

[5] Assume 150 sq.ft./employee

[6] Assume 170 sq.ft./employee

[7] Assume 160 sq.ft./employee

unattractive environment.

Roughly 70,000 people are now employed here, whereas in 1958 the number of jobs was around 90,000. In the goods-handling sectors declines averaging 3 per cent yearly are not unusual. [1]

The typical building is a five-story loft seldom larger than 3,000 square feet per floor, and of non-fireproof construction dating from before 1915. Rents of well under a dollar a square foot are common; even the better lofts seldom rent for over $1.75. Some of this is cheap "incubator" space, but much of it represents space for inefficient or marginal activities which cannot afford higher rentals. Major rehabilitation, in such conditions, would not appear able to pay its way, and little renovation has occurred in a long time except a few isolated conversions to office space.

The area is occupied by eight functional groups as follows:

Butter-Cheese-Eggs Wholesale Market: Once the center of this trade for the region, the area now services primarily Manhattan restaurants, hotels, and independent groceries, leaving the major share of the general market to chain store distributors. Employment is probably no more than 2,000, down by half in the last 15 years. As much as half the space in the area is vacant or virtually unused. Many of its owners are near retirement.

Its future growth potential is not great; on the contrary, a continued decline is anticipated. In time the function may be phased out of the area altogether. There are no significant linkages to the locality now that truck traffic is almost the sole means of transportation.

Dry Groceries and Import Food: Some 2,000 people work in this subdistrict, dealing in specialized foods such as olive oil, paprika, and pistachio nuts. Rents are low, and the businesses are stable but not growing. No important local linkages are indicated. However, these businesses constitute a fairly significant portion of this activity in Manhattan.

Warehousing and Export Packing: These port-related assembly, storage and transfer functions remain here in very cheap space (as little as 30¢ a square foot) employing some 1200-1500 people. Their relationship is to the New York port as a whole, not to local piers. Therefore, this bustling function could be located almost anywhere in the City.

Wholesale Shoes: Perhaps 400 to 500 of Manhattan's 1,500 wholesale shoe employees work here in what appears to be mostly small specialty jobbers operating with unusual stocks. Rents are moderate and upper stories are utilized for storage. There are signs that some of the larger shoe jobbers are moving uptown along with the larger textile firms to a new and growing shoe center.

Textiles: Major textiles have moved uptown to sell directly to the garment industry. This area has increasingly become one of dealers in remnants and specialty cotton goods, accompanied by packers, refolders, import-export agents, and a few small garment makers. About 8,500 people are employed.

There are many signs of long-term vacancy, as well as underutilization of upper floor space. Some textile buildings have been taken over by other marginal uses, and still others have been torn down for parking lots. Continued contraction of the industry in and north of the Worth Street area is expected.

Graphic Arts: About 4,000 employees work in the graphic arts complexes. Rents are in the $1.75 per square foot bracket, for space with 250 lbs. (and up) floor load capacities.

This is a potential growth industry. It has market linkages to the nearby government and financial centers. Rehabilitation of older buildings for printing is in progress in several locations, but no new construction is anticipated. Rents in new buildings are generally higher than the industry can afford.

---

[1] This material is based on a series of interviews with informed realtors and local merchants, conducted in June, 1965, and an analysis of the 1958 Census of business.

Hard Goods: Wholesalers of machinery, electrical goods and hardware employ perhaps another 4,000 people, some with stocks and some without. This total also includes an estimated 1,5000 people in hardware manufacture in substantial loft buildings along Lafayette Street.

Other Functional Specialties: Variety is characteristic of the area: casual employment agencies on Warren Street; clerical garb stores a few buildings west of Broadway on Warren, Murray and Park Row; bail bonds north of the Courts; retail shopping along Broadway and Chambers. Adding in services and retail outlets throughout the area, this miscellaneous grouping probably employs another 10,000 people.

THE MOVEMENT SYSTEM AND THE LOCATION OF ACTIVITIES

Why activities are where they are is largely a function of the movement system. This system is considered at length in Part 2, and is discussed here in summary only. Its performance characteristics explain as nothing else can the tremendously concentrated Core, and the relatively lightly developed frame at its edges.

Regional Position

In spite of certain weaknesses, Lower Manhattan enjoys a favorable position with repsect to the regional and local transportation system. The highly concentrated Core is the expression of the disciplines of movement, the focal point of Gottman's "economic hinge" [1] At a region-wide scale, it is the point of greatest accessibility.

Before 1900, downtown was served by elevated and surface trolleys. Within a 15 year period, the tunnels and 5 subway lines were connected to it.

As a result few urban centers are as dependent on mass transit. Some 95 per cent of its workers reach their jobs by public transportation, 75 per cent by the subway system. [2] Even for New York this is high. In the Manhattan Central Business District, taken as a whole, the corresponding figures are 70 and 60 per cent.

This dense network of subway lines (five abreast at one point) and stations (arranged roughly in four east-west zones or bands), corresponds to the physical configuration of the mass of buildings it serves. The northern band at Chambers Street serves the government center. The Fulton Street and the Wall Street complex of stations serve the Core, along with PATH that connects to Newark.

While this confluence of lines once represented the focal point of the City's transit system, the influence of the commuter lines, the rapid development of the Midtown office center, and growth in regional population to the north and east have shifted the focal point to the north.

Downtown's Capture Rate

The current configuration of journey-to-work movement into the two Manhattan office centers is shown in the accompanying maps. They demonstrate Midtown's higher "capture rate" of workers from Westchester and upper Manhattan. Anyone living in many of these areas must pass through Midtown before he reaches Lower Manhattan. These are exactly those northern parts of the metropolitan area where the growing class of skilled professionals are increasingly concentrated. Thus the Midtown area, whose subways are heavily overloaded, limits the capacity of a large part of the downtown system, and considerably reduces its effectiveness.

Lower Manhattan continues to rely heavily on older areas, with their higher proportion of unskilled workers, to which it has excellent transit connections. Most notable in this regard is Brooklyn. However, these older areas are not expected to grow, and in fact may decline in population.

---

[1] Jean Gottman, Megalopolis, M.I.T. Press, Cambridge, 1962.

[2] Downtown Lower Manhattan Association, A Study Of Travel Patterns, 1961.

**Commuter
Travel Patterns:
East Midtown and
Lower Manhattan**

Legend:

200,000

100,000   50,000

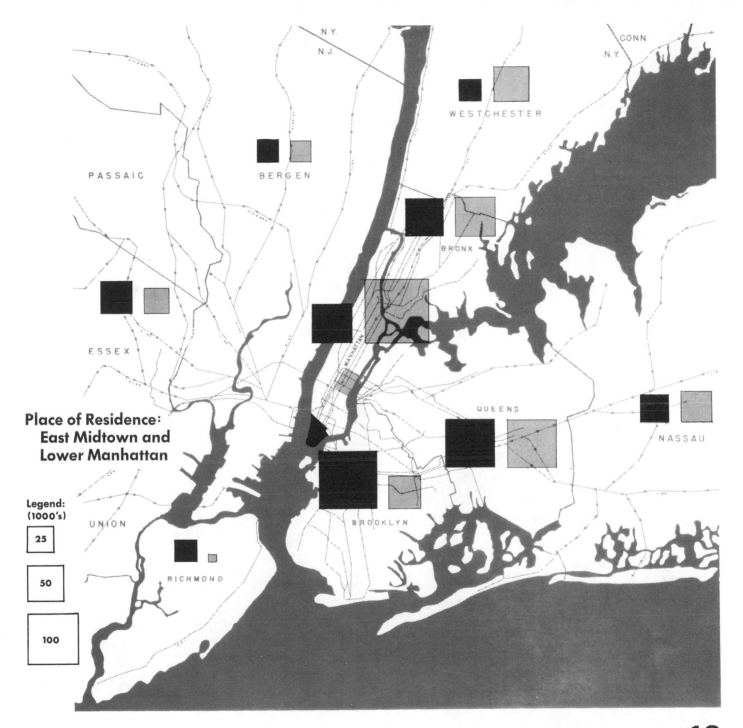

**Place of Residence:
East Midtown and
Lower Manhattan**

Legend:
(1000's)

25

50

100

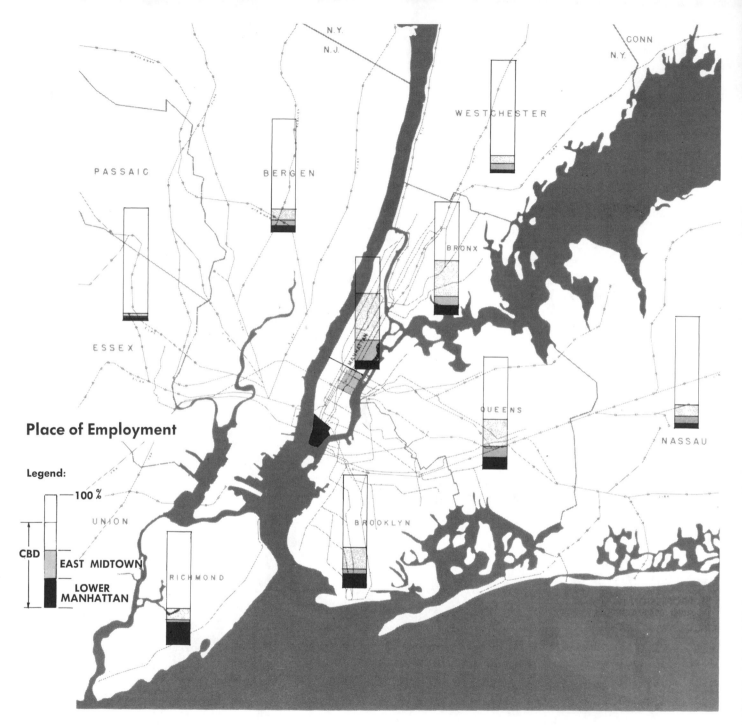

Place of Employment

Legend:

— 100 %

CBD

EAST MIDTOWN

LOWER MANHATTAN

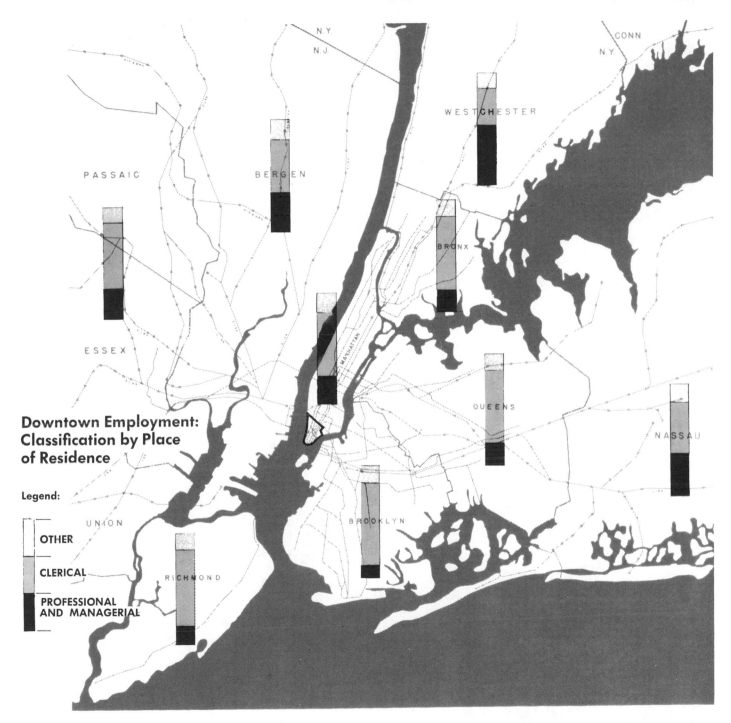

**Downtown Employment:
Classification by Place
of Residence**

Legend:

OTHER

CLERICAL

PROFESSIONAL
AND MANAGERIAL

PASSAIC

BERGEN

WESTCHESTER

ESSEX

BRONX

MANHATTAN

QUEENS

NASSAU

UNION

RICHMOND

BROOKLYN

N.Y.
N.J.

CONN
N.Y.

TABLE   III

Percentages of Persons Employed in Selected
Areas of CBD by Residential Area

COUNTY	LOWER MANHATTAN (a)	EAST MIDTOWN (b)	REST OF C.B.D. (c)	TOTAL C.B.D. (d)
	(Total Number of Employees 1000s = 100%)			
	(408)	(400)	(1100)	(1908)
BRONX	11	12	17	15
BROOKLYN	27	9	18	17
MANHATTAN	13	34	30	27
QUEENS	19	19	17	18
STATEN ISLAND	4	-	1	1
N. Y. C.	77	74	83	90
NASSAU	6	7	5	6
SUFFOLK	1	1	1	1
L.I.	7	8	6	7
BERGEN	4	3.5	3	3
OTHER N.J.*	8	4.5	4.	5
TOTAL N.J.	12	8	7	8
REST OF REGION **	4	10	4	5
TOTAL REGION	100	100	100	100

* ESSEX, HUDSON, MERCER, MIDDLESEX, UNION.
** DUTCHESS, WESTCHESTER, FAIRFIELD

TABLE IV

Percentages of Persons Living in Counties of Metropolitan
Region Employed in Selected Areas of C B D.

(a) RESIDENTIAL AREA	(WORKING POPULATION in 1000s) = 100 %	(b) LOWER MANHATTAN	(c) EAST MIDTOWN	(d) REST OF C.B.D.	(e) C.B.D. (b) (c) (d)	(f) REST OF REGION	(g) TOTAL REGION (e) (f)
BRONX	(572)	3	8	32	48	52	100
BROOKLYN	(1026)	12	4	19	35	65	100
MANHATTAN	(781)	7	18	42	67	33	100
QUEENS	(773)	10	10	24	44	56	100
S. I.	(180)	20	2	10	32	68	100
N.Y.C.	(3232)	10	10	28	48	52	100
L. I.	(679)	4	5	10	19	91	100
BERGEN	(303)	5	5	10	20	80	100
OTHER N. J. *	(1623) (1926)	2	1	3	16	94	100
REST OF REGION **	(652)	2	6	7	15	85	100
REGIONAL	(6489)	6.5	6.5	17	30	70	100

* ESSEX, HUDSON, MERCER, MIDDLESEX, UNION
** DUTCHESS, WESTCHESTER, FAIRFIELD

With respect to the overall commuting situation, Lower Manhattan's position is relatively good for parts of New Jersey, Staten Island, but poor for Westchester and much of Long Island. The improvement of the PATH system since its acquisition by the Port of New York Authority will increase downtown's reach in New Jersey.

Intra-city bus service to Lower Manhattan is also poor. The major Manhattan terminals are all to the north.

Downtown's Area of Interest

Thus Lower Manhattan will benefit from any loosening of the transit situation in the midtown area, although to a lesser degree than midtown itself. These issues are discussed more thoroughly in Part II.

However, by the nature of things, Lower Manhattan will always be at some disadvantage, vis a vis midtown, in reaching potential employees in the northern part of the metropolitan region. By the same token, Lower Manhattan has a strong interest in the development of those parts of the region for which it serves as a natural focus. The growth of residential communities ringing the Harbor is thus of primary concern. Several recent proposals reinforce the belief that such an extended waterfront community is in process of formation -- particularly as obsolete waterside functions are phased out, leaving large tracts of new land for development. Among those areas are Jersey City and Weehauken, where new residential communities for 85,000 people are proposed, as well as a vast new park.[1] Growth is also anticipated along the Brooklyn and Staten Island waterfronts, and several specific proposals have been put forward. Ellis Island is also under construction for new uses more compatible with the Harbor's recreational future.

Capacity of Lower Manhattan's Movement System

Generally, the subway lines leading into Lower Manhattan are not being used to capacity. Overcrowding at peak hours occurs only on two lines, and then for only brief periods. Peak hour in Lower Manhattan, however, is really a peak 15 minutes when 200,000 subway riders arrive and depart from their jobs. Usage of the West Side lines in the downtown area is particularly low.

Whether this excess capacity can be effectively exploited by Lower Manhattan depends on City-wide decisions affecting the system at other critical points, particularly in the Midtown area.

However, this statistical "surplus" can be misleading, for in spite of actual excesses of capacity on the lines, the prevailing impression is one of crowding and discomfort. This is in part due to the design and conditions in most stations, which are old, with confined exits, creating an impression of visual confusion and congestion. Much can be done to improve this situation, as is evidenced where the Transit Authority has been able to remodel old or build new stations.

Special consideration is given in later chapters of this Report to the pedestrian movement system, relating the subway stations and their interconnections to the surface sidewalk system, and to destinations in buildings. This of course in the Core is a particularly important, even critical, part of the system.

Less than five per cent of Lower Manhattan's workers arrive at work by automobile. Lack of parking facilities, traffic hazards on an archaic street system, the availability of mass transit and its wide coverage of this compact area, account in large measure for such a low figure. Even so, less than five per cent of 375,000 people makes for a sizable absolute number, particularly when combined with regional thru-movement and visitors.

Service movement, however, is extremely heavy, especially for the narrow, twisting streets which characterize much of this area. Off-street loading facilities exist only in relatively new buildings, resulting in a constant series of interruptions of normal pedestrian traffic, with vehicles awkwardly maneuvering through the maze of streets.

---

[1] See The Changing Harborfront, Tri-State Transportation Commission, March 1966.

The peripheral highway system is designed primarily to bypass the area -- for traffic bound for the Brooklyn-Battery Underpass, the Brooklyn Bridge, and the ferries. Since Lower Manhattan is a peninsula, its streets carry little through traffic -- that is, most of its traffic is of a local character. The major exception to this condition is the intrusion of heavy volumes of traffic on and off of the Brooklyn Bridge, much of which neither originates in, nor is destined for, Lower Manhattan. This intrusion dominates traffic movement in the northeastern portion of the Study Area, causing major disruptions when combined with local traffic and local delivery and servicing. A solution to this problem represents one of the major objectives of the Study.

Summary of Problems of the Movement System

The principal problem of the movement system is getting pedestrians to subway connections and back which is dealt with in detail later in the Report.

The problem of surface congestion is the conflict of through and local traffic, of local and service traffic, and of vehicular and pedestrian traffic.

The new projects pose special problems of new traffic generators and the impact these will have on the system.

The objective of a plan must be to sort out these movements into clearly articulated and smoothly functioning sub-systems.

EXISTING OFFICE EMPLOYMENT AND SPACE

Analysis of functions and the movement system that serves them leads to a detailed consideration of existing office employment and space and to estimates for the future. In assessing Lower Manhattan's probable future growth, it is also essential to focus on forces which may modify trends in the future.

In office employment, two types of information are sought: numbers of employees, and the amount of office space required to house these employees. As will be indicated, the exact relationship between these two is not very clear. Indeed, there appears to be a striking discrepancy between the two. Office space expansion far exceeds employee growth, not only in Lower Manhattan, but throughout the Manhattan Central Business District.

Thus the addition of 16 million square feet of new space in Lower Manhattan in the next ten years, which would surely have a strong physical impact on the area, might at the same time reflect only a modest increase in employment. Also, the character of the employed population may change significantly in that period.

Employment and space were looked at in three ways. The first was a look at previous estimates of existing employment as a basis for establishing a new estimate. The second was an analysis of these estimates based on various data developed in this study, noting discrepancies, and illustrating that the growth of office space far exceeds any apparent increase in office employment. Third, trends in each of the major economic sectors were studied. Finally, a series of employment and space estimates were prepared.

Estimates of Existing Employment

The Downtown Lower Manhattan Association placed the 1961 employed population south of the Chambers-Worth Street line at 425,000.[1] The Chambers-Worth Street line roughly defines the northern limit of office development. This agreed with figures issued by the Department of City Planning in 1957. The apparent stability of population was surprising considering the substantial new office space placed on the market in the intervening five years.

However, an unpublished door-to-door survey conducted in 1961 by the realty firm of Braislin, Porter and Wheelock, Inc., indicated an employment figure of 390,000, well below the 425,000 cited. These figures and the discrepancy underlined the fact that no clearly distinguishable employment trend was apparent.

---

[1] Downtown Lower Manhattan Association, Major Improvements, Land Use, Transportation, Traffic, November, 1963.

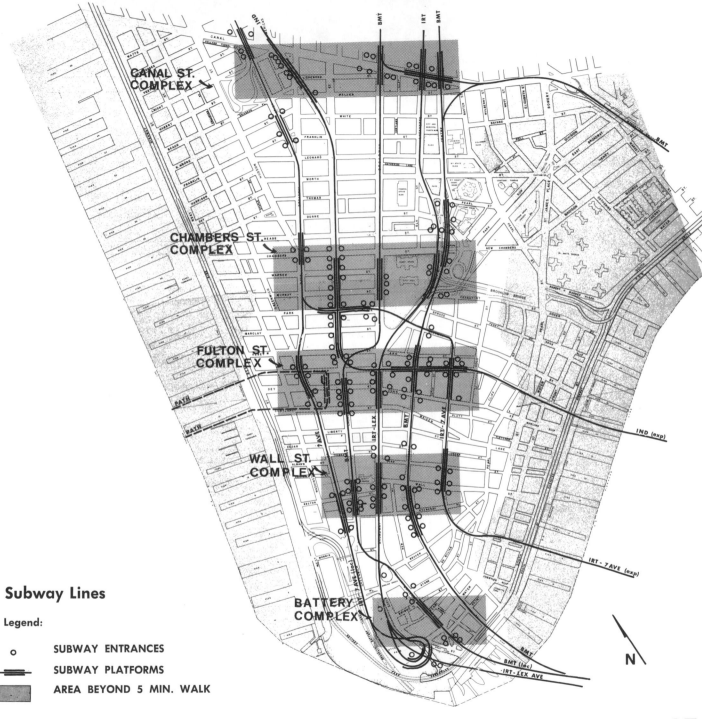

Subway Lines

Legend:

○   SUBWAY ENTRANCES

▬   SUBWAY PLATFORMS

▦   AREA BEYOND 5 MIN. WALK

0'   500'   1000'   2000'

CANAL ST. COMPLEX

CHAMBERS ST. COMPLEX

FULTON ST. COMPLEX

WALL ST. COMPLEX

BATTERY COMPLEX

LOWER MANHATTAN PLAN   **15**

Unfortunately, no business census has been conducted in Lower Manhattan since 1961 (one is currently in progress but results were not available at this writing). However, subway turnstile counts were analyzed year-by-year between 1960 and 1965. Since 75 per cent of Lower Manhattan's employees arrive by subway, and 95 per cent by mass transit, a comparison of these figures should produce reasonable figures.

These counts suggest that 1960 employment was around 400,000, and that by 1965 it had declined to somewhere in the neighborhood of 375,000.

For example, the peak hour (4 P.M. - 7 P.M.) counts for the subway stations south of the Chambers-Worth line dropped from 213,955 in 1960 to 191,338 in 1965. Assuming that everyone who leaves the downtown area between 7 P.M. and 7 A.M. is an employee (an assumption which is justified in downtown conditions) and adding in these additional hours, the following figures for 4 P.M. to 7 A.M. are 262,255 in 1960, and 247,302 in 1965, a decline of 14,953.

The 1961 Downtown Lower Manhattan report "A Study Of Travel Patterns" stated that 4 per cent of downtown's employees leave between 8 A.M. and 3:50 P.M. It is felt that this report underestimated non-peak travel and the time-period here considered is longer, so a figure of 7 per cent for the 7 A.M. to the 4 P.M. period is reasonable. If the figures above represent 93% of the daily subway total, this total would be 282,000 in 1960, and 265,000 in 1965.

To this must be added non-subway riders, which are estimated to be 75,000 and 70,000 respectively for the two years, giving totals of 357,000 in 1960, and 335,000 in 1965. Assuming that 10 per cent of the employees do not report to work on any given day, the total downtown employment would come to 396,000 in 1960, and 372,000 in 1965.

In assessing these figures, certain complicating factors must be borne in mind. First, turnstile decline is not uniformly spread throughout the study area. The Bowling Green, Whitehall and Broad Street Stations have shown a modest increase, while the Brooklyn Bridge and Fulton Street Station complexes have shown a marked drop, probably reflecting the impact of redevelopment.

Second, a portion of the decline has clearly non-office origins; the demolition since 1960 of loft buildings north of the Brooklyn Bridge, plus the evictions of loft tenants already in progress to the south of the Bridge. This may account for perhaps 5,000.

Third, there is a sizable student population in the Study area -- well over 15,000. Many of these students are also downtown employees (probably a majority). Nevertheless, those who are not employees, and who use the subways, should be subtracted from the area totals.

Fourth, the peak-hour decline (22,600) exceeds the 4 P.M. - 7 P.M. decline (15,000), thus indicating that while peak-hour movement dropped off, off-peak-hour movement actually rose by 7,500. Recent observation has confirmed this trend, with such employees as Chase Manhattan working round the clock.

That there has been a decline in total downtown employment seems inescapable. Whether there has been a decline in downtown office employment is not altogether certain. However, it is probably safe to say that, contrary to general impressions, there has been little increase. That is, office employment is approximately stationary.

What makes this conclusion extraordinary is that in the same five years there was a net increase in available office space of some six million square feet. Assuming 150 square feet per office employee, that represents space for 40,000 new employees.

The Space-Employment Ratio Problem

This conclusion confirms the Harvard study of the New York Metropolitan Region (NYMRS) [1] economy which noted

---

[1] Edgar M. Hoover, and Raymond Vernon, _Anatomy of A Metropolis_, Harvard University Press, Cambridge, Mass. 1959

that the growth of Manhattan's office space in the postwar period was greater than the growth in the office population. Taking the financial community and other office employment together, their crude estimates suggested that Manhattan employment grew by about 10 per cent between 1947 and 1956, from 753,000 to 830,000 persons, a net gain of 77,000 persons. During the same period, according to present study estimates, office space grew by 25,000,000 gross square feet. This would represent a net gain of 135,000 persons based on 150 square feet per employee.

Similarly, NYMRS projections as revised on the basis of the 1960 Census, predicted that office employment will increase in the region by 1,273,000 jobs between 1956 and 1985 in the fields of finance, business and professional service and government. In finance, Manhattan is projected to increase from 211,000 jobs in 1956 to 290,500 in 1985, a gain of 79,500; in business and professional services from 559,600 in 1956 to 650,200 in 1985, a gain of 11,000. This equals 189,500 new jobs. Government is unpredictable. Assuming that all of this Manhattan growth will occur in the Central Business District and that it was exclusively office growth, this represents an increase in floor space (computed at 150 net square feet per office employees) amounting to 28,375,000 square feet. However, between 1957 and today, 58,000,000 square feet of new office space have already been occupied or are in construction; by 1970 the total is expected to be 106,000,000 square feet.

This discrepancy between forecast, fact, and employment is common to the entire New York Central Business District. During the same period analyzed above (1960-1965) some 17 million square feet of new office space were added to the East Midtown area, between 34th Street and 62nd Street, east of Seventh Avenue. On the basis of 150 square feet per person, this would mean space for 115,000 new employees.

However, here turnstile counts indicate an increase of only 46,000 people during the peak evening hour. If this represents 60% of East Midtown employees, the actual increase would then be in the order of 75,000, leaving some 40,000 people unaccounted for, and presumably explainable only in terms of changing office space standards. It appears quite

clear that there is a great discrepancy between the apparent rate of growth of office space in the Manhattan Central Business District and the rate of growth of office employment.

Several explanations for this discrepancy between office space and employment growth are possible. First, there has been a distinct upgrading in the space many kinds of enterprises have demanded. Salesrooms have switched from aging loft structures to more elaborate space in office buildings. Demand for future office space will occur because of increased need, as well as a desire to secure prestige office space in new buildings as a result of voluntary relocation (upgrading of space), or involuntary relocation (renewal, etc.)

Such a redistribution is always taking place. A more detailed survey of vacancy rates may be warranted to more accurately gauge its extent. The next few years can be expected to witness a greater acceleration in the redistribution of office space. The World Trade Center conservatively estimates that one-half of its future employees are already in the area. The new office development will undoubtedly move offices from the present Core and may lead to a temporary softening of these areas.

Another explanation has to do with the increasingly high standards of office design. The NYMR Study estimated that an increase of 10 square feet per office worker in the Central Business District could have absorbed one half of the post war growth in office space to 1956. In fact when firms move, they take more space than they immediately need, which can also account for a considerable temporary increase in space per employee.

Attempts by this Study to measure the change in office design standards, with a spot check of key buildings were inconclusive. The variations from one building to another, from one profession to another, are so great as to require an area-wide inventory. Although there is general agreement that standards have changed in the last twenty-five years, many observers feel that the trend towards greater space has been reversed in the last five years. This left the question unsettled.

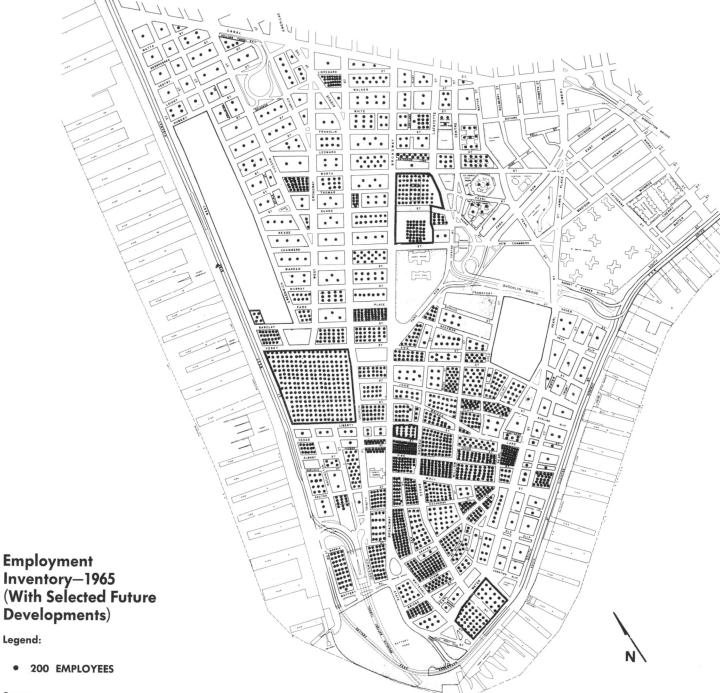

**Employment
Inventory—1965
(With Selected Future
Developments)**

Legend:

●   **200 EMPLOYEES**

Source:
    DLMA, CPD

0'   500'   1000'   2000'

N

LOWER MANHATTAN PLAN   **16**

Another explanation has to do with vacancies in older buildings. Realty specialists have long predicted the growth of such vacancies, although reliable information on this subject is held confidential. A good deal of un-modernized office space still exists in the downtown area with high vacancies.

A final explanation may lie in the changing composition of the downtown office work force -- the decline in the proportion of unskilled "back office" workers who require little space, and the increasing proportion of trained peo-ple, with larger space allocations. This trend was men-tioned by every downtown executive who was interviewed. What seems to be involved is a general upgrading of the work force which, with the assistance of new office mach-inery, can accomplish far more work with fewer people than ever before, but takes more space per employee.

In summary, future space projections must be made on some basis other than as a ratio of future expected office employ-ment.

TRENDS IN EMPLOYMENT FOR LOWER MANHATTAN

Estimates of future employment in Lower Manhattan must be based on reasonable assumptions regarding trends in the following sectors of the Lower Manhattan economy: the fi-nancial district (including the banking and exchange com-munities) insurance, government, maritime, world trade and goods-handling, and the attraction of activities not now represented there.

The Financial District

What actually happens here will be the result of diverse and uncertain trends: (1) The national volume of transac-tions in banking, insurance and the securities markets; (2) New York's share of these activities; (3) Lower Manhattan's share of New York's share, particularly of banking acti-vities; and (4) the impact of computer technology. Faced with this degree of uncertainty, only maximum and minimum figures may be suggested to set design scale extremes.

Three schools of thought characterize the differing views

that have been taken of the financial district's future. One sees a decline in Lower Manhattan banking employment and a consequent forty to fifty per cent reduction in banking space. [1] This may be translatable into a ten to twenty per cent decline in total financial district floor space. The contention is that computer technology, lower rents in out-lying areas, and the relative mass transit inaccessability of Lower Manhattan will combine to send information process-ing operations to places like Long Island City. The Robbins -Vernon approach of the Harvard Economic Study [2] sees New York as retaining an absolutely vast, though relatively declining, volume of transactions, continuing to be concen-trated in Lower Manhattan.

More optimistic views on the Lower Manhattan scene assume that New York's share of all kinds of financial district acti-vity will remain high and concentrated in Lower Manhattan. The range of possibilities generated by these views of the future are summarized in Table II.

They represent little more than orderly guesses about what the various views of the financial district mean in terms of employment and floor space. Low figures represent the low-est employment prospects. High figures represent optomistic views of the future employment level in each sector of the financial district.

The real estate market itself is also likely to legislate against an absolute decline in financial district office space. If the $ 9.00 per square foot of Lower Manhattan space which is being replaced by $ 3.00 space in Long Island City is in fact vacated, then it won't long be $ 9.00 space. It will soon be $ 7.00 space which can be occupied without having to set up a separate cafeteria, a limousine shuttle, and a TV net-work and become more competitive. Also many New York banks, including the Chase Manhattan have a major stake

---

[1] Boris Yavitz, Commercial Bank Operations in Lower Man-hattan -- The Impact of Automation on Location and Space Needs, A Report to the New York Department of City Planning, August, 1965.
[2] Vernon et al, op. cit.

in Lower Manhattan's real estate market that they can't afford to leave.

The real question, then, is not downtown versus Long Island City, but downtown versus Midtown, and New York versus the regional exchanges.

Many intangibles may be at work here; the "magic" of downtown as against the inconveniences of working there, the capacity of downtown to generate (with City assistance but not subsidy) a new diversity and an orderly development of its decaying peripheral areas, downtown's success in overcoming some of its transportation handicaps and capitalizing on some of its potential commuter advantages (in the Harbor area in particular). Also involved are long-range economic factors; regional growth, the increasing independence of parts of the economy of the money market, the role of international finance (in which New York's dominance is almost absolute) in America's economic growth. Considerations of banking and the securities markets follows.

On Banking In Lower Manhattan

Some writers have assumed that banking management can, and therefore should, in its own interests, set up split operations to relocated automated data-processing operations outside the Central Business District.

While there is a certain abstract logic in this argument, most bankers interviewed have stated again the desirability of having full control over their operations in a single location -- for ease of consultation, as an administrative service center, and sharpness of response. The executive vice president doesn't need to see the key-puncher, but he does want daily contact with the manager of data processing who wants, in turn, to see the supervisor of data input, who does need to see the key-puncher.

Although the decentralization argument is based on analogous situations in other modern corporate business operations, it very possibly fails to take into account the special characteristics of a New York commercial bank. By condensing the space needs of data processing, the computer has enhanced the possibilities for further centralization as much as for decentralization. Banks, which once housed hundreds of clerical workers in cheap lower midtown warehouses (Wanamakers at 9th Street, for example) have recently been consolidating. The First National City Bank which moved Midtown has spoken of a dual headquarters, but in fact has transferred real administrative control to its new Park Avenue offices. This Midtown choice is therefore irrelevant to the decentralization argument.

The next generation of computers may eliminate even more low-skilled personnel and further reduce the need for paper as a transfer medium. Optical readers, tape or core storage of accounts plus direct debit-credit methods could enable the banks to concentrate an ever greater amount of work in ever-smaller per-unit space.

Today informed realtors say that banks in response to these changes are looking for building sites for large floor area (30-50,000 sq. ft. per floor) clerical "factory" operations in areas at the fringe of the Core. They say they are tied to downtown by security transfers, by the Federal Reserve Bank, and by Check Clearing House, as well as the so-called face-to-face and decision making functions.

A further factor which may modify the pessimism of some predictions is that programming the computer, necessarily linked to the computer operator, is a function that more and more will become a management and executive one. Like the budget director of the last generation, who often went on to become a policy maker and president of a corporation, the programmer today is the "magic man" who will rise in importance as the importance of the machine increases. Since he can't be let out of sight of the policy makers, the real choice is whether the whole operation moves to Long Island or stays in Manhattan.

The current set of choices in planning by the business community are critical in "locking in" banking as a permanent and expanding activity downtown.

On The Exchange Community

A shift to a lower Broad Street location for the New York Stock Exchange would tend to pull the exchange community south. While this change is at the present writing in doubt, some move is very likely. Possible sites are considered in the Chapter V. Regardless of where the Exchange moves, computer technology has already enabled the large brokerage houses to reduce their paper work and thus keep all operations efficiently centralized in the financial district without sacrificing the face-to-face compactness which is the area's life-blood. One major Wall Street building is already being remodelled for the margin operations of a large brokerage firm. Also few brokerage houses are related in any critical way to the Exchange floors in contrast to the floor brokers who represent them. Centralized accounting service for small firms will soon be provided by the New York Stock Exchange. Central certificate service to permit non-physical transferring of stocks could reduce the space and personnel requirements of this activity. Although at present it is prohibited by law plans are afoot for such a change. If this law were changed it could loosen one of the ties which has kept banks and the exchange community so close to each other.

Even though such legal changes are possible, evidence indicates that the centralized character of the New York exchange community will not be fundamentally altered in the foreseeable future. Although modern communication and computerization make possible a decentralization of many functions, it seems clear under present influences that all of these operations connected with the day-to-day operations of the money market will continue to be concentrated in the downtown area.

Furthermore, the American Exchange, west of Church Street, has been growing in volume of business and has become an important force, such that it has been conjectured that if the New York Stock Exchange were to leave New York, it might take over the "big board" functions. The New York Stock Exchange would simply become the regional exchange wherever it went.

Three distinct types of decentralization must be considered. The first is the separation out of mechanical processing functions into locations outside of the Central Business District

(Long Island City, for example), where land is cheaper, and transportation simpler. The second is the decentralization of the national securities market itself, which is now so heavily concentrated in New York. This would reinforce the role of regional exchanges in Philadelphia, San Francisco, Chicago and elsewhere. The third is the broadening of the base of financial decision making.

The very forces that make this decentralization possible -- technological advances -- seem to make it less likely to happen. Downtown has shown an extraordinary ability to incorporate into its existing structure the entire technological "factory" now available in the business of processing paper; this has meant that the pressures for geographical expansion of the downtown area have been under control. In fact, by condensing the space needed for operations, the computer has enhanced the possibilities for centralization as much as for decentralization.

Further reliable estimates are that the exchange community can double its business capacity without enlarging its geographical coverage very much. A combination of tradition and managerial judgement make this desirable. In fact, the computer can probably keep the space requirements of rapidly expanding volumes of information-processing close to what they are today.

With regard to the growth of regional exchanges, and the decentralization of the money market, the fact is that New York's share of nationwide financial employment has increased in the last two decades and is likely to continue. Advantages the regional exchanges now enjoy may be negated by changes in operation of the New York Stock Exchange, particularly in regard to brokers' fees, making New York still more competitive.

On the other hand, it is undeniable that certain traditional downtown functions can and have been decentralized or relocated. The central administration of commercial banks need not be located in the financial district itself. This is quite clear from the experience of the First National City Bank which has successfully relocated all but its specifically money market functions uptown (6,000 out of 7,000 employees). While the advantages of a Midtown location hardly need to be enumerated, it is also reasonably clear that these administrative functions need not be relocated. The great commercial banks which have invested a quarter billion dollars in new downtown plant between 1955 and 1965 will probably further consolidate their investment rather than decentralize.

The other type of decentralization that has occurred has been the broadening of financial decision-making that was once concentrated in the money market's Core. Reference here is to the substantial influence now wielded by pension funds, university endowments, corporate giants, and insurance companies in the working of the money market. These groups are not located downtown, but they exercise authority through a wide variety of agents. The Federal presence is also felt in a hundred ways, and this, too, is a direct force in the money market, unknown a generation ago.

Following the NYMRS thesis concerning regional growth, it seems reasonable that national security transactions' volume will increase proportionately with Gross National Product. This is confirmed by recent projections made by the New York Stock Exchange.[1] Lower Manhattan's exchange community can probably be expected to keep 85% of that increase. While automation will enable the resultant 90% increase in New York market volume to be handled by perhaps a 40% increase in people, the space needs of these people may be much greater since it will be shared with data processing equipment. Thus, the exchange community might well double its floor area as the exchange function becomes more dominant in Lower Manhattan's compact, face-to-face financial district.

On International Trade and New Activities

The World Trade Center represents the first intrusion of new business activity downtown in a long time. Although it will draw a number of activities from the downtown Core -- beginning with the Custom House, and including many of the freight forwarders and shipping agents clustered around Bowling Green -- it is essentially a much broader operation,

deriving its strength from the City and the World as a whole. One of its purposes is to strengthen the position of New York in foreign trade. As such, its benefits to downtown business will be indirect in the short-run, and its immediate relation to the money market of no greater significance than that of the insurance district.

However, its role in upgrading downtown should be direct and real, particularly in the presently disintegrated fringe of the Core. Some 100,000 new people, both workers and visitors, are estimated to be drawn into the downtown area every day, demanding a higher level of services and more service employees.

The immediate impact of the WTC on downtown real estate is a serious question. While some tenants will be drawn from the marine-occupied buildings around the Battery, the space they vacate may well be taken by businesses moving south, west, or north, to be near the new Stock Exchange; other older buildings may, in fact, drop out of the market. The major impact will probably be on the area around the Civic Center, as well as the financial center, among buildings presently occupied by New York State offices. These will suffer a short-term vacancy.

In the long run, the results will be to upgrade and modernize fairly good space, and to retire really obsolete space from the market. This sets the opportunity for private redevelopment of sites then made available.

On Maritime Activity

In view of the continuing decline of activity in American shipping, and the improved business techniques utilized in Lower Manhattan shipping offices, shipping is a kind of fixed, stable static element, neither growing, or contracting. Estimates are that downtown employment in this sector may

---

[1] See Graphic 6
In the last year the expansion of Stock Exchange trading has exceeded the growth of Gross National Product, but whether or not this betokens a long-range trend is not yet clear.

TABLE   V

<u>WORKING POPULATION - ESTIMATES</u>

<u>AND PROJECTIONS</u>

(Chambers - Worth Line)

Year	Estimate	Source and Comments
1958	425,000 (510,000 south of Canal St.)	N. Y. Department of City Planning, "Employment Distribution in New York City and the Central Business District." Based on data provided by the New York Department of Labor.
1960	396,000	LMP 1966, based on turnstile counts, see pp. 14 - 15.
1961	390,000	Braislin, Porter and Wheelock, Inc., Survey of 1,600 buildings (for Downtown Lower Manhattan Association).
1963	425,000	Downtown Lower Manhattan Association report, "Lower Manhattan," 1963.
1963	415,000	Estimate of Dick Netzer (based on two abovementioned sources).
1965	372,000	Lower Manhattan Plan 1966, based on turnstile counts, see pp.
1975	435,000	Lower Manhattan Plan, based on committed and projected developments (100,000) minus assumed "redistribution" (40,000) on estimated 1965 base of 375,000.
1980	500,000	First National City Bank: committed and likely projects, on assumed 1965 base of 425,000.
1985	475,000	New York Metropolitan Region Study: as interpreted by Downtown-Lower Manhattan Association, 1963.
1985	435,000	Lower Manhattan Plan, 1966, based on individual unit projections (see Table V), assuming no residential community or other improvements.
1985	510,000	Lower Manhattan Plan, 1966, based on individual unit projections (see Table V), assuming realization of residential community and other improvements.

TABLE VI

POPULATION ESTIMATES BY FUNCTION

(South of Worth – Chambers Line)

(in 1000s)

	DLMA-NY STATE DEPARTMENT OF LABOR		LOWER MANHATTAN PLAN		ESTIMATES	
Function	1957[1]	1961[2]	1961[3]	1965[4]	1985[5]	1985[6]
Banking	45	58	55	56	69	75
Securities		55	52	55	74	75
Insurance	33	44	41	40	40	45
Law & Prof.	24	24	22	22	28	30
Business Service	19	19	18	18	23	25
Corporate	33	33	30	26	20	45
Shipping	50	48	45	35	25	30
Communications & Transport	27	29	27	28	32	35
Real Estate	a	9	8	8	9	10
Government	a	42	40	45	60	65
Retail	a	20	19	14	10	25
World Trade	a				30	40
Manufacturing & Wholesale	a	40	38	23	10	5
Others	a	5	5	5	5	5
	425	426	400	375	435	510

[a] not broken down in DLMA analysis

TABLE VII

FUTURE SPACE AND POPULATION ESTIMATES

Year	Workers	Office Workers	Sq.Ft. Worker [6]	Office Space (Sq. Ft.)	Residents	Residential Space (Sq.Ft.)
1965	375,000 [2]	350,000	142	50,000,000 [1]	15,000	4,500,000 [7]
1975	395,000	375,000	165	62,000,000	-------	---------
1935	435,000 [4]	400,000	130	72,000,000	-------	---------
1985	510,000 [5]	480,000	130	96,000,000	100,000	38,000,000

[1] LMP Estimate, See Graphic 5.

[2] See Table V.

[3] Based on Current and committed projects, minus office stock withdrawn (by demolition).

[4] Low Estimate, based on current trends and committed projects, see Table VI.

[5] High Estimate, based on adoption of Report Proposals, see Table VI.

[6] Assume continuation of current trends toward greater space per worker.

[7] Alfred E. Smith Houses, Chatham Village, Chatham Towers, Chinatown.

TABLE VI (continued)

SOURCES

[1] Downtown -Lower Manhattan Association, Lower Manhattan, 1958.
[2] Downtown-Lower Manhattan Association, Lower Manhattan, 1963.
[3] LMP Estimates, revising DLMA figures in terms of turnstile counts, 1960–65.
[4] LMP Estimates, projecting 1961 DLMA figures in terms of turnstile counts, interviews and employment estimates for "northwest" and World Trade Center Area.
[5] Unassisted growth estimate, based on NYMRS projection of 29 per cent gain in downtown financial employment between 1965 and 1985 (Robbins and Terlecky, Money Metropolis, p. 193, Table 36), from 128,600 to 165,200, representing a slight decline in proportion of CBD financial employment (from 48.6% to 47.7%), and more significant decline in CBD's proportion of regional financial employment. In the above Table this 29% was applied to Banking and Securities (taken in combination), Law and Professions and Business Services. Other activities estimated on the basis of current trends as revealed in interviews and field surveys by LMP staff: stabilization of insurance work force, continuing decline in corporate employment, stabilization of shipping office employment but sharp decline in goods-handling maritime activity; sharp increase in government following consolidation of federal, state and municipal administration; continuing decline in manufacturing and wholesale trade, at rate established in northwest field survey.
[6] The figures in this column assume an altered downtown composition following the introduction of a residential community as proposed in this paper. It is assumed that Lower Manhattan has regained a segment of the general office market of the Manhattan CBD (as reflected in the corporate office category) that other downtown office components (world trade, insurance) develop at faster rates than they would otherwise, that a substantial retail trade develops to serve the new residential community.

decrease by 20% from approximately maximum of 15,000 to 12,000. However, shipping firms have been diversifying, and this may tend to counteract the downward trend. The future, therefore, is problematical.

PRELIMINARY POPULATION ESTIMATES

The following tables summarize estimates of employment and space needs insofar as they can be determined:

Table V summarized these estimates on a gross area-wide scale. Table VI gives area-wide total, and breaks up the population into its components, and makes individual estimates for each component. Using the NYMRS basis for the financial components, certain regional and CBD "capture rate" trends are thereby implicitly assumed as possible. For the non-financial components, where local and industry-wide considerations are paramount, a series of assumptions were used (e.g. a virtual standstill in shipping, decline in manufacturing, sharp rise in residential-related retail and business services, etc.)

Table VII deals with office space, and its implications for both the number of workers employed and the floor-space ratios resulting.

No assumptions concerning transportation have been made. With the exception of world trade, no new activities have been assumed. The implications of the assumptions of office space goals are considered later. [1]

Conclusions Regarding Future Employment and Floor Space

In a situation of uncertainty with an indeterminate future, it would appear within the reach of the relatively few decision-makers that influence investment in Lower Manhattan to set the stage for either a long-range continuation of the building renaissance of the past 15 years, or to end it.

If the first decision gains as much consensus as would appear to be the case, then the current investment may well be minor compared to what is possible. If, on the other hand, civic

leaders weaken, are unaided or are unencouraged by events and the Administration, (they need City support at least in policy terms), a kind of self-fulfilling prophecy of deterioration may set in.

It may seem to many that an apparently vital and growing complex such as Lower Manhattan is not as vulnerable as would be indicated by the above statement. A diagnosis of the present building pattern, however, shows the growth was triggered by perhaps no more than five key decisions, and has been continued by constant civic interest and stimulation. The climate that fostered downtown's comeback against Midtown's competition is more fragile than is popularly supposed. At the same time, the potential for growth and strength is there.

A major conclusion of this Study therefore, is that the continued strength and growth of the Core depends on diversifying its base and mix, what the business community and the Administration decide to do about the evident need for broadening downtown's economic base, enriching its mix of activities, and improving its environment.

This diversification is later seen possible if the residential potential of the area is realized to help support new housing-related business, and to create an environment in which other kinds of businesses now concentrated only in Midtown can be attracted.

---

[1] The trends discussed previously were confirmed by the 1959-1961 study of the occupancy of Lower Manhattan buildings conducted by Skidmore, Owings and Merrill. The study showed the following increases in employment in selected economic sectors: security and commodity bankers and dealers, 23%; law and other professions, 10%; banking and credit, 5%; insurance 3% and government 5%. Employment in manufacturing and wholesale trade declined by 7% while there was a 3% decline in people employed in transportation and communications. While the 1959-61 period was one of unusual economic growth in the financial district, the figures confirm the independent estimate of trends in this Report derived through the studies, interviews, research and field work.

REHABILITATION

Although the major emphasis in planning Lower Manhattan is on the Core, certain "frame" areas and activities are important to single out for special consideration.

Industrial Rehabilitation

In previous discussion, it was observed that the average manufacturing and wholesaling firm in the Study area lacked the resources for major rehabilitation; indeed, that the special attractiveness of this area for them lay in its extremely low rentals in a central location suitable to the typical marginal industry still prevalent here.

The one possible expection to this rule may be in the triangle of land in the very northwest corner of the site -- bounded by West Broadway, Canal, North Moore and West Streets. It is an extension of the viable industrial area to its North. Here a program of industrial rehabilitation may yield fruitful results.

The area is suitable for rehabilitation for four reasons. First, it contains a considerable number of the loft structures in Lower Manhattan which may be readily rehabilitated to provide long-term space for industrial uses. These buildings are generally in sound condition, four or more stories in height, with grass floor areas in excess of 5,000 square feet, and with floor loadings in excess of 250 lbs/ square foot.

Second, the area has several locational advantages, particularly for goods-handling. It is adjacent to the concentration or trucking facilities north of Canal Street, the West Side highway, the Holland Tunnel and the planned Lower Manhattan Expressway.

Third, it also contains a number of smaller buildings many of which are both functionally and structurally obsolete. These could be demolished by encouraging private effort to provide vitally needed space for off-street parking, loading and storage areas for remaining buildings. Extensive demolition of such obsolete structures may provide good sites for any future industrial construction which may be warranted. Similarly, the

northern end of the Washington Street Renewal Area has been included to provide immediately available sites for off-street parking, loading and storage or for new industrial construction.

Finally, the suitability of rehabilitation has been demonstrated here. Private interests have recently obtained several large loans for the express purpose of rehabilitating several properties in this area.

Residential Rehabilitation

With one or two exceptions, the entire housing stock of the Chinese- American area (" Chinatown ") is of per World War vintage. Most of these structures are old-law tenements housing cold-water flats. A recent CRP report cites it as being one of the areas of the City requiring direct public action.

The problem here is to achieve a level of rehabilitation without destroying Chinatown's special character -- as much for the residents and merchants themselves, who have naturally resisted publicly-directed renewal, as for the area's annual half million tourists.

The renewal action should be self-generated with the initiative coming from the community, involving the community in planning for its own housing needs. The community is well-organized under lay leaders, and capable of employing its own advisers for the professional, architectural and planning assistance that may be necessary. The goal of "self-rehabilitation" would be to prevent a further decline of the building stock as a means of preserving its essential character. Indefinite delay might make major renewal necessary at some future date. Spot clearance should be encouraged where required. In addition, the possibility of converting some presently underutilized loft space on the Bowery, and Elizabeth and Canal Streets should be explored.

In the Governor Alfred E. Smith Houses next to Chinatown, the interior grounds should be redesigned to provide additional playground space.   The Charles Evans Hughes

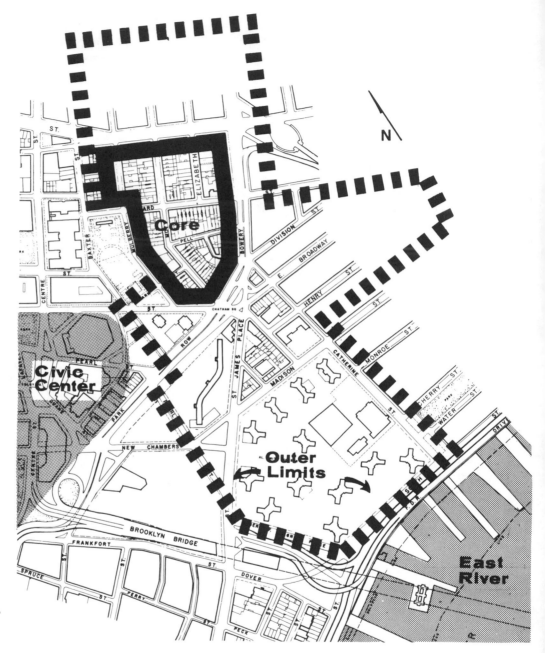

Functional Areas: Distribution of Chinese-American Population

Source:
LMP FIELD SURVEY

0'   100'   200'   500'

Areas and Structures of Permanent Value

Legend:

CLOSED SPACE-
NODAL SPACE

OPEN-ENDED SPACE

STRUCTURES DEFINING
SUCCESSFUL SPACES

STRUCTURES OF INTRINSIC
INTEREST

STRUCTURES DEFINING
LOWER MANHATTAN SKYLINE

Source:
SEE APPENDIX I.

0'   500'   1000'   2000'

LOWER MANHATTAN PLAN   **18**

N

Vocational High School scheduled for demolition in 1972
could be eliminated at an earlier date and replaced by
additional play space.

Self renewal here should be based on the following principles: people should be involved in planning for their
own housing needs, under local leaders; relocation should
be minimized.   Where relocation is necessary, it should
be largely within the present community; clearance of
housing should be deferred until new or rehabilitated housing is available;   sub-standard housing should be rehabilitated, wherever economically feasible, to decent, safe
and sanitary standards;   interference with ethnic and social integration throughout the community should be avoid-
ed; conversion of non-residential to residential uses should
be encouraged where the former are not viable; existing
institutions which serve the neighborhood should be upgra-
ded in quality or replaced within the neighborhood. Facilities or institutions which are lacking should be provided;
renewal programs should recognize the qualities of the
area which have made it a major tourist center and seek to
reinforce them.

CHAPTER III

STRUCTURES AND BUILDING SITES

Growth and change, whether as estimated or not, is affected in terms of its location by many factors. Among the most important is the availability of sites that are appropriately located and adequate for the demands for space. The previous chapter saw the demand for space as primarily related to growth of activities.

The purpose of this chapter is to tie growth to buildings and to appraise the likelihood and desirability of new construction in any particular area based on the life expectancy of existing uses and structures. Those that have a relatively permanent life will act as "givens" around which new growth will occur. Those that are less-permanent but are well located will become the sites for new construction. Those that are less-permanent but poorly located will languish in their present state, or decline gradually, unless some public action intervenes.

Most importantly, site costs for construction with few exceptions must be within the range of economic feasibility for the earning power of the new uses that can be put on them. In the normal market, "write-downs" are rarely possible. [1]

STRUCTURE AND AREA CLASSIFICATION

The factors that are considered here are: age, condition, assessed valuation, historic or architectural value, relation to visually coherent spaces, amount and character of employment, and size. While the study attempted a generalization of these factors on a numerical scale by block or major structure, the end product is a judgemental evaluation of each factor in composite.

If a building was built before 1915, was not fireproof, and had not been modernized (high speed elevators and air conditioning) these factors are considered as militating against its permanence. In addition, if it was small (less than 12 stories), not historically or architecturally important (not on lists established by experts), contained little employment (by block, less than 1000) and/or employment of relative functional unimportance to the Core (or in terms of City policy) and was valued at less than $5/square foot of land, it was considered very expendable (that is, its owner would probably welcome the possibility of another building on the site).

At the other extreme, if it had all or any significant combination of the above characteristics, a building was considered to have a relatively permanent life expectancy. In between was a middle range of buildings with a combination of the above characteristics sufficient to make it a short-range "given." Chapter V on land use discusses how these were used in the future land use assignment. The fixed areas are classed as "hard," the others as "soft".

---

[1] Except where a user makes a non-market decisions, such as a corporation that earns the site rent on a nationally-based activity rather than what is actually conducted on the site.

These factors alone, however, give a deceptive picture of where development might occur. Investor interest may be high in "hard" areas and non-existent in "soft" areas depending on other considerations. In order to take this into account, informed real estate opinion, recent sales and speculative activity [1] were used to clarify areas as very active, active, or inactive. These were characterized as "hot" or "cold". The results are, of course, only guides and probabilistic.

These two area characterizations (hard-soft, hot-cold) were in turn combined to suggest three general kinds of areas: those in which private enterprise can operate effectively with appropriate public planning and zoning regulations; those in which a combination of public and private coordination and cooperation is indicated for optimum development; and those in which public initiative and action is necessary to set the stage for appropriate private investment response.

The Frame of the Core

The basic configuration resulting from these studies may be summed up as follows:

Around the Core is a periphery of older buildings, primarily loft in character, with relatively low assessed valuations. All were built before the turn of the century, very few re-modelled, and only a handful have intrinsic architectural or historical merit (including the first pre-fabricated cast-iron building, built by the engineer Bogardus in the 1850's at the corner of Washington and Murray Streets).

They are generally occupied by older industries, many of them phasing out of the area as has been seen. They frequently don't use the entire space, or use most of it for long-term storage.

Within this loft category is a wide range of building types and uses. Along Front Street, for example, there are a number of interesting buildings built in the 1830's, with attractively simple facades. Many of the five-story textile lofts north of Leonard Street, with large plate-glass windows handsomely framed by iron columns, are also attractive.

Several modern multi-story loft buildings in the Study area -- mostly along Canal Street -- date roughly to the construction of the nearby Holland Tunnel in the 1920s. These buildings are part of a larger group of modern loft and warehouse buildings north of Canal Street, and appear in good condition with heavy floor loadings.

A significant factor in treating many of these buildings as having a middle-range life expectancy is based on the fact that their blue-collar employment is important to the City.

Office Buildings

The other major category of structures in Lower Manhattan is office buildings, whose age, quality and character vary widely.

In the financial and insurance districts, even old office buildings are generally in good condition (either new or modernized), with high tax assessments, high employment and high rentals. Many of these buildings have a certain architectural distinction, forming both the downtown sky-line and the complex, irregular system of "canyon" spaces which give this area its special character.

In the Core, roughly defined as east of Broadway and south of Fulton Street, three-quarters of the rentable office space is either of recent construction (that is, postwar), or modernized; vacancy rates are generally below five per cent. Among the older, non-modernized buildings the vacancy rates are substantially higher.

Rentals are between $4.00 and $9.00 a square foot, depending primarily on the age of the building and on whether it is at the heart of the Core or at its fringe.

Outside the central Core, the office stock is not of such

---

[1] Purchase for obvious resale at a profit rather than use.

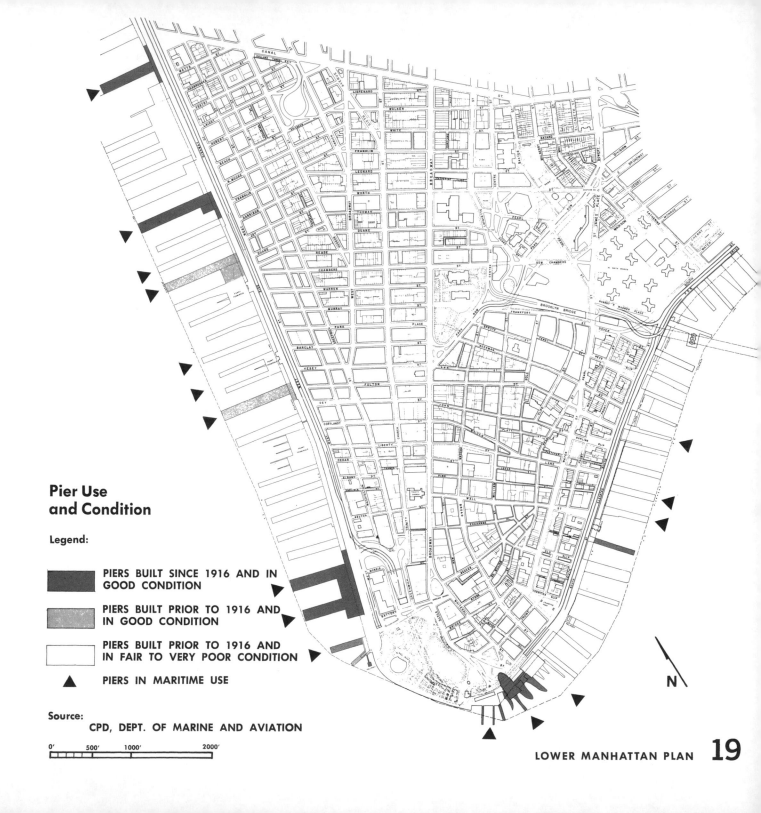

Pier Use
and Condition

Legend:

■ PIERS BUILT SINCE 1916 AND IN
GOOD CONDITION

▨ PIERS BUILT PRIOR TO 1916 AND
IN GOOD CONDITION

□ PIERS BUILT PRIOR TO 1916 AND
IN FAIR TO VERY POOR CONDITION

▲ PIERS IN MARITIME USE

Source:
CPD, DEPT. OF MARINE AND AVIATION

0'   500'   1000'   2000'

LOWER MANHATTAN PLAN **19**

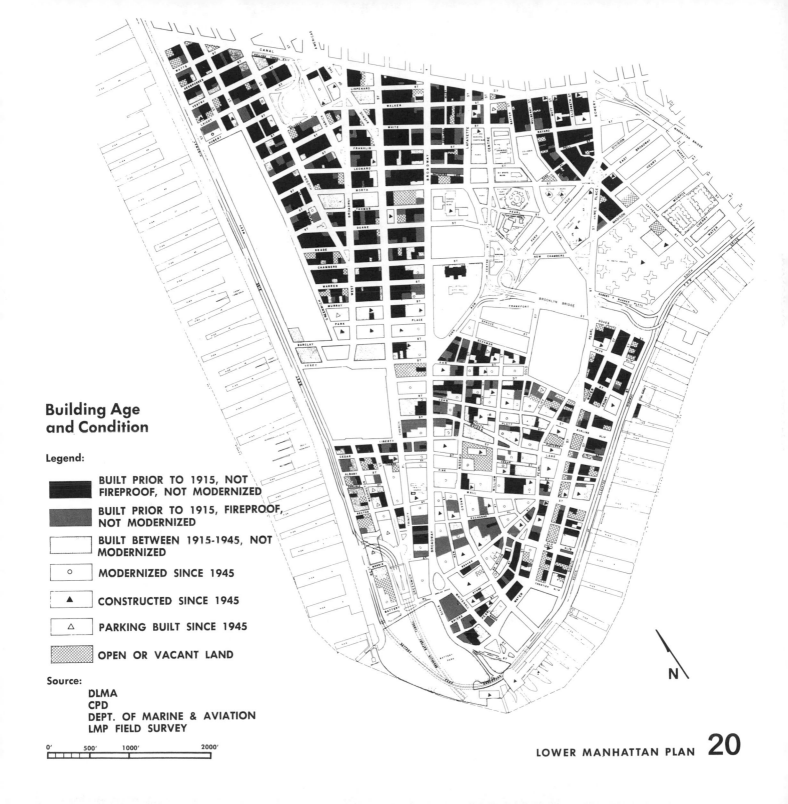

Building Age and Condition

Legend:

■	BUILT PRIOR TO 1915, NOT FIREPROOF, NOT MODERNIZED
▨	BUILT PRIOR TO 1915, FIREPROOF, NOT MODERNIZED
☐	BUILT BETWEEN 1915-1945, NOT MODERNIZED
○	MODERNIZED SINCE 1945
▲	CONSTRUCTED SINCE 1945
△	PARKING BUILT SINCE 1945
▦	OPEN OR VACANT LAND

Source:
DLMA
CPD
DEPT. OF MARINE & AVIATION
LMP FIELD SURVEY

0' 500' 1000' 2000'

N

LOWER MANHATTAN PLAN **20**

high quality. Pockets of older, (often unmodernized) office buildings extend in a line starting from Morris Street on the West Side, along West Street to Liberty Street, then north between Church and Nassau Streets to City Hall Park, and finally along Broadway almost as far north as Canal Street.

In this band only some 40 per cent of the space is either new or modernized, in contrast to 75 per cent in the Core itself. The typical building dates back 40 or 50 years. Rentals run from $ 3.00 to slightly above $ 4.00 a square foot. A good deal of this space is occupied by government agencies and government-related office services. Another large proportion is devoted to professional services related to the declining goods-handling industries in the northwest portion of the Study area. The rest is composed of various marginal office uses unable to afford the higher rents of more prestigous areas.

Major functions of some of the utilities mentioned earlier --Western Union, New York Telephone Co.,etc., are also located in this area.

Postwar Growth

The famous downtown skyscraper profile was formed in the 1920s -- downtown's last great period of growth. The four towers by which that skyline is defined -- two on Wall Street and one each on the streets directly north and south of Wall (Pine and Exchange Place) -- were completed between 1928 and 1932, along with a host of lesser buildings.

This was the period when the prestige and authority of American business was at its height. The soaring towers, each one higher than the next, "symbolized" the successful ambitions of finance and industry of that confident era.

Then came the Depression -- so damaging to Wall Street's image and authority. In the city as a whole construction dropped off sharply, and in the financial district it stopped altogether. In the twenty years between 1932 and 1952 there was virtually no new construction.

The recovery came slowly, more slowly than anywhere else in the city. While midtown office construction was well

under way in the late 1940s, downtown stood still. Many firms moved uptown, including the executive headquarters of three of the area's six largest banks, several major law firms, corporate headquarters. There was some fear of a runaway move uptown which would in time empty the financial district. Few were willing to invest what might prove a failing enterprise.

The change came in the mid-1950s. Two new buildings symbolized the restoration of confidence: the 1.3 million square foot office structure at 2 Broadway and the Chase Manhattan Building. The first represented the successful gamble of the building industry. The second confirmed the wisdom of that gamble, and was followed by a series of similar decisions by the majority of banks: to stay, to consolidate, to rebuild and to modernize. In the following decade the banks alone spent $250,000,000 on new and improved physical plant.

Altogether, some 16 million square feet of new office space have been added to downtown's stock, and some 17 million modernized. Since some three million square feet of older space was demolished in the process, the net gain was in the order of thirteen million square feet. In all, by 1965, roughly three quarters of the total office space south of Fulton and Rector Streets was either of postwar construction or renovated (modern elevators, air-conditioning, lighting, etc.)

The new construction was distributed widely in the downtown office core, serving banking, securities, insurance and the utilities. The heaviest demand for new space came from the exchange community, with banking second. The rapid expansion in the securities business was reflected in the Stock Exchange's decision, in 1961, to build a new trading floor and offices at the end of Broad Street.

Outside of the downtown core, construction and modernization has been on a much more limited scale. North of the Fulton-Rector line only forty per cent of office space is either of postwar construction or renovated. Governmental operations have expanded into older buildings dispersed throughout this area. The need to consolidate operations led to the City's decision in 1957 to build a million square foot tower of office space at the center of a redeveloped City Hall area. This tower, plus the new Federal Building further north, were to form the basis of the planned Civic Center.

Nature of New Space

But it was not merely new space that was required, but a new type of space as well. The composition of the downtown work force was undergoing a change, broadening out the traditionally steep downtown social hierarchies. The older pattern -- a small "elite" with their private elevators and clubs on the one hand and a great mass of ordinary clerks on the other -- has been substantially modified by the upgrading of the entire work force and the growth of the class of technically trained workers.

No clear data exist on this subject, but circumstantial evidence (referred to in the next section), backed up by interviews with many downtown employers, substantiate this observation. The automation of business processes, the increasing use of computers and other office machinery, the increasing professionalization of the work force and the growing use of university-trained economists, has meant a decline in the proportion of "back-office" clerks and an enlargement of the class of specialists. It has also probably meant a change in the average space occupied by the downtown employee. This may in turn explain the apparent decline in downtown office employment at the very same time its physical plant underwent substantial enlargement.

Historically, downtown has been the home, par excellence, of the "back office" worker: an anonymous clerk handling enormous quantities of paper required by complex financial transactions. The dark, canyon-like streets, with their sheer cliffs of masonry, underlined the impression of an invisible business world where decisions are made in isolation, and revealed only when necessary.

Midtown, on the other hand, emphasizes "visibility," that is, the front office, public relations, the public "image". This is among the reasons (there are many others) for its superiority as a location for corporate headquarters, specially when public image is important.

The Chase Manhattan Building, with its abundance of glass, its open plaza, represented the first sharp break with the older downtown tradition. Other plazas have followed at 140 Broadway, the Home Insurance Building, and a huge open space is planned for the World Trade Center. These changes have not, however, been accompanied by the development of the type of luncheon and consumer facilities and amenities of which midtown has so much, and of which downtown is so notoriously deficient.

Directions of Office Expansion

The main thrust of downtown office construction today is to the east and south of the Core, following the lead taken by the proposed move of the Stock Exchange and triggered by the widening of Water Street. Little new investment in the older office area to the north and west is anticipated in the near future, with the possible exception of a large tract on the west side of Broadway now owned by United States Steel Pension Fund.

The future for office expansion (discussed previously) depends on new uses and new functions, most notably on the success of several major new projects in generating a demand for space: the World Trade Center, the Civic Center, the projected expansion of Pace College, and the possibility of new housing along the waterfronts. These projects are of immense proportions, but how soon, and to what degree, they will generate new demand in the area is not yet clear. Their immediate short-term impact will be to increase vacancies in buildings now occupied by government agencies, and thus to depress the competitive ability of existing older space in the market still further.

Downtown Street Pattern as it Affects Design

The Dutch street pattern, to which the peculiar juxtaposition of the famous skyscrapers owes much, was not the accidental chaos which it may seem at first glance. On the contrary, it showed a keen recognition of the configuration of the terrain. The high central ridge running down the middle of the island almost exactly describes the location of its main street -- Broadway. City Hall is located at the

Area
Evaluation
(by block)

Character	Legend	Rating
"SOFT"		0-11
		12-19
"HARD"		20-24
		25-38

VERY ACTIVE		DEGREE OF
ACTIVE		SPECULATION OR INVESTMENT
INACTIVE		ACTIVITY

Source:
    SEE APPENDIX II

0'   500'   1000'   2000'

Building
Life
Expectancy

Legend:

SHORT-TERM

LONG-TERM

Source:
SEE APPENDIX II

0'   500'   1000'   2000'

LOWER MANHATTAN PLAN **22**

**Building
Life Expectancy
(Long Term)**

Source:
SEE APPENDIX II

0'   500'   1000'   2000'

N

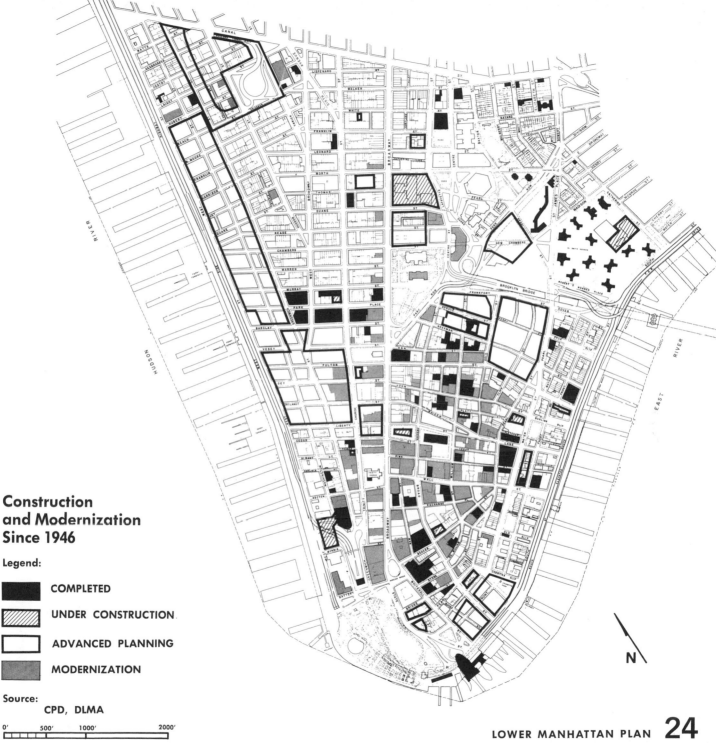

Construction
and Modernization
Since 1946

Legend:

■	COMPLETED
▨	UNDER CONSTRUCTION
□	ADVANCED PLANNING
▨	MODERNIZATION

Source:
CPD, DLMA

0'   500'   1000'   2000'

LOWER MANHATTAN PLAN **24**

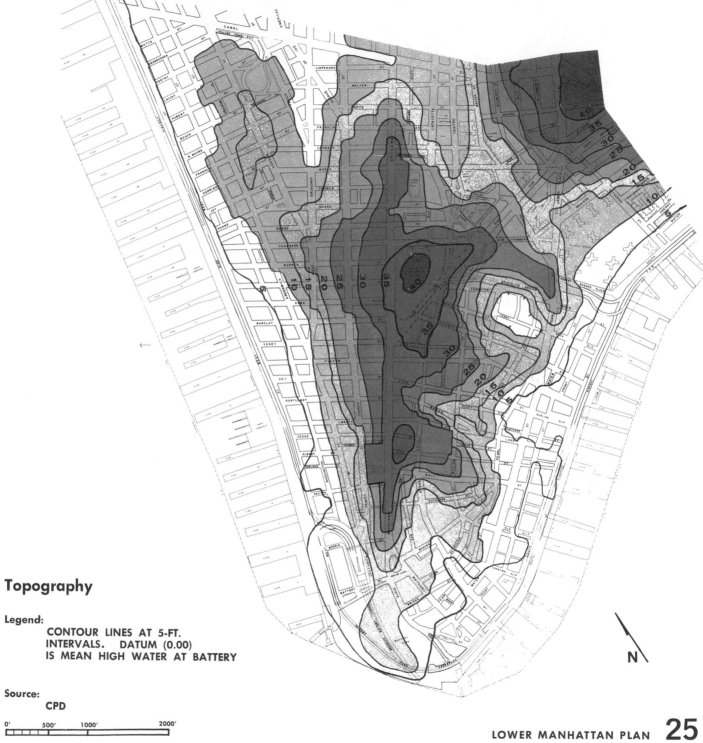

Topography

Legend:
CONTOUR LINES AT 5-FT.
INTERVALS. DATUM (0.00)
IS MEAN HIGH WATER AT BATTERY

Source:
CPD

0'   500'   1000'   2000'

LOWER MANHATTAN PLAN **25**

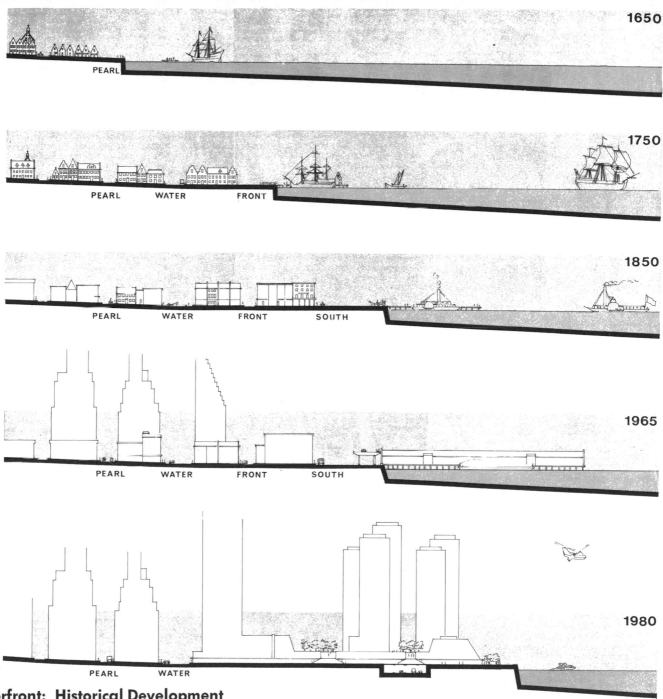

1650

PEARL

1750

PEARL   WATER   FRONT

1850

PEARL   WATER   FRONT   SOUTH

1965

PEARL   WATER   FRONT   SOUTH

1980

PEARL   WATER

Waterfront: Historical Development
1650-1980

0'   100'   200'   500'

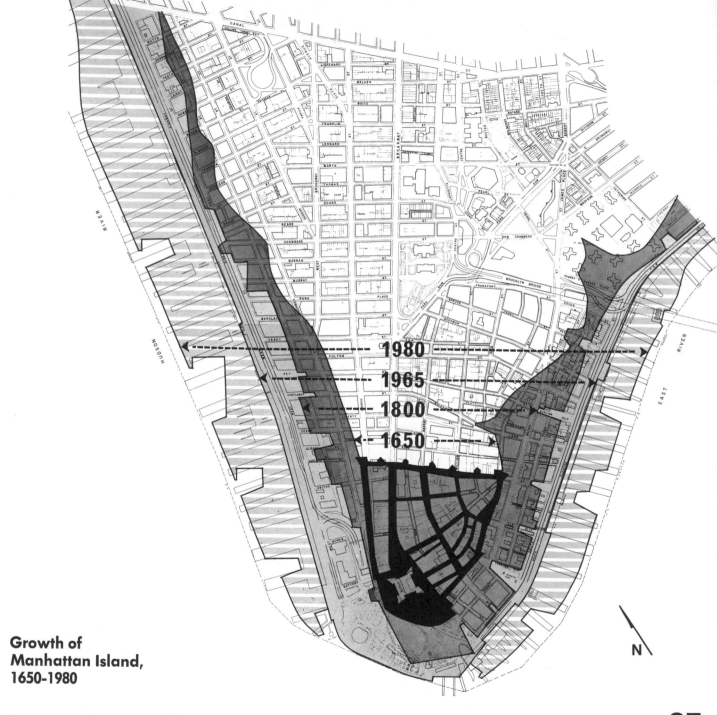

**Growth of
Manhattan Island,
1650-1980**

1980
1965
1800
1650

0' 500' 1000' 2000'

N

LOWER MANHATTAN PLAN **27**

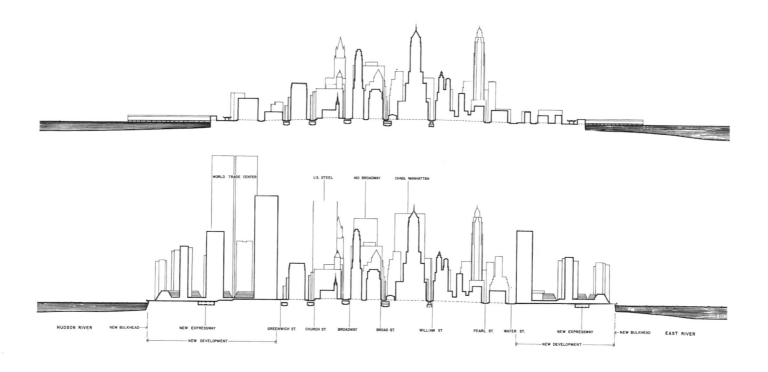

HUDSON RIVER   NEW BULKHEAD   NEW EXPRESSWAY   GREENWICH ST.   CHURCH ST.   BROADWAY   BROAD ST.   WILLIAM ST   PEARL ST.   WATER ST.   NEW EXPRESSWAY   NEW BULKHEAD   EAST RIVER

NEW DEVELOPMENT   NEW DEVELOPMENT

WORLD TRADE CENTER   U.S. STEEL   140 BROADWAY   CHASE MANHATTAN

**Cross-Island
Sections: Looking
North at Wall Street**

1950-1980

0'   500'   1000'

high point along Broadway. It was to this same high point on which City Hall is located that the line of the Brooklyn Bridge was aimed in the 1870's. Broad Street was built over a canal which the Dutch had dug out of a depressed swampland that turned northwest from the East River. Canal Street followed the course of the stream that emptied the small lake (known as "Collect Pond") just north of what is now the Civic Center.

The street pattern abruptly changes east of Pearl and West of Greenwich Streets, from the topographical pattern of the early Dutch system to the rectangular grid adopted by the English for the new land filled beyond Pearl and Greenwich.

The division between the original "core" (the old Dutch City) and the newer filled land persists to this day -- the divide between the high-prestige financial district (which occupies the old Dutch city) and the varier commercial activities that grew up around it -- shipping, warehousing, import and export houses, markets, ferry slips.

In contrast to the "hilly" core, the filled land is generally flat. The soil has poorer bearing qualities, and poses foundation problems where bedrock is not near the surface. This, as well as the existing structures affects where and how new construction will occur.

BUILDING PATTERNS

The corelation of excellent space and high dollar value is one expression of the peculiar genius of downtown. Builders have adhered closely to the irregular street system, filling out carefully to the edge of each property line.

The Old City

The tenacious observance of the old street system has helped preserve the value, integrity and character of the area. Downtown growth has been highly regenerative: older buildings constantly give way to newer ones. The basic form of the streets -- in terms of bulk, setbacks, and openings -- has changed only superficially in 75 years. Almost the entire Broad Street frontage on

both sides has been replaced unit-by-unit since 1900, but the basic street-form is very much the same.

Yet a major change has occurred in stages, as the skyscrapers developed and the new zoning law of 1916 took effect in the 1920's. The Equitable Building on Broadway triggered a reaction against filling entire sites and building to any height at all with no concern for light and air. The squat, commercial buildings of the earlier era gave way to the vertical bands of higher towers. In the space of a decade, the famous downtown skyline was reformed, to the dismay of many for whom the 40-story Equitable and Singer Buildings represented the ideal in vertical proportions and use of site.

The post-World War II change was, however, even more dramatic in character. Here, it was not a question of height or verticality, but of basic spatial organization. For the first time, the old street pattern was set aside. The freestanding tower was introduced, opening up huge new plazas, setting flat planes against vertical spires, and juxtaposing steel and glass against walls of stone. This trend toward more spacious downtown siting was further reinforced by the new zoning code introduced in 1962.

The problem today is how to retain a balance between these new openings and the old canyons. The indescriminate location of adjoining plazas in the downtown area could lead to a breakdown of the traditional spatial sense, transforming Wall Street's canyon into a diffuse pattern like that of Sixth Avenue in Midtown..

The New Zoning Ordinance

140 Broadway and the World Trade Center are the exact expression of building in this pattern to the maximum, within the new floor area ratio and (setback) incentive zoning adopted in 1962. This law encourages large-site assembly. The larger the site, the more possibility for setback, and thence the greater volume and height on any given site. Such buildings as 140 Broadway provide large setbacks and get more height in a market that would have paid a premium for larger floors.

The form of future building patterns is going to be affected greatly by any zoning ordinance, as it has in the past. The effect of the present ordinance will be to introduce a loosening of the "grain"[1] of buildings which, without coordination through a plan, may in turn loosen the Core as well as destroy many of the important semi-enclosed spaces downtown, such as Wall Street, Nassau Street and others.

BUILDING SITES OFFSHORE

Not the least of the potential building sites is the area between the bulkhead and pierhead lines. Offshore conditions at the tip of Manhattan are exceptionally favorable for either land fill or pile-supported structures. Since this area is no longer appropriate for marine-related functions, it is important as an area of potential use for the Core. In determining the possible extent and location of new construction past the bulkhead line, an assessment of subsoil conditions was necessary.

A good deal of data was already available in two reports commissioned by the Department of Marine and Aviation.[2] One report, issued in 1959, dealt with the East River, where the Department's consultants proposed a series of marginal piers to replace the obsolete and underutilized piers now there. The second report, issued in 1962, proposed the complete redevelopment of the land lying off the Hudson River from the Battery to 72nd Street. In the Lower Manhattan Study area, the consultants proposed a combination of piers, apartment houses and office buildings. This was the first serious study of the possibility of offshore housing downtown.

The following is a summary of the information presented in these two reports dealing with sub-surface conditions.[3]

General Conditions: Offshore conditions at the tip of Manhattan Island are exceptionally favorable for either land fill or pile-supported structures. Bedrock (chiefly Manhattan Schist) is capable of providing point bearing resistance to high load piles, piers or caissons, within several feet of its surface.

Soil Conditions: Typically, the strata of materials above bed-rock fall into two broad categories: a) those that are incapable of supporting fill without excessive settlement (compressible materials, either fill or organic clayey materials), and b) those that are capable of supporting fill and offering resistance to friction piles (coarse sands or granular materials). Strata A and B (below) fall into the first category, Stratum C into the second.

a) Non-Load Bearing: Stratum A: Miscellaneous Fill. Mixed Clay, silt, sand and gravel, cinders, occasional boulders, and pockets of organic silt. Stratum B: Silt. Very soft to soft organic clayey silt, fine sand. Will settle under fill loads, must be penetrated to denser materials by piles.

b) Load Bearing: Stratum C: Coarse Sands. Medium compact to very compact, includes gravel, granular soils.

Fill Procedures: In order to provide bearing for fill, Strata A and B must be dredged, then replaced by coarse sands and other materials capable of long term stabilization. In Zones II, III and IV, this process is feasible and economical; an average of some 20 feet of silt must be dredged out. In Zone I, however, where soft compressible material is found as deep as 80 to 120 feet, it is not recommended. In Zone II, for which preliminary calculations were made in the North River study, an average depth of 55 feet of new fill will be required to achieve a new surface of plus 12 above Mean Low Tide. Roughly five million cubic yards of fill are involved.

---

[1] Grain is defined as the texture of buildings and voids.
[2] Department of Marine and Aviation, Redevelopment of East River Piers, Lower Manhattan 1959. Consultants: Tippetts-Abbett-McCarthy-Stratton, Engineers and Architects. Department of Marine and Aviation, Manhattan North River Development Plan, 1962. Consultants: Ebasco Services, Inc. (Management Consultants), Eggers and Higgins (Architects) and Moran, Proctor, Mueser & Rutledge (Engineers),
[3] An additional source of information was Mr. John Wilson of the Port of New York Authority.

Estimated Cost: Costs were estimated at $8.30 a square foot, which included demolition of existing pier structures, dredging, fill, dikes and relieving platform. Retaining walls at the perimeter of the fill would cost roughly $1200 to $1500 per linear foot. This obviously means that the larger the land fill, both in breadth and length, the cheaper the unit cost of the new land. Thus, for a fill 600 feet wide, and 1,000 feet long, the retaining wall would cost around $4.30 per square foot of new land, whereas if it is 2,000 feet long, it would be $3.20 per square foot. On the other hand, if relieving platforms are not necessary and either ordinary platforms on piles or earth embankments will do, edge costs can be cut almost in half. Where structures are founded on fill (in Zone III, for example), deepened dredging should be considered to control settlement. Under exceptional circumstances, fill can be placed over Strata B Silt, but this requires special controls and an extended wait for soil consolidation.

River Flow and Tides: a) East River: According to the U.S. Corps of Engineers, placement of fill must not reduce the cross-sectional area of the riverway by more than two per cent. To achieve this, in the area south of Brooklyn Bridge, the outward line of fill must be kept back 80 feet from the pierhead line. Between Brooklyn and Manhattan Bridges, the comparable figure is 150 feet.

b) Hudson River: No such limitations seem to exist for Hudson River fill. Silting under existing piers is so great that the effective river section is already well under what the nominal width the river would allow. "For this reason," states the North River report, "the proposed land fills create little additional obstructions to the normal river flow."
The same would obviously also apply to pier supported structures. Silting along the marginal wharfs proposed would be substantially reduced in comparison to the slips between the finger they replace.

Pile Construction: Pile-tip elevations are obviously highest in Zones II and III, where bedrock is between 20 and 40 feet below mean sea level. No pile problem exists here and it might even be economical to carry piles for light loads to rock. In Zones I and IV, estimated average pile-tip elevations are about 80 feet below Mean Sea Level. Here various alternatives are open. In Zone III, the soil can sustain friction piles to support

light and medium loads. In Zone I, penetration to bedrock will probably be necessary, unless a small settlement can be tolerated. A lot of variables are involved in such calculations, and each configuration of factors will dictate different solutions.

Piles Versus Fill: The situation can be summed up as follows:

a) Land fill has lower first cost than a pile-supported deck area, without considering the additional costs of pile support for heavy structures in either case. The land fill area has practically unlimited life and is nearly maintenance-free if potential settlements are largely completed during construction.

b) Land fill eliminates certain continuing problems of pile-supported decks, such as long term pile-protection, concentration of organic gases and odors, and fire hazard beneath a deck extending over wide areas.

c) Fill areas provide convenient working space during construction and are flexible for possible changes in location and type of structure.

d) With proper construction procedures, pavements, utilities, landscaped areas, storage yards or light structures may be placed directly either on or in fill: pile support need not be provided. Although batter piles probably would be necessary for larger structures in decked areas, they could be eliminated for the same structures in filled areas.

Disadvantages of Land Fill Schemes: Disadvantages of land fill compared to pile-supported deck are as follows:

a) Land fill is economical where a relatively large area is available for filling at one time. Small areas with a large perimeter to area ratio are not economical for fill because of special problems and added costs for the slope at the fill's periphery.

b) For those structures which must be pile-supported, the foundation cost for piling is superimposed on costs for land fill in the building area. Unless all the compressible silt is removed from beneath fill areas, the pile loads will be significantly increased by drag forces.

c) In areas where fill if to be placed above organic silt, staged construction is required to insure the stability of fill slopes and to minimize settlement. This staged construction might require at least 3 years before structures could be commenced in the area and that time would be lost to revenue production.

Land Fill Construction Techniques and Costs:

In dredging and filling operations, the North River report anticipates the following conditions in Zone II:

Average Elevation of Bedrock Surface............ 47 feet
Average Elevation of Mudline .... 23 feet
Average Thickness of Sand Gravel
        Above Bedrock Surface .... 6 feet
Average Thickness of Strata to be Dredged .... 20 feet
Average Thickness of Fill to Elevation 12 .... 55 feet

Note: Elevations plus and minus refer to Department of Marine and Aviation Datum, 0.0 = Mean Low Tide at the Battery.

Costs for Land Fill in Zone II (called Area I in the North River Study) were calculated as follows, on the basis of 1962 prices:

Demolition	4,650,000
Dredging	3,160,000
Demolition of top of bulkhead	380,000
Fill including compaction of top layer	8,225,000
Perimeter relieving platform including fenders	6,800,000
TOTAL	23,215,000

The area of fill involved is 2,8 million square feet; and this comes out to the aforementioned $ 8.30 per square foot.

If a rock dike is constructed in place of a relieving platform, the cost would be reduced by $ 3,700,000, bringing the cost

of the new land to $ 6.95 per square foot.

If a regular bulkhead is constructed (at $ 1200 a linear foot) the cost would be a little less than the relieving platform ($ 6,250,000 against 6,800,000).

Comparison of costs between pile-supported and fill systems is complicated by the fact that one includes the cost of a finished deck, while the other does not. The North River study estimated the cost of pile-supported platforms in Zone I at around $11.50 per square foot. This included demolition, pier platform and fenders.

The conclusion of this analysis that land fill and new bulkheading, together with basic utilities, will cost around $14 to $15 per square foot of created land if the majority of the area from present bulkhead to pier head is filled. This, in New York terms, is a very modest cost for sites.

SITE ASSEMBLY COST AS A FACTOR IN GROWTH AND LAND USE

The above section demonstrates the very competitive possibilities of off-shore sites. This section continues the consideration of where development is likely to occur. First site assembly costs are considered. Then the utility of various possible uses within the zoning envelope is estimated to compare with costs of sites. Later in Chapter V, the two are put together as a device for determining a minimum, and maximum intensity, and the possible type of use that could be expected on any given site.

A contour map of downtown market values for land and improvements (combined) bears a distinct resemblance to the downtown topographical map. The Core and center have high values. Prices drop off progressively as one moves out towards the rivers. [1]

---

[1] The map itself is based on three sources of information: recent sales; informed opinion of local realtors and developers; and assessed valuations (adjusted to compensate for known discreapancies). It does not pretend to exact accuracy but is reliable as a general tool.

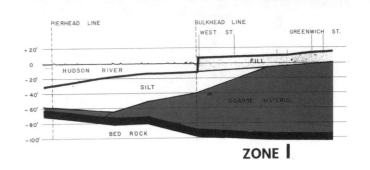

ZONE I

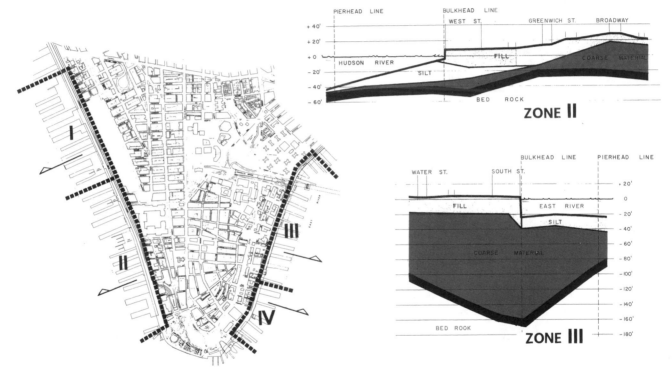

ZONE II

ZONE III

ZONE IV

**Offshore
Subsurface
Conditions**

Source:
CPD, DEPT. OF MARINE
AND AVIATION

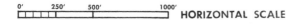

0'   250'   500'   1000'
HORIZONTAL SCALE

**Generalized
Land
Acquisition Costs**

(Dollars per Square
Foot for Land and Buildings)

Source:
RECENT SALES, ADJUSTED
ASSESSED VALUATIONS

0'   500'   1000'   2000'

LESS   THAN   50

50
100
200

50

500

200

500

200

100

N

LOWER MANHATTAN PLAN **30**

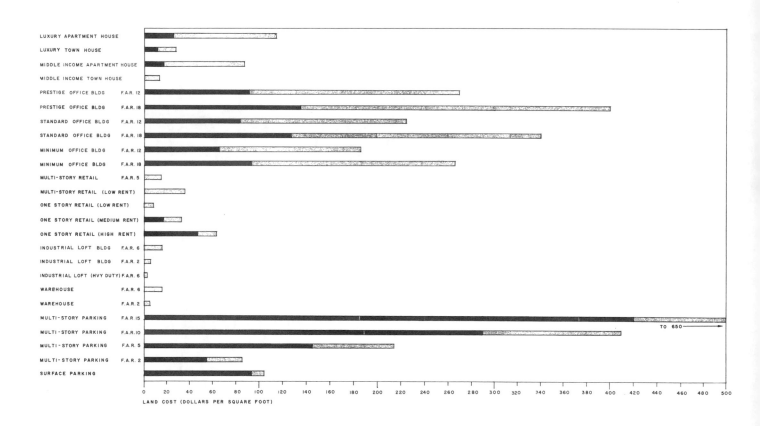

LUXURY APARTMENT HOUSE	
LUXURY TOWN HOUSE	
MIDDLE INCOME APARTMENT HOUSE	
MIDDLE INCOME TOWN HOUSE	
PRESTIGE OFFICE BLDG	F.A.R. 12
PRESTIGE OFFICE BLDG	F.A.R. 18
STANDARD OFFICE BLDG	F.A.R. 12
STANDARD OFFICE BLDG	F.A.R. 18
MINIMUM OFFICE BLDG	F.A.R. 12
MINIMUM OFFICE BLDG	F.A.R. 18
MULTI-STORY RETAIL	F.A.R. 5
MULTI-STORY RETAIL (LOW RENT)	
ONE STORY RETAIL (LOW RENT)	
ONE STORY RETAIL (MEDIUM RENT)	
ONE STORY RETAIL (HIGH RENT)	
INDUSTRIAL LOFT BLDG	F.A.R. 6
INDUSTRIAL LOFT BLDG	F.A.R. 2
INDUSTRIAL LOFT (HVY DUTY)	F.A.R. 6
WAREHOUSE	F.A.R. 6
WAREHOUSE	F.A.R. 2
MULTI-STORY PARKING	F.A.R. 15
MULTI-STORY PARKING	F.A.R. 10
MULTI-STORY PARKING	F.A.R. 5
MULTI-STORY PARKING	F.A.R. 2
SURFACE PARKING	

TO 650 →

LAND COST (DOLLARS PER SQUARE FOOT)

Maximum Land Cost Allowable for Specified Rates of Return for Selected Building Types

Legend:

8% PLUS

5-8%

The wide range of market values of land and improvements in the Study area reflects many of the same conditions analyzed earlier in this section: the extremely valuable Core and the declining periphery.

However, it should be noted that although the range is wide, much of the peripheral land is by no means cheap. This is particularly true of land adjacent to the Core. On the East Side where speculation is great, sites are now selling at between $ 75 and $ 100 a square foot, with some as high as $125 depending on location and assembly. Ten years ago this land could be purchased for perhaps a third as much.

This rise in value reflects the spreading out of Core activity which has occurred in recent years and the effect of the widening of Water Street. Speculative activity to the south and east of the Core has been particularly vigorous. A number of parcels have been assembled, and plans have been filed for several new buildings.

Even on the lower West Side, where little new construction is anticipated soon, land values are relatively high. This is due in part to the World Trade Center, and in part to recognition that the entire downtown area is a potential site for prime office construction.

The Ability of Uses to Pay Site Costs

To determine the economically possible uses in the downtown area, the maximum land costs for a variety of probable downtown building types was calculated, based on a series of assumptions concerning acceptable rates of return, taxes, rents, and expenses. [1]

The calculations were based on the relationship expressed in the real estate formula:

$$\text{Rate of Return} = \frac{\text{(Rents minus expenses) minus Property Taxes}}{\text{Investment}}$$

This rate of return is sometimes called cash flow. It is essentially net income return to full investment after operating expenses and realty taxes. It is measured before considerations of mortgage financing alternatives and income tax situations.

For any combination of building, site, income stream, certainty, and investor, there is a minimum cash flow rate-of-return below which "that" investor won't venture into "that" situation. This minimum rate represents combined returns for the investment itself, management of the investment, anticipations about its future net income stream, and the degree of risk involved. This combination can then be set against alternative investment returns, mortgaging prospects or limits, and income tax considerations. A choice about complex relationships can be made on a one-factor basis.

Very simply, if the rate of return equals or exceeds the minimum acceptable rate for a specific investor, that investor could reasonably be expected to build that building on that site. If the rate of return is less than the minimum rate, then the suggested private market investment is unlikely as specified, without public subsidy in one or another form, such as land cost write-down, realty tax abatement, mortgage financing assistance, or rent subsidy. Alternatively, private "subsidy" in the form of a different private investor with a lower minimum rate limit -- due to concern, or tax position, or both -- is a possible way to make an otherwise unlikely investment more likely.

By working backward from the general relationship, as expressed in the rate of return formula, it was possible to examine each of the variables which affect these general values. [2] The calculations of this investment analysis kept the values of each of these factors constant for each building type. In effect, the results of the analysis show how the actual rate of return will change as land cost changes if all other variables

---

[1] These calculations do not apply to non-competitive corporate buildings where site costs are often much more than the earning power of the building.

[2] The names and relations of the variables were those used in the FORTRAN computer program written to carry out the investment analysis.

remain constant for that building type. [1]

Ten building types were analyzed. They represent those major
building types which most reasonably can be expected as major
uses in the Study area. A summation of results from the investment analysis gives the maximum land cost that could be paid
while still giving an investor an 8 per cent or a 5 per cent return on the total investment. Such a return represents as much
as a 15-to-20 per cent return on the developer's equity investment, depending on the proportion his investment bears to the
total. These calculations refer, of course, to an average
"rational" investor, and make no allowance for the many special situations governing individual cases, where tax and de-
preciation situations may dictate widely varying demands and
needs.

In summary these calculations confirm many widely held assumptions regarding investment opportunities.

For example, unsubsidized industrial and warehouse lofts cannot
provide a sufficient return to pay for construction costs, let
alone land costs at prevailing rents and land costs.

Conventionally-financed residential buildings (except in special luxury situations) cannot be built on land costing much
over $50 a square foot. This maximum pertains to the upper-
middle and to upper-income housing typical of much recent Manhattan construction.

For other categories even this figure is far in excess of the possible.

South of the Worth-Chambers line no such land is available.
Thus it is clear that, without substantial subsidy, housing in the
Core area cannot pay current site costs. In fact, only in the
water front fill area can land be made available for housing at
an economic cost.

---

[1] A change in building cost, rent, etc., was considered to
establish another building type. The actual values for each
of the variables was assembled from two major sources: New
York City departments and agencies especially the Department
of City Planning and the Real Property Assessment Department,
and informed opinion from real estate and architectural firms
familiar with the costs of constructing, financing, renting and
operating each of the building types analyzed.

CHAPTER   IV

CURRENT AND COMMITTED PROJECTS

One of the principal objectives of the Study was to determine what the impact will be of the projects which are either
in planning or currently underway. This impact will set in
motion massive changes, most for the better, in Lower Manhattan. These changes (particularly regarding the movement
system) were evaluated to determine what ought to be the
response of the City to proposed street closures and realign-
ments, and what is likely to be the reaction of the private
sector of the market. The movement response is considered
in detail in Part 2. Here the focus is on land use and functions.

The projects considered are: the World Trade Center, the
New York Stock Exchange, Brooklyn Bridge Southwest Urban
Renewal Project, the Washington Market Area Urban Renewal
Project, and the Civic Center. A number of other important
private projects were also evaluated, but collectively as net
additions to space rather than individually.

It should be noted that two of the current projects--the World
Trade Center and the Civic Center -- have also been the
subjects of special reports by the Department of City Planning to Mayor John Lindsay, and for that reason are dealt
with only generally here.

THE WORLD TRADE CENTER [1]

The prime stated objective of the World Trade Center is
to simplify and expand international trade by centralizing
and consolidating within the Center essential world trade
services and activities. It is anticipated that members of
the world trade community will be able to function more
efficiently by rapid interchange of information, prompt
processing of trade documents and rapid consummation of
exchange and other transactions. The Center's expected
range of world trade services and facilities will constitute
a new and unique headquarters for international trade.

Description of the Project

The Center will contain principally government agencies
and private firms which play a part in international marketing and in the administrative processing of world trade.
The United States Bureau of the Customs, offices of the
Department of Commerce, Port Authority administrative
offices, foreign consulates and commercial attaches, foreign government purchasing missions, Custom House brokers,
international trade associations, exporters, importers,
freight forwarders, international banks, marine insurance
firms and other agencies and businesses related to foreign
trade will be among the occupants. In addition, the State
of New York plans to consolidate most of its principal
offices in Manhattan in the Center. These offices now
account for approximately 1,500,000 square feet of rentable
space at both owned and leased locations. Only those State
offices which are essentially neighborhood service facilities

[1] For a more detailed discussion of the World Trade Center see
Department of City Planning, City of New York, The World
Trade Center: An Evaluation, The Department, March, 1966.

will remain where they are.

The following, with the indicated major occupants and functions are scheduled in the World Trade Center and the distribution of net floor space:

OCCUPANTS, FUNCTIONS AND SPACE IN THE WORLD TRADE CENTER [1]

User	Net Square Feet
State of New York	1,900,000
U.S. Bureau of the Customs	800,000
N.Y. Port of Authority	800,000
Other Government (Foreign and State Functions Related to World Trade)	450,000
Trade Service (customs brokers, freight forwarders, international banks, etc.)	1,700,000
Export-Import Firms	2,300,000
Auxiliary Services (consumer services)	750,000
Exhibit Space	185,000
Information & Education Center	80,000
Hotel (550 Rooms)	200,000
Parking (subsurface) (2,000 cars)	800,000
Storage (subsurface)	200,000
TOTAL	10,165,000

The proposed World Trade Center will be located on the largest commercial superblock in Manhattan, to be created by closing all internal streets: its length and width about equal to the midtown blocks between Fifth and Park Avenue. The 16-acre site in Lower Manhattan is bounded by Vesey Street on the north, Liberty on the south with West and Church Streets, respectively, the western and eastern boundaries.

Transit access will be provided by three subway lines with direct connections by underground passageways to a covered concourse level directly underneath the plaza. The new PATH station, to be relocated under the present Greenwich Street (six levels below grade), will also connect directly into the concourse, which will contain shops, restaurants and other consumer services, as well as direct access to all of the elevators serving the buildings above. The Center's designers have assumed that a great majority of the Center's 100,000 visitors and 50,000 employees will pass through the Concourse. To facilitate access to the Concourse level from the west, a new underpass will be constructed under Church Street, supplementing the two underpasses (two levels below grade) now in operation.

The paved five-acre pedestrian plaza above the concourse is conceived of primarily for exhibitions and noon-time strolls, rather than as a part of the primary pedestrian circulation system. From the west it can be reached only by crossing Church Street itself, which is over 100 feet wide; and from the major office units it can be reached only by rising by escalator from the central pedestrian circulation level, the Concourse. The Plaza itself will be about ten feet above the level of Church Street, and (since the ground slopes off to the west) about 28 feet above West Street, approximately at the level of the elevated Miller Highway.

Once within the World Trade Center sites vehicles and pedestrians will be completely separated. The plaza and the concourse levels will be exclusively for pedestrians. Under these levels will be parking for 2,000 cars, building service and storage, and Customs examination areas. These

[1] Source: Port of New York Authority, February, 1966

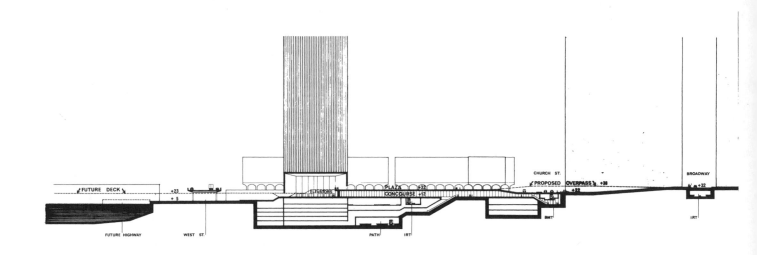

FUTURE DECK   +23
+ 5

ELEVATORS   PLAZA +32
CONCOURSE +12

CHURCH ST.
PROPOSED OVERPASS +38
+32

BROADWAY
+32

FUTURE HIGHWAY   WEST ST.   PATH   IRT   BMT   IRT

**Section Through
World Trade Center:
Looking North**

0'   100'   200'   500'

areas will be entered from vehicular tunnels from West Broadway, Liberty and West Streets.

Taxis and other Center-generated traffic will be provided for in separate drop-off lanes, out of the main flow of traffic. Traffic not destined for the Center will circulate around the superblock on the peripheral streets which, except for West Street, will be doubled in width.

Existing Land Use and Structures

This area is now occupied by a polyglot of old delapidated loft structures, with retail office, manufacturing, automotive, and some small amount of residential use.

Many of the small retail stores are in older loft buildings, using the basements or upper floors for storage. A large proportion of the upper floors of these buildings have been vacant for many years. There are a small number of transient hotels. Two fire houses, and auto service and parking lots make up the rest.

The most substantial structures in the area are the office buildings along Church, Liberty and Vesey Streets. Some 61 per cent of the structures in the area were built before 1858; 22 percent were built between 1358 and 1914; 15 percent between 1915 and 1929; and only 2 percent after 1930. Most are in poor condition.

A spine of retail business runs along Greenwich Street, extending on most of the cross-streets to the east and west. With few exceptions the distribution of light industrial and warehousing uses follows the same pattern.

The site of 15 acres presently consists of 14 small unevenly shaped blocks. The streets themselves, many of them awkwardly aligned, occupy almost half of the site.

Current Employment

Of the total number of 17,200 persons employed on the site in 1958 [1], the largest single number, 5,850 were engaged in services. This category covered a wide variety of professional, business and personal services from barbering and management consultation to telephone-answering and legal. The second largest group of workers, 3,150, were employed in light manufacturing.

Retail stores employed 2,550 persons. These stores had given this area its distinctive quality: home electronic goods, food specialties, vegetables and fruits, coffee and tea, discount and hardware appliances, florists, pet shops, bargain clothing apparel.

Other employment included 1,750 workers in wholesaling, mostly with stock, and 1,700 workers in financial, real estate and insurance. Transportation, communication and public utilities employed 1,200 construction industries 700, and government offices 200.

It is now estimated that the total employment in the site as of mid-February 1966 is between 4,000 and 5,000, including workers employed by PATH. This represents a 75 per cent decrease in jobs over the 1958 employment.

Analysis Of Effect On Lower Manhattan

Real Estate And Future Growth: Of course, it is not possible to precisely guage the impact of the World Trade Center on the overall market for new office space and the occupancy of existing space. However, it is possible to make generalized observations.

There is little evidence to suggest to date that anticipation of the World Trade Center is having any serious negative

---

[1] Department of City Planning, study of wage and salary employment in Manhattan CBD, 1958.

effect on the rate of new building construction downtown. In the long-run it is likely that the World Trade Center's 8,000,000 square feet of competitive space will be absorbed by a currently expanding market for office space in the Manhattan CBD. The introduction of this new function into Lower Manhattan -- international trade -- and the Port Authority's investment of over $500,000,000 together with the improvement of PATH, will very likely have a generative "throw-off" on future office growth in Lower Manhattan. Already there is evidence of land speculation in the area to the north. In addition a successful Center can enhance New York's growing role as the center of international finance. Over time a functional connection to the financial community is expected to develop. This could manifest itself in the expansion of banking east of Broadway and north of Liberty Street, its traditional boundaries until now. In addition to the supporting service that will be provided within the Center other ancillary activities are anticipated near or adjacent to the Center. These areas will ultimately assume greater value as prime office sites than they now enjoy.

The immediate impact, however, may be very significant on the market for existing office space in older buildings downtown. As has been seen, about three-quarters of the office floor space, or about 40 million square feet, is pre-World War II. Half, or 20 million square feet, is still unmodernized. In 1963, vacancy rates in non-modernized office buildings south of Chambers Street averaged about 13 per cent. Almost all of the tenants of the Customs House, 45 and 346 Broadway, 80 Centre Street and 270 Broadway are already scheduled to move to the Center. Customs brokers, freight forwarders, State offices in rented space, Marine Insurance firms and international banks will be attracted to the Center leaving office **space behind**. The Port Authority has said that one half of its 50,000 Center employment is already in Lower Manhattan.

The response of the market to this will be as it has been elsewhere. Vacancies in buildings that have good locations and can be modernized will stimulate competitive remodelling. Where structures are not so well located, rents will drop. Owners of older buildings will face the choice of remodelling, dropping rents, or considering alternative uses. As elsewhere, it is expected that the result, in the long-run, will be to upgrade the office stock, improve the environment, and increase taxes to the City.

Transit: The World Trade Center with its 150,000 daily visitors and employees is advantageously situated in relation to the subway system. Passing through the site is the Seventh Avenue IRT. On the east is the BMT Broadway Line and just to the northeast the entrance to the IND. A short block away is the Fulton Street-Broadway complex of stations which provide access to two additional lines. Platform lengthening resulting in increased capacities has already occurred on the Seventh Avenue IRT. Studies of train capacities of all the lines in Lower Manhattan indicate considerable additional available capacity in the lines on the West Side. It is anticipated that the Center will not overload the subway system.

Pedestrian Circulation: Port Authority planners estimate that a little under one half of its workers and visitors will arrive by the three subway lines (and PATH) directly connected to the below-grade Concourse level; the remainder will arrive from subway stations to the west, crossing Church, Liberty and Vesey Streets to reach the Site.

The pedestrian routes from the east therefore are of critical importance. Question may be raised concerning the adequacy of this access, particularly with regard to the Church Street crossing, which involves a complex two-level drop on one side, and a one level rise to the Concourse on the other. It is difficult to believe that, except in bad weather, this underground route will be extensively used. The easier, more natural route will be to cross Church Street on-grade, and to continue on-grade into the center, across the great open plaza, and from there directly into the office buildings.

This route is not only easier, but it has the virtue of making maximum use of the huge plaza, with its handsome paving, its attractive displays.

The problem with this route, however, is Church Street itself. Heavy pedestrian crossing will pose difficulties for both pedestrians and the anticipated large volumes of vehicular traffic, each slowing the other up considerably. This would become further exacerbated if the World Trade Center

---

[1] Similar massive changes on a smaller scale have been observed in Pittsburgh, Chicago, Baltimore, Philadelphia and many other cities.

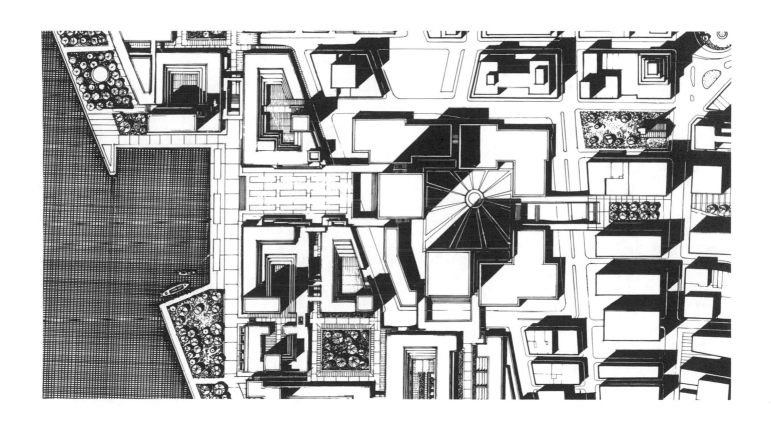

**Waterfront
Development:
World Trade Center**

0'   200'   1000'

plaza should become part of a pedestrian route from the interior of the island to the waterfront development area.

For these reasons an overpass at Church Street, described in more detail among recommendations should be considered.

Vehicular Circulation: The Center, a significant vehicular generator itself, will be adjacent to four major traffic routes: Barclay and Vesey Streets to the north and Liberty Street to the south provide east-west movement. Church and West Streets on the east and west provide north-south movement.

Many currently important streets such as Fulton and Greenwich will be closed to create this large commercial superblock. To compensate for this, peripheral streets are being doubled in width. The proposed traffic pattern -- a modified traffic-circle -- while not providing the highest quality of service, appears to satisfy adequately traffic circulation requirements. Off-street parking for 2,000 cars and 75 to 100 truck berths will help solve the servicing and parking problems. The Center will be a significant generator of trucks particularly to the Customs examination areas. Curb cuts and turnarounds will adequately provide for buses, cabs and other temporarily stopped vehicles.

Urban Design: The World Trade Center establishes a new scale, both horizontal and vertical, in the skyline and streetscape of Lower Manhattan. Its partial symmetry, large paved open plaza, and the horizontal line of its low buildings against aluminum-clad 110-story towers contrast strongly with the older downtown community. The five-acre plaza will provide a major urban open space and the lower five-story flanking buildings almost completely enclosing the plaza will help provide a sense of human scale at the pedestrian level.

At first glance the 110-story towers seem to overpower the skyline, and architectural reactions have been voiced strongly. Historic examination of change reveals, however, that this is the old idea only bigger and bolder. The Lower Manhattan skyline was created to some extent by corporate egos of the past. These new towers can be considered no

more out of scale than were the Woolworth Building and Empire State Building in their day.

Perhaps the most startling contrast is between the squared-off towers and the spires of most of the older buildings. Buildings of a similar kind and close to the Center in height are needed to form a transition between it and the old scale.

Recommendations

1. Integration.

If the World Trade Center is to function as an integral part of the downtown community, the design of its many peripheral pedestrian connections should be given further consideration.

Recent modifications of the relationship between the towers and the low-rise units have facilitated connections to future raised pedestrian levels to the west and south, the probable elevation of these future pedestrian levels has been established in the optimum site plan (at +24) and this elevation should be taken into account in the further design of the connecting elements.

To the east, however, the problem is more complex, and more immediate, and here an overpass should be planned as part of the current design.

2. Overpass.

The proposed overpass would require a minimum of vertical movement. Following the line of Dey Street, it would ultimately form a connection between Broadway and the World Trade Center Plaza, which are roughly at the same elevation. In traversing Church Street itself, the overpass would have to rise some six feet (for clearance).

The construction of this overpass would have several important by-products. By making it easy for pedestrians to move across the plaza, it could enhance usage of what should be an exciting, useful and busy space. The relocation on the Plaza of a portion of the consumer services now planned exclusively for the below-grade Concourse might thus also be considered.

This, in turn, may raise the question of whether it is desirable for the Center's elevators to load and unload at the Concourse level. The decision to place the elevator entrances at the Concourse level was based on the assumption that some 80 per cent of the Center's employees and visitors would arrive through the underground Concourse, and only 20 per cent across the plaza.

3. Concourse and Plaza

This assumption, if correct, will mean a virtually empty plaza during the very periods of the day when it should have the most intensive use.

Closer investigation indicates that, with close to 50 per cent of the Center's employees walking on-grade from the east, the 80 per cent figure for the Concourse is probably very high -- even if no direct overpass is constructed at Church Street. With an overpass, however, the distribution might well be nearer 50-50, and this may suggest some rethinking of the relationship of the two major pedestrian levels and the elevators, along with a broader conception of the role of the great plaza itself.

Or it may suggest that, if the Concourse is to be the major pedestrian level of the Center, handling some 130,000 people daily, it should be treated as such: perhaps as a monumental covered space, fifty or sixty feet high, or even higher, in which the functions of the Concourse and the Plaza are combined.

4. Intra-Bus

A further consideration, along these lines, concerns the routing of the low-speed Intra-Bus. The most desirable route would be one which passes directly across the plaza, depositing its passengers at the entrances to the Towers. In the future, it would continue past the Center and onto the waterfront deck beyond. The proposed Church Street overpass (running along Dey Street from Broadway) would facilitate such a route.

A less preferable alternative would be to route the Intra-Bus around the Center, on Vesey and/or Liberty Streets. This would detract from the usefulness of the plaza, and also reinforce the

Center's physical "isolation" from the city's fabric.

THE NEW YORK STOCK EXCHANGE SITE

At the present writing the proposal to impose an additional stock transfer tax has upset the plans of the Stock Exchange to locate at the foot of Broad Street. Although alternative choices are available to the Exchange[1], the original plans to which the Exchange may return are analysed here, as they will more or less obtain on many alternate sites.

The Exchange is making a significant expansion move for the third time in its history. The need for more room on its trading floor and the need to introduce more automated equipment require a site area of considerable size for the Exchange to accommodate its growing volumes of business. Its strong physical links to banks and brokerage houses require a site within walking distance of the financial core.

Description of Project

The Exchange proposed to build a trading floor, with office space and adjacent meeting rooms. It would accommodate a projected employment of 3,700, up from its present employment of 2,400. Added to this daily total will be 2,500 tourists, 500 traders and 2,000 business visitors. The adjacent office building to have been built by the Atlas-McGraw Co. would undoubtedly house predominantly member firms of the Exchange, would contain about 5,000 employees in about 1,200,000 square feet of space. Parking for 200 cars and retail facilities are to be provided in a below-grade concourse and garage. The Exchange's investment would be about $ 50,000,000, while the adjacent office building would cost $ 27,000,000.

The proposed Exchange site (of 100,000 square feet) is located about 1,200 feet southeast of its present location in the center of the financial district. The private office building

---

[1] 20 Broad Street was designed to permit removal of thru floors for expansion of the Exchange.

would occupy a site of 110,000 square feet, just to its south across Broad Street. Four historically significant buildings are to be moved from the sites to the Fraunces Tavern block where they will be restored and, in combination with a rebuilt replica of Stadt Huys, will be the downtown Museum of the City of New York. Together with the tourist attraction of the Exchange, this will be a highly popular place and strengthen the Battery area as a tourist attraction.

Previous Land Use

The site originally contained 3 residential buildings with 9 families and 91 commercial buildings with 250 tenants. These buildings were used for office, manufacturing and warehousing. Marine supplies with other maritime functions predominated. At present the majority of the area is being used temporarily for parking. Historically it has been related to the commerce of the adjacent waterfront.

Analysis and Effect on Lower Manhattan

Real Estate and Future Growth: The decision of the Exchange to move has precipitated a wave of real estate speculator activity in areas heretofore considered "out of the office core". This area, particularly from Whitehall to Maiden Lane between Pearl and South Streets, is being assembled by a few investors, because of the Exchange's move, the sale of City-owned land, the widening of Water Street and expansion needs of the financial district. On the west side, the World Trade Center has not appeared as yet to have precipitated any spectacular activity similar in scope to the Exchange, probably because it is a new concept without the institutionalized linkages of the Exchange to the financial community.

The immediate effect of this move would be to almost double the perimeter of the financial community. However, although its historic compactness will be loosened, it will not be destroyed by this enlarged core. Over time, a gravitation of member firms and other related activity to the now underdeveloped areas around the Exchange, can be anticipated.

Pedestrian Circulation: The Exchange combined with the City Museum will be a significant generator of pedestrian movement.

In addition to 3,700 employees, the Exchange expects over 5,000 daily visitors.

To reach existing adjacent subways such as the IRT involves circuitous movement through an area of vehicular-pedestrian conflict because of the vehicular approaches to the Staten Island Ferry. Also there is an absence of pedestrian connections to the Ferry Terminal and the proposed new developments on the waterfront. A solution to this problem must ultimately involve a separation of pedestrian and vehicular movement around the western and southern perimeter of the site.

Probably the most significant pedestrian impact of the relocation of the Exchange will be on Broad Street, which will act with Wall Street as the central pedestrian arteries of the financial community.

Transit: The Exchange is served by the IRT Lexington and Seventh Avenue Lines and the BMT Broadway. These lines make the Exchange relatively well-served by rapid transit. In contrast, however, its former site on Broad and Wall Streets was served by five different lines within a four-minute walk. However the Exchange's employment and new future office development at this site would not present any problem as far as transit riders are concerned.

Traffic: The Exchange and the adjacent office building are following the current downtown pattern of the street closing, development of superblocks and the widening of peripheral streets. Local traffic circulation in the area is complicated by the access streets to the elevated F.D.R. Drive. The completion of the widening of Water Street should considerably improve circulation. In addition, South Street and Coenties Slip will be widened to increase street capacity in the immediate area. Because of the alignment of the F.D.R. Drive, Broad Street is the major entrance to the financial district from the north, while Coenties Slip provides access to the Battery Park Underpass.

Local traffic circulation in the area will be improved by these changes and will be adequate for the Exchange development. However, the access to the F.D.R. Drive will continue to be a problem, because of the awkward alignment, and increasing traffic volumes will further complicate access to the Drive and perhaps overall circulation in the area. Further consideration of this is given in Part 2 of the Report.

Urban Design: The Exchange's location adjacent to the waterfront and the Bay will afford it a significant place in the downtown foreground. Its proposed massing in the latest scheme is an appropriate symbol of its importance.

Immediate Recommendations

1. The Water Street widening should be completed, extending to Whitehall Street.

2. Future pedestrian connections to the waterfront should be planned for by extension of the proposed plazas across South Street.

3. Broad Street should be considered (for the future) as a pedestrian street to facilitate movement to the Exchange. The long-range proposal to relocate and redesign F.D.R. Drive below-grade will release this street for exclusive pedestrian movement.

4. Pedestrian connections to the Staten Island Ferry area and subways should be improved. The proposed raised plaza along Whitehall Street suggests the possibility of a pedestrian overpass or an underpass from its below-grade concourse level.

5. If the New York Stock Exchange does not locate on this site consideration should be given to including it, along with its waterfront, as part of the East Side Urban Renewal Area.

BROOKLYN BRIDGE SOUTHWEST

This federally-assisted 27 acre urban renewal project administered by the Housing and Redevelopment Board will provide for the expansion of two important institutions - Pace College and Beekman-Downtown Hospital. In addition it will introduce a middle-income residential population into Lower Manhattan south of the Brooklyn Bridge providing housing within walking distance of the Core , the Civic Center, and the World Trade Center.

Description of the Project

The apartment development will contain 1,650 units (5 percent three bedroom, 33 percent two bedroom, 50 percent one bedroom and 12 percent efficiency apartments). A parking garage for 600 cars will permit 40 per cent of the tenants the possibility of parking their cars. Commercial buildings will provide about 200,000 square feet of retail shopping space while an additional office building is planned for 400,000 square feet of space. The apartments will occupy seven acres while commercial uses occupy four acres.

Pace College will build a new campus to provide for 10,000 students (a doubling of its enrollment) a new graduate school with 1,500 students, a library, a 600 seat theater, a gymnasium with 2,200 seats, computer and communications centers, a dormitory for 600 students, 60 new classrooms and a cafeteria and administrative space.

Beekman Downtown Hospital will expand from 200 to 300 beds with the possibility of adding 200 beds at a later date including facilities for 300 ambulatory patients per day. One third of its patients are from downtown (mostly emergency cases with many from Chinatown). Twenty five percent are welfare cases. A longer-range plan includes a separate building for long-term care. Together all these uses occupy four acres.

The four 30-story residential towers with connecting six and seven story lower units are interconnected by an elevated plaza. Underneath this plaza are two levels of parking. The open areas, some of them planted, provide the necessary recreational and community facilities in a relatively quiet and isolated area two levels above the street. The long six to seven story buildings provide an intermediate scale between the towers and the low rental structures.

Pace College is developing its long narrow site into a multi-level college and campus. The first three to five stories of this sharply sloping site (three stories at Park Row and five at Gold Street) will be developed into academic facilities with the "campus" on the roof, while a 23 story tower near Gold Street will accommodate administrative and faculty offices with the student dormitory.

Beekman Hospital will expand its existing buildings by adding a wing to the east, extending each floor of the existing building.

Existing Land Use

The site now contains 11 blocks on which are 171 commercial and industrial buildings. 143 are deteriorating. Over 700 businesses are being relocated including 15 individuals (mostly artists) living in warehouses in the area. The area contained a mixture of uses including offices on Park Row, the "swamp" (an historic leather wholesaling area) printers and other manufacturing including some automotive uses. Thus the trend toward the decline of goods-handling activity from below Chambers Street is being accelerated by this project. It also was the place of origin of "pop" art in America.

Total public investment in land acquisition, administration and relocation is expected to be $22 million. Total resale value of the site averages about $25 per square foot. The City contribution, after land writedown and sale, will be about $3 million. The sponsors will pay $5.5 million for land. The residential developer, Pace College and Beekman Hospital will invest about $50,000,000 on the site.

Analysis and Effect on Lower Manhattan

Real Estate and Future Growth: Brooklyn Bridge Southwest is in a polyglot neighborhood unusual for a housing project. To the south, across a half block of non-descript commercial structures, it faces the insurance district. To the east across a widened Water Street is the Fulton Fish Market, and to the west is Pace College and Beekman Hospital. To the north of the Brooklyn Bridge are public and middle income housing projects.

While the location is not now prepossessing, it is a dynamic one quite different from the homogeneous residential surroundings of other housing. Because of the solid wall of the Brooklyn Bridge, the project stands somewhat isolated in the midst of a dense business and industrial area. It will have to provide many of its own supporting retail and recreational facilities. Its expected population of 4 to 5,000 persons and high proportion of

downtown workers and few children. Here will be the first bridgehead of housing in Lower Manhattan and it will provide a test for the concept of housing-office intermixture. It will serve as the starting point of additional middle-income housing in Lower Manhattan.

Pace College's ambitious $16,000,000 expansion will provide more cultural and educational opportunities to the downtown business community through its educational programs and new theatre-library-auditorium facilities. The diversification of Lower Manhattan's predominant use -- business -- will be furthered by this development. The area to the South of the new campus along Nassau Street toward the "soft" area around Fulton Street can be considered an "expansion" area for this prime growth industry, education. The College realizes that it may outgrow its projected facilities in a few years and will have to purchase buildings to its south. The school has been able to fill classrooms as fast as they can be made available.

Beekman Hospital will expand its services for the residential community and its City clientele south of Canal Street was well as the business area to the south. About 75 percent of its cases come from this area.

Transit: The institutional and residential sites are well served by subway. Within a five minute walk are all the subway lines in the City located in the Fulton Street complex. Any additional load on the transit system should be predominantly in the reverse direction from the daily heavy incoming movement.

At present buses run on Water Street and Park Row. The possibility has been discussed of extending an existing line down Madison Street, under the Bridge to Gold and Fulton. This could provide an additional connection to the residential areas to the North.

Pedestrian Circulation: If the experience from Chatham Green Houses holds true here, over 50 percent of BBSW residents who work will be employed in Lower Manhattan. An even higher percentage of walk-to-work employees can reasonably be expected here because it is much closer to the financial Core. The experience of people who actually walk-to-work and the distances involved will provide a real clue to the effectiveness of such a policy.

Pedestrian access to the south will be simplest, while access to the North is impeded by the Bridge and its access ramps. Access to the Civic Center, in spite of an existing underpass and a proposed overpass (at Park Row), will be difficult. The site slopes 20 feet from Park Row to Water and it would have been possible to provide continuous level pedestrian access within the site.

Fulton Street to the south of the residential block is to become an important pedestrian street with service access in the overall circulation system developed for Lower Manhattan. Both Pace College and the housing have been developed as "islands" and their pedestrian areas will be above and separated from street level.

Traffic Circulation: Peripheral streets, including Gold, Frankfort, and Fulton will have their rights-of-way widened. Traffic circulation in the area should be improved and off-street parking and loading will improve the curbside situation. The continuation of Madison Street -- Gold Street into this area will provide an additional entrance to the financial district and serve principally as a connector street with the residential areas to the North.

Immediate Recommendations

1. The widened right-of-way of Fulton Street should be designed in conformity with the recommended use of Fulton Street as a pedestrian-service street.

2. A future pedestrian connection to the area to the east (future housing) should be designed so that these housing areas can be connected by a walkway system. This may be an at-grade solution, or if it proves feasible an overpass over Water Street.

WASHINGTON STREET URBAN RENEWAL AREA

The history of this project goes back seven years, involves a large number of groups, interests and changing market conditions, and reflects all the complexities and problems of New York's industrial development.

Description

The gross land of the renewal area is 38 acres, the net land 23 acres. It is now owned by the City, and its present users -- the produce market -- are in the process of leaving for the new Hunt's Point Market in the Bronx. In six years of effort the city has not yet found a suitable sponsor for the site's redevelopment, and the prospect looms for the site to become a stretch of deserted land along West Street for some years to come. It would thus join the Flatlands Industrial Park in Brooklyn, a similar development area taken over by the City for which no suitable use has yet been found.

The total cost of acquisition, demolition, management, and site preparation, will come to around $ 44 million. The City will pay a third and the Federal Government two thirds of this $ 44 million less whatever the eventual resale value of the land is. This comes to a little under $ 44 a square foot cost of the land available for redevelopment.

The original plan called for a combination of offices in the southern half of the site and warehouse-loft space in the northern half. However, the first sponsor had difficulty obtaining rentals which would cover his costs, and he withdrew in 1962. Subsequently, the land-use designation was changed to exclude office space.

In the next few years the potential for industrial loft and warehousing in the area was investigated by several developers who after exhaustive surveys decided against going ahead. Few industries in Manhattan were able to afford the high costs of new space and they were expanding very little. Other industries were either contracting, or uninterested in high land costs. Furthermore, a good deal of modern loft space, renting well below the probable rentals of this project, was vacant elsewhere. This made the prospects of successful development here even more discouraging.

In 1965 several new proposals were made, all of a different character from the previous. One developer sought to use the area for a one and two-story warehousing-distribution center. But this low-density coverage meant a high tax write-down to which the City was legally unable to commit itself. The City was very reluctant to go ahead with a development which would bring so little return to the City -- in jobs and taxes -- after such a heavy investment on its part.

Two other developers proposed residential usage -- one in combination with commercial on the first few floors, the other without any commercial. According to the official designation of the site, the Housing and Redevelopment Board could not actually consider either of these proposals without further policy decisions by the City.

Immediate Policy

In these circumstances, the initial response of the Study has been to caution against hasty action -- particularly with regard to the low-density warehousing proposal. The area is changing rapidly, and within a year or two several major projects will substantially alter the complexion of the neighborhood. Among these are the World Trade Center, the Civic Center, the development of an acceptable plan for the Lower Manhattan Expressway, and the adoption by the City of a plan for redevelopment of the downtown Hudson waterfront.

Most of these plans are, of course, individually known to the general public. However, their cumulative impact may not be easily apparent today, since many of them are still on the drawing boards or clouded by uncertainty. As definitive decisions are reached, new possibilities will open up. Clearly in the long run the City will gain more in three or four years than the minimal return possible today.

Long-Range Policy

Nevertheless, the question still remains: is there now, or is there likely to be in the future, a demand for loft space in Manhattan renting for $ 3 ro $ 5 a square foot? The answer seems to be no.

There may, however, be other possibilities and it is desirable to rethink the basic assumptions of the project. In the first place, the area need not be thought of in terms of a single use. It falls into one piece only because it was originally laid out to serve the piers that supplied the fruit and vegetable markets directly across West Street. However in terms of current linkages, it breaks up into three areas, each related to neighboring predominant uses: the World Trade Center (office) at the south end, warehousing or printing at the north end and butter-eggs-cheese in the middle. It is in this middle area on either side of Chambers Street that may prove to be the key to the entire development.

Secondly, it may be useful to remove any preconception concerning usage, abandon the original industrial-commercial assumption altogether, and start over.

The City has on its hands 31 acres of land, near the waterfront, within walking distance of three subway lines, the Civic Center, the World Trade Center, and ten minutes from the heart of the financial district.

What function might take maximum advantage of such a site, with a high priority in the City's overall scheme of things? The concept would be to use a public function, if appropriate, as a part of a strategy to set the stage for waterfront development and ultimate renewal of the northwest itself.

Probably no single topic of recent municipal policy has occupied as much attention as education -- both because of the new importance of educational institutions in an increasing technical-professional society, and because of the particular significance of education in providing full opportunities for the city's disadvantaged minorities.

The use of this excellent site for educational purposes therefore deserves serious consideration. [1]

Educational institutions throughout the country are expanding at a very fast rate and are a "growth industry"; indeed, the general trend is for colleges and universities to outpace their own expansion plans. This is true in New York as well, where the City universities, public and private, have been expanding into a host of old buildings at various distances from any central campus.

Overall City policy may indicate that current investment should be put elsewhere -- in Harlem perhaps as a device for improving the environment in investment possibilities there. Without taking a position on such a policy, it should be noted that Lower Manhattan represents a great opportunity to have integration in both schools and housing because the area has no residents now, and requires no relocation to create sites.

The proposal is to set aside the central portion of the Washington Market site as an educational reserve -- for institutions now seeking space, for joint facilities of several institutions, or for an entire campus if that seems possible.

The area involved is some 25 acres; three times as much space can become available when waterfront development occurs. The opportunities for expansion are clearly very good. The area calls for a user with strong growth tendencies; education obviously falls into this category. The idea need not be limited to, or even be essentially higher education. It could also be a site for university-related private research organizations, and data processing centers.

Education could provide that focus for residential development in the area which all current proposals lack, a focus essential in an area as isolated as this one is now. The nearest existing residential development is nearly a half mile away. It seems doubtful that an isolated stand of new housing, in the midst of a goods-handling neighborhood, could be successful, nor would it be good policy to try it. There are other locations downtown which are far preferable for housing now -- particularly on the East Side, adjacent to Brooklyn Bridge Southwest or on new filled land past South Street.

A proposal for residential development in this site should be part of a larger plan for the West Side -- including offshore development. An educational park would appear to be an appropriate part of such a plan.

[1] At this writing, the Board of Education is proposing a study of such a possibility.

Development of Duane Street Park

While not part of the Washington Market Renewal Area, one of the few fine urban spaces in the northern part of the Study area is Duane Street Park. It is a small triangle formed at the intersection of Duane and Hudson Streets, bounded by a small office building and 4-5 story loft buildings housing butter-cheese-eggs merchants. Further study of the market could include it as an adjacent area.

With the development nearby of institutional uses in the Washington Street Market Urban Renewal Area, and with the eventual phasing out of the butter-cheese-eggs businesses, this Park might become the nucleous of a small residential-student-faculty enclave. Some of the neighboring buildings might be rehabilitated and converted to new uses: for restaurants, studios, clubs, small apartments. The triangular space itself will relate at the western side to a waterfront plaza, and connect to the educational use proposed for the central portion of the Washington Street Market Urban Renewal Area.

Land costs in the area are now probably too high to justify extensive low-density redevelopment. However, if educational functions develop to the west, the expectation is that a high-density residential growth may in time be expected to follow here. This high-density development may thus, in effect, make possible the development of the Duane Street Park as a project, whose value lies in the preservation of the scale and character of the old, low-density structures which now surround it.

By adding to the value of the neighboring development, giving distinction to the area for which it serves as the nucleous, the preservation of Duane Street Park could easily be justified as a special rehabilitation project.

Immediate Recommendations

1. Concur in and urge the carrying out of the study of the Central portion of the Washington Street Market Urban Renewal Area as an educational complex. Conceive of it as related to the waterfront residential development.

2. Promote development of the northern end of the project for use by the graphic arts industry or for research and development related to the educational use.

3. Reserve the southern portion of the project area for future intensive office use related to the World Trade Center. An interior use is of course parking and as a construction material site.

4. Include a study of the preservation and development of the Duane Street Park as an extension of the renewal project.

THE CIVIC CENTER

The purpose of the Civic Center Project is to consolidate City and Federal agencies now in scattered locations principally in Lower Manhattan. The result is expected to increase the efficiency and operation of these sectors of government and to provide a more suitable and functional working environment than they now have. The Center will also be a tangible symbol of the City's pre eminence as a great world metropolis. An important consideration is the money now expended annually on rentals for City agencies in private buildings. At this writing the City administration is reviewing all the program and physical planning of this Project.

The principal elements of the proposed Civic Center are:

The Federal Office Building and Customs Court: (including a proposed extension) 1,750,000 square feet of office space containing 11,000 employees, and a 300 car garage;

The Municipal Office Tower: 900,000 square feet of office space containing 8-9,000 employees, 150,000 square feet of retail space and a 500 car garage;

Police Headquarters: 670,000 square feet containing 2,500 employees, and a 200 car garage;

Family Court Building: 270,000 square feet of space containing 920 employees.

Description of the Project

The City area of the Civic Center was designated in preliminary drawings by Edward Durell Stone and Eggers and Higgins, Associated Architects. This plan, a further refinement of a former diagram called the ABC plan, combined the Executive Office Building and the Municipal Building into a single 54 story tower on axis with City Hall between Chambers and Duane Streets. A paved pedestrian plaza from the rear of City Hall to Duane Street was proposed. This would have removed all the trees in historic City Hall Park and changed its character from an earth park to pavement. At Duane Street because of topography the plaza would be 13' above grade, while at Chambers Street it would be at present grade.

The square tower 160 feet on a side would be set on a plaza 450 by 650 feet. The tower was moved south from an earlier location away from the Federal Office Building (FOB) and was placed close to the Hall of Records. It was then recommended that this latter building (recently designated as a landmark by the Historic Buildings Commission) be demolished, along with 2 Lafayette Street (an office building) and that the plaza and parking be extended east to Centre Street. Underneath this plaza was to be located a concourse which would contain City offices serving the public, 150,000 square feet of retail space and 200,000 square feet of circulation area. This concourse would also serve as indoor connection to the three subways that immediately serve the area as well as City Hall.

A rectangular reflecting pool would occupy a good part of the depressed area and provide an attractive setting for restaurants, etc. At Duane Street the concourse would be at street level while at about Chambers Street it would be completely below grade. Beneath this pedestrian concourse was to be a parking garage for 500 City-owned cars, and loading space for 12 trucks for the retail and office space.

The plaza itself would be planted with trees (in boxes) and paving and would become one of the largest urban open spaces in the City. It would be a monumental setting for the Civic Building.

The Federal Office Building and Customs Court (under construction) between Duane and Worth Streets creates its own plaza level a few feet above Duane Street but almost a full level below the plaza of the Civic Center. Entrance to the FOB and the Civic Centers' underground parking and service was planned to be off Duane Street and is the most satisfactory location for service if thru-traffic is eliminated.

Because of serious mid-block pedestrian conflict at Duane and Chambers Streets, a carefully designed loop road and ramp system was developed as part of this Study with the architects for both building complexes and the Department of Public Works.   This consisted of a set of ramps in the middle of Duane Street peeling off left and right to underground areas. Around these ramps is to be a loop road at grade for drop-offs and taxis. This loop stopped short of the location of the mid-block pedestrian movement. The present FOB ramp on Duane Street (already built) is designed so it can be depressed to meet the new grade of the access ramp in Duane Street.

Previous Land Use

The Federal site contained a mixture of office buildings along Broadway with some manufacturing and loft buildings on Centre and Thomas Streets. These contained about 180,000 square feet gross of office and 640,000 of loft type space.

The Civic Center site, still occupied, contains a similar mixture, with office functions predominating. Businesses in the area consist of law and other service functions, retail shops, printing firms, manufacturing wholesalers and business sales and service.

Analysis and Effect on Lower Manhattan

Real Estate Activity and Growth: These are already indications of a resurge of real estate activity in the immediate vicinity of the Civic Center particularly along Broadway. Some buildings have been renovated. A previously high

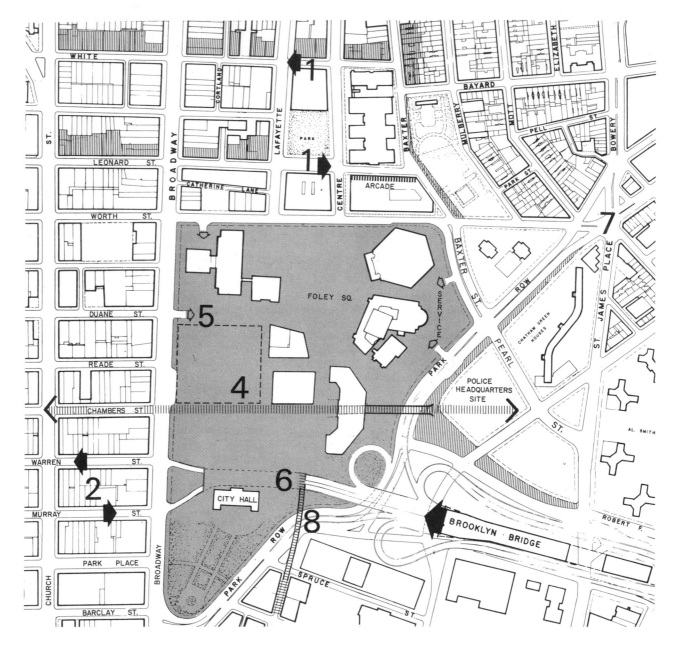

Map labels:
WHITE — LEONARD ST. — BROADWAY — CORTLAND — CATHERINE LANE — WORTH ST. — DUANE ST. — READE ST. — CHAMBERS ST. — WARREN ST. — MURRAY ST. — PARK PLACE — CHURCH — BARCLAY ST. — ST. — LAFAYETTE — CENTRE — PARK — ARCADE — BAYARD — BAXTER — MULBERRY — MOTT — ELIZABETH — BOWERY — PARK ST. — PELL — FOLEY SQ. — BAXTER ST. — ROW — COLUMBUS — PARK — PEARL — CHATHAM GREEN HOUSES — ST. JAMES PLACE — POLICE HEADQUARTERS SITE — CITY HALL — ROW — PARK — SPRUCE — ST. — NASSAU — BROOKLYN BRIDGE — ROBERT F. — AL. SMITH

1 · 1 · 5 · 4 · 2 · 6 · 8 · 7

Civic Center:
Problems and Proposals

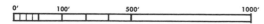

0'   100'   500'   1000'

1. WHITE-LEONARD COUPLE
2. WARREN-MURRAY COUPLE
3. POLICE HEADQUARTERS SITE
4. MUNICIPAL TOWER SITE
5. DUANE ST. SERVICE COMPLEX
6. CITY HALL UNDERPASS
7. CHATHAM SQUARE ALTERATIONS
8. NASSAU ST. OVERPASS

LOWER MANHATTAN PLAN **34**

vacancy rate showed signs of dropping by 1965. This was undoubtedly due in part to relocated occupants of the Federal and City building site areas. Concentration of approximately 15,000 additional employees on these sites will also have a positive effect on adjacent business and personnel services. The related private activities that service and receive business from government will concentrate and expand to the west across Broadway and toward the World Trade Center as the area to the north is preempted by Courts, and by the textile center. Thus the natural functional expansion area of office related activities to the Civic Center will be to the west while the courts are expanding to the north.

Substantial increases in government employment and related services has occurred over the past five years and is, together with finance, the major growth sector of the Lower Manhattan economy.

Transit: The Civic Center is directly served by the BMT, Jamaica, IRT Lexington Avenue and the BMT Broadway subway systems. Located further west on the Chambers Street axis of subway stations are the IND and IRT 7th Avenue, about a five minute walk. Additional employment in the area, (actually a redistribution within Lower Manhattan) should be adequately accommodated by this major concentration of subways, along with bus routes that also serve it, particularly from the Lower East Side.

Pedestrian Traffic: One of the important concepts adapted from the ABC plan for the Civic Center was a traffic-free pedestrian "superblock". This would stretch from Worth to Barclay Streets and Broadway to Park Row in a triangle with a base of 1,300 feet and a north-south dimension of 1,800 feet, certainly the largest "superblock" in the City. Within this area separate City buildings would be more effectively related if vehicular traffic were excluded. An additional 7 acres of open plaza and park land would be added to the present.

However this "superblock" did not encompass the area to the north of Worth Street where a substantial number of government employees work. In fact it proposed to re-route traffic from the area to Leonard and White Streets to the north. Detailed analysis of existing peak hour pedestrian movement showed the importance of Duane and Chambers Streets through the area as not only traffic but major pedestrian routes to the sub-

way stations. In addition Centre Street carries pedestrians to the subway entrances in Foley Square across a very complicated traffic pattern.

Projections of these pedestrian movements were made to show conditions after the Civic Center and Federal Office Building are in place. They demonstrated the importance of a mid-block, north-south crossing of Duane Street especially between the FOB and the Civic Center concourse with its retail shops and connections to the subway. It was decided that an effective connection should and could be worked out between the pedestrian levels of the FOB and the Civic Center at Duane Street.

Vehicular Traffic: Initial examination of the vehicular traffic problem in the Civic Center area indicated a far higher traffic volume than had been anticipated in 1962 by the ABC plan. In particular, question was raised concerning the routing of traffic around the northern end of the new pedestrian island, both from operational and land use points of view. It had been assumed that a widened Worth Street, plus one additional street to the north (probably Leonard) could handle the increased volumes caused by the closing of Chambers, Reade, Duane, Lafayette and Centre Streets; closer examination showed that this solution would require the widening not only of Worth Street, but of both Leonard and White Streets to the north, entailing substantial demolition and relocation of existing functions and displacement of important blue-collar jobs in the textile area.

Alternative solutions were therefore sought out. In the process five alternative plans were developed and evaluated. Criteria for judgement included directness and speed of traffic movement, service access to Civic Center buildings, ease and freedom of pedestrian movement, cost to the City, and impact on neighboring properties.

An electronic computer network was used, which is described in detail in Part 2 of this Report. This technique made it possible to quickly test each of many alternatives, assigning different traffic volumes to the street system (as they would occur during various construction stages), including traffic

Generated by new developments. The Lower Manhattan Expressway was assumed in, under construction, or not in, as three alternate conditions. The volumes and turning movements resulting from the initial assignments were carefully checked against actual traffic counts to ensure maximum accuracy. Certain minor errors in assumptions were thereby corrected. The period for which the network was built was the morning peak hour, 8:00 to 9:00 AM.

The network analysis indicated that traffic volumes moving around the northern end of the Civic Center pedestrian superblock will require 7 to 9 moving lanes, assuming that the Lower Manhattan Expressway was completed by the time the streets are closed. These lanes could clearly not be accommodated on Worth Street, even after widening. Therefore, four alternative solutions were explored.

Alternative I: A Leonard-Worth Couple plus White Street.

This proposal, a variation of the original ABC plan, called for the widening of the following streets: Worth, Leonard, White and Baxter (including the taking of a slice from Columbus Park).

The widening of Leonard and White Streets would require the acquisition and demolition of buildings now housing about 400 firms and close to 2,000 employees. It would cost about $12,000,000 (exclusive of relocation costs).

This routing would solve the basic east-west traffic problems created by the new pedestrian island, but its long, circuitous path makes it an awkward and inflexible solution. The heavy volumes of traffic on all sides of the Civic Center superblock make internal servicing off these streets very difficult. Pedestrian movement would be quite hazardous.

The required demolitions and relocations along Leonard and White Streets, cutting through the heart of the textile district, would leave a wide scar of excess property taking, unsightly rears of buildings exposed to view, and dislocate many businesses in an already shaky area.

Alternative II: A Duane-Worth Couple.

This proposal is a modified version of a plan worked out by the Department of Traffic.

But instead of a two-way system, it is only west bound, thereby making possible a satisfactory pedestrian solution between the FOB and the Municipal Tower.

The Duane-Worth Couple would reduce pressure on Leonard Street, but not eliminate the need for its widening, with the necessary demolition, relocations, etc. However, it would make unnecessary the widening of White Street.

It would result in a partial interruption (at the south end of Foley Square) of the pedestrian island and an extremely cumbersome design of the intersection of Broadway and Duane Street, where the already-complex service-taxi ramps and the new high-speed underpass must be brought together. As previous investigations emphasized, this area lying between two buildings with roughly 20,000 workers, is an extremely critical one where intensity of pedestrian movement is expected to be (in fact already is) far greater than anywhere else in the Civic Center.

Traffic service for Alternative II is slightly better than for Alternative I, but the advantage of the direct connection to Broadway is offset in part by the complexity and tightness of the resulting design. Redevelopment of a traffic-free Foley Square is made extremely difficult if Duane is a through street.

The high ramp coming off the Brooklyn Bridge, clearing Park Row, makes virtually impossible a direct pedestrian connection from the Municipal Building to the new Police Headquarters. This connection would therefore have to cross Park Row at the rear of the Federal Court House, a less desirable solution.

Costs for this alternative were estimated at $8,000,000.

Alternative III: A Chambers-Worth Couple

This proposal is similar, in many respects, to the Duane-Worth alternative described above: it requires the widening of Leonard and Baxter Streets but not White Street, and it breaks sharply through the pedestrian island, this time at the Municipal Building itself.

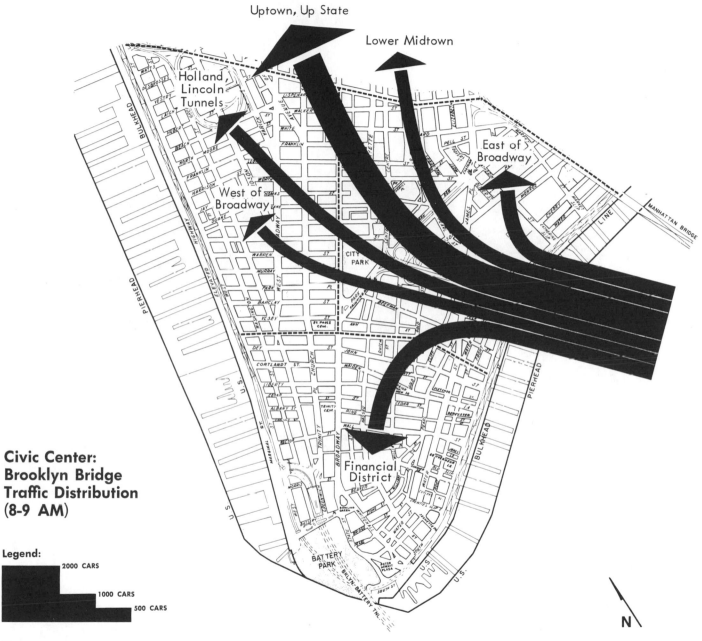

Uptown, Up State

Lower Midtown

Holland
Lincoln
Tunnels

East of
Broadway

West of
Broadway

MANHATTAN BRIDGE

Financial
District

**Civic Center:
Brooklyn Bridge
Traffic Distribution
(8-9 AM)**

Legend:

2000 CARS

1000 CARS

500 CARS

Source:
AMV TRAFFIC COUNTS
DEPT. OF TRAFFIC

N

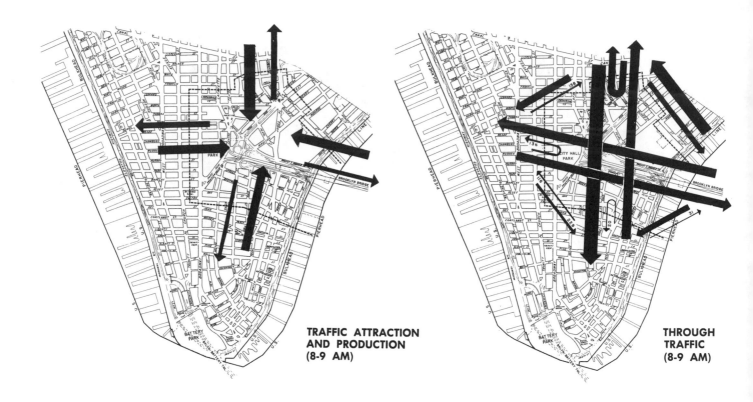

TRAFFIC ATTRACTION
AND PRODUCTION
(8-9 AM)

THROUGH
TRAFFIC
(8-9 AM)

Civic Center:
(Network Area)

Legend:

2000 CARS
1000 CARS 500 CARS

Source:
AMV TRAFFIC COUNTS
DEPT. OF TRAFFIC

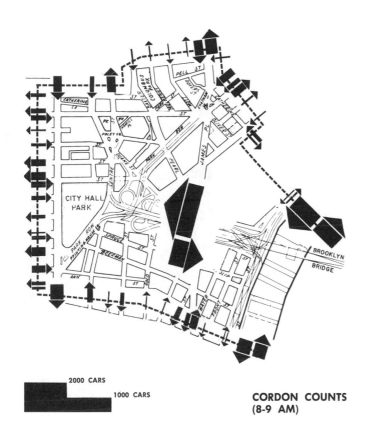

2000 CARS
1000 CARS

CORDON COUNTS
(8-9 AM)

2000 CARS
1000 CARS

PRESENT TRAFFIC
VOLUME ASSIGNMENTS
(8-9 AM)

Civic Center:
(Network Area)

Source:
    AMV TRAFFIC COUNTS
    DEPT. OF TRAFFIC

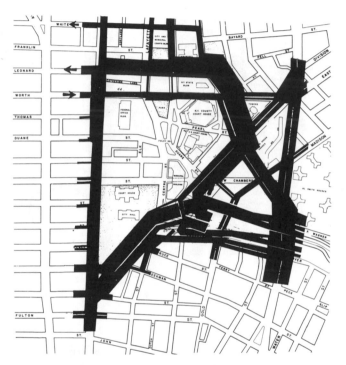

WORTH-LEONARD-WHITE

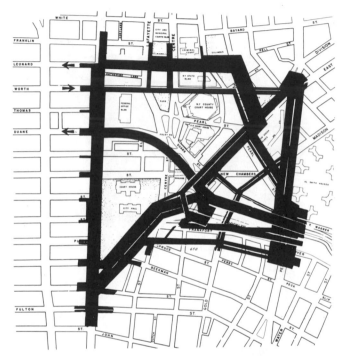

WORTH-DUANE-LEONARD

Civic Center:
Traffic Volume
Assignments
(8-9 AM)

Legend:

1500 CARS
1000 CARS
500 CARS

Source:
COMPUTER NETWORK
ANALYSIS

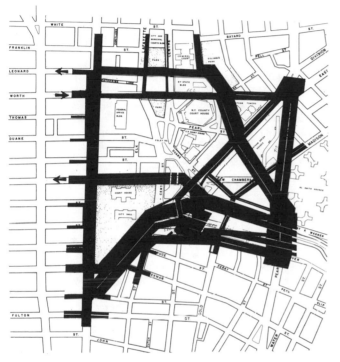

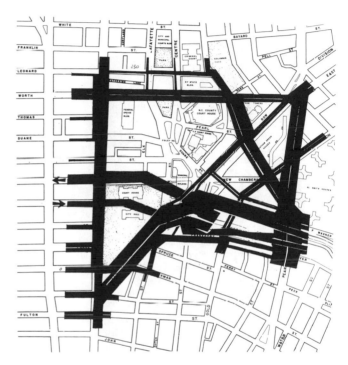

WORTH-CHAMBERS-LEONARD   **CHAMBERS-WARREN**

Redevelopment of the forecourt of the Municipal Building, a potentially valuable space, would not be possible, but Foley Square would be left free for redesign.

This scheme had one advantage over the Duane-Worth solution: it separated Brooklyn Bridge traffic from local service to the new federal-municipal complex at Duane Street. Like Alternative IV below, it required a reconsideration of the design of the concourse level of the Municipal Tower.

Its cost was estimated at about $ 8,500,000.

Alternative IV: A Chambers-Warren Underpass.

This solution, an underground connection directly across City Hall Park, provides the highest level of overall service, disperses traffic effectively, retains the pedestrian island, and eliminates altogether the need for land acquisition and relocation north of the Civic Center island. Chambers and Warren Streets align directly with the existing ramp entrances to the West Side Highway, and would provide relief to the Barclay-Vesey-Broadway intersection, as well as better access to the World Trade Center area. A significant land use advantage is that it allows a substantial enlargement of the Police Headquarters site. In an area where land is valued at least at $30 per square feet this is no small saving. Vehicular access to these sites will also be improved.

A direct pedestrian on-grade connection from the City Hall Park to the Brooklyn Bridge walkway can easily be constructed. A pedestrian route through the center of the Municipal Building at Chambers Street to the new Police Headquarters can be developed in place of a more remote one suggested across Park Row further north. This pedestrian overpass design would be coordinated with the design of the Park Row off-ramp from the Brooklyn Bridge. If possible pedestrians should be kept at or near grade. If an above-grade solution is necessary, major pedestrian entrance to Police Headquarters should be that level.

Worth Street would be widened, as planned, and serve as a two-way street for east-west traffic north of the Center. Since volumes on Worth are now such that it can operate as a two-

way street, there would be no need to widen Leonard or White Streets, or cut a strip from heavily-utilized Columbus Park. The resulting lower volumes on Worth Street, Park Row, and Baxter Street will ease service access from these streets to Civic Center buildings, including the new Police Headquarters (a major traffic generator itself).

This solution, and Alternative V, are the only ones which adequately solve the vehicular traffic problem created by the pedestrian superblock.

Preliminary study of the Warren underpass indicates that it can be so aligned as to preserve some of the larger trees in the rear and to the west of City Hall. The descent from the Bridge will require modifications of the City Hall IRT Station, relocating one entrance and one (no longer needed) crosswalk, but in no way interfering with the headroom of the trains or the station platforms.

This solution has two defects. In common with alternative V below, it requires two exits at Broadway, acting as barriers to free flow of pedestrians.

The second defect is that Chambers Street is already a major pedestrian route from the subway entrances to the Civic Center. Its use as a major arterial would be in conflict with pedestrian flows. While the possibility exists of treating Reade Street to its north as the pedestrian route, Chambers will undoubtedly remain the major pedestrian thorofare.

The estimated cost of this Alternative is $ 5,000,000.

Alternative V: A Warren-Murray Couple.

This solution is similar to the Chambers-Warren Couple, except that the Chambers underpass is shifted one block to the south to Murray Street. It has several advantages and disadvantages in relation to the Chambers-Warren solution.

One advantage is that it is slightly cheaper to construct, since for a large portion of the route, only one trench and one set of retaining walls need to be dug. Furthermore, it concentrates the damage to City Hall Park within one area, thereby reducing the scope of refurnishing and planting necessary.

Its major advantage is that it leaves the Chambers Street axis free for future pedestrian development -- both within the Civic Center itself and later on along the line of Chambers Street to the West. This axis ties together a number of important elements in the long-range plan for the area: starting from the west, the proposed Chambers Street waterfront plaza, the line of subway stations along Chambers, the old Municipal Building, and finally, the new Police Headquarters.

By eliminating the open cut of the Chambers underpass, this solution also solves a serious siting problem in locating the new Municipal Tower, allowing for a wider range of solutions, and permitting easy access to the Tower along Broadway, should the tower be located at Broadway.

Its disadvantages may be summarized as follows: Taken by itself, it is not quite as direct a vehicular route as the Chambers-Warren Route. It must make a turn on the west side of City Hall, coming close to City Hall itself. To conceal the open cut to the west will require careful planting. This solution also means that few of the fine stand of trees behind City Hall can be preserved, while the Chambers-Warren solution might have permitted the saving of some of them.

Recommendation

Taking these factors all together, the Consultants recommend the Warren-Murray solution. The development of the Chambers Street pedestrian axis is so important to the long-range plan for the entire area, from the new Hudson shoreline all the way to the Gov. Alfred E. Smith Houses, that it should take precedence over the minor (and soluble) problem created at the Murray Street open cut west of City Hall. No street other than Chambers -- with its many shops, bars and restaurants, its subway stations, and its visual climax in the arch of the old Municipal Building-- is capable of serving this function.

Suggestions for Consideration

Both the retail facilities and those City agencies requiring easy public access might well be placed on the new Municipal plaza, rather than under it. Such a change could intensify usage of what could otherwise become a lifeless expanse of open space. Since a grand pedestrian plaza is being created at grade, the advisability of putting most of the public activity in 400,000 square feet of space under that plaza, with over half of it devoted to circulation alone is questioned. The vast bulk of subway-bound movement, destined for the IRT-BMT complex to the east (the Broadway BMT is a minor station), can be handled by a more modest underground system, if such direct connections are deemed necessary.

The need for new parking facilities in the overall area is beyond dispute. Closer study may show, however, that only a portion of it (say 200 cars) must be located directly in the Municipal complex; space for the other 400 cars might be added to the parking garage tentatively set for the block adjacent to the new Police Headquarters (which can be enlarged substantially beyond its mapped size to accommodate larger capacities). Such a plan would have the virtue of keeping traffic out of the heavily congested Broadway area, and near the major arteries to the east.

Another point to be noted in the reappraisal would be the possibility of preserving City Hall Park in its entirety. If the underground concourse must now be terminated at Chambers Street there would be no reason to carry the paved Plaza across the northern half of the Park to the rear steps of City Hall. This park, the second oldest in the City, with its fine old large trees is the traditional setting and symbol of municipal government in New York. Its partial demolition in favor of a formal paved plaza deserves serious reconsideration.

The location of the Municipal Tower itself is also deserving of some further thought. The present plan, placing the building squarely in the center of a great open plaza, clearly calls for the ultimate demolition of the Hall of Records. Yet this architecturally interesting building has been designated by the Landmarks Preservation Commission as a permanent landmark.

If the Hall of Records is to be retained, relocation of the tower should be considered -- perhaps it could be shifted over to Broadway, where it would reinforce the line of towers which carries up all the way from Battery Park. Instead of

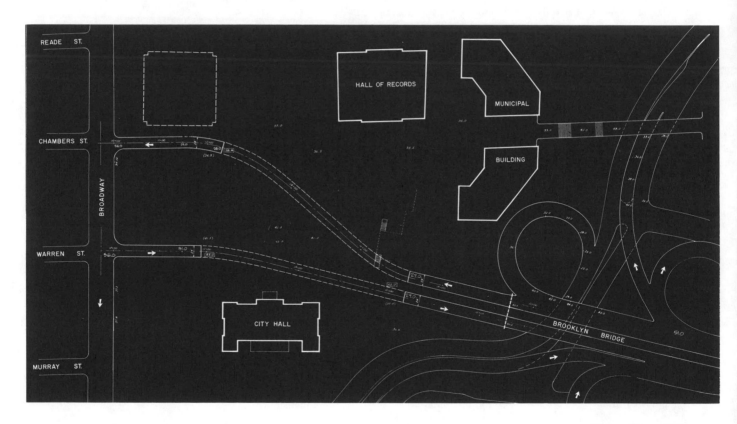

Chambers-Warren

Civic Center:
Underpass Alternates

0'   100'   200'   500'

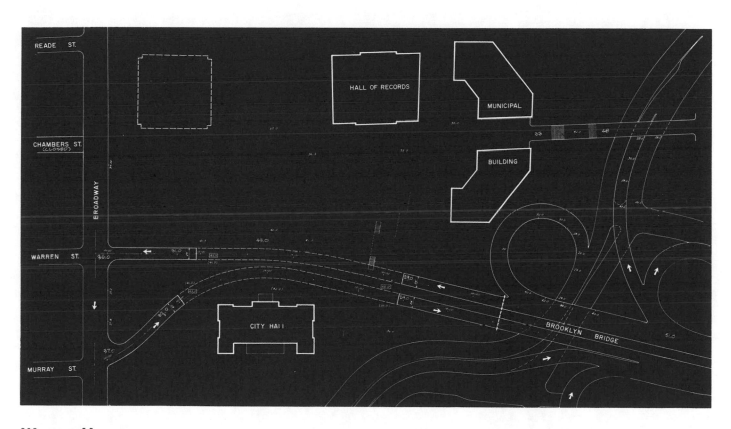

Warren-Murray

N

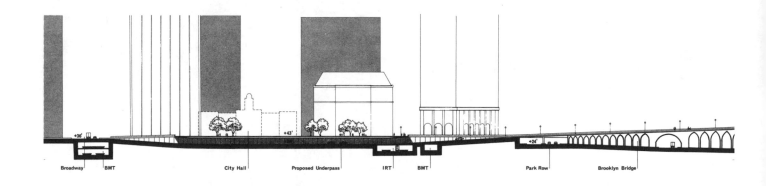

Broadway   BMT   City Hall   Proposed Underpass   IRT   BMT   Park Row   Brooklyn Bridge

**Civic
Center:
Section Through
Underpass**

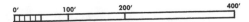

0'   100'   200'   400'

setting the new tower on axis with City Hall (which then looks out of scale), a better sense of scale might be achieved by the development of low service-retail buildings at the north end of the Municipal plaza, echoing the scale of City Hall.

This would, in turn, make possible a direct, focal relationship to the old Municipal Building, whose great space-receiving bulk could form an important element in the Civic Center design. Indeed, if the Hall of Records is ever taken down, a direct line of construction could be established with the Municipal Building.

Preliminary analysis indicates that, at present rates of governmental growth (with the City Budget expanding 7% annually), the need for new municipal administrative office space will not be permanently exhausted by the present phase of construction. Expansion should probably occur within the new pedestrian island, rather than to the north of it, as originally implied in the ABC plan. With the great open spaces soon to be developed in the Civic Center, the need will be for increased activity rather than for greater dispersal. It is urged that this matter be given consideration in any further assessment of the Civic Center.

Recommendations for the Civic Center

As mentioned earlier, the Civic Center is now under detailed review by the City Administration. This review may produce a revised program, and call into question some of the assumptions under which the present plan was derived. Nevertheless, certain basic problems will remain, whatever new solutions are evolved, and the following is a list of basic principles developed from the Study which can be of use in the process of review:

I. If a Civic Center superblock is considered an important objective, the Brooklyn Bridge traffic should be handled within the superblock itself, and not thrust off onto neighboring areas. In these terms an underpass through City Hall Park appears the most direct and economical solution.

2. Even if a superblock is not deemed necessary, the vehicular-pedestrian conflict in and around Chambers Street--

slicing through the heart of the Civic Center -- is so severe that the underpass as proposed should be considered as the long-term solution to the problem created by the Brooklyn Bridge traffic as it moves into Lower Manhattan.

3. The preservation of as much as possible of the City Hall Park, as an open, green area should be a major goal.

4. Service traffic to the Federal Office Building and the Municipal Tower should be consolidated in the Duane Street area in such a way that pedestrian movement across the service area is simple and direct and does not come in conflict with service traffic.

5. In consideration of the designation of the Hall of Records as a historical monument, its permanent position in the Civic Center should be recognized. This may be reflected in a decision to move the new Municipal Tower to Broadway, north of Chambers Street.

6. As a general principle, the bulk of the programmed municipal parking should be located outside of the Civic Center, to the east of the old municipal building on the expanded Police Headquarters Site, where it will be closer to highways and away from the congested core.

7. The feasibility and desirability of extensive below-grade retail facilities, concourse and parking, as now planned should be re-examined carefully.

8. Two basic pedestrian routes should be considered as central design elements: First, Chambers Street, running across the Civic Center, through the Municipal Building, and then by overpass to the expanded site of the Police Headquarters. Second, an extension of the Broad-Nassau pedestrian route, across Park Row, and into the heart of the Civic Center joining there with the pedestrian path of the Brooklyn Bridge.

**Hudson Skyline:
Present**

**Hudson Skyline:
Future**

LOWER MANHATTAN PLAN

CHAPTER   V

GOALS FOR LOWER MANHATTAN

Chapter II of the Report emphasized the difficulty of trying to forecast the future of the financial and governmental communities on the basis of past performance or present trends. The conclusion was drawn that the future of Lower Manhattan will be determined more by what people want and take collective action to get, than by unseen market forces whose cumulative impact is beyond the community's capacity to influence. This conclusion points up the critical role that planning can play and the importance of spelling out in the Plan the possible and appropriate goals. This chapter summarizes the goals for Lower Manhattan and its role in the region, considers each in some detail ,and describes briefly the process of plan development showing how the proposals in the Plan relate to the goals.

APPROACH TO TAXES AND CENTER OF PLANNING

As has been stated, a major purpose of the Plan is to provide an organizing concept to guide present and future growth --

an organizing concept that as nearly as possible expresses the optimum achievement of all goals in combination. It must also describe a process whereby the means and the goals can be constantly reappraised in light of degrees of achievement and changes in circumstances.

In considering a list of such goals, questions must include: What is Lower Manhattan's proper role in the City, the region and the nation? What are the appropriate specific goals for Lower Manhattan, and how do such goals become translated into alternate means for achievement? Whose goals are they and how does their achievement affect other goals held by the same people? What must be given up and by whom, for an optimum achievement of all goals that might be valid for this important -- yet still small -- piece of New York?

To deal with these questions the approach of the Study assumed that the Plan must have four important ingredients. First, it must be a problem-solving course of action which can be carried into effect and whose outcome will be expected both to solve problems and attain goals. Second, it must be comprehensive even though Lower Manhattan is only a small part of the City and the region; that is to say, the Plan must spell out the main actions by which all of the most important goals are to be achieved. Third, the Plan must indicate the choices of actions (and the implications of each choice) that will be probable and feasible over as long a time as possible. Finally, the Plan must create an image of what the achievement of the long-range goals can look like, an image that will fire imagination and enthusiasm and at the same time appear achievable.

In response to the above questions, the aims of the Study were to develop a plan that would be doable, comprehensive ,long-range and exciting. In a situation of uncertainty about trends and the nature of future problems and goals, the City is inevitably committed to incremental planning that proceeds in stages, beginning with what is feasible and necessary and then expanding the area of action as knowledge increases and needs are better known. However, prudent incremental planning also requires a set of long-range goals that serve as a constant guide against which short-term decisions are screened and evaluated.

These specifications were used to develop a planning process that combined incremental and comprehensive planning methods with an end-state group of goals set forth in three-dimensional clarity to illustrate their implications. The following considerations of goals have come out of that process.

NATIONAL GOALS WHICH LOWER MANHATTAN CAN SERVE

If the assumption is made that the money market function in the United States can best be served by a centralized, efficiently operating nucleus, and this appears to be the case, then Lower Manhattan can serve this national goal by performing that function as well as possible. Further, with international trade becoming an increasing activity, this also behooves Lower Manhattan to carry out its potential to the maximum extent to help the nation.

REGIONAL GOALS WHICH LOWER MANHATTAN CAN SERVE

The statement that Lower Manhattan has an appropriate role to play in the region means that by virtue of its central location, history, and unique characteristics -- both physiographic and functional -- it has certain obligations to the region. Planning for Lower Manhattan must recognize this basic fact. The regional goals that relate to Lower Manhattan are similar to those in any large metropolitan area and its downtown. In New York they take on particular significance because of Lower Manhattan's importance to the Nation.

The first such goal considered is efficiency of transportation. It would seem at first glance that work trips could be reduced by decentralizing jobs closer to where people live. On this thesis, Manhattan should not be encouraged to grow. The disadvantages of such a pattern of land use in a metropolis are not as obvious as the seeming advantages. An inevitable result would be great increases in auto travel and additional traffic congestion, as well as reduced efficiency of business now based on economics of scale. While the average trip of the suburbanite who works in the suburbs is now shorter than that of many downtown workers, if everyone lived and worked in the suburbs, the overall average would be considerably longer than now. Los Angeles is an example.

In point of fact, a very large number of New Yorkers and New Jerseyites already do live very close to their jobs in Manhattan. Since the great job concentration already exists and is supported by a sunk investment in subways and commuter lines, the reduction of the journey-to-work is more easily accomplished by putting more housing close to downtown, than by decentralizing jobs. Therefore:

Regional Goal # I: The reduction of the journey-to-work, then, is an important regional goal to which Lower Manhattan can contribute if appropriate places for housing are made available.

An additional regional goal related to the first is to maximize everybody's choice of both work and residence. Theoretically, to have everyone working in the same place would provide for maximum job interchangeability. This is to say that if one decided to change jobs, this decision could be made without influencing where one wanted to live, since both jobs would be in the same place. Job interchangeability is one of the major reasons for living in large cities, and the goal of maximizing choice of job is best served by concentrating a wide variety of jobs, not by decentralizing them.

If one assumes that place of residence is fixed, then broadening choice of place of work would be better served by job decentralization, not by job concentration. However, people move almost as frequently as they change jobs, and of course what they do is optimize [1] on their own between the goals of where they want to live, where they want to work, and how much time and money it takes to get between the two.

---

[1] Optimize is used here to mean trading-off between the satisfaction of conflicting goals to get the most aggregate satisfaction.

While a theoretical discussion of this aspect might not lead to practical conclusions, a realistic way for Lower Manhattan to serve both goals is to provide for as much and as varied a job concentration as possible, and at the same time to provide for as much nearby housing variety as possible. Therefore: Regional Goals Numbers 2 and 3:

Regional Goal # 2: Broadening choice of work is an important regional goal to which Lower Manhattan can contribute by providing a wide variety and an intense concentration of jobs. And,

Regional Goal # 3: Broadening choice of place and type of residence is an important regional goal to which Lower Manhattan can contribute by making available its unique site characteristics for housing a wide variety of income groups and families.

The next problem concerns Lower Manhattan's position in the regional transportation network -- insofar as many of its important vehicular and transit lines must pass through Lower Manhattan itself. The improvement of these facilities can thus serve a double purpose: to upgrade service to Lower Manhattan and to facilitate regional movement through it. This problem relates particularly to the peripheral highways, the Brooklyn-Battery Tunnel and the Brooklyn Bridge. The principle is expressed in:

Regional Goal # 4: Efficient and unimpeded movement throughout the region is an important regional goal to which Lower Manhattan can contribute by increasing the ease with which people go through or around it with as little conflict as possible with the needs of local movement.

Lower Manhattan's impressive natural site, at the head of the New York harbor, and its extraordinary physical plant, represent a combination of urban resources which have not been fully realized. The water and its edge have significant potential for both recreational and residential development, serving Lower Manhattan and the Region. As long as downtown shipping was strong, trade dominated the waterfront ; today this use has sharply declined. Therefore:

Regional Goal # 5: Utilization of sites of great natural beauty and uniqueness for as many people as possible is an important regional goal to which Lower Manhattan can contribute by making its water's edge accessible to the general public. [1]

ALTERNATIVE REGIONAL CONCEPTS

It is next necessary to examine fundamental questions of regional form in relation to these regional goals in order to focus on the Study Area. A major consideration touched on before at a regional, City-wide and Manhattan level is whether Manhattan ought to be encouraged to grow, if growth is possible. The extremes of a decentralized and centralized region are considered.

A Decentralized Region

At this level, an extreme alternative is to reduce overall congestion by reducing, as has been discussed, the concentration of employment in Manhattan, redistributing it to regional sub-centers. To an extent this is happening anyway, as the region grows and Manhattan's capture rate of activity becomes relatively smaller (although still absolutely large) than it has been for most functions.

While this is probably a theoretical but not an operational alternative for Midtown -- that is, Midtown's growth is beyond the influence of individuals or even government to alter -- it may be a real alternative for downtown. As has been pointed out, Lower Manhattan's growth has been the result of general market trends. These relatively few decision-makers might very well be able to reestablish by inaction, or by policy, the stagnation that set in in the 1930's. If, for example,   the World Trade Center,   The Civic

---

[1] This and the other goals are in accord with statements by the Regional Plan Association.

Center and the Stock Exchange were to be halted, Lower Manhattan's considerable vulnerability, due to its singleness of function, would suddenly be exposed. The "critical mass" necessary for its continued "fission" and growth might be lost. The beginning of the dispersion of the financial center could accelerate. An analogy is that of a tightly-wound ball of string whi ch could unravel rapidly once started. In contrast, Midtown is a complex mass [1], not easily influenced.

In such an eventuality, the growth that would have occurred in Lower Manhattan would probably be redistributed largely to Midtown, rather than to regional sub-centers. Little of it would be within the power of public policy to influence, assuming that such a policy was seen to be desirable. Although it would be possible, and perhaps even politically popular, to distribute the functions of government now envisioned for the Civic Center to areas throughout the City, most of these functions have few reasons for citizen contact and can benefit by centralization; dispersion would appear to be the detriment of good governmental coordination. [2]

The notion that Lower Manhattan can very well "take care of itself" without the kind of activity proposed in this Plan is contradicted by the evidence presented, and is based on a lack of understanding of the area's vulnerability as a "one-industry town".

The decentralization concept was rejected therefore as immediately irrelevant, partly because it is unworkable as public policy, but also because it is clearly in conflict with the stated goals of the people most concerned with what happens to Lower Manhattan.

A Concept of Concentration, Diversity and Growth

The alternative concept -- of a region highly concentrated at its center and organized hierarchically -- is conceived as most effectively meeting the stated goals of the region and the City as a whole. (Midtown will continue to grow with congestion being an increasing problem). For Lower Manhattan this means further growth and diversification of function assuming it can be achieved without more congestion. The interests of the City and region appear to coincide with those of Lower Manhattan.

A recent paper of the Regional Plan Association phrased it this way: "Our working hypothesis is that anything which importantly weakens the central city's functioning weakens the Region. And given the importance of the NYMR to the entire nation, the CBD's rapid deterioration has obvious adverse extra-regional implications as well." [3]

For Manhattan as a whole, the choice of either regional concept has few short range consequences. Further growth will continue in Midtown in any event. Only in the long run would public policy based on either choice have any significant effect on land use patterns. For Lower Manhattan, however, a general concensus that there is too much activity concentrated there now could trigger a public and private series of actions and policies regarding currently p roposed projects that could become a self-fulfilling prophecy that favors Midtown if not decentralization.

In light of this and in the interests of the City's tax position, encouragement rather than discouragement of business would seem the better policy, particularly if such a policy is not in conflict with larger social welfare considerations.

In fact, aside from a number of fairly crucial decisions -- for the World Trade Center, the Civic Center, and possibly the Stock Exchange -- the public policy recommended in the Plan of creating a new residential community and making the water's edge available to the region, are consistent with e ither concept of regional form. If, in spite of a choice for

---

[1] In ecology, simple systems are basically unstable where complex and diverse systems are stable.

[2] This is not to discredit the idea of "little city halls" located where people can use them for the increasing services that government is expected to provide.

[3] Regional Plan Association, Memorandum, "Forecast and Analysis of Past Trends," May 3, 1966, page 94.

concentration, downtown's Core does not grow, the areas not utilized by business would be available for other choices, presumably more housing.

The concept of a high concentrated regional core was therefore adopted for purposes of the Plan, with the proviso that concentration not exceed the limit of capacity of Lower Manhattan to absorb growth, based on transportation facilities, land available, and liveability.

SUMMARY OF THE PROBLEMS

The problems of Lower Manhattan have been identified through evaluation of the present situation in light of these regional and local goals. The means to resolving the problems become goals themselves at the next level of consideration. They are not necessarily listed in order of immediate importance or ease of solution.

Problems of Functioning: the need for cohesiveness of the Core; its vulnerability to change; the need for diversity and enrichment of activity.

The problem of how to strengthen the Core and reduce its vulnerability can be approached in a number of ways, none mutually exclusive. First, diversifying activities so that the total emphasis is on more than a few functions will both reduce Lower Manhattan's "one-industry" character, and help enrich the activities that are there. With the exception of the World Trade Center, recent trends in Lower Manhattan have all been in the opposite direction.

This diversity can take the form of new types of businesses and corporate headquarters appropriate to the Core and its supporting activities of law and accounting. It can also take the fore of selected new harmonious non-office uses. Housing and commercial recreation rank high as such symbolic uses. Industry or wholesaling-with-stock rank low.

Problems of Environment: obsolete physical structures: declining functions inharmonious with new growth in key sections: decayed piers: the Chinese walls of the elevated expressways.

The elimination of the many environmental deficiencies such as the elevated expressways, decayed piers, obsolete buildings, and (ultimately) declining and inharmonious functions is necessary to the achievement of a strong Core, and of Lower Manhattan's performing an optimum role in the City, the region and the Nation.

Improvement of the environment and achievement of the regional goals are seen as having at least three means for achievement. Each seems either compatible, or at least not in conflict with other possible regional and City goals. These means are (I) diversification and strengthening of the business Core, (2) development of a residential community particularly at the water's edge; (3) the introduction of regional recreation at the water's edge. Such actions consistent with the concept of a strong Core would take maximum advantage of Lower Manhattan's unique natural and locational characteristics.

Problems of Access and Movement: inadequate internal transportation; awkward relations between streets and land uses, a too-long and uncomfortable journey-to-work: pedestrian-vehicular conflicts; through and local traffic conflicts and congestion (anticipated further traffic bottle necks as the streets in the Civic Center are closed).

A second way to strengthen the Core is to improve access and divert and ease through traffic by such facilities as a lower manhattan expressway. Along the same line the reduction of the mass transit bottlenecks in Midtown, and the connection of downtown subways directly to the suburbs, by-passing Midtown, are seen as major City-wide means to reduce vulnerability and increase Lower Manhattan's competitive position. Local means include improving the subway stops and internal circulation and reducing goods-handling conflicts.

CITY-WIDE AND LOCAL LONG RANGE GOALS FOR LOWER MANHATTAN

Shorter-range goals particularly at a City-wide level in some instances act as constraints on the nature and timing of the means for achieving the long-range goals. The specific constraints or determinants are outlined in the next chapter.

LM Goal #1: Create a Strong, Coherent and Diversified Core

Perhaps the most far reaching goal for Lower Manhattan, and that with the greatest multiplier effect, is a strong, efficiently functioning Core in an attractive working environment. The Plan must provide diversity to the Core which will give its business owners, managers and workers that quality of life and richness of environment which is necessary for modern working conditions. As the need to attract skilled office workers increases and the number of "back office" jobs declines, conditions of the working environment become more critical. More recreation, more restaurants, more entertainment, more parks, better shopping, new urban services and new urban excitement are needed. This renewed environment can only be achieved and economically supported by a further diversification of Lower Manhattan's currently limited activities.

LM Goal #2: Provide For Prime Office Space Expansion

The goals for Lower Manhattan, concerned both with form and function, are ultimately directed toward and reflected in the office towers. As the Core is strengthened and diversified, the demand for office space will rise. Provision for major expansion of prime office space close to and a part of the present Cire is a major goal of the Plan.

On the basis of analysis, major new areas for office growth can be expected around the World Trade Center, the new Stock Exchange, and west and south of the Civic Center. Continuity between these areas of new growth and the older parts of the Core must be carefully planned, lest the Core be diffused to its disadvantage. Moreover, continued regenerative construction within the older Core must also be accommodated, particularly as the standards of office space continue to improve and older buildings lose their competitive position. This internal growth is needed to help maintain a balance between the Core and its periphery.

LM Goal # 3: Develop a New Lower Manhattan Residential Community

The demand for housing relatively close by the Core is already substantial: Brooklyn Heights, the Palisades, Staten Island. None are as accessible as would be housing in Lower Manhattan itself. The potential for housing in the core area will increase substantially in the 1970s. Many City-wide goals as well as those for Lower Manhattan would be met by people living adjacent to the dense urban Core, and within easy range of prime City attractions. The addition of business and retail functions that housing supports are a key part of a strategy of diversifying the Core.

In order to meet the combined goals of the region, the City and Lower Manhattan, specifications for this housing should include that it should be large enough to be a viable total community with a full range of income groups, family sizes and diversified backgrounds appropriate to urban living. It should take full advantage of views of the rivers, permit easy physical integration with places of employment to reduce the journey-to-work and to permit housing and offices, working together to support restaurants and shopping, have a full complement of community facilities, be close to major transportation routes, provide a hierarchy of private and public open spaces, and have as full a range as possible of housing types including those for family living.

LM Goal # 4: Improve Regional and Local Transportation

Improvement of transportation should be geared to the following major objectives.

Vehicular: Elimination of all non-essential traffic in the primarily pedestrian Core, re-routing through traffic on separate thorofares designed specifically for this use, and classifying and adjusting the internal street system to serve as distributors and service streets.

Pedestrian: The fact that vehicular traffic is not as intense as in Midtown, makes this area a feasible beginning place for the separation of pedestrian and vehicle traffic. It is also an area whose walking scale and character has not yet been destroyed by parking lots and traffic. A goal for all the users of Lower Manhattan, where everyone is a pedestrian, is the creation of pedestrian "precincts" and pedestrian streets in a pattern consistent with dominant usage.

Internal Movement: The expansion of the Core and the intensity of pedestrian movement makes necessary a consideration of a supplemental new intra-downtown mass transit system to ease pedestrian flows. Subways do not serve this internal movement.

Mass Transit Access: Improvements in Lower Manhattan's transit links to Westchester, Staten Island, Queens and New Jersey as well as to the rest of New York, are important goals. Where such major changes are compatible both with Lower Manhattan's goals and with those of the region, they should be an integral part of the Plan. Improved stations, and local linkages can increase ridership and greatly enhance the transit environment.

LM Goal # 5: Take Maximum Advantage of the Waterfront

New York is gradually awakening to the great natural resource which its 800 miles of waterfront represents. Nowhere else but in Lower Manhattan, however, in all this mileage, is there such a great working population so close to the water. The pressure for its use gives a high priority to the renewal of Lower Manhattan's waterfront. The fact that almost the entire waterfront is now under single ownership makes possible an unusual freedom in planning normally found only in outlying suburban areas. Cleaning up and opening up the waterfront for regional as well as local access is an important goal. The resource is so great that significant regional recreation needs can be met as well as local.

LM Goal # 6: Protect Existing Jobs

Supporting the Core will act significantly to protect its existing jobs.

However, large scale urban improvement plans have all too often eliminated low-paying jobs. The blue-collar working areas of northwest and north Lower Manhattan cannot be duplicated; the economics of new construction would cause their disappearance, and these jobs employing semi-skilled and unskilled workers are in short supply in the City. In the northwest goods-handling area, this strongly suggests a goal of postponement of radical change which overrides any other possibility. In the long range a number of alternate uses are considered on the assumption that the City policy will no longer dictate this action so strongly here.

LM Goal # 7: Enhance the Old Form of Lower Manhattan With the New

The skyline of downtown is so famous and evocative that it is often thought by visitors to be the profile of Manhattan itself. In the redevelopment of Lower Manhattan this pyramidal form, with great towers in the center and lower buildings at the edge, should be respected.

This does not mean that the skyline will not undergo alteration, enlargement, and change. The World Trade Center will soon rise, at the island's edge, on a wholly new scale, significantly changing the downtown form. At first glance the old scale seems destroyed, but appropriate development in the vicinity of the World Trade Center, both inland and offshore, can reincorporate these towers into the larger downtown scale. The need now is for towers which are close to the giants in size, located close to them to form a transition between the Center and the old scale. The Center can thus form the nucleus of a cluster as significant as the old one.

The second form problem concerns internal scale: the street-canyons from which planners recoiled when they wrote the 1916 ordinances to prevent their repetition. Today these deep cleavages of space are held in high favor and if the new design standards of open space threaten to destroy the older form, they should be revised to allow tighter construction in the downtown area.

LM Goal # 8: Enhance the City's economic and tax base.

By development of Lower Manhattan to its full potential, consistent with sound planning principles and a good quality of environment, the area can enhance the City's economic and tax base. That combination of activities which represents the highest and best use of Lower Manhattan should be sought.

THE ROLE OF THE CONCEPT PLANS

The Concept Plans were developed as a forward look at a future schematic picture of how the various goals (listed above) might be translated -- an image of what life could be like in Lower Manhattan. They were conceived as a hypothesis to be tested against the policy, market, and capacity determinants discussed in the following chapter, to be tested against the principles and specifications for a residential community and against processing and staging possibilities and alternative choices over time. They consist of both land use and movement systems illustrating how optimum movement is intimately related to the land use concepts.

A Strategy to Achieve the Goals

Part of the Concept Plans is a strategy followed by tactical considerations. The range of alternate means to achieve the overall goals, while broad in the long run, is fairly narrow in the short run, when the determinants discussed later are taken into consideration. The choices narrow down to four sets of major actions: transit and pedestrian movement improvements to the circulation system in response to immediate problems primarily in the Core; defensive actions in the industrial northwest and the present residential area; the vigorous promotion and development of current projects; and the development of a major new residential community of a size and character to achieve the greatest possible multiplier effect in diversification of other activities to enrich the Core and improve its environment. This last is seen as the key strategic move, the "key to the kingdom" in military terminology. [1]

The defensive actions -- industrial renewal, and residential self-rehabilitation -- are geared to short-range goals. The transportation elements of the Plan fit both the short and long range goals. The majority of elements and actions can and should be begun immediately. They set the stage for the land use changes proposed and for the new residential community.

With a strategic decision to create a new residential community, the next consideration was with the tactical question of how and where moves should be made. It was concluded that the goal of ultimate diversity of income groups and housing types can be most easily achieved if the initial beachhead of housing is established in the upper range of the income scale rather than in the middle or the lower. Subsequent development can work down the scale; the reverse is difficult once the character of an area has been established. Since initially there are policy limits on provision of public community facilities, it also seems best to introduce housing whose occupants can best fend for themselves.

A second consideration was that of size. To establish a significant new environment of its own in an area formerly identified as totally commercial, it was felt that the minimum number of dwelling units at the start should be in the range of 2000 to 3000 with an optimum of perhaps 6000. The minimum might be marketed over a three to five-year period at the rate of perhaps 600 a year, well within the feasible project-size in New York.

The final consideration was location. Factors discussed in Chapter VI suggest the East River waterfront from Wall Street to Fulton Street as the location in which the housing would most easily meet the specifications of the goals.

DETERMINANTS OF ACTION

The goals, the Concept Plans and the strategy and tactics for carrying them out all must operate within certain constraints on action. These are limiting factors on choice, some of which the City can control, such as the allocation of resources and policy. Some, however, such as the market demand for space and housing, the economics of building, and changing technological requirements are beyond influencing, at least in the short run.

Together, these are referred to as determinants of action. They are considered in detail as they affect the possibilities for action in the following chapter. They include the previously considered goals and, collectively, establish a kind of "decision model," to serve as a conceptual tool to explain the selection of recommended actions.

The determinants include policy determinants such as clients' goals, the allocation of public resources, City Housing, employment and parking policies, design and planning principles (including zoning), and considerations of historic and symbolic importance. Market determinants include the

[1] Strategy is used here as a long-range allocation of resources to gain an overall set of objectives (goals), as contrasted with tactics, a short-range set of moves or actions. Together they are in a sense synonymous with planning.

demand for space, the cost of sites, the character of the environment, the life expectancy of existing uses and structures and technological change. Capacity determinants include minimum land area needed for a viable residential community, and capacity of the movement systems to efficiently deliver the numbers of people.

LAND USE ASSIGNMENT, DESIGN PROGRAMMING, AND TRANSPORTATION TESTING

The process of design and planning next involved seeing how, and whether, the goals could be achieved and the concepts carried out within the limits of the outlined determinants. These possibilities were conceived as a kind of "solution area" which changes dimension over time as current determinants may be relaxed or tightened, or as new determinants may be imposed. The resultant Plan is for a sequence of choices over time.

The process of land use assignment to particular areas described in detail in the next chapter served four purposes. First, the assigning of land use, population and space to each area in accord with the Concept Plan, served as a test of the feasibility of the Plan within the limits of the determinants. Second, these allocations, each in effect the recommended alternative outlined in previous steps, served as a basis for testing the internal consistency of the decisions as well as the responses to them. The third purpose served was to establish a design and planning program for each area which would be consistent with the long-range and short-range goals. These programs included types of use, amounts of space, required ancillary facilities, and specific design and planning criteria.

The fourth purpose of the land use assignments was to load the movement system model and see whether the traffic thus generated exceeded the capacity of the system. Part 2 on transportation elaborates on this test and on considerations of mass-transit, pedestrian movement and service responses to the proposed land use changes.

CHAPTER VI

DEVELOPMENT OF LAND USE AND CIRCULATION PLANS

In the preceding chapters, the long-range goals for Lower Manhattan are seen to be the maintenance and growth of a strong, cohesive, diversified business and government Core, the improvement of access to it and its internal circulation , reduction in the journey-to-work, the public utilization of the waterfront and the creation of a major residential community to take advantage of the area's unique natural characteristics and excellent location.

Certain specific improvements can be immediately instituted in the transportation system and are discussed in detail in Part 2. These, along with the addition of the residential community are seen as a critically strategic way to achieve the strong and diversified Core. They will create demands, opportunities and an environment for commercial, cultural and public activities that will expand the present limited functions. These in turn will provide an atmosphere which will attract additional kinds of general office, commercial and corporate tenants.

This chapter combines the conclusions reached regarding the development potential for the major uses to be attracted, describes the alternate and recommended concepts and principles of overall land use and movement, and reviews the determinants of development as they affect the short,middle and long-range alternate choices for each sub-area of Lower Manhattan.

This is followed by a detailed description of land use,space , employment and housing, and the assignment process and design program that devolved. The design program is then used as the basis for the illustrations of the optimum development in Chapter VII and VIII.

As a test of the feasibility of the principles and the program, and of the possibilities for immediately establishing a large, integrated residential area, a more detailed study of the East River Waterfront is then undertaken. An outline of an implementation process for it is developed. This test case is extrapolated to illustrate how the optimum development of Lower Manhattan might look, if all of the recommended decisions were carried out over time. The function of the Optimum Development Site Plans is not to show how the future will look with a pretense at precision, but rather to serve as visual representations of the goals outlined earlier.

SUMMARY OF DEVELOPMENT POTENTIAL AND LOCATIONAL PREFERENCES

The present market demand for space and activities is summarized here under the categories of office, government, other non-residential uses, special areas, are residential. These are first considered in the context of the New York region.

Regional Location Considerations

The importance of Lower Manhattan's central location in the region has been stressed before. Historically this has been the reason for the great "sunk" investment in the transportation plant that now supports it and Midtown. Its central location establishes both regional obligations and regional opportunities that have only begun to be capitalized.

The first of these, Lower Manhattan's regional role as an office, financial and government center has been realized over the years, and is anticipated to continue and grow. A second and as yet undeveloped aspect of this role is a result of Lower Manhattan's key location at the head of the Upper Hudson Bay. In fact, it is now possible to think of the peninsula as a part of the land   bounding the Bay itself, with Brooklyn, the Verrazano Bridge, Staten Island, Port Elizabeth and the Palisades at Jersey City creating a huge amphitheater that is the Upper Bay. This amphitheater is dotted with Governor, Ellis and other smaller islands as events within it. World shipping is constantly in movement or at anchor in the great roadstead.

Such a reorientation of land and activity toward the water has been recognized by the Regional Plan Association as a new way of looking at this precious asset. A result has already been seen in proposals for housing along the Jersey waterfront, in Brooklyn, for the development of Ellis and Governor Islands, and at the approaches to the Narrows. The possibilities for exciting places to live along the water, combined with the regional goals outlined, (in particular the reduction of journeys-to-work bringing housing close to Lower Manhattan) thus makes proposals for housing along the East and Hudson River banks of Manhattan consistent with the regional context.

Office Space Demand and Locational Preferences

The immediate demand for office space is generated almost entirely by firms already located in Lower Manhattan. It consists of three kinds: corporate and business expansion and upgrading; some small-firm needs for space in speculative buildings; and expansion for mass clerical and machine operation functions. The first two need prestige location and identification, while the last is best accommodated in large, undivided floor areas with somewhat different building requirements than the other two.

A considerable part of this immediate demand is for buildings with floor areas of 30,000 to 50,000 sq. ft. Banks seek places for stock transfer activities [1] linked to the corporate headquarters, the brokers and corporations who have stock issues, the Federal Reserve Bank and the Check Clearing House. Much of this is tied to locations south of Chambers Street, and the Water Street area is a logical choice. Business services expansion is related to all three in terms of growth potential.

All of this demand translated into net additions of space required for present functions is still modest (for perhaps 50,000 employees). However, if the objective of diversification can be achieved and new functions added, Lower Manhattan's share of regional growth can be substantially increased by new firms (by the addition of a goal of another 75-85000 employees). [2]

Locational preferences are expected to continue to be in or near the Core. The "natural areas" of expansion are assumed to be where market demand now indicates: to the east in the short-range, adjacent to the World Trade Center in the middle-range, and further in-filling in the long range.

Although considerable in-filling of the present Core is now taking place [3] a major share of this new construction is in response to the widening of Water Street and the availability close to the Core of relatively cheap sites. Water Street shifted the traditionally inward focus of the financial community outward to the East River, but it is a kind of backing movement with continued focus on Wall and Broad Streets as prestige addresses as expansion occurs.

---

[1] See e.g. New York Times. Op. cit.

[2] See supra, Table V

[3] As evidenced by the planned and committed buildings shown on the map of immediate recommendations.

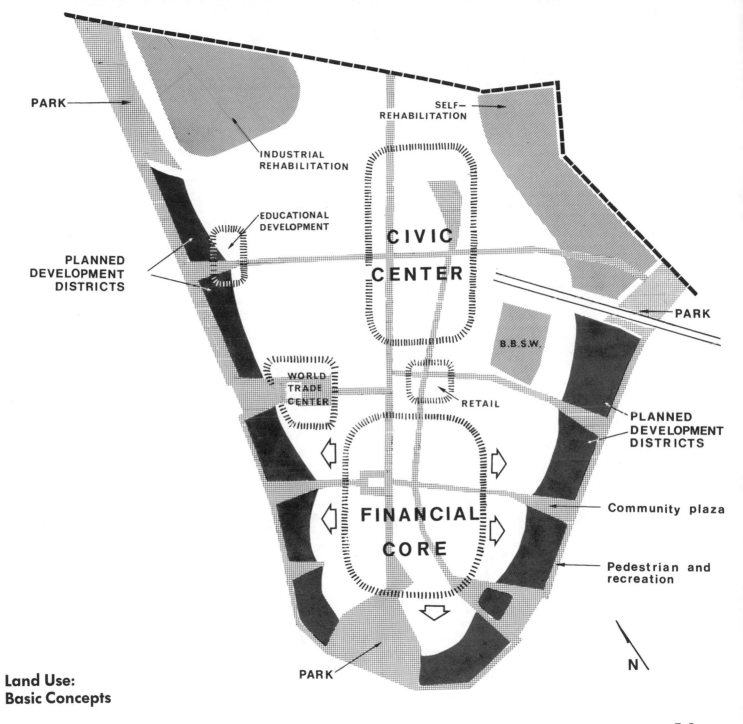

PARK

INDUSTRIAL
REHABILITATION

SELF—
REHABILITATION

EDUCATIONAL
DEVELOPMENT

CIVIC
CENTER

PLANNED
DEVELOPMENT
DISTRICTS

PARK

B.B.S.W.

WORLD
TRADE
CENTER

RETAIL

PLANNED
DEVELOPMENT
DISTRICTS

Community plaza

FINANCIAL
CORE

Pedestrian and
recreation

N

PARK

**Land Use:
Basic Concepts**

0'   500'   1000'   2000'

A major function of the Plan is to work with these market forces, to guide them and to insure that the Core does not become too diffuse as a result. Thus housing interposed at Front and South Streets and in the pier area is seen as a counter-move to help prevent this diffusion.

In the middle range, the World Trade Center is assumed to have been completed, along with the development of the U.S. Steel site. By then the capacity of the Water Street area will have been reached and the influence of the W.T.C. will be to generate interest, activity and new functions in that direction. As a consequence the Plan should foresee making use of this anticipated direction-shift of the investment thrust and assign space and growth to areas to the north, south and east of the Center site.

In the long-run, the assumption is made that the additional office space demand will come from new kinds of activities --sub-centers of advertising, general office, housing-oriented business services and the like -- and these will be accommodated by further in-filling in the Core and in transition areas between housing and office areas.

These assumptions are the basis for developing a tactical program and assignment of space illustrated in the staging maps.

Government Space and Locational Preferences

Government policy can be influential in the short-run, but Lower Manhattan's monopoly on government administrative space and related government services is likely to provide for a continued expansion via a rental/construction cycle similar to that which is now happening. Although demand for new space would appear to be largely satisfied by the Civic Center and World Trade Center, it is worth noting that even in the short time of its development the federal space requirement has gone up 50%.

Locational preferences are assumed to continue to be on the major subways and on both sides of Broadway, generally to the west and southwest of the Civic Center. In the future, business services related to government should move forther west and south, attracted by the World Trade Center. The assignment of space is not broken down by government versus private space, but the assumption is that a substantial portion of it will be occupied by government and related business service expansion.

Other Non-Residential Activities

It appears clear that the space demands for most other existing non-residential activities have been declining and will continue to decline. Manufacturing, food distribution, and wholesaling-with-stock with few exceptions have found other areas in the City and region more appropriate to their needs and within their economic reach. Retail activity has been displaced by project after project; in the future it is dependent on an immediate market of residents supplemented by the workers in the Core. The ultimate demand will depend on how much housing is created, and on how attractive the environment will be for restaurants, theaters and shopping.

Locational preferences for shopping will be at points on or near subways, future housing and major employment centers. At the level of general land use planning, assignment of retail space can be ignored, as it will undoubtedly be the first floor activity of buildings with other uses.

Institutional uses, however, are a source of demand that can have a great impact on Lower Manhattan, Beekman Hospital, and Pace College are only two of many possible. Columbia College (later University) was once located near the World Trade Center site. With a major residential community, an educational complex that takes advantage of the great subway concentration appears a logical new use.

Again, why an educational complex? Studies of the Washington Market Area indicate as stated in Chapter IV that this is a site for which there is little demand without a substantial subsidy of some kind over and above the renewal write-down. In the meantime, the City University is looking for places to develop new educational campuses of various kinds. In a way this is an expediency, a site looking for a use and a use looking for a site. Detailed analysis now underway may indicate the site unsuitable.

Clearly, the case for an educational complex here must depend primarily on City policy. However in an area where public decision must be made, such a decision could be a public action, within public control to make, that would have a fantastic multiplier effect as a precedent to upgrading the area to its east, and to setting preconditions for the best kind of development on the piers.

Special Area Demands

Three special areas were considered as to the long-term appropriateness of their present uses: the warehousing and distribution area around Canal and West Streets and the Holland Tunnel; the area north and west of the Civic Center, and Chinatown.

The first is well located, the buildings are appropriate to their uses, with many designed for well over 250 lbs, per sq. ft. floor loading, and with up-to-date freight elevators and air-conditioning. The area has shown considerable growth and vitality in recent years and is more related to the similar area to its immediate north (north of Canal Street) than to the declining food center to the south. Here a program of industrial renewal is considered feasible and desirable. The long-range use of this area is therefore assumed to be its present one, with the demand for such space continuing strong.

The second area -- the industrial "blue collar" area of the northwest -- has been discussed in detail in Chapter II. The conclusion was that it should continue in its present use for the indefinite future, based on the City policy of protecting its jobs. Special programs for helping the businesses and for job-retraining seem advisable.

The third, Chinatown, has a much greater potential as a tourist attraction and residential area than is now realized. With some physical and social changes, the market can support much more activity there.

Demand for Residential Space

With the region increasing by all estimates from 12 million to 20 million people by the year 2000 the total demand for residential space is expected to be large. New York defies housing market analysts because demand in most sectors of the market is so great that developers often dispense with their services.

What little experience developers in the northern part of Lower Manhattan have had (Chatham Green, etc.) in marketing housing indicates that even with a somewhat lonesome atmosphere, the demand is relatively strong. The assumption is made therefore that the developers of a really viable and attractive community can almost write their own ticket. This assumption also indicates the real possibility that public policy can mold the composition of the result in terms of desired housing income and racial mix. [1]

Within marketability limits, such a mix rather than a single-income group for large projects is also of advantage to developers. It permits them to rent and sell more rapidly by reaching into many housing sub-markets at the same time.

The initial demand in a new area not yet identified as a desirable neighborhood should be for relatively specialized groups: people for whom the normal amenities of family life are not essential. Included would be bachelors, "young marrieds," second apartments for executives, etc. In time, as community facilities are developed, the nature of the demand can change, and the mix could be broadened by making available middle-income housing money. The area can then be attractive for family living.

Informed real estate opinion holds that middle-income housing can be built on land costing up to $10 a square foot at top densities, and "luxury" housing (depending on the degree of "luxury") on land ranging from $50 to as high as $100 a square foot of actual site. [2] On existing land, with site costs averaging from $75 to $125 per square foot, there are only few situations along the downtown riverfronts where unaided housing is feasible. These situations will be primarily for "luxury" housing, perhaps combined with office structures. As has been mentioned however, these possibilities are realistic, with the Brooklyn Heights and other Bay sites as exciting examples.

---

[1] See Wallace, McHarg, Roberts and Todd, Trenton Housing Policy Study, for the Department of Planning and Development, Trenton, N.J., 1966 for a study of the implications of rent levels and housing types on viable economic and racial mixes.

Future Land Use
Legend:
RESIDENTIAL
OFFICE
INSTITUTIONAL
INDUSTRIAL
PARKS AND RECREATION SPACE
PEDESTRIAN WALKWAY AND COMMUNITY PLAZA
RETAIL
TO BE DETERMINED
N
0′
500′
1000′
2000′

**Generalized
Functional
Areas: Future**

0'   500'   1000'   2000'

LOWER MANHATTAN PLAN **43**

In contrast , in newly-created areas beyond the bulkhead the actual cost of developed land (including the cost of the relocated and depressed highway) can be in the neighborhood of $25 a square foot. This means that a certain variety of conventionally-financed housing is economically feasible.

In terms of market for this a major immediate source of the downtown housing demand is the 400,000 employees in Lower Manhattan. In light of the goal of reducing the journey-to-work, the ultimate income mix should bear a close relation to the effective demand of this group. [1]

Market locational preferences today are for housing at the edges of the Core, on either side of the Brooklyn Bridge approach and along the water on the East River. [2]

THE CONCEPT PLANS

With the above summary as background, along with detailed analysis of the existing situation in each sub-area of Lower Manhattan outlined in Chapter II alternate Concept Plans were developed which made initial land use assignments. These constituted a "leap" into the future, putting together the above market considerations with the application of relevant basic principles.

The Land Use Concept Plan

As has been stated, the function of a Land Use Concept (or Sketch) Plan is to provide a long-range basis for preliminary assignment of land use and activity; it also serves as a preliminary test of the possibilities for implementing the strategy of adding a major residential community to the Core. Would such a community be simply an "alien" graft on the Core, unintegrated and not able to effect the enrichment of activities desired? Or could it be sufficiently large and tightly related to become both viable on its own and of real benefit to the Core?

The Land Use Concept Plan shown in detail is a clear statement of the proposed land use relationships. The business Core is enlarged slightly to the east along Water Street and the west to the World Trade Center, but the Core remains basically tight. The government center extends a short distance to the west of Broadway and is occupied by intense business and government services. The residential community is essentially a linear one extending along both waterfronts, organized into planning and development units. These are joined together at community center plazas that serve to unite the social and economic life of the residential and business worlds. In them would be located a wide variety of community facilities.

The selection of the locations of the community center plazas was influenced by the existing major pedestrian streets and connections to subways, by the geometry of the service connections to depressed expressways, and by the population size of the residential units.

Where residential areas join the office Core, housing and office are proposed to be actually mixed in the sense that they will be side by side, or in some cases residence on top of office, they share common open spaces and community facilities and use the same movement system. Thus each residential planning "node" is tied closely to a business or institutional use inland. Both are served by the peripheral expressway system, and share an internal park and open space nucleus. These nuclei will serve as local open spaces, primarily available to the residents and employees they serve, containing tot-lots, swim clubs, handball courts, and other small scale facilities.

Major institutional growth is conceived around Pace College in the center of the peninsula and in the central portion of the Washington Market Area. These are intended to serve both Lower Manhattan and the region as a whole.

---

[1] Little is known about the income stratification of the employment pool today. As projects are marketed, special surveys of the demand are desirable to gear the mix to this group.

[2] From investor inquiries and informed real estate opinion.

Although current plans indicate leaving the northwest as it now is for an indefinite time, the area from Church Street to the Washington Market area is expected to be ultimately renewed for residential use, in part by new structures, in part by conversion of existing warehouses and offices to housing. Remaining industry near Canal Street and the self-rehabilitated area of Chinatown is compatible with the adjacent new uses.

At the community, city and regional scale, the water's edge is completely available, entered from the community plazas and from the adjacent housing. The regional parks form a system of open space which broadens at the Brooklyn Bridge to serve the Governor Alfred E. Smith Houses and the new housing to the south, as well as to serve regional recreational demands with active sports such as tennis, model airplane flying fields, etc. It broadens again and includes Battery Park, a large public esplanade in front of the World Trade Center and finally another major regional park between Hubert and Canal Streets.

The Movement Concept Plan

The Movement Concept Plan presumes major improvement for mass transit access to the Core. In terms of auto access it presumes the existence in the not-too-distant future of a facility of the performance characteristics of the Lower Manhattan Expressway to divert through traffic from local streets. This, while perhaps not critical to the system, is a very important element.

The performance characteristics for the F.D.R. Drive and the Miller Highway are significantly modified in requiring more points of access to the major arterial system at Maiden Lane-Liberty Street and Barclay-Vesey, and Worth-Leonard on the west. It is these points of access which will improve the distributor function. They become a major traffic reason for considering depressing the expressways.

The initial movement system developed in response to current problems (discussed in detail in Part 2) was found to be consistent with this land use pattern and with minor modification served as a Movement Concept Plan. The peripheral expressways perform the major by-pass and distributor function, an internal

**Circulation
System I**

Legend:

██	**PEDESTRIAN**
——	**ARTERIAL**
– – –	**SERVICE**
‖‖‖	**PARKING**

0' 500' 1000' 2000'

Canal St.

Manhattan Bridge

Worth St.

Park Row

Chambers St.

Warren

Murray

Barclay

Vesey

Fulton

St.

St.

B'klyn Bridge

Liberty

Broadway

Nassau St.

Wall St.

Broad

Water

St.

N

LOWER MANHATTAN PLAN **44**

north-south and east-west major arterial system and a local service system act as distributors. Parking garages are tied to the peripheral system at points where expressway exits occur. The concept intends the internal street system to be largely for service and taxi access.

Connected to the community plazas is a major pedestrian street system -- Chambers, Fulton, Wall and Broad, in an east-west direction: and Broadway, the north-south ceremonial street serving both as a pedestrian and vehicular artery. Nassau-Broad Street is the other major north-south pedestrian thorofare. The pedestrian streets connect to the major subway exits, and form a structure on which internal open space, both existing and proposed, is located.

Alternate Concepts

In terms of form, the concept alternatives range from a massive development along the edge of the water that clearly expressed the linear nature of its development, to a pattern of towers in parks -- objects in space like the Governor Alfred E. Smith Houses. The first extreme cuts the City off from the rivers and the second is basically non-urban and sterile, a relic of obsolete design concepts and standards.

The most desirable form appears to be a modified combination of towers and terraces, a mix of residential and commercial that has a visual expression more like San Gimignano in Italy than either of the two extremes.

The visual solution to the scale-upsetting World Trade Center was felt to be the development of towers close to it in height that would provide a transition between it and the present complex. At the same time the total shape should continue as much as possible to be the pyramidal, albeit slightly off-center, skyline profile of today.

Major alternate land use concepts were possible only if the determinants outlined below were substantially relaxed. For example, one involved limiting housing to the area north of Fulton Street and in the Washington Market Area. The piers would be eliminated and either replaced by park or left as water. The housing developed on inland sites would require both urban renewal and middle-income subsidy; the first because of the high land costs, and the second because luxury housing,

politically unlikely to be placed on urban renewal land anyway, would require a better environment than could be provided without removing the elevated expressways. Their removal is unfeasible without building out into the water, as will be shown in the East Side Case Study in Chapter VII.

A major reason for rejecting this alternate was that the residential areas could not be integrated with the Core. As a result, the commercial activities that they would generate would depend for their support on the residents alone and could not tap the market of Core employment. The Core in turn would not benefit by enrichment of mix. A final reason was that the activities and jobs that would have to be relocated to make sufficient room for such housing, are and will be in critical demand in the city for a considerable time to come.

Summary of Principles

In summary of the adopted Concept Plans, the underlying principles intended to serve the previously outlined goals are as follows:

A. Movement

1. Classification and assignment of each element of the street and expressway system to the function is should perform; and the treatment of each accordingly as: a) Streets for major movement of traffic, designed as a peripheral by-pass and distribution system; an internal arterial system; and a local service and access system, b) Pedestrian streets for free movement of people over short distances.

2. Integration of pedestrian streets into a structure of feeder subway stations and zones, major internal open spaces, community plazas and the park system for public access to the water's edge.

3. Location of parking -- except that for short turnover -- at the periphery of the peninsula and keyed primarily to the expressways to reduce internal traffic as much as possible.

4. Improvement and integration of public transportation into a system to distribute people consistent with land use concentrations.

5. Provision of pedestrian connections from all residential units to job centers to take maximum advantage of a shorter journey -to-work.

B. Land Use And Activities

1. Maintenance and enhancement of a strong, coherent concentrated Core, along with as intense uses as possible consistent with a tolerable level of congestion.

2. Close integration of residence and office uses at the periphery of the Core, not just grafted on, but interwoven with each other.

3. Provision of a new major residential community with full community facilities organized into viable planning and development units, served largely in terms of access by the peripheral expressway system.

4. Within each residential planning unit, complete separation of pedestrian and vehicular traffic.

5. Development of a system of public community plazas and open spaces to serve as the meeting places for the social, economic and cultural life of Lower Manhattan.

6. Development of the waters' edge into a variety of recreation facilities with full pedestrian public access to all.

7. Provision of inland views to the water from as many points as possible to maximize the advantage of Lower Manhattan's unique location.

8. The gradual elimination of activities that are competitive and inharmonious, particularly goods-handling and low-intensity uses, consistent with:

9. The retention, for an indefinite period, of jobs now in critically short supply.

C. Shape and Form

1. Arrangement of zoning envelopes and development controls and intensive activities at the key points of major access, the

subway zones, and the central spine of Broadway.

2. New building so arranged as to provide "transition" towers between the new form of the World Trade Center and the old form of the familiar silhouette.

3. Preservation of downtown "canyon" scale and spatial organization at the same time allowing for utilization of modern technology, economic disciplines in new construction.

SPECIFICATIONS FOR THE RESIDENTIAL COMMUNITY

Out of these principles come certain specifications for development of each of the land uses. Because of its central role in the Plan's strategy of change, and because of its being an "introduced" use, the specifications for and implications of the residential community are singled out for special consideration. These must be viewed, of course, in light of general housing goals for the City. [1]

The most desirable community from the standpoint of City-wide policy would be composed of a mixture of economic and ethnic groups, from upper income to lower, as a long-range goal. The specific mix of such groups is beyond the scope of this Study, and in light of the City policy of no subsidy in this area the subject is perhaps academic at the present time. It is felt that later study, particularly of the employee market in Lower Manhattan, should determine an appropriate mix. Ultimate decisions on this mix will not materially change the housing types and intensities, although they will affect the amounts and kinds of community services needed.

In developing the preliminary specifications for the proposed residential community, the considerations that were examined are outlined below.

---

[1] See e.g. Department of City Planning, City of New York, Toward a Strategy for Urban Renewal for New York, Department of City Planning, City of New York, 1966.

Regional Trends for Downtown Housing

The immediate market for downtown housing concentrates on that increasing portion of the region's middle-to-upper income population which seeks multi-family housing in the Core and in what the Regional Plan Association has referred to as the "inner ring".[1] In 1957, only 20 percent of the housing units in the "inner ring" were multi-family; by 1964 this proportion rose to almost 60 percent.

For the most part, these units represent two household types: relatively young families with few or no children, and an older group (generally over 45 years of age) whose children are now teenage or adult and who have therefor gained a considerable mobility. Both groups are growing in the region, and their housing decisions have had a strong impact on the distribution and categories of the housing stock being added. It is estimated that between 1965 and 2000, the number of one-and-two person households will rise by 84 percent compared to 46 percent for three-or-more person households. There will also be a shift toward younger households, a group which, in certain income categories, is amenable to central city living. The capacity of the Core to attract this group -- or significant segments of it -- depends on its success in creating good housing in a good environment.[2]

A third group consists of the well-to-do with the means to select and influence their own environment and who can set the tone of any area they decide to move into. This group will play a major role in downtown housing, particularly since it is will represented in downtown employment.

Out of the 100,000 - 130,000 dwelling units added annually to the regional stock,[3] these three groups account for roughly 25,000 to 35,000 units. If as many as 2,000 of these households were to locate in Lower Manhattan annually, this would represent a "capture rate" of some 8 per cent of the market. In the development period envisaged, such a rate would mean the addition of 40,000 new dwelling units, or roughly 80,000 to 120,000 people, depending on household size (2 to 3 per household).

Desirable Mix Based On A Midtown Example

In the course of the analysis of anticipated downtown residential growth, a survey was made of the existing mixture of employment and housing in the East Midtown area (between 30th and 60th Streets, east of Fifth Avenue). This area was selected because it is probably the most successful existing prototype of mixed office-residential use in the country. It was not assumed that this prototype would function as a "model" for downtown development, but only that it might offer some clues as to the nature and composition of viable mixed areas.[4]

Some 595,000 people are employed in this East Midtown area, while the residents in the same area number 102,500. The ratio is therefore about six employees to one resident. This ratio varies widely from one part of Midtown to another. For example, along the East River a predominantly residential area, the ratio is three or four employees to one resident. South of Central Park, in a predominantly office area, the mix is almost exclusively office, with only a scattering of residential-hotel population.

The residents are not organized in typical family units. There are 96,476 adults and 6,086 children (14 years or less), well below the City average. Of the adults in the area, a relatively small proportion are married -- 39,940 out of 96,476 or 41 percent. This too is below average.

The pattern of this development emerges as small apartments with a heavy concentration of bachelors, unmarried women, plus married people with few or no children. These are largely people who want direct day-and-night involvement with the Core of the city, or who want walk-to-work housing. In addition, the well-to-do enjoy the benefits and convenience

[1] This includes Manhattan, the near in portions of Long Island, Staten Island, and New Jersey.
[2] R.P.A., op. cit.
[3] R.P.A. op. cit.
[4] Some significant differences should be noted at the start: the Midtown residential community is actually part of a larger residential area extending up the East Side to 96th Street. It therefore cannot be treated in isolation. Also, the Midtown housing stock was built up over a long period, and ranges greatly in quality and character. The downtown development, on the other hand, will be somewhat "isolated" for some time to come, and it will be more difficult to market it for a heterogeneous group.

of Midtown living; at the same time, through country homes and beach houses they have the best of a variety of residential environments.

In certain areas, the proportion of women to men is very high, in particular between Park and Third Avenues. This suggests young career women, as yet unmarried, walking to work, living together in groups of two, three or four, near their jobs, restaurants, theatres and other amusements.

Minimum Community Size

Assuming a goal for the downtown development of a working population of 500,000 (up from 375,000 today), a minimum residential population of 83,000 would provide a ratio of six workers to one resident; a three to one ratio would require 166,000 residents. The lower figure would be sufficient to support a wide variety of local activities, including a major high school in the downtown area to serve the new population as well as a portion of the Lower East Side. A high school would be important in the development of a strong community self-image and would help to anchor the community to the downtown area. However, it is clear that a high school involving a major allocation of City funds would not be indicated until the later stages of development. In conclusion, a goal of approximately 100,000 residents is sought.

Density and Coverage

Much downtown residential zoning is currently the equivalent of R-10, the highest category of residential zoning in the code, providing a room count of about 1,450 per acre, or roughly 1,200 people per acre. At between 2 and 3 people per dwelling unit, this would be about 500 dwelling units per acre.

In light of probable land costs and in view of the existing business densities, this zoning has been used for the initial land use calculations although R-9 turned out to satisfy the economic requirements. High densities are both economically necessary and aesthetically appropriate to the area because of the goals of intensity and maximum use of the sites. Later planning for facilities and a desirable environment tended to cut back these totals to a degree. As a result neighborhood density, including public open space comes to between 400- 600 people per acre. Building coverage consistent with the zoning code would be about 40 percent with the remainder in open space or public use.

Neighborhood Unit Size

A number of neighborhood clusters or development nodes was fixed on a trial basis, at six in accordance with the "natural" area divisions along the periphery. Each is centered between two major pedestrian arteries and constitutes a major building unit. The pedestrian arteries are part of the internal pedestrian street system. For identification these units are referred to as: 1) (on the Hudson River) Chambers Street, 2) World Trade Center, 3) Rector Street, 4) (and on the East River) Fulton Street, 5) Wall Street, 6) Broad Street. The neighborhoods are roughly equal in size, except for the Fulton Street unit which is considerably larger than the others and encompasses a renewal project (Brooklyn Bridge Southwest) already underway.

Each of these neighborhood units ultimately should be large enough to have its own residential shopping, which is to say at least around 12,000 people or enough to support a small super-market. Added together, this would suggest a minimum downtown residential population of 80,000, not inconsistent with the minimum based on the office-residential ratio criterion.

The preparation of the land use programs and later design studies acted as tests for the feasibility of these principles and specifications.

Supporting Facilities

Playgrounds and Playlots: Basically, two kinds of local recreation space are necessary for the residents: 1) Playgrounds distributed at a maximum of a half-mile from residential areas, and 2) local facilities (including playlots) for each residential office cluster. No fixed national standard can be used to determined the amount required; properly distributed, a large number of small units, supplemented by several field-size playgrounds, will meet the needs of the population to be served based on an ultimate detailed analysis.

The location for small scale "backyard" parks or units is proposed for platforms over the service areas in each residential unit, surrounded by low-rise buildings, with easy access to the residential towers.

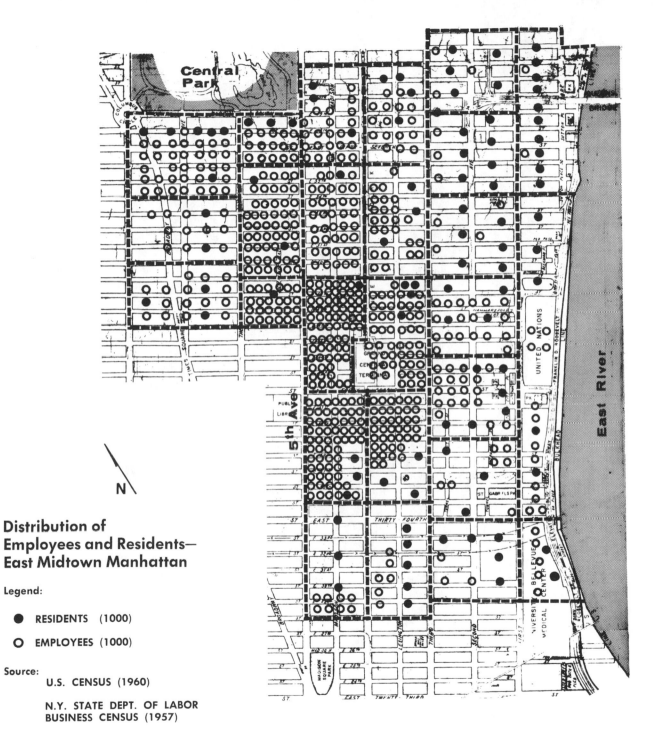

**Distribution of
Employees and Residents—
East Midtown Manhattan**

Legend:

● RESIDENTS (1000)

○ EMPLOYEES (1000)

Source:

U.S. CENSUS (1960)

N.Y. STATE DEPT. OF LABOR
BUSINESS CENSUS (1957)

0'   1000'   2000'   3000'

Present Zoning

0' 500' 1000' 2000'

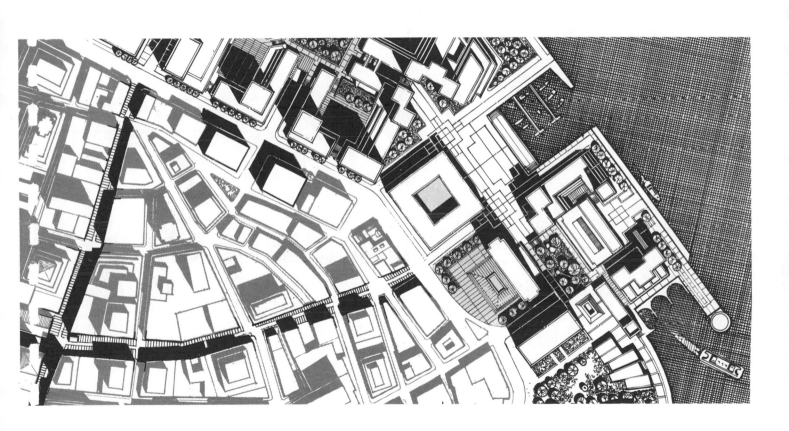

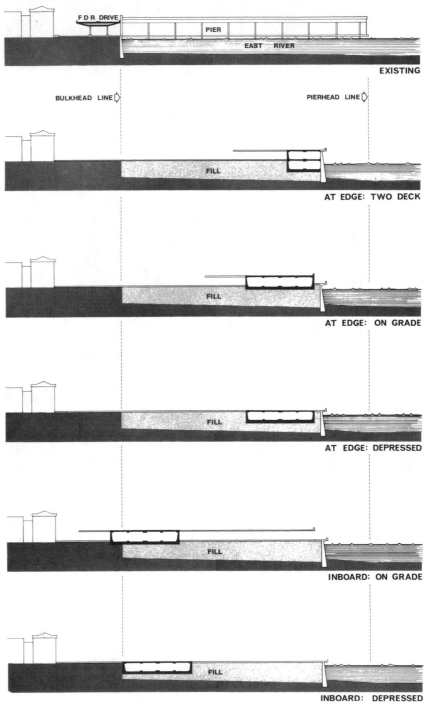

EXISTING

F D R DRIVE
PIER
EAST RIVER

BULKHEAD LINE ▷
PIERHEAD LINE ▷

FILL
AT EDGE: TWO DECK

FILL
AT EDGE: ON GRADE

FILL
AT EDGE: DEPRESSED

FILL
INBOARD: ON GRADE

FILL
INBOARD: DEPRESSED

**Waterfront
Development:
Highway Alternatives**

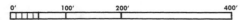

0' 100' 200' 400'

LOWER MANHATTAN PLAN **49**

On these raised terraces, a degree of isolation suitable to playlots and pre-school activity will be assured. These areas will be used primarily by residents of adjacent buildings.

Parks: Three major parks are indicated, two new ones at the northern end of each shore development, and one old one (Battery Park) enhanced and partially used for active recreation. The total space involved is somewhat over ninety acres.

The East River Park, on new fill between Peck and Catherine Slips (partly under the Brooklyn Bridge), will serve both the new community and the existing Alfred E. Smith Homes to the north. This area is presently deficient in playfield area, although the Two Bridges Neighborhood Association has plans for the enlargement of existing facilities.

The Hudson River Park will be located north of the proposed institutional reserve (or educational park)and north of Hubert Street. It will also be on new filled land. It might serve the proposed downtown high school and other educational facilities suggested for this area. It is considered an appropriate location here for three reasons. First, it should be designed for teenage and adult recreation, and therefore its users would be highly mobile and able to travel to it. Second,the character of active recreation makes it an "attractive nuisance" not desirable too close to dense housing. Third, it will form a good transition or buffer between the housing to its south and the industrial area to its north and east.

Schools: As previously mentioned, it is anticipated that two primary schools will be required, one for each side of the island, with a capacity of 1200 children each. An intermediate school will be required for the East Side development, as well as an additional one for the west side. The primary schools are seen as easily accommodated in several floors of multi-use structures. The intermediate schools will probably require separate sites, and it is anticipated that developers can integrate these schools into their plans in such a way as to relieve the City of any site costs.

A senior high school ultimately will be needed. It can serve the areas to the north of Lower Manhattan as well. A possible location for it would be part of the educational reserve proposed for the Washington Market Renewal Area. It is desirable that it be located on or near a good subway access and with play space; it could be designed as a special-emphasis or "magnet" school related to the employment needs and activities of the Core.

Shopping Facilities: Some local shopping and community halls may also be provided, [1] but these should principally be at the plazas. Each community plaza can take on a special character: the Fulton Fish Plaza with oysters sold from boats, etc.

Specifications for a New Peripheral Movement System

It was evident that the existing waterfront street system would have to undergo significant modification and expansion to accommodate the new growth. The new system should meet the following requirements.

1. Express traffic on the peripheral highways should be provided so that it no longer constitutes a physical and visual barrier between the area inside and outside the present water's edge.

2. Access must be provided directly from the expressway to distributor arterials and the service system for the waterfront development districts.

3. Servicing of any new development area should impose no additional burden on the arterials, but should be handled in a separate system designed expressly for service purposes.

4. New residential parking facilities should be tied primarily to the peripheral highway system, and as little as possible to the existing internal street system.

_____

[1] The prototype for this is the Brooklyn Bridge Southwest housing now being designed on this principle.

5. Direct on-grade pedestrian access should be provided between the business Core and the waterfront community.

As a general principle, the new circulation system must be designed to establish physical continuity between the existing Core and the new off-shore development. The best solution would be the one which creates the most added land value in relation to cost. To what extent can the existing system be adapted or must there be a new system?

Alternatives for the Expressways

The first question has to do with the existing elevated highways. Designed originally to allow on-grade truck access to the now obsolete and underutilized piers, these highways are not only a blighting influence on the surrounding areas but also a barrier between the Core and the new waterfront. In addition they were designed primarily for through traffic and have poor service connections for the waterfront area. [1] Their ultimate reconstruction is therefore the key to the highest possible development of the new areas.

In studying this question, a number of alternative solutions were explored: a highway on grade, elevated (relocated) or depressed. Several alternative locations were also studied: on South and West Street inside the bulkhead line, past the bulkhead line, and at the pierhead line (both single or double -decked).

These alternatives were evaluated in terms of approximate and comparative initial cost, engineering feasibility, links to the existing elevated system, design implications and contribution to land value.

An on-grade highway at the pierhead line was one of the first alternatives investigated. This solution had the advantage of removing the highway altogether from the area of greatest pedestrian-service concentration. However, its connections to the existing highway system were complex and awkward and it required raising access to the water above the percent grade, an impediment to pedestrians. It was not deemed a feasible solution.

A much simpler solution was an on-grade highway on South and West Street, to be built immediately outside of the present lo-

cation of the existing elevated structures.

This solution, however, has several fundamental weaknesses. Pedestrian movement past a new on-grade highway would require a rise of one level, thus defeating the goal of "continuity" and creating a division between the Core and the waterfront community.

This rise might be accomplished in the form of a continuous deck across the new highway. But if the deck were, in fact, not built, the new on-grade highway would constitute an even stronger barrier to free movement than the elevated highway it had replaced. Experience has shown the difficulties of integrated development where people are required to climb over or pass under a highway at grade.

A further difficulty was that access ramps from either side would have to rise over the expressway to the arterial distributors and these would be a formidable problem to design around.

A final difficulty was the cost of relocating or of accommodating the underground utilities. The possibilities of encasing the present highway, or of double-decking it at the edge of the water, were studied in detail. In every case the ramping problems, when adequate access points were included, prevented integration of land uses.

The Depressed Expressway

This led to the detailed consideration of a depressed highway -- the only solution which, in downtown's special topography, would make possible a fully integrated development with free pedestrian movement across the highway. The entire area, including the air rights over the highway, would be available for development. Maximum utilization of the water would be possible.

Costs of Depressed Expressways

A depressed highway is, of course, an expensive engineering

---

[1] It should be noted that two new ramps have been proposed on the Miller Highway at about Harrison Street by the Triborough Bridge and Tunnel Authority.

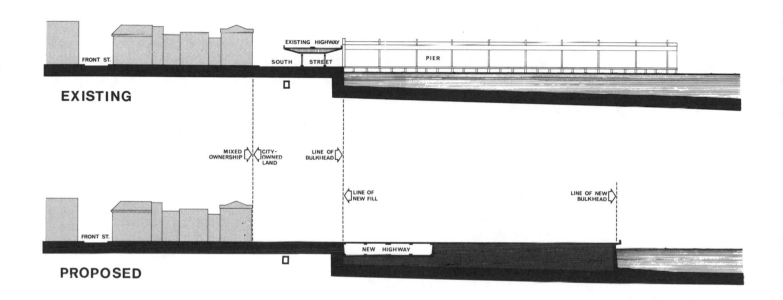

EXISTING

FRONT ST.

SOUTH STREET

EXISTING HIGHWAY

PIER

MIXED OWNERSHIP | CITY-OWNED LAND

LINE OF BULKHEAD

LINE OF NEW FILL

LINE OF NEW BULKHEAD

FRONT ST.

NEW HIGHWAY

PROPOSED

**Proposed
Highway
Relocation**

0'   100'   200'   300'

solution--both because of the excavation required and (in this case) the hydrostatic pressures to be overcome. The road surface acts as a boat, and must be both supported and held down to prevent "floating".

Depressed expressways have been considered in somewhat analagous waterfront situations in Philadelphia, Pa. [1] and Norfolk, Virginia. Costs rise to perhaps double an on-grade solution. However, the particular situations are undoubtedly special and different, and short of a detailed engineering study for Lower Manhattan, only general figures could be used.

Detailed cost estimates for a depressed expressway were beyond the scope of the study. However, certain analagous recent experiences both in New York and elsewhere were helpful in arriving at generally reliable figures. [1] They indicated that the depressed expressway will cost in the range of $7,000 per linear foot on the East Side (where the express portion will be four lanes plus four service lanes), and in the range of $9000 per linear foot on the West Side (where it will be six express lanes plus four service lanes). [2]

It was only after analysis of the total costs involved -- both of the depressed expressway and the land fill -- that its advantages and feasibility became apparent. That is to say, by adding substantially more and higher-quality land to downtown, the depressed expressway is, in the long run, the most economical solution.

Several factors tend to keep down the total cost of the depressed expressway. After study, it was seen to be most easily located outside of the existing bulkhead -- on new fill, There it will be entirely on City-owned land and would be free of most utilities and other encumbrances. It can be built while the existing elevated highways are still in operation. On new filled land excavation costs would be at a minimum. While these factors do not cancel out the extra cost of depressing it, they help substantially. South and West Street representing a considerable strip of land would be freed for building sites. The inclusion of this land in the total development "package" substantially lowers the per-unit cost of the newly created land.

Cost Estimates for the Expressway and Land Fill Combined

Total cost would be in the neighborhood of $34 million for the East Side and $66 million for the West Side, making an overall cost of about $100 million.

The fill itself, plus the new bulkhead, will cost between $8.00 and $10.00 a square foot, depending on a variety of factors. Including utilities, the basic capital cost is estimated to be conservatively in the neighborhood of $15.00 a square foot.

Adding the cost of the land fill and bulkhead of $8.00 to $10.00 a square foot considered previously, the cost of newly created land to the pier head line, (including the new expressway) on the East Side would be approximately $22.00 per square foot. [3] These figures assume no subsidy or grants of any kind, City, Federal or State.

It is clear that if the area between the bulkhead and pierhead were made available, desirable sites could be prepared that would compete very favorably with sites inland, even after absorbing the cost of the depressed expressways.

Sequence of Development

Since the relocation of the peripheral highways represents a substantial investment, attention was given to the question of whether this investment could be spread out by developing only sections of each highway at a time, as development proceeded.

---

[1] The cost of the Delaware Expressway, comparable to the West Side depressed and covered facility, including the cost of the cover is approximately $8000 per lineal foot. Costs were estimated by Amman and Whitney, Engineers, New York City; see Philadelphia Architects Committee and the Committee to Preserve Philadelphia's Historic Gateway, The Proposal For a Covered Below Grade Expressway Through Philadelphia's Historic Riverfront, 1965, p. 24.

[2] These figures also checked out with updated costs for the Battery Underpass (around $75 a square foot), which encountered many of the same subsurface problems which will be met with in this proposed relocation.

[3] These figures were arrived at by calculating the per lineal foot cost of new fill, new bulkhead, highway and basic utilities (around $13,000 per linear foot on the east side and $21,000 on the west) and dividing this total by the number of square feet of new land per linear foot thus created (575 feet on the east side and 975 feet on the west side).

It was finally concluded that such piecemeal development, while plausible in certain situations, would produce a decidedly inferior final result, both in terms of design and land values.

Such a procedure would minimize immediate investment, but it would mean that great sums of money were tied up in an underground system which was (except possibly for temporary parking facilities) providing little benefit.

It would also mean retention of the existing elevated highways in their entirety until completion of the entire project. This is turn would prohibit development of a three-hundred foot swath of land between the "property line" and the outside edge of the future highway, some seventy-five acres of extremely valuable land.

Furthermore, this "swath" might thus become a permanent ribbon of open space, dividing the Core from the new development areas, thereby diminishing the potential benefits to both of the continuity emphasized in earlier discussions.

Then new peripheral highways then should be built one shore at a time, east or west. The development agency's financing must be sufficiently long-term in character to "support" the entire highway cost even while portions of it are not yet producing the anticipated revenue.

However, this time-gap should not be exaggerated. It seems unlikely that the highway relocation will be undertaken until a number of private developers have committed themselves to major portions of either shore. This would have the further benefit of maximizing the possibilities of coordinating the circulation system with the buildings overhead -- in terms of footing locations, entry and exit points, and soforth.

The Service and Parking System

The next problem was to relate this express system to the proposed waterfront development -- to work out the performance characteristics and design implications of a feeder and service system.

One alternative was to treat the peripheral highway as a self-enclosed independent unit, designed primarily to deliver and take away vehicles, and for through movement. Service would be handled by an "inland" system -- Water, Greenwich Streets -- with "prongs" reaching out to the offshore developments.

The second alternative was to line the peripheral highway with its own set of service streets, serving both a "feeder" function for the express highway and a direct "service" function for the development areas.

After study, it was felt that the second alternative was the more flexible arrangement. Also, it minimized the impact of the newly-generated traffic on an already overloaded inland street pattern.

The proposed "connecting points" between the service roads and the inland major traffic arteries are shown in the Circulation Plan.

The service roads rise at each interval to meet the arterial roads, as determined by analysis of the internal traffic patterns.

Both the service and express roads are below grade at the "waterfront plazas" which represent the major downtown pedestrian ways. It is at these six plazas, each at the heart of a "neighborhood," that uninterrupted pedestrian access to the waterfront is essential.

The principle adopted earlier regarding parking may be summarized as follows: insofar as new parking is to be introduced downtown, it should tie directly into the peripheral system, and not further congest local streets.

Parking facilities should therefore be designed adjacent to, or above, the highway, capable of directly feeding into the two peripheral service streets.

As shown, the parking facilities would serve primarily the waterfront residential communities. City zoning requires that at the proposed category (R-9 or -10) parking space must be built for 40 percent of the dwelling units. This would amount to 16,000 parking spaces for the residential develop-

**Waterfront
Development:
New Highway
Alignment**

EXTENT OF
CONSTRUCTION

PROPOSED
DEPRESSED
HIGHWAY

EXPRESSWAY
SERVICE - FEEDER

EXISTING
ELEVATED
HIGHWAY

EXTENT OF
CONSTRUCTION

N

0'   500'   1000'   2000'

LOWER MANHATTAN PLAN **51**

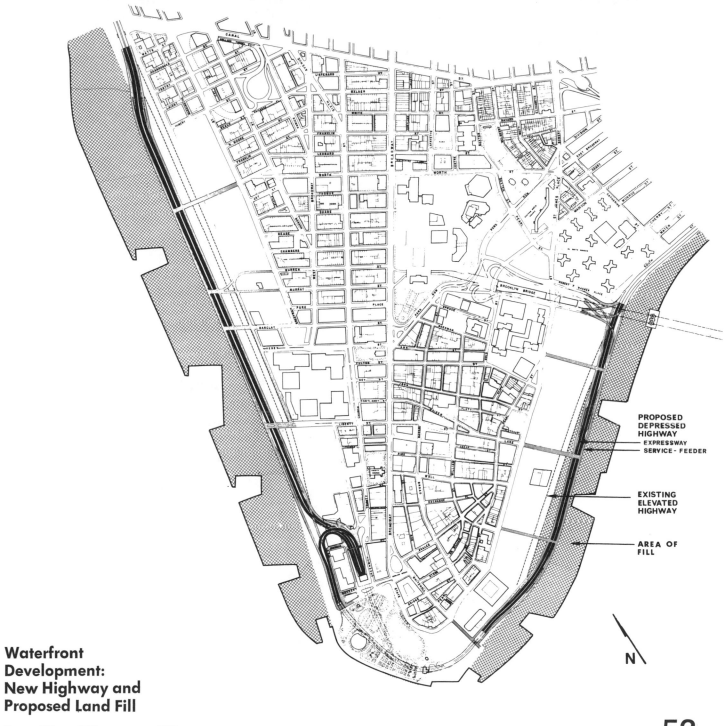

**Waterfront
Development:
New Highway and
Proposed Land Fill**

PROPOSED
DEPRESSED
HIGHWAY
— EXPRESSWAY
SERVICE- FEEDER

EXISTING
ELEVATED
HIGHWAY

AREA OF
FILL

N

0'   500'   1000'   2000'

LOWER MANHATTAN PLAN **52**

SERVICE AREA

Chambers
Plaza

**SERVICE
AREA**

World
Trade
Plaza

**SERVICE
AREA**

Trinity
Plaza

**SERVICE
AREA**

Fulton
Plaza

**SERVICE
AREA**

Wall
Plaza

**SERVICE
AREA**

Exchange
Plaza

**Waterfront
Development:
New Highway and Service Areas**

Legend:

═╪═ AT-GRADE SERVICE ROADS

≡≡≡ DEPRESSED HIGHWAY

0'   500'   1000'   2000'

SERVICE
ROADS

SUBWAY
STATIONS

DEPRESSED
EXPRESSWAY

PEDESTRIAN WAY

N

**Circulation
System II**

0'   500'   1000'   2000'

LOWER MANHATTAN PLAN **54**

ment around the perimeter. In most cases, approximately two levels of parking must be provided if multi-story parking were not included.

Multi-story parking would also be possible, but the high value of the land for multiple uses as well as the functional complexities of such an arrangement, strongly suggest the superiority of a horizontal deck solution. This is also more popular for self-parking which most of it should be.

Service for Development Units

As shown in the accompanying sketch, service to the development unit can be handled by means of a loop system, allowing maximum flexibility of building location and entrances to them.

Separate areas would be established for goods-handling and passenger delivery and pick-up. Vertical transportation would rise from this level. The passenger-elevator areas would, in almost all cases, be at the periphery of the unit, allowing natural lighting and direct access to the esplanade or plaza. In such an arrangement, building sites would be most logically grouped around the perimeter of the "loop," schematically indicated. Such an interlocking scheme would require a high degree of coordination among the various developers involved.

The central service elements -- the service loop, the parking ramps and the garage itself -- might be constructed and maintained by the general development agency, while the site parcels would be developed individually.

Many variations of this fundamental type of organization are possible; this diagram presents only one.

Levels

As the accompanying diagrams indicate, the several levels of service activities over the "connecting point" result in the creation of a higher pedestrian elevation in the inner or "core" side of the residential development units.

Generally, this level would be between 20 and 30 feet above the community "waterfront" plazas. Its height will vary from one situation to another.

So will the use to which this rooftop is put.

The basic concept here is that these areas will be specifically developed to serve the local residents -- a "backyard," as it were, with sandlot recreation, small courts, possibly some local shopping, rest and sun areas. In certain situations schools can be located here using the open space for recreation.

While the waterfront plazas are large, relatively open, full of community bustle, with restaurants and shops and theatres, thronged with office workers and tourists, the "upper plazas" will be small-scale, intimate, slower in pace, and confined largely to use of local residents. This distinction will be reinforced by the difference in levels. Nevertheless, passage from one level to another should not be difficult, whether by elevator, ramp or stairs.

DETERMINANTS OF ACTION AND CHANGE

The real test of the above specifications is whether they can be achieved within the limits of a number of determinants or constraints. Chapter V listed briefly the various determinants assumed in the development of the Plan. Some are short run only; others are relatively permanent. Some are determinants over which the City and private decision-makers have little, if any, control; others can be controlled. In this latter category are City-wide policies that, if adhered to, preclude or make available resources and determine the possibility or impossibility of achieving many local goals, at least in the short-run. They are considered further here to establish the ground rules on which the recommended land use pattern was based.

The determinants considered as operative on Lower Manhattan are summarized under three categories: policy, market and capacity.

Policy Determinants

Policy Determinants include local client goals: the allocation of public resources; city housing, employment, and parking policies; design and planning principles. Each sets conditions or is a precedent for action, and combined, they set both an upper and a lower limit on possible development.

Local Client Goals: Many local business and civic leaders consider the development of a residential community a means of strengthening the Core. They feel strongly that it should begin with upper and middle income groups that will most immediately stimulate the development of a richer mix of activities. Since they also believe in the value of a tight-knit Core, which precludes early use of the pier area for office development, the local client's goals can only be achieved by primary non-office development beyond the present bulk-head line. With a further mandate against subsidy, this limits any immediate practical choice to upper-income and relatively dense housing that can support the costs of site preparation at least.

Allocation of Public Resources: At least for the short-run, the City has allocated all of the currently available public money through its various housing and urban renewal programs. This has been accepted by the Study as a constraint for the short run. The result is that new growth must be able to absorb all costs of site acquisition and preparation. This sets minimum intensity and requires a kind of activity that will generate enough land value to pay the site costs. It virtually eliminates the possibility of middle-income housing under the Mitchell-Lama formula. The prohibition on subsidy is consistent with the local client goals outlined above.

Other public money such as Federal open space programs, gas tax for highways or public money provided on a self-supporting, (revenue-producing) basis has been considered as potentially available and it is believed a case can be demonstrated for it.

An important public policy determinant that affects potential development is the City decision not to redevelop the piers for shipping. The resources of the New York Port Authority are being concentrated in Port Elizabeth and Brooklyn where there are better back-up facilities than could ever be achieved in Lower Manhattan. The City Planning Commission concurs in this decision and further has urged that any new passenger line activity be centered around 42nd Street. [1]

Critical Employment: The City-wide policy to protect industrial and blue-collar jobs available to minority groups and the unskilled has been taken into account. This, combined with the vulnerability of some activities such as the remaining food wholesalers and textile manufacturers, was the policy behind the short-range recommendation not to disturb the areas they occupy. Since there is presently little market interest in these areas anyway, this policy does not have a restricting effect on the Plan.

Parking: Current public policy severely restricts parking in Manhattan. If this had not been the case, chaos would have resulted since parking can pay as much as or more than almost any other use for sites. Consideration was given to this policy in providing for only a relatively limited amount of parking in the Plan.

Design and Planning Principles: The concept of the most effective shape of the skyline, the pyramidal buildup from the water's edge to the Core and the way in which the shape of Lower Manhattan expresses the functions, relations and processes that constitute form, all were considered as determinants in the development of the Plan. The concept adopted expresses the goal of a tight Core.

In this same category, two planning principles that act as determinants were 1) the outlined minimum specifications for a residential community and 2) a park system large enough to contain general regional leisure-time activities. A third planning principle that acted as a determinant was the need to integrate the residential areas with the commercial core. This integration could be achieved it was found only be removing the elevated expressways and putting housing along the rivers edges. Design principles at a finer scale were utilized in developing and protecting spaces and areas of unusual quality.

A fourth planning-policy determinant of form and development potential is zoning which establishes limits on intensity and kind of use, and tends to set a lower as well as an upper limit on land values. In using zoning as a short-run determinant, it was assumed that no new zoning classifications would be available that were not now in the code. Still,

---

[1] Department of City Planning, The Port of New York, Sept. 1964.

variances might open the possibility (with the Plan as justi-fication) of intensifying development in certain areas on a planned unit basis. However, as an initial limit, the maximum intensity of any given use classification was adopted in the land use allocation, with planning considerations later modify-ing the intensity.

Structures and Areas of Historic or Architectural Value: A final public policy determinant had to do with structures and areas of historic or architectural value. Retaining such buildings and areas is a value judgement that must be weighed in each case against other values. Structures considered range from City Hall, whose permanency none would dispute, to old warehouses. The location of such structures acts as a limiting factor to varying degrees on possible development.

Market Determinants

Each of five market determinants acts in different ways. They are 1) the demand for space, 2) the cost of sites, 3) the char-acter of the environment (both natural and man-made), 4) the life expectancy of existing uses and structures, 5) and new technology.

The Demand for Space: Total demand (and Lower Manhattan's capture rate within the total demand) sets a shifting upper limit that is fixed at any point in time. Demand can fluctuate drama-tically, however, in a relatively few years, so that it operates as a varying determinant. In taking this into account land use assignments were quantified in the aggregate, measured against reasonable estimates of demand and scaled back where suspected of being unreasonable. An alternative to scaling them back was to anticipate a longer time span for Plan realization, but this was not found necessary in the process.

The Cost of Sites: As the demand for space sets an upper limit on development, the cost of sites sets a lower. The current cost of sites was estimated for the entire area, and economically feasible uses, without site write-down, were determined. [1] Holding to the public policy of no subsidy, the preferred uses were selected for any area from the list of possible uses. This set a lower limit on intensity and type of development, and to a

large extent restricted even very intense and expensive hous-ing to cheaper new land beyond South and West Streets.

The Character of the Environment: Existing enviroment either encourages or discourages specific types of develop-ment. The present environment in Lower Manhattan limits new residential development to existing residential areas or to land on the East River, where a new environment can be easily established. Combined with the previous constraint of site cost, such new development is also forced out beyond Front and South Streets. However, once a new environment is established as a keystone, it can then be easily expanded into areas too blighted to be acceptable as sites for the first stage. This sets up the possibility of housing adjacent to the World Trade Center under certain conditions.

Particular attention was paid to the blighting and inhibiting effects of the decayed piers, the unsightly elevated express-ways, the Fulton Fish Market and the eggs, butter and cheese market; these last two are in deteriorated structures, generate truck traffic, smell and are functions generally inharmonious with new uses.

Life Expectancy of Existing Uses and Structures : Existing uses and structures serve a variety of goals for their owners and businesses. Their relative resistance to change becomes a constraint on any possible action. In the short-run, those areas not occupied by structures resistant to change were assumed to be available for new uses. In the longer run, only the structures with an indefinite life expectancy were assumed as "givens". In the process of land use and space assignment, the successive relaxation of the "givens" as constraints was the basis for calculation of land available in the short, middle or long run.

Technology as a Determinant: Present technology acts as a limiting factor. However, breakthroughs in movement, building and communications technology were considered in terms of their impact on actions and choices over time. Such conceptual breakthroughs as the elevator system for the World Trade Center, if successful, can open up possibilities

---

[1] See infra Tables VIII, IX.

of a variety of new structure types.

Capacity Determinants

The land available in areas not occupied by "givens" has physical limits of capacity. A maximum zoning classification for any particular use was assumed for each area in the assignment process as discussed. Two further capacity determinants were considered: necessary minimum sizes for the residential community and its neighborhoods (also a planning principle); and the adequacy of the movement system to perform its function for the populations assumed.

Residential and Office Capacity: At maximum zoning the population that would occupy the land considered available for residential use was calculated. This was then progressively cut back to allow for area taken up by community facilities, by auxiliary parking and, to be in accordance with the specification of variety of type, for a mix of some lower-intensity housing types. The resulting residential population was then compared to the minimum ultimate size of 80,000 to 100,000 people. It was found that the community population figure can range as high as 150,000 assuming the ultimate availability of larger parts of the northwest.

Movement Capacity: In the analysis of the movement system, the traffic generation characteristics of the future as well as existing land uses were estimated. The resulting traffic was then assigned by the computer to test the adequacy of the proposed street and expressway system to handle it. This was a check on internal consistency of the Plan.

ALTERNATE AND RECOMMENDED LAND USE CHOICES

The Concept Plans and principles of development must, at least in the short run, operate within the determinants listed above. These determinants tend to limit the real choices in the immediate future to a relatively narrow band of alternatives. As time goes on and as the Plan is carried out, a progressively new and better environment will be established and the range of choice is expected to broaden. The reason for considering these alternative land use choices at this point in the Report is to pin down as many of the land use assignments as possible, at least for the short and middle range. These designations are then the basis

for developing the design program.

The alternates are in four phases: immediate actions, first, second and third stage development. No attempt is made to suggest actual time periods, although the market determinants would suggest a total length of twenty to thirty years.

Immediate Actions and Responses

The recommendations for immediate action are outlined in the Summary of the Report. They are assumed here as implemented, setting in motion the process of change and development.

Movement System: The changes in the movement system are designed as a response to currently planned improvements: the Civic Center, the World Trade Center and the Brooklyn Bridge Southwest. It is assumed that the reclassification and directional changes proposed will all be made and act to ease traffic flow, improve both pedestrian and vehicular access, and, with the subway and station improvements, have an immediate positive impact on business activity.

The intra-Core vehicle service is particularly important to start. It should, as the stages develop, expand to include the first residential units on its route. It should be self-supporting.

Land Use and Activity Changes: The industrial renewal program will take special study and further definition as will the residential self-rehabilitation of Chinatown. Each of these will require considerable planning time, with local businesses and residents intimately involved in the process.

The educational complex is already under study as a possible use for the central portion of the Washington Market Area. As these studies take place, the City will remove all the piers possible on both waterfronts, particularly in the area of the East Side Case Study area.

Development Process: In this area, the Planning Department and H R B will have completed basic studies of how to designate portions of the East Side as an unassisted urban renewal area, the appropriate City departments and the civic groups involved will set up the necessary organizational mechanism.

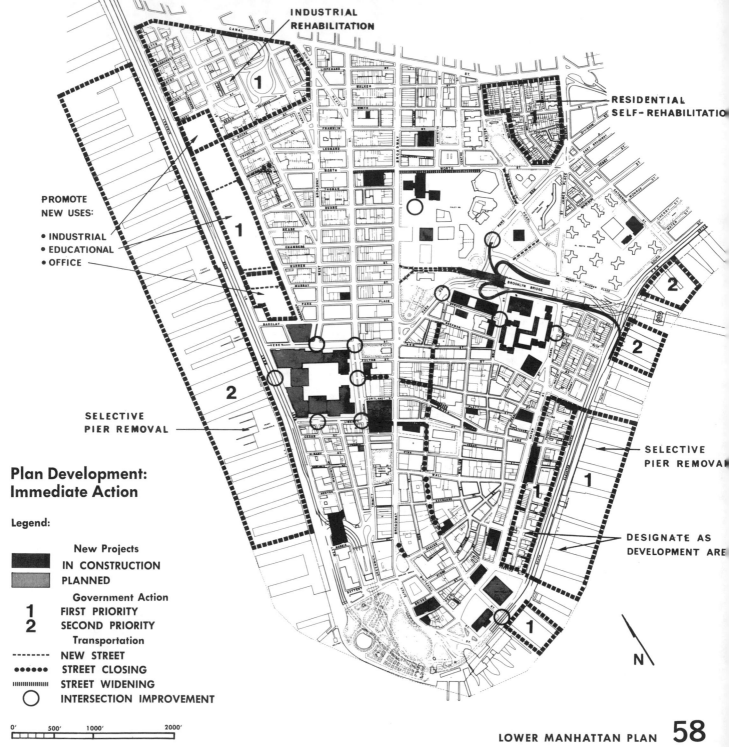

INDUSTRIAL
REHABILITATION

RESIDENTIAL
SELF-REHABILITATIO

PROMOTE
NEW USES:

• INDUSTRIAL
• EDUCATIONAL
• OFFICE

SELECTIVE
PIER REMOVAL

SELECTIVE
PIER REMOVA

DESIGNATE AS
DEVELOPMENT ARE

Plan Development: Immediate Action

Legend:

New Projects
IN CONSTRUCTION
PLANNED

Government Action
1 FIRST PRIORITY
2 SECOND PRIORITY

Transportation
-------- NEW STREET
•••••• STREET CLOSING
|||||||| STREET WIDENING
◯ INTERSECTION IMPROVEMENT

0'   500'   1000'   2000'

N

It is assumed here that a formula can be established to achieve the objectives outlined in Chapter VII, an organization set up and the development process set in motion.

The First Development Stage

The map shows currently committed projects as they would appear completed in the first stage, as a result of the immediate actions. These are the Civic Center, Police Headquarters, the World Trade Center, Brooklyn Bridge Southwest and the Stock Exchange. Other private projects now underway and planned will, of course, also have been completed. Five areas of action are considered here.

East Side Renewal: This area has been indicated as the best place to begin development based on the determinants considered. (A location further north is inhibited by the Fulton Fish Market and the decayed piers it still uses). Speculative office potential is already greatest here. Most important, unless this opportunity is seized now, the chance to integrate in-shore and off-shore development at this key point will be lost as additional development occurs along Water and Front Streets and preempts the space. If too much is built not in accord with the Plan, it will rule out the possibility of carrying out objectives of the Plan.

Alternate choices considered were between no fill, partial or full land-fill out to the pierhead line; and between a combination of commercial and recreation, or commercial residential and recreation uses. The latter mix clearly serves the combined goals better than a choice with no housing, and there is no reason to limit new land short of the pierhead line. The Water Street portion of this area should and will be used for office development based on current market interest and what is likely to happen anyway. Residential development can be integrated with it between Water Street and the strip of recreation along the water's edge. Office construction farther east than Front Street will tend to diffuse the Core and is therefore not recommended.

Brooklyn Bridge Park Removal of the piers in this area can immediately make possible a park needed by the current residents. This is the beginning of the regional system. No real

alternates are possible, assuming the determinants listed. Recreation development here depends on the availability of funds. Since this will be relatively cheap recreation land and can tie into the major regional park system, it is very possible that federal and state grants may be available.

West Side Renewal: The World Trade Center established the preconditions for a number of choices of development to its west offshore. One choice is for regional and commercial recreation, another for industry, and a third for mixed commercial, recreation and residence.

The World Trade Center like Rockefeller Center a generation ago will, when completed, establish an environment in which many things will be possible to its north, south and east, but particularly to its west as it faces the river. Immediate possibilities include new office space, but this would tend to diffuse the Core and detract from the World Trade Center as an anchor at the west end of the financial community with which it may not have much immediate linkage but whose future it will strongly influence.

The possibilities for use of the Washington Market Area as an educational complex would be considerably enhanced if a residential beachhead was also being programmed on the Hudson River. In turn, a residential development would be more feasible, if the educational complex were successfully promoted.

One of the World Trade Center's concerns has been its relation to the water, blocked now by the piers and the elevated expressway which cuts across its west face at exactly the pedestrian plaza level. The Plan suggests opening up this important symbolic connection and expanding the plaza to the west with a complex of residential and commercial development and water-oriented recreation uses.

The Port of New York Authority should consider joining with the City and its civic leaders in planning for such an important aspect of its own environment. It is considered that a mixture of residential, commercial and recreation is the best possible mix and is recommended.

The Washington Market Area: A special study was made of the possible choices here because of the area's imminent availability. Uses considered ranged from institutional to industrial although the latter, and housing, are ruled out because of City policy against further subsidy.

At present, no choices are really feasible on an economic basis, yet it is clear that if other actions on the waterfront are taken, intense office and residential use would then be feasible. However, the City has been and is under pressure to do something to "unload" this area and complete the renewal project.

In this context, a public institutional use that does not have to provide an immediate return on the investment in the site suggests itself. While this might appear a choice of desperation, in the long run it would set up optimum conditions for the development of areas around it, and in the short-run could exist even with the cheese, butter and egg distribution continuing to its immediate east. The site is near the mass transit network and, with the development of Chambers Street or Reade Street as a pedestrian route, is within easy walking distance by students of the Civic Center.

The recommended choice is therefore an educational institution for the central section, with a transitional area of industry at the north end and a transitional area of office use at the south because of the proximity of the World Trade Center. A precondition to successful development for any of these choices except industrial is the development of the pier area for housing.

On the other hand, if the choice here is industrial (presuming tax abatement or some other such subsidy), then the logical choice for the piers is industrial development during later stages. In turn, industrial development of both would narrow the ultimate choices for the northwest "blue-collar" area to industrial in the third stage when retention of these jobs would no longer be necessary because of the decline of acti-

vities.

Finally, should city policy preclude the educational complex, the area should be developed as residential along with the off-shore.

Broadway-Cortlandt-Dey-Church Block: A major part of this area is now under consideration for development, but high site costs and a weak market to the west of the financial community have thus far prevented it.

William Zeckendort originally assembled the U.S. Steel site at a cost of over $300 per square foot of land and proposed it for the Stock Exchange. Many long-term leases still have to be bought as a further cost. However, the critical holdup in its development is the lack of a major corporate tenant thus far. All of the banks and other corporations now in Lower Manhattan are firmly tied to existing situations. The area west of Broadway and Church Street has always been considered far removed by the financial community.

It is assumed that the combined influence of the World Trade Center and the enrichment of the Core will make it possible to attract a major corporate tenant or owner here from elsewhere in the region or the country, once the plans for the future are set in motion. In fact, it is again a real contender for the New York Stock Exchange now that the Exchange has given up its option on the Broad Street site.

By adding an additional block to the site (Maiden Lane to Dey Street) and providing a pedestrian connection to the World Trade Center, development may be more feasible, and have more impact on the area. This is a key area to build a tower close in scale to that of the World Trade Center as a visual transition to the present Core. With the costs involved, there is no likely alternate to intensive office development.

The Second Development Stage

The first and second stages will, of course, overlap in time sequence. For discussion purposes they are considered as separate time periods. Five areas are considered ripe for

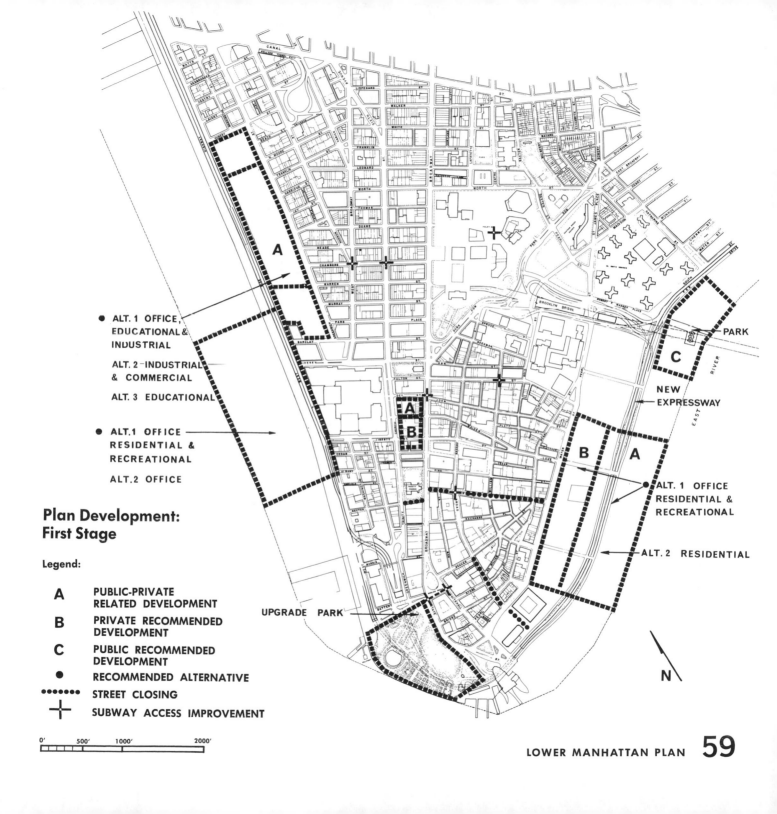

ALT. 1 OFFICE,
EDUCATIONAL &
INDUSTRIAL

ALT. 2 INDUSTRIAL
& COMMERCIAL

ALT. 3 EDUCATIONAL

ALT. 1 OFFICE
RESIDENTIAL &
RECREATIONAL

ALT. 2 OFFICE

PARK

NEW
EXPRESSWAY

ALT. 1 OFFICE
RESIDENTIAL &
RECREATIONAL

ALT. 2 RESIDENTIAL

UPGRADE PARK

**Plan Development:
First Stage**

Legend:

A   PUBLIC-PRIVATE
     RELATED DEVELOPMENT

B   PRIVATE RECOMMENDED
     DEVELOPMENT

C   PUBLIC RECOMMENDED
     DEVELOPMENT

●   RECOMMENDED ALTERNATIVE

••••••• STREET CLOSING

✛   SUBWAY ACCESS IMPROVEMENT

0'   500'   1000'   2000'

N

LOWER MANHATTAN PLAN **59**

action in the second stage. Three complete the East River development on the assumption of steps successfully taken in the First Stage. The other two are new.

The New Stock Exchange Area: Speculative interest has been high in this area since the announcement of the move of the New York Stock Exchange. [1] Real alternate choices include: (a) transportation uses (the ferry and heliport); (b) a combination of transportation, commercial and recreation; and (c) a third choice which would add some residential attached to the residential community to the north.

The presence here of the Exchange or a similar major development and the successful development of the East Side Case Study Area broaden the choices considerably. When the Stock Exchange gave up its option on the site in response to the proposal of an increase in the stock transfer tax, it is reported that there was considerable market interest in the site at higher prices than the option. Nevertheless, in light of the goal of mixing uses, of keeping the Core intensive, and of taking maximum advantage of the waterfront, a mix of transportation, housing and commercial and recreation would appear as the best alternate, assuming the mix can be achieved without disadvantage to each of the activities.

The Fulton Fish Market Area: This area will be available after relocation of the Fish Market itself [2] and the retirement of the piers that it uses. Residential use for it would be a logical extension of the beachhead of housing in Brooklyn Bridge Southwest. The principal alternative consideration is for office space, particularly of the "clerical factory" variety. This presumes relatively cheap land and large floor areas for the mass clerical and machine activity of the financial community.

By the second stage it is likely that some subsidy through urban renewal may be available to write down the cost of sites, but for purposes of the Program developed later this constraint was assumed.

The recommended alternative is for residential and open space for recreation. Income mix is desirable and may be achieved here without subsidy by the device of cooperatives and condominium apartments which can support the land costs envisioned. Some units can be bought for public housing tenants.

Office space is excluded because, when it was included on a test basis in the programming, it was found to add up to more total office space for all of Lower Manhattan than seemed reasonable. Putting office space there also tended to diffuse the Core. Such possibilities as warehousing or industrial uses were rejected because of high land costs with no available subsidies. These latter uses are also inappropriate to combine with the Brooklyn Bridge Southwest housing.

One final possible use relates to the retail and restaurants anticipated in the Community Plaza at the end of Fulton Street. It should be feasible and desirable to continue a small and much more elegant fish-market activity geared to the seafood restaurants and specialty stores. In an atmosphere of drying nets and other maritime paraphernalia, and seafood sold from permanently-anchored fishing boats, the community's shopping center can take on a unique flavor.

West Side Development: Choices of alternate land uses on the West Side depend very much on the choice made in the first stage. If the recommended actions were successfully carried out, the Washington Market Area would be committed to an educational institution in the center, office use in the south, and industry to the north. Residential, commercial and regional recreation would have been established on filled-land to the west of the World Trade Center. In this case, the choices then include extending the residential-recreation area to the north and south or in either direction, depending on the market for housing.

A less desirable alternate to this is to combine a platform of industrial use with residences above. This could be a way of

---

[1] Although at this reading there still may be considerable question as to whether the Stock Exchange will move here, the successful development of the area to the north will set up conditions that will permit the suggested choices.

[2] The relocation of the Fish Market has been proposed to Hunt's Point, the City's new regional food distribution facility.

subsidizing industry by developung the housing at a density sufficient to support the entire land re-use value, plus the extra costs of constructing a platform over the industrial use. Thus the industry would have to support only its own construction, or perhaps not even that. With taxes based on the earning power of the package the result could approximate the tax abatement necessary for industrial development. The structural, mechanical, access and service problems that would result are considered to be serious enough to outweigh any advantages.

However, the choices narrow rapidly if the Washington Market Area has in the meantime been developed for industry (assuming a necessary 50 per cent tax abatement to make it work). This would definitely commit a pier area either to no development or to industry as well, because nearby industrial development would inhibit residential or institutional uses. If residential-recreation development had been successfully carried out west of the World Trade Center, on the other hand, the option would still remain to extend residential northward, even with the disadvantage of leaving the elevated expressway and thus no connection to the inland area.

In-Filling of Land Made Available in the Office and Government Service Area: Unrelated to government intervention and more or less independent of other action, the effect of the World Trade Center will be to commit two areas as shown on the maps to more intensive private office development than now exists. These areas are now occupied by numbers of relatively small and older buildings. They are assumed to be susceptible to private renewal. No alternates are considered appropriate and it is really a matter of the strength of the market for such uses that will determined whether growth will occur in this stage, later, or not at all. Growth is assumed here as a goal but also as a logical prediction in light of the increased access from east and west that will result from adoption of the new traffic plan.

The Third Development Stage

Completion of West Side Development: As before, decisions in the second stage set conditions which either broaden or narrow the choices in the third stage. If the recommended choices were made in Stage Two, then the City has the option for the remainder of the West Side development of residential and/or regional recreation. Some additional commercial development in the

southern end of the West Side will probably be desirable, close to the City's new parking garage and Battery Park. Even though industry might be suggested as a possible choice, the residents who have moved in to the north during the second stage may well resist development for anything except more housing and recreation.

This latter mix is the recommended use. An alternate of office development might be possible by then, on the assumption that the Core would not become too diffuse thereby, and that the market for office space would remain strong. On the other hand, if previous choices have been either for no action or for industry, then the choice at this future time may well narrow to industry or port-related activity with some office use. Obviously the full waterfront need not be considered as a unit and a combination of choices are possible, with the northern end used for industry and the southern used for residential and regional recreation. In this third stage of West Side development, it will very likely be both possible and desirable to introduce relatively low-income housing at the same densities.

Area South of Brooklyn Bridge Southwest: This area may become committed as early as the second stage to either office expansion or institutional and government use. Beekman Hospital and Pace College will likely need more room and while the insurance area to the south is substantial it is not likely to grow much unless new insurance headquarters are established. The result of stage two activity around it will be to accelerate development and private renewal for some of the new business activities hoped for as a result of the strategy of the Plan.

A possible alternative in this area is for an extension of Brooklyn Bridge Southwest housing. This would probably involve considerable further introduction of subsidy for site write-down. Although it may prove ultimately desirable, as City policy changes, it is not recommended now.

Northwest Renewal and Rehabilitation: The greatest leeway in terms of choices in the long range is in this area - whose potential today is very small within the limits of the determinants. If the jobs and functions have continued to decline here as anticipated, fairly dramatic renewal may be possible and desirable. Its nature will depend on preconditions and choices set in the first two stages.

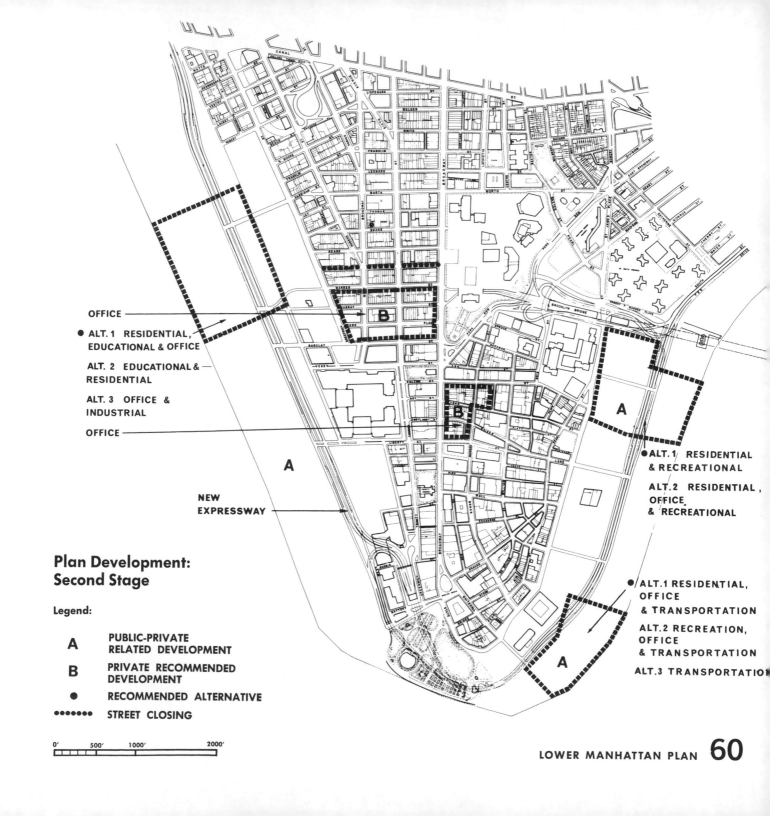

OFFICE

● ALT. 1 RESIDENTIAL,
EDUCATIONAL & OFFICE

ALT. 2 EDUCATIONAL &
RESIDENTIAL

ALT. 3 OFFICE &
INDUSTRIAL

OFFICE

A

NEW
EXPRESSWAY

B

B

A

A

●ALT. 1 RESIDENTIAL
& RECREATIONAL

ALT. 2 RESIDENTIAL,
OFFICE
& RECREATIONAL

●ALT.1 RESIDENTIAL,
OFFICE
& TRANSPORTATION

ALT.2 RECREATION,
OFFICE
& TRANSPORTATION

ALT.3 TRANSPORTATIO

**Plan Development:
Second Stage**

Legend:

A   PUBLIC-PRIVATE
RELATED DEVELOPMENT

B   PRIVATE RECOMMENDED
DEVELOPMENT

●   RECOMMENDED ALTERNATIVE

••••••••   STREET CLOSING

0'   500'   1000'   2000'

LOWER MANHATTAN PLAN 60

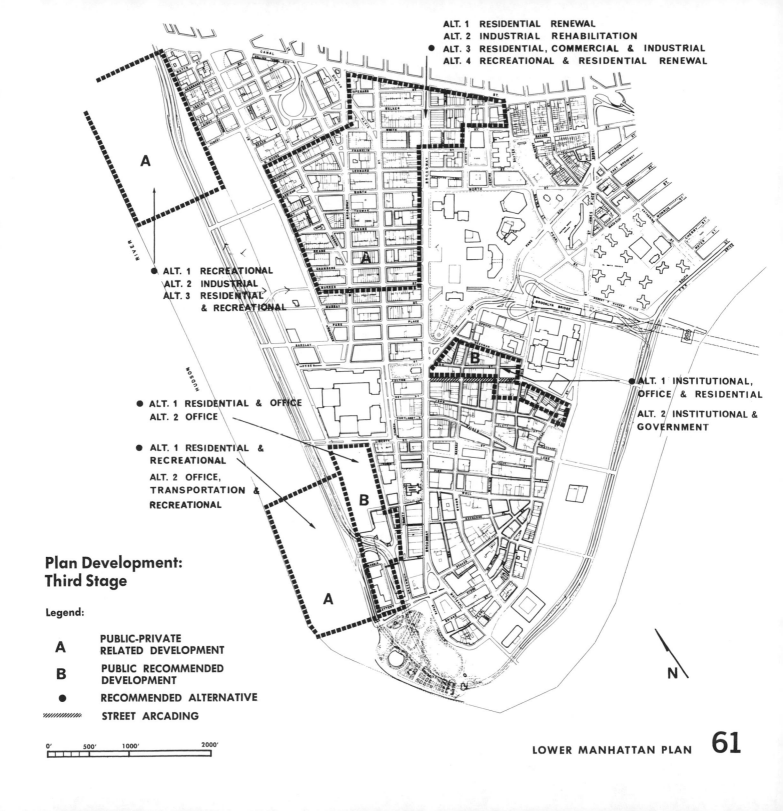

ALT. 1   RESIDENTIAL   RENEWAL
ALT. 2   INDUSTRIAL   REHABILITATION
● ALT. 3   RESIDENTIAL, COMMERCIAL & INDUSTRIAL
ALT. 4   RECREATIONAL & RESIDENTIAL   RENEWAL

● ALT. 1   RECREATIONAL
ALT. 2   INDUSTRIAL
ALT. 3   RESIDENTIAL
& RECREATIONAL

● ALT. 1 RESIDENTIAL & OFFICE
ALT. 2 OFFICE

● ALT. 1 RESIDENTIAL &
RECREATIONAL
ALT. 2 OFFICE,
TRANSPORTATION &
RECREATIONAL

● ALT. 1 INSTITUTIONAL,
OFFICE & RESIDENTIAL

ALT. 2 INSTITUTIONAL &
GOVERNMENT

**Plan Development:
Third Stage**

Legend:

A   PUBLIC-PRIVATE
RELATED DEVELOPMENT

B   PUBLIC RECOMMENDED
DEVELOPMENT

●   RECOMMENDED ALTERNATIVE

//////////   STREET ARCADING

0'   500'   1000'   2000'

N

LOWER MANHATTAN PLAN   61

A previous commitment of the Washington Market Area to industrial use will, however, narrow the choices either to clearance for industrial use involving substantial subsidy or to industrial rehabilitation of an extensive kind.

On the other hand, if the Washington Market Area has been committed to educational or residential use (along with the piers) , the choices broaden and permit a combination of residential, commercial and/or industrial rehabilitation.

The recommended alternative very tentatively put forward (not considered in the calculation of residential population for later programming) is ultimately to commit the area to predominantly residential use with a large park for recreation, located in such a way as to tie together the West Side and the Civic Center. The area is well situated for residential use. Of course any alternate, to be feasible, will require a major allocation of subsidies but the choices are a long way off. What is envisioned as possible and desirable is the remodelling of many of the industrial and office buildings suitable for housing to enrich the area, make maximum use of the physical stock and reduce the unit costs to bring them within range of middle and lower-income families.

Conversion of Selected Building Space to Residential Use:
Along the same line, in the long-range the life expectancy of many buildings close to new residential areas will decline to a point where they cannot command high or even moderate rents for office use. This is particularly true for towers with small and uneconomic floor areas. At the point where residences can compete successfully on a dollar rent per square foot per year with such office space, it would appear perfectly feasible to convert space to residential use. | Although this is now prohibited by codes, it can become a way of making use of these old but structurally sound buildings or parts of buildings, consistent with the objectives of the Plan.

This is one way of saving older office buildings with architectural or historic interest. In fact the narrow towers of many office buildings would make excellent luxury apartments. Such residences can pay upwards of $6/square foot a year which is competitive with high office rents.

Recommended Allocations As The Basis For Ultimate Lane Use

From the previous discussion it is clear that no single prediction is possible of what is likely to be the ultimate land use pattern in all of Lower Manhattan. The choices are many. However, land use in some sections such as the World Trade Center and Civic Center is reasonably predictable. In other sections, such as the waterfront, the future is not predictable but what is desirable is clearly evident. The purpose of considering alternate choices over time was to illustrate that the nature of the Plan is primarily a program and guide for action and decision and not a set of expected decisions for the long range that once made are irrevocable. Each choice was considered in relation to the extent that it achieved the goals, was within the limits of the determinants and broadened or narrowed future choices.

There are many combinations of choice over time, most of which do not have to be or cannot be committed in the present; however that combination of choices which appears to add up to the most aggregate satisfaction of the goals outlined in Chapter V, has been recommended in successive development stages. It is summarized on the accompanying map of recommended land use.

As public and private choices and decisions are made and development occurs in the future in Lower Manhattan, it will provide reality and "givens" around which future development must occur. The choices outlined above will then have to be restudied to see whether they still appear as conceived in this Report. Perhaps other choices and problems not now thought of will then be evident.

Land Use Assignment And Development Of Design Program

The summary of recommended land uses is translated in this section into square feet of office space, numbers of dwelling units and acres for each use. In the process of the Study this translation was first done on a trial basis for all of Lower Manhattan and then added up. The total was compared with

---

| In fact, artists had converted warehouse space in the Brooklyn Bridge Southwest site to studios and makeshift apartments.

reasonable capacity and capture rate figures and market and planning considerations; it was then readjusted where judgement indicated serious excesses or conflicts. A more detailed description of this process follows.

As has been frequently emphasized, it is not possible to predict in detail what the future of Lower Manhattan will be or even what it ought to be. The purpose of the succeeding sections leading to the Optimum Development Site Plan is to spell out what the implications (in three-dimensional, people, economic and organizational terms) would be if all of the recommended choices were followed. The result is a realistic program for immediate action that is clearly consistent with the goal-image for the long-run.

The Process of Program Development

Lower Manhattan was divided for purposes of the process into sub-areas called land use zones (LUZ). Each of these was further subdivided into land use units (LUU). The zones had major streets, obvious divisions between areas, etc. as boundaries. The units consisted of several blocks of relatively similar existing contiguous development. Later, these units or zones were reassembled into planning units in conformance with the recommended land use pattern.

Three limits were used to set the range of calculations. The first was the amount of land available for reassignment to a more intensive, or other, use. For this the Building Life Expectancy Map was used. Those areas, blocks or sites not pre-empted by a relatively permanent structure were assumed to be available in the long-run.

Second, the site acquisition cost for a new structure with no subsidy was assumed, which set the lower limit of intensity. This frequently eliminated many potential uses entirely, at least for the short run, since quite intensive uses are necessary to develop enough land value to pay for all current site costs, including existing structures and their demolition.

Third, the maximum zoning class for each use was adopted as a first trial run. That is, wherever residential use was assigned, R-10 (F.A.R.-12 with incentives) the highest in the City's zoning code, was applied. In some cases, even this intensity com-

bined with an assumed high-rent level did not throw off enough land value to absorb the site costs. In other cases, R-9 was possible. Thus zoning set the upper limit, and site costs set the lower. The same process was used for commercial zoning.

Obviously, these three limits might have set a range within which no sound planning and design solution could be found.

A fundamental purpose of the East Side Case Study and of the Optimum Development Site Plans was to show that there is not only a design and planning solution, but a considerable variety of solutions.

The land available in each LUU was thus measured, the selected zoning envelope calculated and translated into office space based on analysis and judgement of the market possibilities. [1] Areas initially designated for office or office-residential were then reassigned to residence or other uses and the total office space increases lowered to the "reasonable" goal of a total ultimate figure of 500,000 employees in 85 million square feet of space.

The accompanying table describes the results of this process. They also list the various auxiliary activities that will be necessary or desirable -- community facilities, recreation, parking requirements, etc. In the design process these are inserted and in some cases the total space assignment further reduced to allow land for them. For much of the northwest, the figures that resulted are not shown because they are felt to be irrelevant at the present time in light of the immediate recommendation to leave this area untouched.

Once the totals of space, employment and residences were derived for the LUU's for the long-run, they were then superimposed over blocks occupied by buildings that are relatively permanent in the short-run. The land occupied by these as indicated by building life expectancy was measured, and the result totalled and subtracted from the long-run space and activity figures. Since most of the proposed development is at or near the water's edge where there are few structures of even short-term permanence, it was not a

[1] In fact, the initial assignment would have almost tripled the present employed population.

**Land Use
Zones and Units**

Source:
        SEE CHAPTER VI

0'   500'   1000'   2000'

N

LOWER MANHATTAN PLAN 62

IDENTITY		Land Area (Acres)					Space (Sq.Ft. 1000s)			Population (1000s)				Parking (Spaces)			Dwelling Unit Characteristics				Active Recreation Areas	Community Facilities	Retail Facilities (Sq.Ft.)	CHARACTER OF COMMUNITY PLAZA
		Total Area	Sites To Be De-veloped	Res.	Off.	Other	Res.	Off.	Other.	Exist-ing Empl.	Fut. Empl.	Exist-ing Res.	Fut. Res.	Res.	Off.	Total	No. Of D.U.'s	Av.D.U. Size	Child/D Ratio	No. Of Child				
I	CHAMBERS STREET	68.0	35.1	6.6	-	28.5	4,000	-		20.0	23.0	-	9.3	1,200	-	1,200	3,100	3.0	.3	900	11.6	Inter-mediate & Senior High School	32,000	EDUCATIONAL
II	WORLD TRADE CENTER	67.0	47.3	14.4	21.7	11.2	9,100	12,000		35.0	74.0	-	20.9	4,100	2,300	6,400	10,500	2.0	.1	1,100	26.2	Primary School Library	71,000	FOREIGN TRADE
III	TRINITY-RECTOR STREET	41.0	26.0	10.2	3.6	12.2	6,200	2,300		20.0	29.0	-	14.1	2,900	900	3,800	7,000	2.0	.1	700	17.6	-	48,000	RESIDENTIAL SERVICE
TOTAL WEST SIDE		176.0	108.4	31.2	25.3	51.9	19,300	14,500	SEE TEXT	75.0	126.	-	44.3	8,200	3,200	11,400	20,600	-	-	2,700	55.4	-	-	-
IV	STOCK EXCHANGE	47.0	32.7	7.5	17.1	8.1	4,500	9,000		14.4	47.5	-	10.2	2,000	1,800	3,800	5,100	2.0	.1	500	12.6	-	35,000	BUSINESS SERVICES
V	WALL STREET	27.0	21.1	7.1	7.0	7.0	4,000	5,100		14.0	26.9	-	9.3	1,900	1,100	3,000	4,600	2.0	.1	500	11.6	Library	32,000	MARITIME ACTIVITIES HISTORIC SHIPS
VI	FULTON STREET	60.0	49.0	34.2	5.1	9.7	14,400	1,400		7.0	7.0	-	33.5	4,500	200	4,700	11,000	3.0	.3	3,400	41.9	Primary & Intermed-iate School	114,000	RESIDENTIAL SERVICES
TOTAL EAST SIDE		134.0	102.8	48.8	29.2	24.8	22,900	15,500		35.4	81.4	-	53.0	8,400	3,100	11,500	21,700	-	-	4,400	66.1	-	-	-
GRAND TOTALS		310.0	211.2	80.0	54.5	76.7	42,200	30,000		110.4	207.4	-	97.3	16,600	6,300	22,900	41,300	-	-	7,100	121.5	-	-	-

Waterfront Development Districts: Program Estimates

INNER AREA   OUTER AREA

Land Area (Acres) Sites To Be Developed	Res.	Off.	Other	Space Res.	Space Off.	Exist. Empl.	Fut. Empl.	Fut. Res.	No. Of D.U.'s	Av.D.U. Size	Park Res.	Park Off.	Park Total	Land Area (Acres) Sites To Be Developed	Res.	Off.	Other	Space Res.	Space Off.	Exist. Empl.	Fut. Empl.	Fut. Res.	Net/Gross Residential Development Density	No. Of D.U.'s	Av.D.U. Size	Park Res.	Park Off.	Park Total	IDENTITY
18.6	–	–	18.6	–	–	20.0	22.0	–	–	–	–	–	–	16.5	6.6	–	9.9	4,000	–	–	1.0	9.3	1400 / 480	3,100	3.0	1,200	–	1,200	I
24.6	2.5	20.0	2.1	1,800	11,100	35.0	69.0	4.1	2,100	2.0	800	2,100	2,900	22.7	11.9	1.7	9.1	7,300	1,100	–	5.4	16.8	1410 / 740	3,400	2.0	3,300	200	3,500	II
5.3	1.6	1.6	2.1	900	1,000	20.0	22.5	2.2	1,100	2.0	500	700	1,200	20.7	8.6	2.0	10.1	5,300	1,300	–	6.1	11.9	1380 / 580	5,900	2.0	2,400	200	2,600	III
48.5	4.1	21.6	22.8	2,700	12,100	75.0	113.5	6.3	3,200	–	1,300	2,800	4,100	59.9	27.1	3.7	29.1	16,600	2,400	–	12.5	38.0	–	17,400	–	6,900	400	7,300	TOTALS WEST SIDE
15.5	.6	14.9	–	400	7,600	14.4	41.0	.8	400	2.0	100	1,600	1,700	17.2	6.9	2.2	8.1	4,100	1,400	–	6.5	9.4	1360 / 550	4,700	2.0	1,900	200	2,100	IV
8.1	2.1	6.0	–	900	4,400	8.6	23.7	2.2	1,100	2.0	500	1,000	1,500	13.0	5.0	1.0	7.0	3,100	700	–	3.2	7.1	1420 / 550	3,500	2.0	1,400	100	1,500	V
33.0	22.5	5.1	2.4	10,700	1,400	7.0	7.0	25.2	8,300	3.0	3,300	200	3,500	16.0	8.7	–	7.3	3,700	–	–	–	8.3	950 / 520	2,700	3.0	1,200	–	1,200	VI
56.6	28.2	26.0	2.4	12,000	13,400	30.0	71.7	28.2	10,800	–	3,900	2,800	6,700	46.2	20.6	3.2	22.4	10,900	2,100	–	9.7	24.8	–	10,900	–	4,500	300	4,800	TOTALS EAST SIDE
105.1	32.3	47.6	25.2	14,700	25,500	105.0	185.2	34.5	14,000	–	5,200	5,600	10,800	106.1	47.7	6.9	51.5	27,500	4,500	–	22.2	62.8	–	28,300	–	11,400	700	12,100	GRAND TOTALS

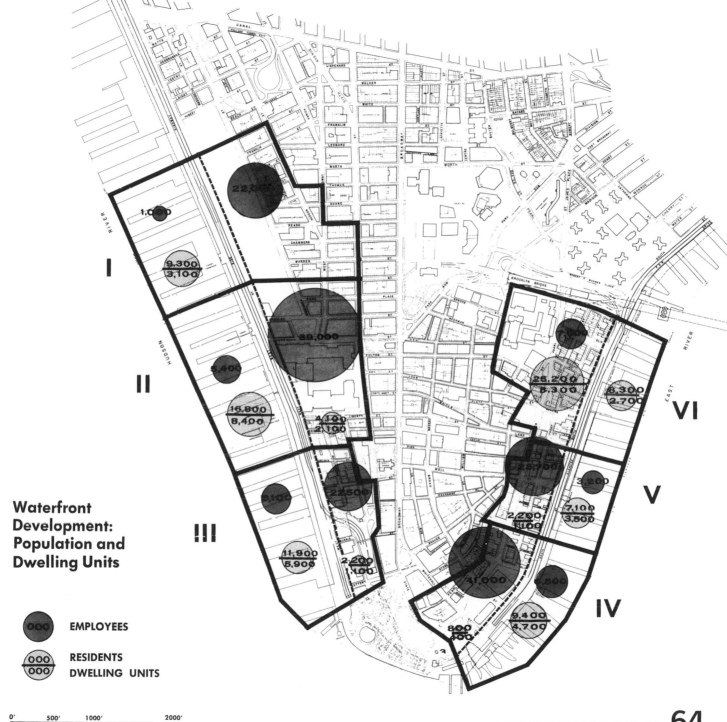

**Waterfront
Development:
Population and
Dwelling Units**

○ **EMPLOYEES**

⊖ **RESIDENTS
DWELLING UNITS**

0' 500' 1000' 2000'

LOWER MANHATTAN PLAN **64**

significant factor in the development potentials.

The program for each area was then detailed by planned unit development districts established in accord with the Concept Plans, [1] with the designer being required to test whether the space and dwelling units of the program could be accommodated in the land available in accord with good planning and design principles, and in accord with the concepts of form and shape discussed earlier in the Report.

Finally, as described in Part 2, the employed and resident population figures were analyzed for their traffic generation characteristics. These were introduced into the computerized coded network to see whether they would overload the movement system. It was found, as described later, that they did not, but that capacity was reasonably above the figures used.

Thus they were close to capacity but with a margin for flexibility.

The resulting Program is of course only a general guide for the long-run. Its development established a process, however, which can and should be repeated as time and actual development occurs.

For example, if substantially more office space is ultimately developed in any particular area than that programmed, other areas will decline in their growth expectation if the overall growth estimates continue valid. If, on the other hand, the overall capture rate and/or general demand for space increases above a reasonable anticipation, then the aggregate space totals can be assumed higher without internal inconsistency.

The next chapter examines and tests in detail the validity of this programming method by applying part of the Program to a particular development unit -- the East Side Case Study.

The Program can thus serve as an overall framework within which any particular proposal can be viewed. It also shows the feasible development potential that achieves the goals set forth, within the determinants assumed. At the same time, it should not be construed as something "sacred" or not to be changed. It is a tool only, albeit a useful tool, to guide the consistent and rational process of change.

---

[1] These divide the waterfront areas into basic development units such as the East Side Case Study Area.

LOWER MANHATTAN PLAN

CHAPTER VII

THE EAST SIDE RENEWAL CASE STUDY

In the last chapter the Program was set for the specific
amounts of space, dwelling units and ancillary requirements
for each area. This section describes the analysis, planning
and design process of the part of the development unit along
the East River recommended for immediate action. The purpose
of this special study in depth was to test the principles of the
Concept Plans and the Program, to study the special problems
of integration of in-shore and off-shore development, to determine the preliminary costs and implications of such development
and to design a prototype for the perimeter of the peninsula. It
also served as a basis for outlining a development process
whereby that part of the Plan can be carried out.

EXISTING CONDITIONS

Existing conditions are considered under the following head-
ings: selection of the area, current state of the site, present
zoning, subsurface conditions offshore, and the feasibility
of creating new land (considered in detail in Chapter IV).

Selection of the Area

The area selected is bounded by the pierhead line on the
east, Water Street on the west, Fulton Street on the north
and Wall Street on the south. Reasons for picking it have
been discussed briefly before. First, it is the area of present expansion of the financial Core and has been undergoing active site assembly and speculation, particularly
between Water and Front Streets. This is both a disadvantage and an advantage. It is a disadvantage in raising site
costs, but an advantage in that it is an area of great investment interest.

Second, the area, while still in multiple ownership, has been
assembled to such an extent that only a relatively few owners
are involved. This simplifies dealing with them for coordination and planning.

Third, 42 per cent of the area from Water Street to South
Street is already in public ownership in the form of streets,
excess taking from the recent Water Street widening or
occupied by public buildings. If South Street itself and the
bulkhead-to-pierhead area are included, public ownership
rises to 81 per cent. With this large proportion of land in
public control the City's role in this development is easily
apparent.

A fourth reason for selection of this area is that much of
the land is vacant, occupied by deteriorated and/or small
structures and with few important activities. The landside
is very probably eligible under state (and federal) legislation for renewal activity. In addition the pier area will
also qualify in all probability as a renewal area, a potential aid to assembly and site improvement.

Finally, private renewal, although not yet at full speed,
is proceeding apace on a small-lot, fractionized and unintegrated basis. Clearly the opportunity for development
in accord with a master plan is here and now; otherwise
it will quickly be dissipated as private development occurs
It is reasonable to assume that a planned result will be

superior to what might take place without some concerted action.

Public involvement is justified here partly because of the large ownership of public land and rights, and also because it can be demonstrated that the optimum achievement of the goals for all is substantially beyond the legal, organizational and financial capacity of unaided private enterprise. Leadership by both private and public sectors in a joint venture is clearly in the larger -- and longer range -- general interest.

Current State of the Site

Data from recent sales and appraisals indicate land costs here range from $ 70 to $ 120 a square foot, depending on the size of parcel, structure on it, and assembly factor. These costs are based on assumptions regarding the potential availability of zoning changes and on the possibility of closing public streets and adding them to enlarge the zoning envelope.

One major building is now in the early planning stage, but has not proceeded so far as to preclude its being influenced by a master plan than might be adopted.

The only substantial buildings in the area are 110 and 120 Wall Street around which it is assumed any future development must plan.

On the southern side of Fulton Street, between Front and South Streets, are a group of older loft buildings which deserve serious consideration as permanent landmarks of New York's commercial and maritime history. Unlike many of the equally fine historic buildings along Front Street itself, which are scattered here and there between parking lots, these buildings form a coherent grouping capable of successful incorporation into future planning efforts.

The dominant structure on the site is of course the Franklin Delano Roosevelt Drive, a six lane expressway elevated over South Street. It is on steel columns and girders. It looms 20 to 30 feet overhead and constitutes a major visual barrier to the river from the west.

Beyond the bulkhead (in poor condition) are four dilapidated wood and/or concrete platform piers. Two are used intermittently.

Underground is an important network of utilities, including a large storm and combined sewer interceptor now being completed in South Street, along with a major steam main that services much of downtown.

Present Zoning

Present zoning is C6-6 (Residential equivalent is R-10) in the inland area and MI-4 from bulkhead to pierhead. This would allow a development of perhaps four million square feet over the present private properties. However, the site costs that speculators have been paying for land is based on the assumption that the city will close streets, making possible a higher allowance for space.

Subsurface Conditions Offshore

A detailed description of offshore conditions is found in Chapter III. Here they are summarized:

Offshore conditions at the tip of Manhattan are exceptionally favorable for either land-fill or pile-supported structures. This is particularly true of the area at the very end of the island where bedrock depth ranges between 30 and 40 feet below mean sea level. In contrast, bedrock depths in Zones I and IV range between 80 and 150 feet; and to the north, along both rivers, bedrock depths are generally much greater.

The area between Wall and Fulton Streets ranges between 40 feet on the south to 80 feet on the north.

In Zones II, III and IV the process of land fill is economical and feasible. In Zone I, however, where soft compressible material is found as deep as 80 to 120 feet, fill is more expensive and may not be recommended, except possibly for park and recreation activities. Where solid foundation is required, pile-supported structures will probably have to be relied on. The Case Study site falls in Zone III.

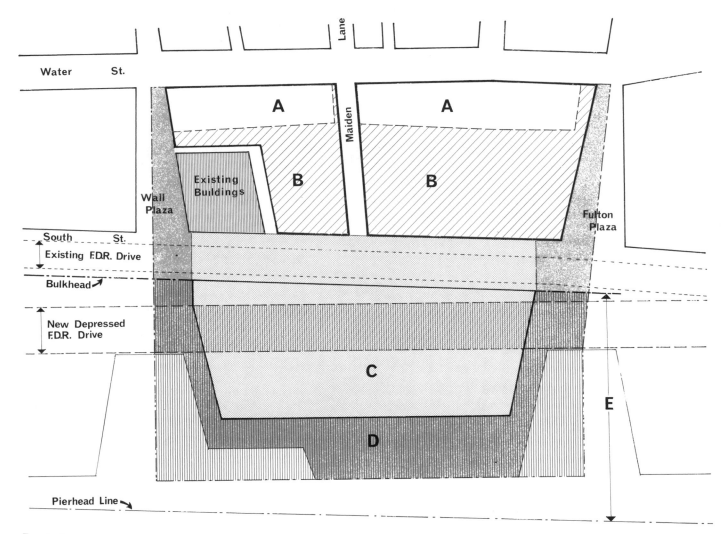

**Prototype
Development
Sequence: I**

Planned Development District

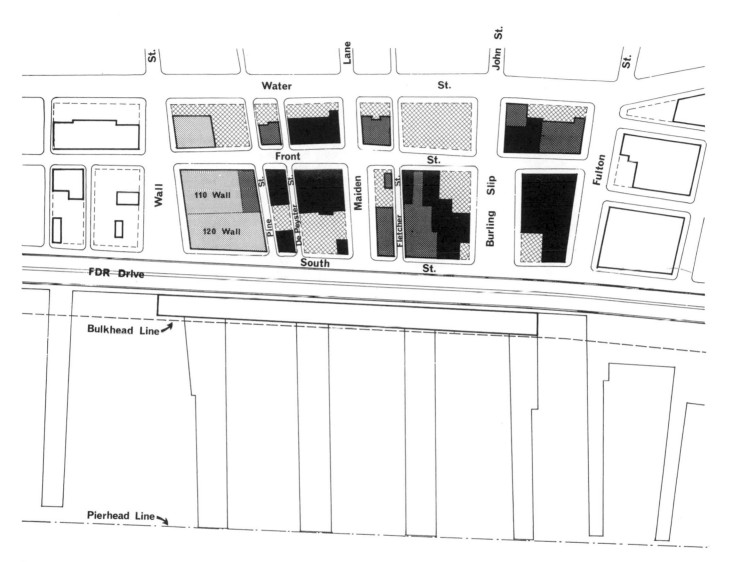

St. **Lane** **John St.** **St.**

Water St.

Front St.

Wall

110 Wall

120 Wall

Pine St.

De Peyster St.

Maiden

Fletcher St.

St.

Burling Slip

Fulton

South St.

FDR Drive

Bulkhead Line →

Pierhead Line →

**Prototype
Development
Sequence: II**

Existing Conditions

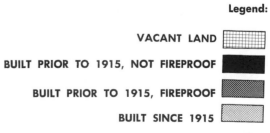

Legend:

VACANT LAND

BUILT PRIOR TO 1915, NOT FIREPROOF

BUILT PRIOR TO 1915, FIREPROOF

BUILT SINCE 1915

0'   100'   200'   500'

The Cost of Creating New Land

The cost of creating new land at this part of the edge of Lower Manhattan was estimated to be $8.30 per square foot. This figure included demolition of existing piers, dredging of soft materials, new fill; it did not include a perimeter relieving platform, a regular bulkhead or a rock dike. It also did not include the cost of utilities for the new land, which in this case study are presumed to be paid for by developers.

The total cost of creating new land including all of the above is estimated to be between $13 and $15 per square foot, depending to a degree on the distance from pierhead to bulkhead. That is, Hudson River costs will be lower per square foot because of the wider area involved over which the lineal cost of bulkhead will be spread.

THE EAST SIDE CASE STUDY ILLUSTRATIVE SITE PLAN

The Program in Chapter VI indicated about 2,200,000 square feet of office space, 6,000 luxury high-rise, garden apartments and town houses, and 2,700 parking spaces as the basic space assignment to the East Side Case Study area.

These have been designed diagrammatically as shown in the Optimum Development Site Plans in accord with the basic principles for movement and access outlined before. Each is based on the same principles, but as shown, there is much variation possible within the concept.

As the sketches indicate, the several levels of service activities over the expressway-arterial "connecting point" result in the creation of a higher pedestrian elevation in the inner or park side of the residential development units than the adjacent street grade. Generally, this level would be from 15 to 30 feet above the community "waterfront" plazas. Its height would vary from one situation to another, as will the use to which this deck is put.

The basic concept is that these areas will be specifically

developed to serve the local residents and office employees - a "backyard park" as it were, with recreation consisting of handball courts, skating, possibly some convenience shopping, rest and sun areas. In certain situations nursery schools can be located here, using the open space for plan space.

In relation to zoning, these open spaces form a cluster that pools the open space for each apartment building, into a relatively private park. These would be accessible mainly from the residential and office buildings at the upper level, so that people could come down by elevator, and would not have to climb up ramps or stairs from the main streets to reach them.

The intensity of office activity is shown concentrated principally along Water Street. Some housing also appears there to get an intermixture. In terms of shape of silhouette, development slopes upward from the park and esplanade at the water's edge to perhaps 60 and 80 story towers along Water Street.

Expanding the Example

When enough of the special problems of the Case Study had been worked out it was extrapolated as a system of growth over the entire waterfront, with adaptation wherever necessary because of differences in topography, program and the current street system to be retained. The expansion process resulted in the Optimum Development Site Plans shown later.

THE DEVELOPMENT PROCESS

A vision of the future , however seductive, is illusory and frustrating unless a way to get there from here is also presented. In order to suggest a process by which this development can begin to take place in accord with the goals, the problems, costs, procedures and organizational mechanisms necessary to take action were examined.

Insofar as possible, normal market development processes

must be utilized to implement large-scale plans such as these. From the preceding analysis and recommended development of the East Side prototype, it is clear however that a number of special conditions indicate the need for a combination of public and private action in partnership, if anything close to the optimum achievement of the goals is to be reached.

Requirements For The Development System

The proposed development breaks down into two basic categories: first, those elements which can and should be in the hands of private developers: second, those elements which must be planned and/or constructed either directly by City agencies or through some delegated authority.

Wide variations in administrative mechanics are possible and there are many different precedents in recent urban experience. The critical necessity is the delegation (with appropriate safeguards) of sufficient authority in some central body to assure a coordinated plan and its proper execution, with clear fiscal responsibility for development.

The balance between "public" and "private" segments of the development can take a number of forms. While financing and construction of the individual building units -- residential, retail and office space -- are clearly the job of private developers, guided by a general plan, the area of needed centralized responsibility is not as easy to define, especially in a project requiring substantial public actions and perhaps improvements before private development can properly begin.

This responsibility begins with the project planning itself: the establishment of standards and architectural and financial controls, determination of the exact new bulkhead location and extent and nature of landfill, definition of public and private parcel boundaries, the final alignment of the new highway system including service roads, service areas and parking facilities, the arrangement of basic utilities and other elements of the "capital web", and the devising of the lease or sale system of individual parcels for private development.

It is assumed the individual building parcels are to be privately developed and the basic "capital web" although under a central authority to be primarily paid for by private developers. There

still remains a "grey area" of overlapping interests where the ultimate disposition can be determined only in the course of actual development. This "grey area" consists of the parking facilities, the waterfront plazas, local recreation areas and other publicly used portions of the scheme closely connected with individual development units.

Organizational Alternatives For Detailed Planning and Development

These difficulties and many others not yet detailed point up the need for close coordination and planning between the various organizations responsible. The device for bridging the apparent organizational gap between business and government can take a number of forms, ranging from private advisory and planning groups to quasi-public and public development corporations and foundations. An example of the first is that of the Old Philadelphia Development Corporation, a private, non-profit, non-taxable corporation sponsored and financed by Philadelphia businessmen. Its primary purpose is to act as consultant and advisor to development and planning agencies. It is responsible for much of the success of Philadelphia's downtown renaissance and its executive vice-president is a close advisor to the city administration on all aspects of renewal and development.

Somewhat similar in operation is the Charles Center-Inner Harbor Management, Inc., a non-profit organization in Baltimore, Maryland. It was created to act as agent and consultant for the city in the promotion, development and management of that city's downtown renewal program. Unlike the O P D C above whose funds are largely private, the C C I H M receives its major funds from the city under contract to perform its work and is closely supervised by the administration.

As example of a quasi-public agency is the Philadelphia Industrial Development Corporation. It is a non-profit corporation created by the city whose role is the promotion and development of industry in the city. In a typical activity, the city deeded an unused city-owned airport to P I D C for a nominal sum and the Corporation planned an industrial park for it. Through an industrial real estate firm, it sells, builds, leases, arranges financing for and promotes industry

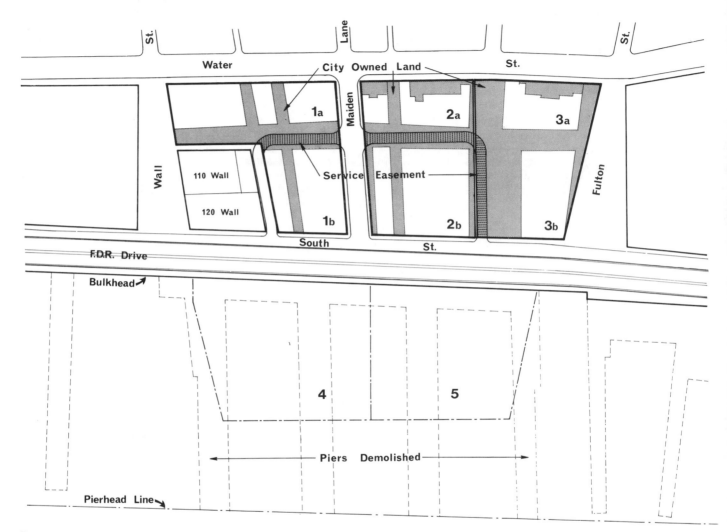

**Prototype
Development
Sequence: III**

Inland Site Organization

0'   100'   200'   500'

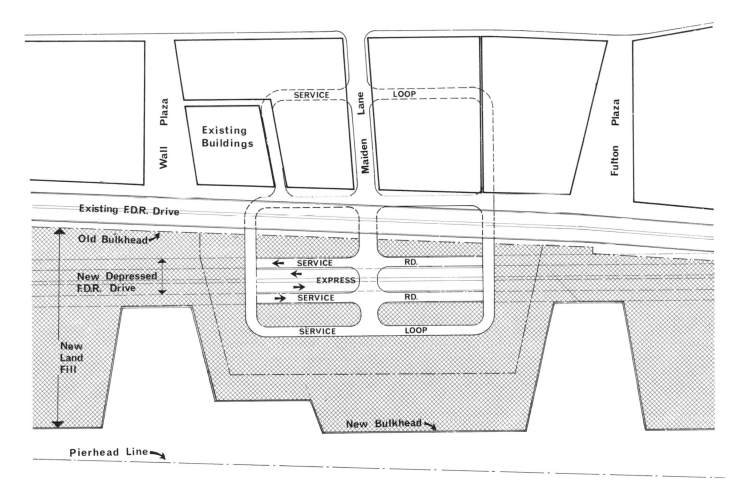

**Prototype
Development
Sequence: IV**

Public Construction (1)

0' 100' 200' 500'

for the site, in accord with city policy.

P I D C's board has both public and private representation, and the corporation has private enterprise freedom to act combined with responsibility for the public interest.

All over the country other examples can be found of variations on these and other arrangements.[1] Of particular interest are examples using development revolving funds. One such is the Cleveland Development Foundation that has sponsored a number of that city's renewal projects and has also undertaken private development in the general public interest. Missouri legislation has permitted the creation of public development corporations organized by owners of a majority of private property in an area to carry out a plan approved as in the general public interest. Another aspect of this law permits forming corporations such as Kansas City's Downtown Redevelopment Corporation (a development fund) which has the power of eminent domain. In this case the city lends its power of eminent domain where necessary to implement a plan it has approved, but the city does not involve its own funds.

The Pittsburgh Development Fund of ACTION-Housing, Inc. Oklahoma City's Urban Action Foundation, the Purdue-Calumet Development Foundation of East Chicago, Indiana, and the Citizen's Redevelopment Corporation of Detroit, Michigan, are fascinating examples of creative and flexible use of business and civic leadership applying their know-how to carry out ventures in the public interest.

Relevant New York Legislation and Devices

New York legislation already provides some relevant devices and possibilities. Under the 1963 Community Development Corporation Act [2], non-profit corporations that are empowered to build civic, cultural and recreational facilities can be formed and can qualify for state mortgage loan assistance. Under an earlier 1951 act, redevelopment corporations can be set up and, where the corporation acquires 51% of the land in a designated area, the municipality can lend its power of eminent domain to help implement the corporation's redevelopment plan.

Still more recently redevelopment companies have been authorized whose role is primarily to provide low and middle-income housing. Again the municipality can condemn land for them;

they are limited-dividend in nature with a maximum 6 per cent return on investment.

It is quite possible that one or another or combinations of the above devices can meet the specifications needed for the activity outlined below.

The Specifications for Organizing the Development of the East Side Example

It can be concluded that the most appropriate organization for development will depend on three factors: the nature of the people involved and their goals, the existing organizational context and the kind of job to be done. Consideration of the first two in New York must perhaps wait on a later stage of Plan review and implementation process. It is certain there is no single magic formula. However, the kind of job to be done can be specified in some detail using an hypothetical procedure to examine the necessary specifications for organization and power.

The objective of the kind of coordination outlined below is to attain an optimum development in the general public interest and to maximize the opportunity for private enterprise contribution. Since large areas of publicly owned land (both existing streets and filled areas) are involved, the public responsibility is clear. Further it can be demonstrated that without public-private cooperation of a high degree, the objective of integrated development at an optimum level cannot be fully realized. Neither partner can achieve alone what both can do together. In other cities this is so patently true as to be a truism. "Those communities which have had an effective civic organization, supported by business and working in cooperation with government, have been able to make effective strides to combat economic adversity, advance redevelopment, stimulate better planning, and

---

[1] See Seymor Baskin and Bernard Loshbaugh, A Critical Analysis of Private Development Funds, ACTION, INC., May, 1964. Although New York suffers from a kind of reverse provincialism in sometimes being unwilling to learn from experiences elsewhere, New Yorkers have been centrally involved in the creative developments along these lines in other cities.

[2] See Article 6-A, Book 23, General Municipal Section, the Kinney's Statutes.

generate urban growth." [1]

An organization which would appear to combine the necessary features would be a private, non-profit, non-taxable corporation or foundation, with representatives of the City Administration as ex-officio members of the Board of Directors. This corporation should be able to enter into contracts, to acquire real estate or any interest therein, to borrow and lend money and to receive gifts. Its financing could be established by subscription through loans and grants.

Its function would be to plan, promote and in some instances execute various portions of the development; in most instances, however, it would be acting as agent for the City. It should have the freedom to act of private enterprise but with the sense of responsibility of a public authority. It would work under contract to such City agencies as the Housing and Redevelopment Board, the Department of Traffic and the Planning Commission, it would and could act independently.

Planned Unit Developments

The purpose of such an organization would be to provide a device for treating large tracts as planned unit developments to ensure the implementation of the Plan's objectives. By planning on a unit rather than a parcel basis, it is possible to provide an intensity of development for open space, parking and other requirements, consistent with the appropriate overall zoning for the unit; but each element and intensity could be distributed in a coordinated way without each individual property being inhibited by restrictions, and zoning having to be applied on a parcel-by-parcel basis. The alternative of a property-by-property type of development (as in now happening in the waterfront area) will not produce as flexible, integrated or well planned results.

The minimum size for such a planned unit development should be from the center of one community plaza to the center of another, or a single "node". This is not to say that the community plazas themselves should not be planned as entities; they should. In terms of development, however, the node should be the unit.

METHOD OF DEVELOPMENT

There are five possible ways of going about the development of the Case Study example. The first would be to have the City simply fill and sell or lease the land beyond the bulkhead, subject to restrictions. Owners of Areas A and B (see diagrams) would be encouraged to develop in accord with the Plan with the incentives of adding the street areas to their property if they conform. This method has the disadvantage inherent in a property-by-property development where, for example, a parking garage might have to extend over two properties to work properly. The costs of this method are summarized later.

At the other extreme is the treatment of the unit in its entirety as an unassisted urban renewal area [2] with the City acquiring all property, through eminent domain if necessary, and reselling it to developers subject to the controls of the Plan. Present property owners could have first refusal options to act as developers.

Under normal urban renewal circumstances this method would require an advance of funds as a loan from the City or Federal Government until the land was resold. An alternative to this would be for the City to deed the resulting publicly-owned land to a development foundation or corporation for a nominal sum (à la P I D C) and have the foundation borrow the money, with the land as collateral. This money could be used both for payment of owners and for preparation of the off-shore land. Another alternative would be for the foundation to raise the money privately as a loan, like some of the examples cited in other cities.

Private Property

Between these two extremes are at least three alternatives

---

[1] IBID, p. 36
[2] An unassisted urban renewal area is one in which the resale value of land is expected to equal or exceed the cost of planning, acquisition and site preparation; therefore no subsidy is involved.

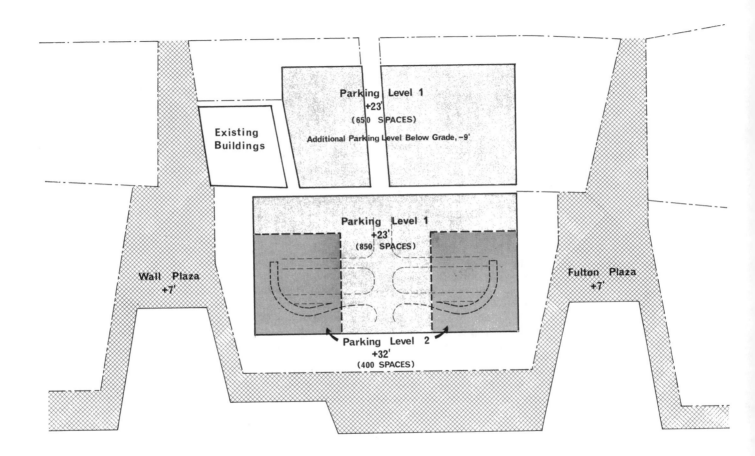

Parking Level 1
+23'
(650 SPACES)

Additional Parking Level Below Grade, –9'

Existing Buildings

Parking Level 1
+23'
(850 SPACES)

Wall Plaza
+7'

Fulton Plaza
+7'

Parking Level 2
+32'
(400 SPACES)

**Prototype
Development
Sequence: V**

Public Construction (2)

0'   100'   200'   500'

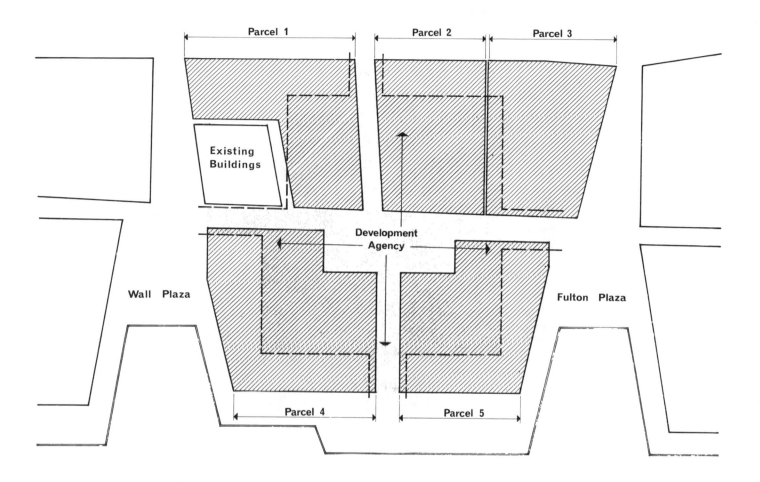

Parcel 1　　　Parcel 2　　　Parcel 3

Existing
Buildings

Development
Agency

Wall　Plaza

Fulton　Plaza

Parcel 4　　　Parcel 5

**Prototype
Development
Sequence: VI**

Private Construction

0'　　100'　　200'　　　　　　500'

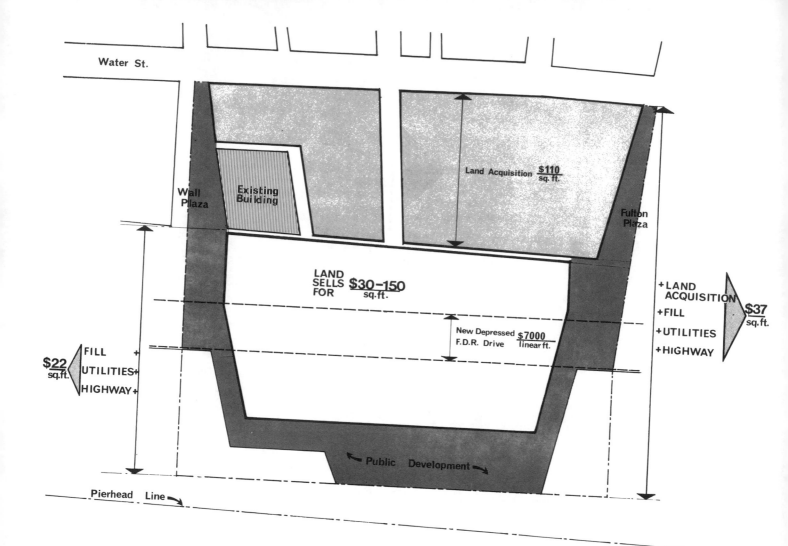

Water St.

Land Acquisition $\underline{\$110}$ sq. ft.

Wall Plaza

Existing Building

Fulton Plaza

LAND SELLS FOR $\underline{\$30-150}$ sq. ft.

+LAND ACQUISITION
+FILL
+UTILITIES
+HIGHWAY

$\underline{\$37}$ sq. ft.

New Depressed F.D.R. Drive $\underline{\$7000}$ linear ft.

FILL +
UTILITIES+
HIGHWAY +

$\underline{\$22}$ sq. ft.

← Public   Development →

Pierhead   Line →

**Prototype
Development
Sequence: VII

Costs and
Figures**

0'   100'   200'   500'

based on acquisition by the City of less than the fee simple for various portions of the private property. The basic idea to be explored in that of designating the entire site as an urban renewal area, preparing an urban renewal plan for it that contains architectural and planning controls and restrictions, and inducing or in some cases requiring private owners to conform to the Plan. The three variations consist of acquiring rights in various parts of the site, leaving the rest unacquired and uncontrolled.

The urban renewal plan (for unassisted renewal) would have the force of law because it would have to be adopted by the City. In the optimum situation, all development rights (but not necessarily the fee) would be acquired by the City or the foundation acting for the City, probably by negotiation, expect those which allowed development in conformity with the Plan. To the extent that the loss of these rights reduced the value of an owner's property, he would be equitably compensated.

An example would be a parcel whose present zoning allowed approximately 400,000 square feet of office space. Under a plan, this site might be reduced to 200,000 square feet or to residential development with a 50 per cent or so loss in value. The owner would receive compensation and be encouraged through a variety of possible incentives to develop under the new controls.

Where a property should be developed at more than the present parcel-by-parcel zoning allowance this converse situation should probably be dealt with by acquisition and deed-back at a raised price, reflecting the expanded development opportunity. In effect this would be a "betterment" charge. The overall zoning of the unit would be adhered to, but the distribution of intensity within it would be in accordance with the renewal plan for the unit.

Land Fill and Site Preparation

Although acquisition of private property rights has been discussed first, the land fill and site preparation might well precede it because it would be from the sale or lease of the prepared land that the development foundation would receive its funds for acquisition of the rights. As has been stated, the City would deed the right to off-shore development to the foundation at a nominal sum. The foundation would prepare the urban renewal plan, have it adopted by the City, and enter into agreements of sale or lease with developers. Either the foundation or the developer would carry out the land fill and build that portion of the expressway according to specification.

With the extra money from the sale or money borrowed on the strength of the leases made available to the City, the City could negotiate for the development rights with owners of private property. Payments would be made by the foundation as appropriate and the private owners would have a specific time period in which to build in accord with the Plan. If after a period the owner did not conform, the full fee could be acquired and after the City had turned it over the foundation could resell the property to a developer to proceed.

Alternate Areas of Control and Acquisition

All the site is recommended for control. Whether it all must be acquired outright is not known. The most expensive property is along Water Street and Wall Street. The Water to Front Street area (Area A) might be subject to controls only, with full acquisition for Area B. Another possibility would be to impose controls on both A and B and acquire only the development rights that are not in accord with the Plan. This would reduce the costs considerably in the most expensive area.

A final alternative -- to hope that individual owners would agree to develop in conformity with the Plan -- is anticipated as feasible only where the Plan calls for about the same intensity of development as was possible within present zoning. Only the area from South Street to the pierhead line would be assured of Plan conformity, and integration would be unlikely.

---

[1] Legally zoning could be used to set new use limits, but it is the wrong instrument because it could not be used to get the required degree of conformity to design controls, and could not entail a reimbursement or compensation.

Development Procedure

On the parcelling plan (Diagram 3) the public construction and closing of streets is shown as the first stage of site preparation. Stage II(Diagrams 4 & 7) show a variety of ways of parcelling,based on different detailed site plans. The ground level use and parking decks are shown in Diagrams 5,6, and 8.

When development is ultimately complete,the land occupied by the expressway can be deeded back to the City. Development over it can be treated as air rights, or the expressway can be considered a public easement. Some developers will have purchased land rather than lease it,but for those who have leased it(probably with options to purchase)ownership of the leaseholds will be transferred from the foundation to the City when the development is completed.

The foundation, in the meantime, can use both the money over and above costs made on sale of land and rights, the difference between low interest borrowing, and market rate lending, and the lease-hold income to carry out a number of public objectives. The development of the community plazas, public parking garages, the construction of streets and utilities, where they are not handled by developers, and the provision of a wide variety of community facilities such as nurseries, tot-lots,the operation of small parks and the like, may well be the job of the foundation acting as agent for an improvement association of owners and residents, as well as the City.

Finally, if all of the objectives of the Plan are reached, the non-profit foundation can be dissolved and its assets can revert to the City, which has of course in the meantime been getting the real property taxes from the completed development.

Financing the Expressway

Two key assumptions underly this method. One is that it is appropriate and politically feasible to utilize urban renewal powers in an imaginative and creative way. The second is that State and Federal agencies will permit an expressway to be built by developers, the foundation, or by the City financed by payments from developers.

A variation to building the expressway by this method is of

course possible. The City can float revenue bonds for the expressway, build it all at once on the East Side, and attach an assessment charge on the foundation or on the land, to be collected from developers with the proceeds to retire the loan. This would raise the total cost of the expressway by interest charges, but would have the great advantage, if the assessment were spaced over years, of lowering the immediate cash requirements to developers who would be paying for the expressway "on time". It would also have the tremendous advantage of building the new expressway at once and thus accelerating the whole undertaking.

A less desirable alternative is for the development foundation either to borrow the money and build the expressway at once or to collect and invest the expressway assessment as it is levied, leaving the area for the expressway vacant and eventually build it all when there are sufficient invested funds. This latter has the disadvantage of increased construction costs that may be balanced by cumulative investment income. [1]

Sequence of Development

As indicated earlier, the development of Lower Manhattan's new waterfront districts may require some twenty years or more of effort. The recommended staging of this development, from district to district, as well as the alternative involved, was also discussed earlier.

---

[1] In a simpler day, east side offshore development could be handled more directly: "During the last decade of the 17th Century , while New York was under English rule, it was determined to fill in the shore along the East River which had hitherto not been encroached upon. The Corporation therefore sold the water lots from the City Hall at the present Coenties Slip, to the present Fulton Street. These lots were laid out with a frontage of about forty feet each. Provision was also made for the erection of a wharf along the water side, of thirty feet in width, which should be a free street. This was the origin of the present Water Street."(New York, the World's Metropolis , New York, 1924. p. 367).

An interim stage in this evolution is shown in the Site Development Plan (Stage I). The two peripheral highways have been relocated, and development has occurred in two areas, one centering around the World Trade Center, and the other around Wall Street. The new bulkhead has been constructed throughout the perimeter of Lower Manhattan, but substantial areas are still in the process of site preparation. The three good piers in Lower Manhattan are still in operation, along with the Staten Island Ferry terminal.

This map represents a "guess" about future staging, based on anticipated levels of demand; needless to say, many factors will intervene that will be reflected in a more complex course than can be foreseen today.

ECONOMIC FEASIBILITY

Detailed study of costs of carrying out such a development is beyond the scope of this Report. However, preliminary estimates indicate that the sales value of the land to developers would aggregate enough income to pay for all acquisition costs of private property, for the depressed expressway, for fill and new bulkhead, and for necessary site improvements such as utilities. This statement is conditional of course on the provision of luxury housing at the densities proposed as well as first class office space. Less intensity or quality will not generate enough land value.[1] Land for office space would range from $100 to $200 per square foot of actual building coverage and land for residence would produce as much as $35 to $50 per square foot. Depending on policy, land for parking can develop very high per-square-foot values.

Table VIII shows that total site acquisition and preparation costs may range from as high as $37.0 to $18.5 million, depending on whether the full fee simple of all private property is acquired or only the development rights as discussed above. For purposes of this economic analysis, full fee acquisition was assumed.

The next question to be addressed was whether the programmed intensity of uses would generate enough land value to pay all of

these costs. Tables IX and X show that under either alternate (full fee acquisition or development right acquisition) it would appear that the programmed uses will generate enough land value to pay for the full site acquisition and site preparation costs. That is, if all of the site is acquired, developed and resold, the sale of land will bring about $37.0 million. If only development rights are purchased from private property, no resale value is possible from that part of the site. The remaining area of filled land and streets, however, will return enough sales value ($18.5 million) to return all costs. In that situation, demolition of private structures is not included in project costs.

An important aspect of economic feasibility is the tax return the City can expect from any development. Table XI shows that annual taxes from the East Side Case Study investment of some $250 million would be about $10.7 million. While some of this might have happened here, and some might have occurred in the City anyway, it is certain that a significant portion -- perhaps as much as a quarter -- is a clear gain for New York in its competition with the region.

Zoning Implications

Part of the feasibility of the envisioned development method depends on the assumption that within the development district itself only the overall zoning limitation (probably R-9) need be adhered to, and that for individual parcels a flexible variation of "envelopes" and subdivision regulations can be devised. This will make possible the "pooling" of space referred to earlier in connection with joint recreation areas, as well as the development of design controls and limits regarding height, bulk, plaza levels, etc., particularly as it affects the desired stepped-down form-relationship at the water's edge (see Graphic 69).

A number of factors suggest strongly the adoption of an entire development area as a single planning and zoning unit through

[1] This does not mean that all of the housing must be in the luxury class. The East Side Case Study area is the most expensive private property. Therefore these figures can presumably be scaled down considerably in other areas. Introduction of condominiums can provide apartments for middle-income families with no subsidies.

unassisted urban renewal designation. By this device special
controls necessary to shift the intensity of development within a legal zoning envelope are possible, with the concurrence
of zoning authorities, either as special variances or as special
renewal restrictions of both. Also possible is the kind of architectural quality control so necessary to this kind of integrated
development. The present zoning of the Water to South Street
area, which is C-6(F.A.R. 15), combined with a presumed
R-9 (changed from M-1) for the area of South Street to the pierhead line allows the intensity of development that is proposed.[1]

SUMMARY

Although the cost estimates are rough ,   it is evident that the
East Side Case Study is economically feasible. Examining the
cost figures, it appears that there is not much net difference
in cost between outright acquisition and acquisition of development right. That is, in both cases the uses generate as much
value as the cost of the site. However if no rights at all were
acquired west of South Street, the proposed development still
would generate some $5 to $6 million in sale of land over and
above the land fill and expressway construction costs. Since
all cost estimates used were intentionally conservative, this
conclusion is optimistic.

In essence, the cost of integrating in shore and off shore development would be about $6 million -- the cost of the rights ac-
quired. The proposed development intensity will support this
additional cost and it would appear that the City and Lower Manhattan can, if agreement can be reached on method, proceed
with development within the concept of the Plan.

While it is clear that both the staging and engineering of the
highway relocation require considerably more investigation than
was possible in this Report, it is the present judgement that the
sale value of the off-shore land will be substantially enhanced
by the removal of the expressway's blighting influence -- very
possibly $6 million greater, due both to the new land made
available for construction and the removal of a major physical and
visual barrier. In fact, under present conditions, it is doubtful that
a high-value housing community could be successfully developed
on this site at all.

[1] See Section of Residential Density - Appendix III

TABLE VIII

EAST SIDE CASE STUDY – ESTIMATED PROPERTY ACQUISITION AND SITE PREPARATION COSTS

Property Acquisition	Area	Total Cost Of Fee Simple	Development Rights Only 6
Private Property [1]	234,000 sq. ft.	$ 23,500,000	$ 5,600,000
Blocks 1, 2, 7, 4	125,600	15,300,000	1,500,000
Blocks 3,5,6	109,400	8,200,000	4,100,000
Public Property [2]	---	---	----
Sub-Total		$ 23,500,000	$ 5,600,000

Site Preparation			
Demolition [3]		$ 1,000,000	$ 400,000
Expressway [4]		8,000,000	8,000,000
Land Fill [5]	316,000 sq. ft.	4,500,000	4,500,000
Landscaping	100,000 sq. ft	500,000	500,000
Sub-Total		$ 13,500,000	$ 12,900,000
Grand Total		$ 37,500,000	$ 18,500,000

[1] Assumed cost of $110 per square foot. Estimates in parts of the area range from $75 to $125.
[2] It is assumed the City will deed all of the publicly owned property along with the right to develop the filled land for a nominal sum.
[3] Demolition of F.D.R. Drive and existing structures.
[4] Expressway assumed at $7000 per lineal foot for 1150 feet.
[5] Land fill and utilities assumed at a cost of about $15 per square foot for 316,000 square feet.
[6] Development rights assumed to average at 1/2 of fee for 3,5 & 6 and 10% for 1,2 and 4, based on distribution of space.

TABLE IX

EAST SIDE CASE STUDY - ESTIMATED LAND VALUES GENERATED BY PROPOSED USES
(ASSUMING ACQUISITION OF ENTIRE SITE)

Proposed Development		
Office	2,200,000 sq. ft. x $25/sq. ft.[1] x .2 [2]	= $11,000,000
Residential	6180 du's @ $4000/du. [3]	= 24,750,000
Retail	100,000 sq. ft. @ $5.00 sq. ft.	= 500,000
Parking	2500 spaces @ $500/space	= 1,250,000
	Total	$ 37,500,000

TABLE X

EAST SIDE CASE STUDY - ESTIMATED LAND VALUES GENERATED BY PROPOSED USES
(ASSUMING ACQUISITION OF ONLY RIGHTS TO A & B)

Proposed Development		
Office	200,000 sq. ft. x $25/sq. ft. x .2	= $ 1,000,000
Residential	4000 du's @ $4000/du	= 16,000,000
Retail	100,000 sq. ft. @ $5.00	= 500,000
Parking	2500 spaces @ $500/space	= 1,250,000
	Total	$ 18,750,000

[1] $25/sq/ft is assumed as an average speculative office constructions cost.

[2] It was assumed that office development can pay 20% of construction cost for land.

[3] Land costs per room and per dwelling unit were assumed as follows:

Mitchell-Lama Max.	$ 225/rm	775/du @ 3 rms
Middle-Income	$250-350/rm	750-1050/du @ 3 rms
Luxury	$1000-1500/rm	3000-4500/du @ 3 rms
Prime Luxury	$2000-2500/rm	6500-7500/du @ 3 rms

Source: Dr. Frank Kristof, Director of Research, Housing and Redevelopment Board, City of New York

TABLE XI

EAST SIDE CASE STUDY ESTIMATED COST, VALUE AND REAL PROPERTY TAX RETURN

	Construction Cost	Land Cost	Total	Assessed Value (90% of Market Value	Annual Tax ($4.63/$100 of Assessed Value)
Office	$55,000,000	$11,000,000	$66,000,000	$59,400,000	$ 2,750,000
Residential	154,500,000	24,750,000	180,250,000	162,225,000	7,510,000
Retail	2,000,000	500,000	2,500,000	2,250,000	104,000
Parking	7,500,000	1,250,000	9,750,000	7,375,000	365,000
	$ 219,000,000	$ 37,500,000	$ 257,500,000	$ 231,750,000	$ 10,729,000

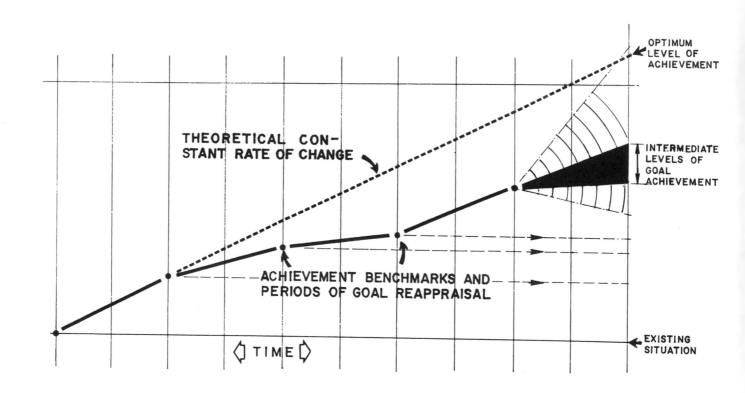

Rates of Change:
Goal Achievement Levels

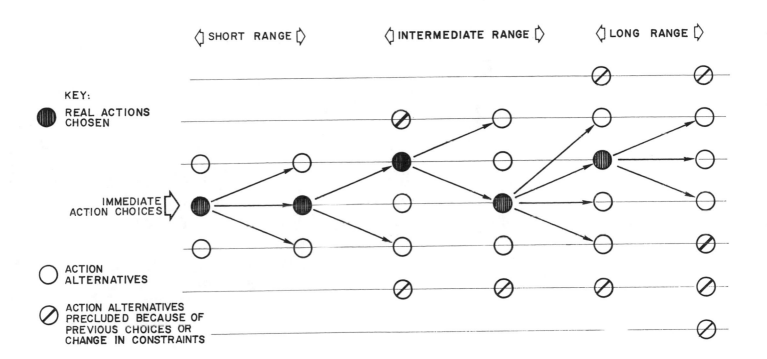

SHORT RANGE〉 〈INTERMEDIATE RANGE〉 〈LONG RANGE〉

KEY:

REAL ACTIONS
CHOSEN

IMMEDIATE
ACTION CHOICES

ACTION
ALTERNATIVES

ACTION ALTERNATIVES
PRECLUDED BECAUSE OF
PREVIOUS CHOICES OR
CHANGE IN CONSTRAINTS

**Action Choices
Over Time**

LOWER MANHATTAN PLAN **75**

LOWER MANHATTAN PLAN

CHAPTER VIII

OPTIMUM DEVELOPMENT AND NEXT STEPS

If all of the choices of alternate land use are selected over time in accord with the recommendations of the Plan the resulting land use pattern will be as shown in the proposed land use map. It must be borne in mind that there is an interdependence to many of them so that a decision for a different use -- in the Washington Market Area, for example -- affects adjacent areas.

RECOMMENDED LAND USE

The Core itself is expanded somewhat in geographic extent. Office space has increased from the present 50,000,000 net square feet to a total of 72,000,000 net square feet. The process of change anticipates retirement of 9,000,000 net square feet, an addition of 31,000,000 net square feet for a net gain of 22,000,000 net square feet. Government and related business services is not estimated separately but is included in the total change in office space.

Residential space is shown as having increased from approxi-

mately 4,200 dwelling units and 15,000 people today to 45,000 du's and 112,000 people.

Regional open space has become a major use, occupying 90 acres along the water's edge. The new park at Brooklyn Bridge accounts for 11 acres, Battery Park for 25 acres, and the new Park south of Canal Street on the Hudson for 23 acres. The remaining 31 acres are in the strip park and open space at the water's edge.

The northwest area is shown as still in its present industrial use, to be designated for other use some time in the future. No attempt is made to add up all land uses to the total area of Lower Manhattan because of the interlocking and mixed nature of many of the uses.

Land use plans are primarily of value as devices for translation of program and principles into zoning controls -- which are necessary, but a negative and limiting kind of concept. Since it is anticipated that zoning will be used in new and creative ways, it is necessary to spell out in three dimensional terms the principles to be followed and objectives sought. Otherwise zoning is arriving at what is wanted by preventing what is not wanted -- what developers can't do rather than what the City would like them to do.

A positive and design-oriented approach is therefore called for as a means of spelling out in three dimensions the principles and the goals of the Plan. These then will be explicit and can be the basis on which new zoning along with other controls can be considered as implementing devices.

LOWER MANHATTAN AS AN INVESTMENT

The costs to the City of carrying out all of the steps outlined, even assuming the eventual availability of highway and housing subsidies, will be substantial. The schools and other community facilities alone would require major sums even though developers may build the smaller ones. Without attempting to estimate these, since many of them would be incurred in any event, it is possible to estimate the future real property tax return from the development shown and compare it with the present.

The total value of the new investment in Lower Manhattan would be in the neighborhood of two billion dollars, of which roughly 1.3 billion would be in residences and 0.7 billion in offices. On the assumption of a self-financing development, these figures include the cost of "public" investments, in particular the relocation of the peripheral highways, new land fill, waterfront plaza, utilities, etc., which should cost in the neighborhood of two hundred million dollars. Assuming the taxable portion of the new development therefore at 1.8 billion dollars, and based on present tax rates and methods of assessment, the annual tax return from the new development should be around 90 million dollars.

This is an investment whose major part will be private and whose early stages at least require no public money at all, as shown in the example.

The public investment in schools and other community facilities will be substantial, but in relation to property taxes and other benefits, not great at all.

Implications of Relaxing Constraints

What would be the changes in the Plan and alternative choices if various constraints were relaxed? This is particularly relevant to location and intensity of use. For example, the high densities of residence at the water's edge are required if their development is to be entirely self-supporting. Probably the acquisition of most of the property in-shore and the filling of the land as a site improvement could be partially supported by subsidy, if it were available. In any event, the potential of the water's edge is so great that subsidy of site cost is unnecessary and would not lower the market resale value of the land.

Subsidy for middle-income housing would make it possible to get a broader economic and racial mix. However, to do this, a land subsidy would also be necessary, as the land costs envisioned here are above what can be supported under the Mitchell-Lama program as has been shown. The result of subsidy should be to lower rents and thus broaden the range of families, incomes and ethnic groups rather than to reduce the intensity or nature of use.

If funds were available for parts of the open space system, it would result in a substantial reduction in cost of land sold because the park costs would then bear a proportionate share of the bulkhead costs, etc. This could be an effective way of reducing land costs to middle-income levels without urban renewal subsidy.

The Form of the Future

The final test of the investment, however, will be the quality of the working environment, the improved transportation, economic diversification, a change in the whole quality of working in Lower Manhattan, a change which will result in a more intense and valuable business community.

The sketches at the end of the Report are designed to offer a hint of this future downtown -- a new type of "total community," composed of 500,000 workers and some 85,000 residents, with interpenetrating residential, office and recreational activities, for which Lower Manhattan is uniquely suited.

Historic streets like Wall and Broad, now reconstituted as pedestrian ways, carry people directly to waterfront plazas at the city's edge. There residential towers rise to look out at the river and back at the great business power they adjoin.

The waterfront plazas: physical extensions of the canyons within, lined with shops and restaurants, low-rise apartments above; the junction-place of business lunches and residential shopping. Along the water's edge, areas for strolling and play are suitably interspersed.

The new world of leisure will leave its mark on the old world of all work. Tourists will move through the towers of Wall Street. The line between work and play will have lost some of its sharpness, and in the ever-expanding ease and plenty of the new society, the two may become natural neighbors.

Steps for Implementation

The Plan for Lower Manhattan represents a formidable undertaking -- requiring a degree of administrative coordination and public concensus rarely seen in New York.

ACKNOWLEDGMENTS

Because it was felt that the results would be of interest
and value to many departments of the City, a special
advisory group to be concerned with the transportation
aspects of the study was appointed. This group, the
Street Technical Committee, consists of representatives
of the Departments of City Planning, Traffic, Highways,
and Public Works as well as the Office of the Borough
President and the Transit Authority. They reviewed the
Consultant's findings, and each participating agency
contributed information valuable to the Study.

Particularly helpful was the large amount of informa-
tion made available by two agencies, the New York
Transit Authority, and the Department of Streets and
Traffic.

The interest and support of the City Planning Department staff contributed immeasurably to the successful
completion of this study. Three members of the staff
were particularly helpful: Jack C. Smith, Joseph McC.
Leiper and Arthur Wrubel. In addition to obtaining
data, reviewing drafts and serving on the Street Technical Committee, these men maintained close contact
with the study staff and each made significant contributions to the plan.

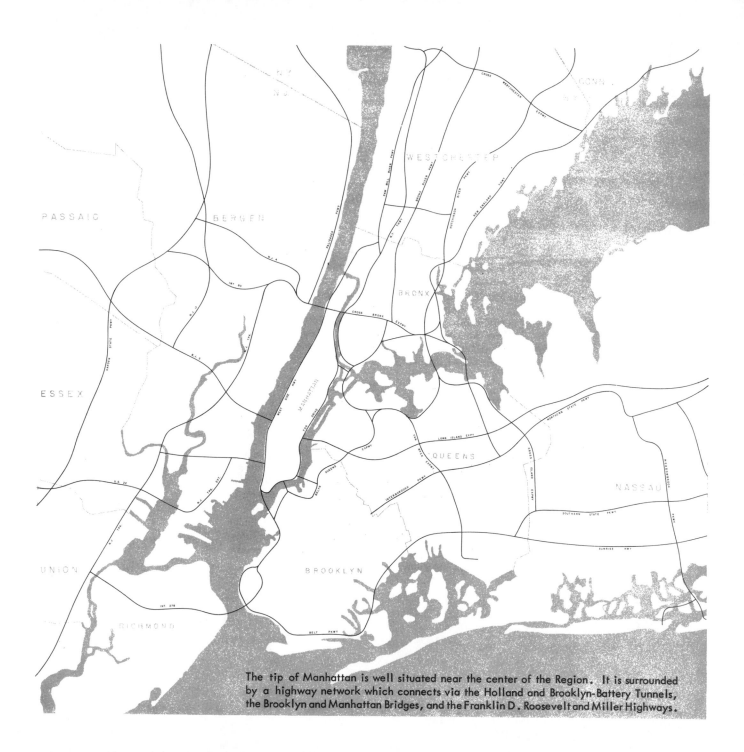

The tip of Manhattan is well situated near the center of the Region. It is surrounded by a highway network which connects via the Holland and Brooklyn-Battery Tunnels, the Brooklyn and Manhattan Bridges, and the Franklin D. Roosevelt and Miller Highways.

Site Development: Stage I

Yet it should be remembered that the Plan is, first and foremost, a guide for decision-making rather than a set of specifications for a series of projects.

Therefore, it is not appropriate to conceive of its "adoption" as a single legislative or administrative act.

Rather, an organization should be created capable of completing the process of cons ensus begun by this Report. This agency (a development committee), presided over by civic, business and governmental organizations, will be the focus for the many refinements and reappraisals required before the Plan can be transformed into legislation, ordinances, institutions, etc.

This plan, which has been developed in coordination with the Department of City Planning, now needs the assistance on implementation proceedures of many other municipal agencies -- such as the Department of Traffic (street classification), Board of Standards and Appeals (zoning changes), Housing and Redevelopment (unassisted urban renewal concept), Department of Marine and Aviation (offshore construction , schedule of pier demolition), Department of Public Works (utilities and construction), Department of Highways (highway relocation), Board of Education (schools), and the Borough President's Office.

At the same time, both State and Federal agencies will be consulted regarding the highway system, navigation channels, possible subsidies. Important Civic groups will also be brought more closely into the planning process.

Depending on the pace and sequence of events, this group could become the nucleous for the central development agency proposed in this Report -- the agency that assumes responsibility not only for general planning, but implementation of major plan objectives as well.

When the major elements of the Plan are thus codified, in actual legislative and organization terms, these elements must, of course, be then presented, in formal terms, for adoption by the appropriate groups: the City Council, the New York State Legislature.

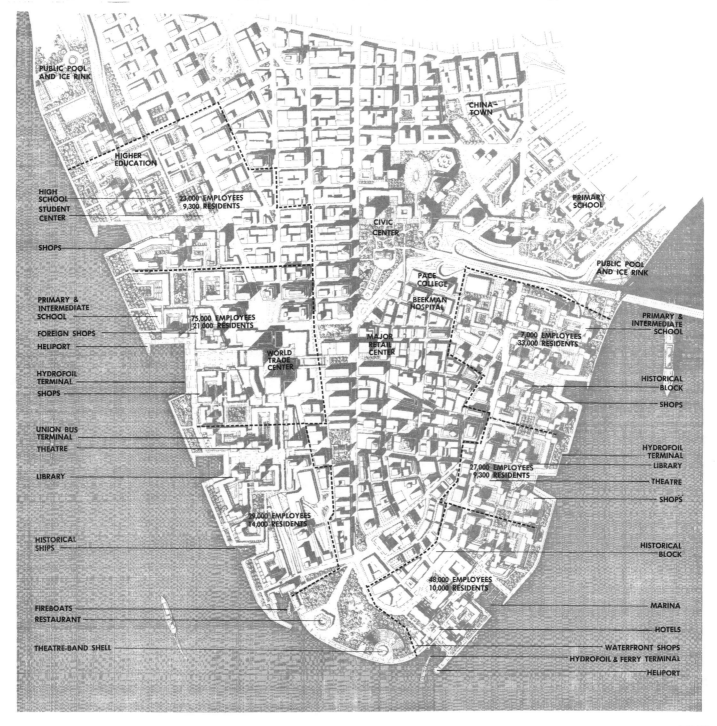

PUBLIC POOL
AND ICE RINK

HIGHER
EDUCATION

HIGH
SCHOOL
STUDENT
CENTER

SHOPS

PRIMARY &
INTERMEDIATE
SCHOOL

FOREIGN SHOPS

HELIPORT

HYDROFOIL
TERMINAL

SHOPS

UNION BUS
TERMINAL

THEATRE

LIBRARY

HISTORICAL
SHIPS

FIREBOATS

RESTAURANT

THEATRE-BAND SHELL

CHINA
TOWN

PRIMARY
SCHOOL

CIVIC
CENTER

PUBLIC POOL
AND ICE RINK

PACE
COLLEGE

BEEKMAN
HOSPITAL

PRIMARY &
INTERMEDIATE
SCHOOL

MAJOR
RETAIL
CENTER

WORLD
TRADE
CENTER

HISTORICAL
BLOCK

SHOPS

HYDROFOIL
TERMINAL

LIBRARY

THEATRE

SHOPS

HISTORICAL
BLOCK

MARINA

HOTELS

WATERFRONT SHOPS

HYDROFOIL & FERRY TERMINAL

HELIPORT

23,000 EMPLOYEES
9,300 RESIDENTS

75,000 EMPLOYEES
21,000 RESIDENTS

7,000 EMPLOYEES
33,000 RESIDENTS

27,000 EMPLOYEES
9,300 RESIDENTS

29,000 EMPLOYEES
14,000 RESIDENTS

48,000 EMPLOYEES
10,000 RESIDENTS

Special Functions and Services

LOWER MANHATTAN PLAN **78**

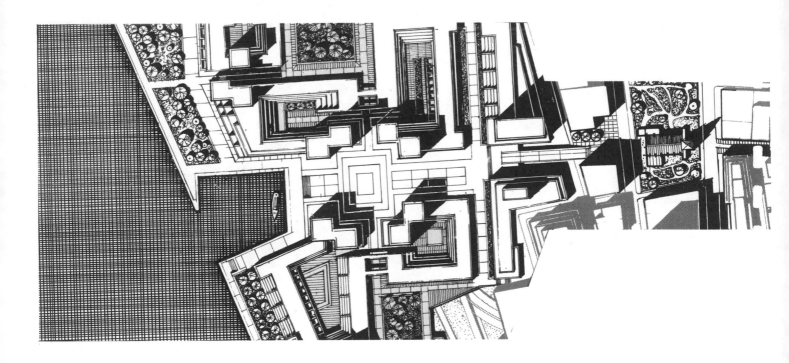

**Pedestrian System:
Wall Street and Waterfront Plazas**

0' 100' 200'   500'

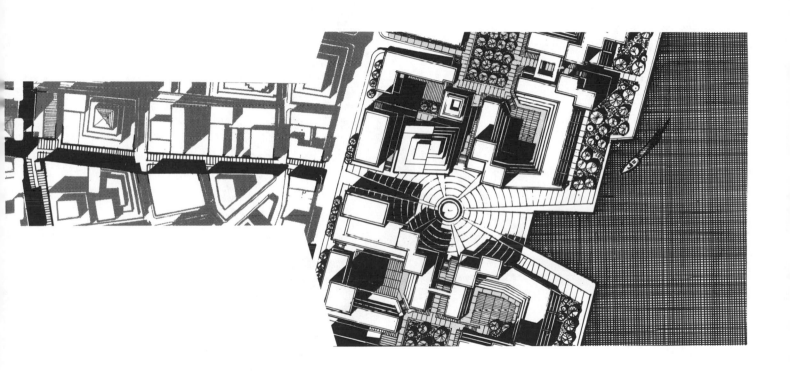

LOWER MANHATTAN PLAN **79**

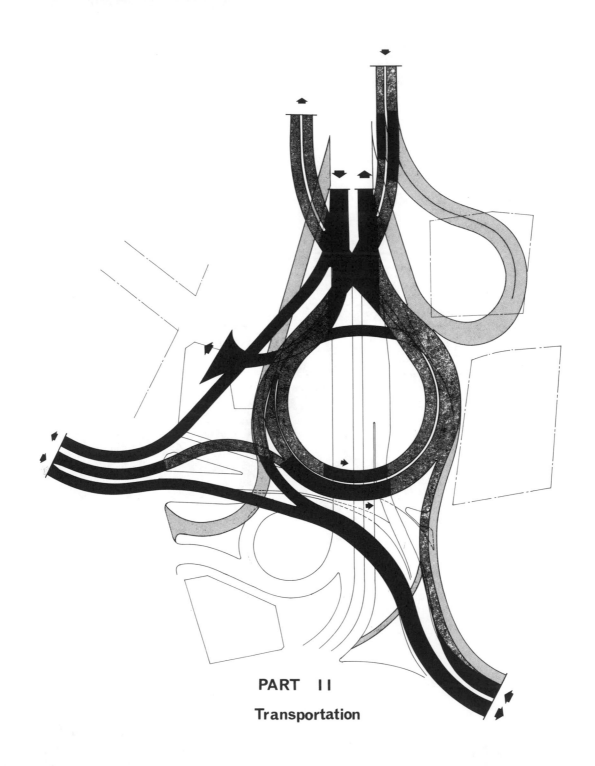

PART II

Transportation

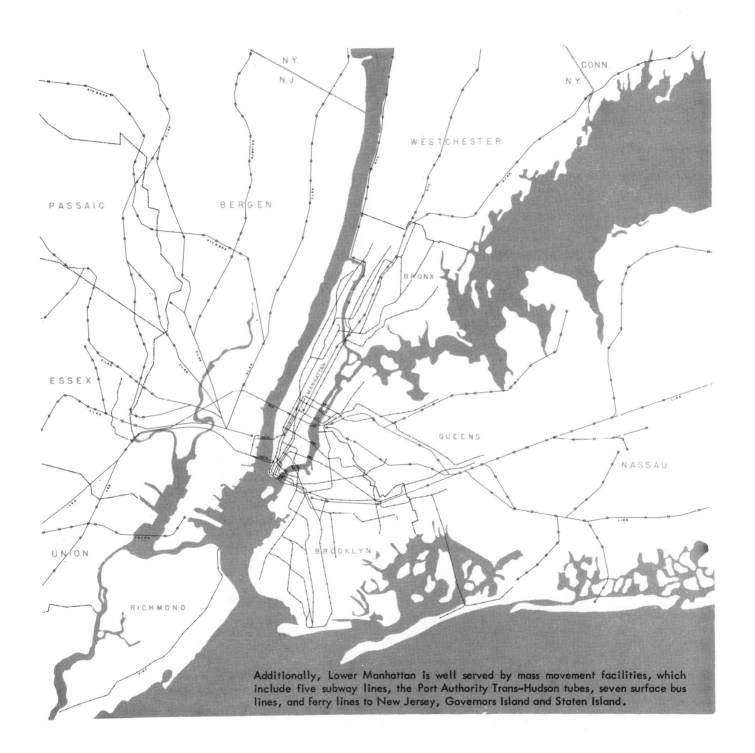

Additionally, Lower Manhattan is well served by mass movement facilities, which include five subway lines, the Port Authority Trans-Hudson tubes, seven surface bus lines, and ferry lines to New Jersey, Governors Island and Staten Island.

CHAPTER IX

INTRODUCTION

As the oldest area of the city, Lower Manhattan has inherited a street system which still reflects many of the paths, squares, and winding streets of the early Dutch and English settlement.

In recent years the area has undergone a massive renewal through renovation and construction, and it stands now on the threshold of another decade of even more dramatic change. Yet, almost incredibly, there is still no accepted plan for development of the street system in the area. This is particularly unfortunate because, without exception, every major project currently proposed for Lower Manhattan calls for street closures and street widenings. The map in Figure 1 shows the street closures which have been proposed for current projects. The absence of a street plan for Lower Manhattan means that there is no basis for evaluating these proposals.

Quite apart from the impact of current project is the problem of providing decent service to the established

core and adjusting to potential changes in land use in the remainder of the area. The streets in the core are intensively used by pedestrians, automobiles and trucks, and the service they provide is deficient by any reasonable standard. Around the edge of the Island, the highways and streets were developed to serve maritime activities when the piers were productive elements of the port. But the port activity has steadily declined, and the piers are now decaying. North of Chambers Street, the gridiron of narrow streets is choked with trucks competing for precious curb space, while motorists trying to cross town creep along at three or four miles an hour.

It is clear that the street system must be improved. It is equally clear that there must be some rational plan for that improvement. Cooperative planning that represents the viewpoints of architecture, land use, and transportation has resulted in a recommended plan that is a bold, dramatic look at the future. On its completion, the original settlement will have an entirely new look and life. Gone will be the rotting piers replaced with a new park and esplanade along the water. Instead of the nine-to five life its streets now know, there will be activity around the clock. Workers will no longer be forced to commute from distant areas of the city but will, instead, be offered a choice of places to live within walking distance of their offices.

The continuation of ad hoc project planning without reference to broad goals and needs will only lead to further deterioration of service and, ultimately, to declining property values, employment, and investment throughout the area. For an area with so many opportunities for significant contributions to New York's economic, social and cultural life, such a dismal prospect is unthinkable.

People will move about the area on a new form of transit, one designed for their special needs, connecting their destinations, and freeing them from the constant conflict with cars and trucks which now characterizes even the shortest walk.

The growth of Lower Manhattan will be made up of many actions by many public agencies and private individuals. One of the chief functions of the city, and one which must be started early, is the development of the pedestrian and vehicular system described in this report. This will provide the framework upon which private development can grow.

Getting from today to tomorrow is, of course, the rock upon which many promising plans founder. With this hazard in mind, the plan is so designed that it and Lower Manhattan, itself, may grow apace. Thus, the interior of the area constitutes a self-sufficient development system, even without the waterfront. With the addition of the related waterfront development, it becomes even more effective.

Clearly, the need for a planned street system stems not only from such proposals of a distant nature as the use of the pier area, but also from projects which are now planned. Such projects have led to increasingly frequent proposals of street closure and the assembly of land into so-called "super blocks."

Of these, extreme examples are the World Trade Center and Civic Center plans, which are of scales large enough to produce significant impact upon the circulation of traffic in the area. Also important to circulation will be the combined impact of such smaller developments as Brooklyn Bridge Southwest and Washington Street.

As such proposals approach fruition, the need for criteria against which to evaluate their impact grows greater and greater. This study, then, had as one of its prime objectives the development of such a rationale, a process which included the definition of regional goals, the description of a basic transportation system, and the definition of the functions of the various elements of that system.

The land use and design plans proposed in Part I represent a limited number of the many alternative ways in which Lower Manhattan might develop. The transportation plan, however, could not be as flexible in its design, although it was developed with an eye to permitting several types and densities of development on the land which it serves. The street system may, however, be altered to adapt to land uses the intensities not foreseen in the land use plan, as long as the basic concepts of function are maintained.

Functional definitions of the elements of the system was necessary for two reasons. First, the function determines the design standards to be met by the system element in question, i.e., a "major arterial" would require more moving lanes than would a "service street." Second, function helps determine the proper relationship of any section to the system as a whole. That is, a "service street" is, by definition, directly related only to the particular building or group of buildings which it serves. It can, therefore, be moved or otherwise altered in any way that still provides service to those buildings. On the other hand, an arterial street is, by definition, related to the transportation system as a whole. Any change in it must, therefore, maintain both its "function", the movement of traffic, and its function in the system, the connection of two areas.

In order to assure the proper interconnection of the sections of the proposed system, it was important to correctly classify all parts of the existing system according to their functions. This was done by observation and research that began with the following inventories of existing conditions.

First, it was necessary to measure actual street and sidewalk widths and translate these into a base map of the study area.

An inventory was then made of existing traffic flows. For this, recent traffic counts by the Department of Streets and Traffic and by the Port Authority were supplemented by manual counts at intersections throughout the study area.

SCALE: 0 200 400 800

**Existing
Street System**

Legend:

▨▨▨▨ **Proposed Closure**

LOWER MANHATTAN PLAN **2-1**

The capacity of the street system was also measured. Nineteen "critical" intersections which govern the continuity-of-flow of the entire system were the subject of careful study.

Because parking near an intersection directly affects its capacity, it was necessary to observe actual parking practices at the nineteen intersections. Capacities were computed according to the parking, legal and illegal, which actually occurred and also according to the parking which would occur if existing parking restrictions were obeyed.

It was also necessary to determine the numbers of pedestrians using various sidewalks at various times of the day. Heaviest hourly volumes were found to occur at the noon hour (although the absolute peaks occurred during periods of less than an hour in the morning and evening), and moreover, this noon-hour traffic moved in all directions, not just to or from subway stations. Because of this characteristic, it placed the heaviest strain on the pedestrian system. Noon-hour volumes, then, were counted at locations throughout the study area, and the resulting figures were supplemented with information from studies made by the Downtown Lower Manhattan Association.

In the field of parking, two types of inventory were made. First, counts were made of usage, by time-of-day, of parking lots and garages in the study area. Second, counts were made of on-street parking, both legal and illegal, at block-faces throughout the study area.

A study was also made of the movements of goods and services by truck. This was done through actual counts and with the aid of information gathered in earlier studies. Service-vehicle volumes were determined for all sections of the system and related to capacities and total volumes of vehicles.

Information on public transportation came from several sources, the New York City Transit Authority, the Port of New York Authority, certain previous studies of the system, and on-the-spot counts by study personnel. From all these were derived the usage of the system, by line and by station, and its capacity, also by line and station. Careful comparisons of the two were used to indicate areas of deficiency and/or overcrowding.

All this information, then, permitted the functional definition of every section (link) of the system and the determination of its capacity and usage. Next, it was necessary to look at these figures in the light of the land uses to which they were related, in order to establish the rates at which various land uses generated trips on the system.

The two such relationships found most important to the operation of the overall system were those between land use and pedestrian trip generation, and between land use and goods-and-services trip generation. These were determined by observation of actual behavior within the system and by the application of the resulting figures to established techniques for determining trip generation.

The ratios thus established were used to determine the ability of the system to handle satisfactorily the traffic which would be generated by various proposed developments.

Along with the functional definitions and trip generation ratios, it was necessary to develop a third tool for the planning and evaluation of the transportation system, a computerized network. This meant the reconstruction, within the memory of a computer, of the entire study-area street system, link-by-link, so that a trip made through the computer network would duplicate one made through the "real" street system.

In order to check this duplication, counts of actual traffic were compared with those estimated by the computer. When the two had been made to agree, it became possible to alter the simulated network to represent proposed changes in the real transportation system. The behavior of the network was then used to analyze the implications for the transportation system of these proposals. This procedure is explained in detail in the section on "Network Assignment."

Continuing analysis of sets of proposals, and of their interaction and consistency with each other, has led to the development of a planned transportation system within which all functions may be served, all future traffic accommodated, and all sections of the system properly interconnected. This has been done in the context of, and in sequence with, the expected redevelopment of Lower Manhattan.

It must be recognized that the proposed street system is not so "hard and fast" that it must be adhered to at all

costs. On the other hand, the flexible system concepts advanced in this report should endure the passage of time. One need only look at recent events to see why a rigid plan would be inadequate. The World Trade Center was first proposed for the East Side, not the West Side. The Stock Exchange only recently began to seriously consider the foot of Broad Street as a possible site for a new exchange building. The Civic Center is even now being re-studied, and the Lower Manhattan Expressway has been "off and on" for thirty years.

Such an atmosphere of constant change and re-evaluation means that the city must be ready to quickly evaluate alternatives. The techniques used in this study offer a means to do this for proposed large changes and the system concepts provide a framework for the evaluation of smaller projects.

CHAPTER X

STREET TRAFFIC

General

Vehicular traffic to or from Lower Manhattan may use any one of seven possible routes. They are:

1. Brooklyn Bridge
2. Manhattan Bridge
3. Brooklyn Battery Tunnel
4. Holland Tunnel
5. Miller Highway (West Side)
6. Franklin D. Roosevelt Drive
7. Streets and Avenues north to Midtown

Approximately 24,000 vehicles enter the study area during the morning peak hours. Of those only one-half or 12,000 are actually destined for Lower Manhattan--the remainder pass through without stopping.

Traffic Volumes

The financial district is largely a terminal area. Most through movements are carried around it either by the elevated highways along the rivers or by Chambers and Canal Streets. Figures 2 and 3 show existing traffic volumes on all streets. Volumes on the surface streets are not unusually high. Church Street and Broadway serve north-south traffic in the center of the Island, and Water Street[1] serves local traffic on the East Side. Cross-Island movements are almost insignificant below Chambers Street. Chambers is, however, currently serving heavy through volumes, by virtue of its close relationship to the Brooklyn Bridge and the ramps on Miller Highway; Canal Street also carries heavy cross-Island volumes.

Unlike that of most places, traffic in the area is not characterized by established "peak hours." The peak hour in Lower Manhattan frequently occurs at an hour of the day that does not correspond to either the opening or closing of business. This is particularly true of streets which carry heavy trucking movements. In spite of this, most major commuter routes behave in a more consistent pattern and, generally speaking, any street designed to accommodate the heavy morning and evening traffic flows will accommodate those occurring during the rest of the day. The fluctuations of traffic during the day are illustrated in Figures 26 through 29 in Appendix A. These illustrations also show the proportion of truck traffic to the total. On some streets, trucks represent as much as 75 percent of total traffic. The amount of trucking is declining as the port and market activities go down but trucking is still a large percentage of total traffic and will continue to be so.

Street Capacity

The capacity of the street system was determined by a special study. The techniques used are explained in

---

[1] For simplicity, Water Street refers to Water, Pearl, and St. James south of Chatham Square.

Appendix A. Results for nineteen key intersections (which effectively control the capacity of the system) are shown in Figures 4 and 5.

Parking is a key element in capacity, since standing vehicles deprive moving vehicles of street space. Flagrant violations of parking regulations in Lower Manhattan were observed, and their effect on street capacity is demonstrated by the two figures. Figure 4 shows the relationship between capacity and volume with parking as it was observed, while Figure 5 shows the same relationship as it would exist if the existing parking regulations were observed. Note that there is excess capacity available at most intersections, but that it cannot be used because illegal parkers pre-empt the space.

The signal modernization program will provide increased "effective" capacity by allotting green time at signalized intersections on the basis of need. Now the signals allot time to each street according to a preset pattern which is often inefficient. Better enforcement of parking regulations, together with the improved signal system, could dramatically improve traffic operations on the street system.

Travel Speeds

The speeds shown in Figure 6 are directly related to congestion and are a good measure of traffic service. For example, speeds on Canal Street--notorious for paralyzing congestion--are very low, while those on Broadway and Church Street are moderate and those on Water Street are relatively high.

Speed and delay runs were made to determine average running times on most major streets in the area. This data (compiled for the morning peak hour) was obtained with a vehicle equipped with a Data Compiler leased from a manufacturer. (The equipment was invented by an employee of New York Department of Traffic.)

In addition to providing insight into problem areas of the system, this information was used in the traffic assignment technique described later. The future street system was planned to eliminate the bottlenecks which now bring traffic to a virtual standstill. In part, congestion and delays result from a basic lack of capacity but private auto and truck parking also play a large part. Therefore, truck service areas and parking are recommended as well as street improvements.

Parking

Particular attention was given to parking in Lower Manhattan. Studies were made of available spaces, parking usage, peak hour trip generation, costs, and parking requirements of different land uses.

In total there are 9,700 spaces south of Chambers Street, the bulk of them in garages, with some parking lots on the East and West sides. One of the largest facilities, the Battery Park Garage, operated by the Tri-Borough Bridge and Tunnel Authority, is soon to be expanded. Curb parking provides approximately 1,000 spaces for short-time parkers.

Parking for residents in proposed housing areas was estimated on the basis of car ownership in a comparable section of Midtown. The Tri-State home interview study found that car ownership in Midtown on the East Side averages 0.28 vehicles per dwelling unit. This figure does not include vehicles which are not owned or leased by the resident. Examples are company cars provided by an employer but garaged by an employee at his place of residence. Allowing for similar rates of car ownership, business vehicles, rental vehicles catering to large residential units, and some visitor parking, brings the total parking related to housing to a figure of 0.40 parking spaces per dwelling unit.

Parking for workers was estimated on the basis of providing only for those few who are not well served by transit, who require a vehicle for business uses during the day, and for key executives who require private transportation for their work trip. Based on existing patterns, about five percent of the total work force comes to the area by private auto or taxi.

**Existing
Traffic
Flow
8:00-9:00 AM**

LOWER MANHATTAN PLAN **2-2**

**Existing
Traffic
Flow
4:30-5:30 PM**

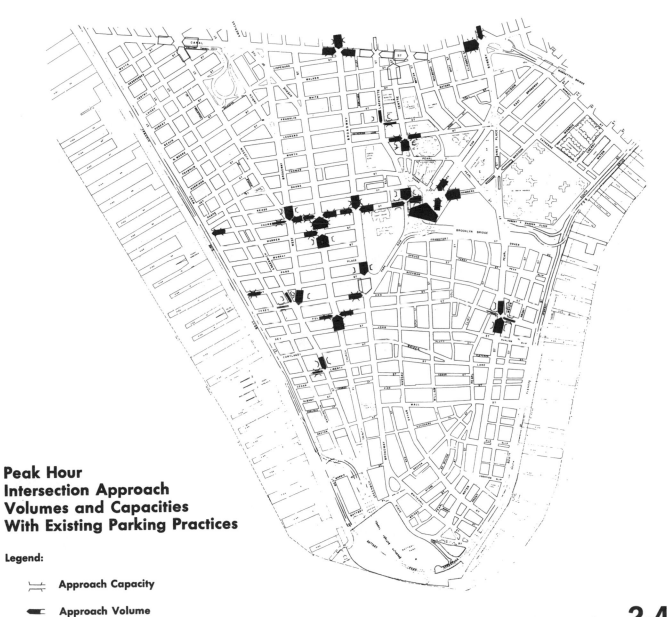

SCALE: 0 200 400 800

**Peak Hour
Intersection Approach
Volumes and Capacities
With Existing Parking Practices**

Legend:

⊐⊏ **Approach Capacity**

◄▬ **Approach Volume**

LOWER MANHATTAN PLAN **2-4**

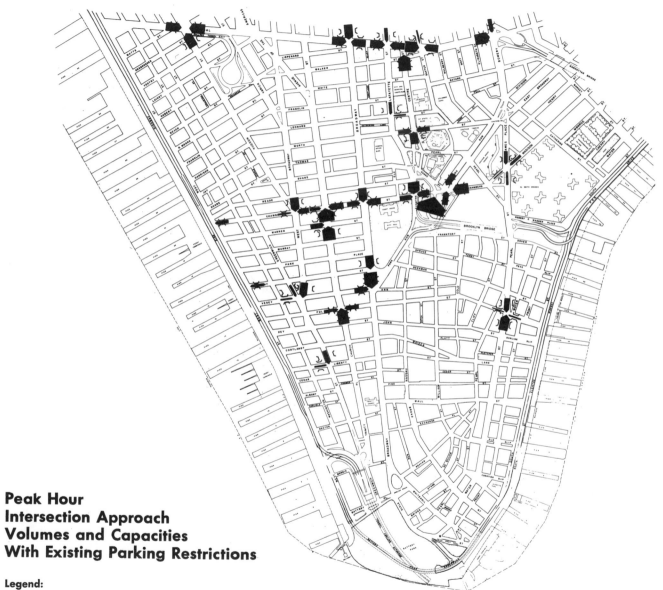

SCALE: 0 200 400 800

**Peak Hour
Intersection Approach
Volumes and Capacities
With Existing Parking Restrictions**

Legend:

⋈ Approach Capacity

◄▬ Approach Volume

LOWER MANHATTAN PLAN 2-5

SCALE: 0 200 400 800

**Travel
Speed and Delay
Runs
8:00-9:00 AM**

LOWER MANHATTAN PLAN **2-6**

Although the trend appears to be toward greater use of the private auto for work trips, there is a practical limit to the amount of parking which can be provided. This practical limit is set in part by the cost, which is clearly beyond the reach of most workers, by the capacity of the roads and streets which now serve Lower Manhattan, and by the ability of the local street system to serve the parking garages.

These limits are not easily defined. For example, the capacity of the roadways which feed Lower Manhattan is easy to measure, but, they are used by motorists from other sections of the Island as well as by through trips. Thus, both existing capacity, and capacity provided by new construction, must be allotted to each of the different users. Clearly Lower Manhattan can not expect to obtain all the total capacity available. Additionally, Miller Highway and FDR Drive have capacity restraints in the Midtown area, and while there is an apparent excess of capacity on the periphery of Lower Manhattan, the truth is that there is a deficiency of capacity for trips originating north of Midtown.

Another problem is the span of time over which capacity can be used for work trips. There has been in recent years a significant shift in work hour patterns which is apparent in the turnstile counts for the subway stations. Work trips on the subways are spread over three hours in the evening rather than being concentrated in one peak hour at the end of the normal business day. This may be the result of greater use of data processing machines which now make it possible to summarize a days activities in the evening rather than on the following day. Certainly there are many "odd-shift" workers who drive to work, as evidenced by the parking during evening hours.

Despite the problems of defining capacity and need, there are indicators which point to a rational policy for worker parking. These were to be found in the amounts of parking now provided, (two to three spaces per 100 workers), the amounts of parking being planned for in current developments (generally three spaces per 100 workers), and the amounts of traffic which would be generated by varying amounts of parking space.

Taken together these factors indicated a need for three spaces for every 100 workers. This amount of parking plus additional short-term parking, was provided in the plan and is the basis for the traffic assignments. New long-term parking was located along the edge of the Island in permanent structures replacing surface lots which are generally only an interim use. The majority of it was planned to be served by the peripheral highway system. There will be, however, a need for additional parking at more central locations, primarily for high turnover parking to serve business trips and visitors.

The most acute shortage is in short-term space; a need which is now met primarily by curb parking and illegal spaces. This need can best be met by spaces located at strategic places throughout the area. A new garage for this purpose is proposed at the intersection of Wall and Water Streets. Residential and worker parking, on the other hand can, and should be, located near the edge of the Island where peripheral highways and major streets can serve them. This will reduce internal street traffic leaving the internal streets available for deliveries, taxis, buses, and other service uses.

A special study of peak-hour parking garage and lot usage, for a selected sample of parking facilities, was conducted to develop trip generation data for the traffic forecasting and assignment phases of the study. The findings are described in Appendix A.

Goods and Service Requirements

The more lightly used streets function primarily to provide service for abutting land. Although trucking is essential to the area, there are very few off-street loading facilities. A survey of off-street loading bays and sidewalk elevators was made for the Core area. These permanent loading facilities are shown in Figure 7.

Off-street loading bays are found primarily in newer buildings and because the zoning ordinance now requires them, they should be more common in the future.

The absence of loading facilities does not mean that there is a small amount of loading. Precisely the opposite is true. At mid-day, when truck parking is near its peak, there are usually 1,500 trucks parked at street curbs in the area. Figure 8 shows generalized street volumes and the number of parked trucks for each street.

Note that the concentration is the heaviest in the northwest section of the city where manufacturing, warehousing and other truck generating activities are located. Only 400 of 1,500 total are parked south of Fulton Street reflecting the lower attraction for trucking of office buildings in contrast to manufacturing, marketing and wholesaling which are concentrated in the northern portion. Since these latter functions are expected to be replaced by offices, housing and other uses which produce fewer truck trips, the amount of trucking in the future will be less for the Study Area as a whole. But truck service will continue to be an essential element of the total transportation needs.

A special study of truck trip generation was undertaken to make it possible to accurately forecast this change.

Goods and Service Trip Generation

The special studies of trip generation for goods and services were conducted at ten buildings to determine the amount of truck traffic related to various buildings by functional type. The study included the recording of data on times of arrival and departure of each truck visiting the building to obtain hourly fluctuations, average duration of parking and peak accumulations. Each building was observed from 7:00 a.m. to 6:00 p.m.

The data were analyzed to estimate the number of trips generated by buildings of various types in relationship to square footage and number of employees. These were used in developing the trip tables for the traffic assignments, both existing and future.

Each vehicle was classified according to the following code:

Vehicle Type	Code #
Single Unit Truck:	
2 axle single rear tires	1
2 axle dual rear tires	2
3 axle dual rear tires	3
Tractor Trailer Combination:	
3 axle	4
4 axle	5
5 axle	6
Other Types:	7

Of the 323 trucks observed, only two were trailer combinations and only 21 had three axles. Delivery service in Lower Manhattan is confined primarily, to two axle trucks due to the narrow streets and tight intersections where turns by long vehicles are, at best, difficult and in some cases impossible.

The average parking duration was 35 minutes but this ranged from two minutes to 450 minutes (all day).

Average attraction rates for all ten buildings was 8.5 trucks per 1,000 employees or 4.7 trips per 100,000 square feet of gross floor area. Retail space attracted far more trips than office space, the average being about 70 trips per 100,000 square feet.

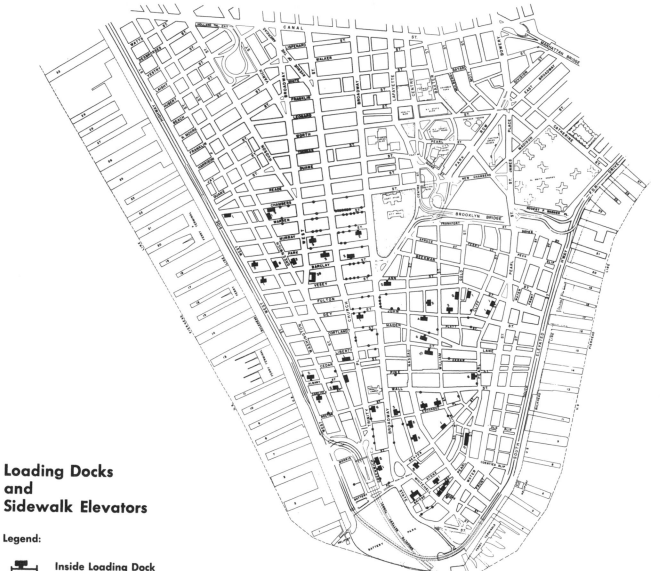

SCALE: 0 200 400 800

**Loading Docks
and
Sidewalk Elevators**

Legend:

🛏 Inside Loading Dock

🛏 Outside Loading Dock

🛏 Sidewalk Elevator

x Number of Loading Docks

LOWER MANHATTAN PLAN 2-7

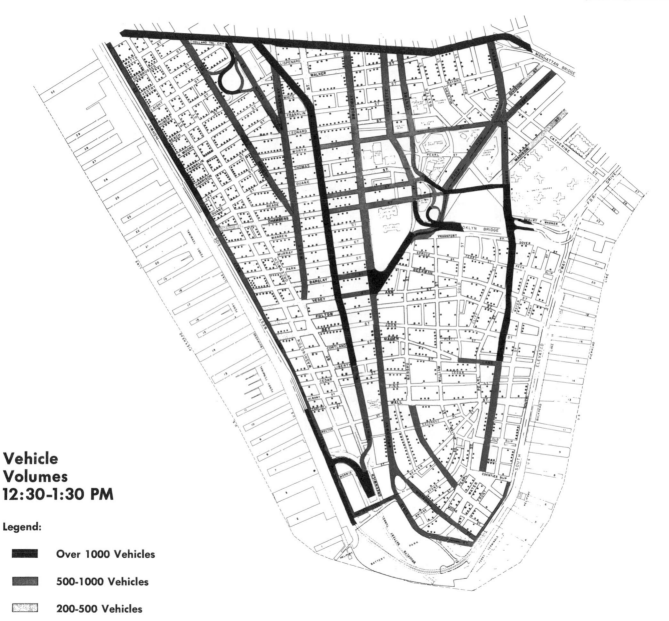

SCALE: 0 200 400 800

**Vehicle
Volumes
12:30-1:30 PM**

Legend:

Over 1000 Vehicles

500-1000 Vehicles

200-500 Vehicles

Under 200 Vehicles

Each dot represents one (1) parked truck.

LOWER MANHATTAN PLAN **2-8**

Individual breakdowns are shown below:

Type of Use	veh./day 100,000 sq.ft.	veh./day 1,000 empl.
Insurance	4.4	4.0
Lawyers	1.0	2.0
Banking: home office type	6.0	10.0
branch office type	4.0	4.0
General Office	4.0	5.0
Maritime	2.0	3.0
Government	3.5	6.0
Brokerage	2.0	2.0
Retail	70.0	120.0

Additional tabulations and illustrations are shown in Appendix A. The specific buildings are not identified by name to avoid disclosure of occupancy, usage, etc.

From the data collected and from review of other studies in Manhattan and elsewhere, a complete tabulation of trip productions and attractions were developed for the different land uses in the Study Area. They are shown in Table 1.

Pedestrian Volumes

Pedestrians are the other principal users of the street system. The heaviest volumes—which approach 7,000 persons per hour in some blocks—are to be found on Broadway, Chambers, Nassau, Broad, Fulton, Church and Wall Streets. These are shown in Figure 9. The number of parked trucks, repeated from Figure 8, indicates the multiple uses to which each street is put.

The principal generators of pedestrian traffic are the subway stations. The movement of people to and from work which occurs in the morning and evening peak hours places a considerable strain on the limited sidewalk spaces available in the financial district. However, the heaviest usage of the sidewalks occurs during the mid-day when there are many visitors in the area and when the workers are moving about for lunch,

business and shopping trips. Although the volumes at that time of the day are not as high as they are in the rush periods, the mid-day is critical because the movements tend to be in many directions and street traffic and loading are also near their peak.

The majority of heavy pedestrian movements occur on east-west streets due to the north-south orientation of the subway system. These trips also tend to be longer, on the average.

Major shifts in pedestrian patterns will result from the World Trade Center, relocation of the Stock Exchange, new office, residential and recreational uses along the waterfront and general growth of office activity in and around the financial district.

In addition to the crowded sidewalks, the joint use of intersection areas by people and vehicles results in delays to both. Vehicles attempting to turn are delayed by pedestrians and pedestrians are delayed by vehicles blocking cross-walks. Several alternative ways of resolving these conflicts at major points in the area were studied. These studies dealt not only with existing conditions but with estimated future conditions.

The capacity of a sidewalk is about 1,000 to 1,200 persons per hour for each 2.5 foot of width, or 400 or 500 per foot. To illustrate the areas which are congested, pedestrian volumes observed during the mid-day hours were converted to densities or pedestrians per foot of sidewalk width per hour. The results are shown on Figure 10. This Figure clearly shows the portion of the street system where additional capacity for moving people is needed. Those areas are Nassau Street, Fulton Street, Cortlandt Street, and Wall Street.

Pedestrian Trip Generation

The same ten buildings mentioned earlier in the Goods and Service Study were used for a pedestrian trip generation study. Data were collected at all building doorways for three time periods; 7:00 to 10:00 a.m.; 11:00 to 2:00 p.m.; and 4:00 to 6:00 p.m.

The studies gave the number of people coming to and going from each building for each time period. From these, it could be seen that the expected patterns of hourly fluctuation do occur. Mid-day counts are clearly influenced by the type of employment in the building and by the availability of food service. In all, over 156,000 people were counted in the study. The average one-way door count at mid-day was 0.92 times the number of employees, although this ranged from 0.60 to 1.40. The average for the entire day was 4.00 times the number of employees, with a range from 2.30 to 5.80. The results for three typical buildings are shown in Appendix A.

SCALE: 0 200 400 800

**Pedestrian
Volumes
12:30-1:30 PM**

Legend:

▬▬▬ Over 5000 People

▬▬▬ 2000-5000 People

☐ Under 2000 People

Each dot represents one (1) parked truck

LOWER MANHATTAN PLAN 2-9

SCALE: 0 200 400 800

**Pedestrian
Densities
12:30–1:30 PM**

Legend:

■ Over 500 Persons/Ft. of Sidewalk

■ 300-500 Persons/Ft. of Sidewalk

▨ 150-300 Persons/Ft. of Sidewalk

☐ Under 150 Persons/Ft. of Sidewalk

LOWER MANHATTAN PLAN **2-10**

TABLE 1

Trip Attraction and Production Averages   for Lower Manhattan

Type of land use	veh./day, 100,000 sq.ft.	veh./day 1,000 empl.
Insurance	5.0	5.0
Lawyers	1.0	2.0
Banking: home office type	6.0	10.0
branch office type	4.0	4.0
General Office	8.0	10.0
Maritime	2.0	3.0
Government	4.0	7.0
Brokerage	2.0	2.0
Retail	60.0	100.0
Commercial	50.0	100.0
Gross parameters	7.0	14.0

Car ownership (middle to higher income): 0.28-0.4 veh./DU

Densities: DU/acre

Person trips per day and DU: 1.7 to 2.0 trips/DU, day

Truck trips for residential units: 30 trucks/1000 person trips

3.0% employees by car or car pool: occupancy rate = 1.2 persons/car

0.5% employees by taxi: occupancy rate = 1.0 persons/taxi

5 to 10% visitors by car: occupancy rate = 1.2 to 1.5 pers/car

5 to 15% visitors by taxi: occupancy rate = 1.0 to 1.2 pers/taxi

Parking times: -visitors, customers at office bldgs: 90 minutes

-visitors in residential developments: 120 minutes

Trucks at berths: - in residential area: 60 minutes

- in commercial developments: 30 minutes

- in office buildings: 30 minutes

CHAPTER XI

FUNCTIONAL CLASSIFICATION OF STREETS

It can be seen that the streets of Lower Manhattan serve many different kinds of trips by many different kinds of vehicles. Some pass through the area without stopping; others are work trips or those by trucks bringing goods or services to buildings or of taxis bringing businessmen or visitors. The list could be carried on almost indefinitely. Further, the street system must serve trips by pedestrians, either between buildings and subway or parking facilities, or among buildings to eat, visit, shop or sight-see.

Since conflicts among these uses often occur, and are often severe, it is clear that the answer to serving them does not lie in designing all streets to serve all purposes. Moreover, such a solution would require the designing and construction of a totally new street system.

It was necessary, then, to determine just how, and how much, each street section was used. To this end, special studies were made of the trips generated by indi-

vidual buildings and of the traffic occurring on each section of street. The findings of these studies were summarized in Figures 8 through 10. The first of these, (Figure 8), shows the volumes of traffic using each street. It is apparent that the few streets that carry really heavy volumes are: Broadway, Church, Canal, Worth, Chambers, Park Row, Water, Vesey, and Barclay. Figure 8 also shows the number of trucks parked in each block during the mid-day illustrating very heavy usage of some streets for deliveries.

Pedestrian movements are shown on Figure 9, in terms of persons per hour using each street, and on Figure 10, in terms of persons per foot of sidewalk width. In both cases, the volumes shown are for the mid-day peak hour. Higher pedestrian volumes occur in the morning and evening peak hours, but they are not as critical because they tend to extend over only part of the hour and because they tend to be highly directional. On the other hand, mid-day volumes of pedestrian traffic extend over two full hours, and movements are in all directions. This period of the day places heavy demands on pedestrian facilities.

The information on street use was then translated into a study map showing those streets with light usage for different purposes, and those with heavy usage. (See Figure 11.) From this map was developed a system of streets for each use. Where one function clearly exceeds all others, the street is designated for that function. Where two or three functions are about equal, the street is designated for multiple usage.

Having developed possible classifications, the next step was to create a "system" from a series of street sections. Streets designated primarily for pedestrians were thus put together to connect important pedestrian generators, including subway stations, ferry terminals, and large buildings. Such a system should attract pedestrian trips from less-desirable streets, hence leaving them more available for other uses.

Similarly, the service system is planned to make service available to every building in the area and connect directly to the arterial streets. The system design is such that each service trip would use the arterial streets to a point within one or two blocks of the building for which it is destined, and then use the service streets for the last portion of the trip.

The arterial street system was planned to connect major roads and streets entering Lower Manhattan, to collect and distribute service traffic, and to provide good access and circulation within the area.

This articulated system gets maximum use from the ancient street system with minimum cost for street improvements. It is suited to a staging process so that it can be developed over time with minimum disturbance of existing travel habits. Finally, it establishes a system that is suited to the core of the area and can be expanded as future growth occurs, either in the fringe around the core or in the area now occupied by piers.

As the core expands, the pedestrian system can expand to provide more efficient service, thereby maintaining the cohesion of the area. In addition, designation of arterial streets and service streets provides a framework within which decisions on street closings can be made.

Lower Manhattan Expressway

The northern boundary of the study area was drawn at Canal Street, well south of the Lower Manhattan Expressway. Analysis of the street system took into account the probable effect of the Expressway and the proposed system was developed with the assumption that the Expressway would be constructed (or a satisfactory alternative).

The Expressway was planned to connect the Williamsburg and Manhattan Bridges on the east side to the Miller Highway and Holland Tunnel. In addition, it would serve vehicles using the tunnel and the bridges which wish to partially cross the Island. By removing these large volumes from the city streets, the Expressway would eliminate the bottleneck to north-south movement which now exists in a broad band across Manhattan. It would also reduce congestion at the bridge and tunnel terminals, thereby effectively increasing accessibility to Lower Manhattan.

One alternative to the Expressway, which has been proposed, would route trips around the tip of the Island. This is not a practical solution to the problem. The depressed highways around the tip of the island proposed in this report could not handle the additional traffic. In addition, most of the traffic involved doesn't really cross the island but distributes itself over the north-south avenues to many points in Manhattan. However, it is possible that alternatives in location and design could be developed by a careful study of the traffic movements, costs, design alternatives and community impacts.

It is also possible that some change in the recommended street system would be called for by a new location of the Expressway or a combination of new facilities to serve the Expressway's functions. Even so, those changes are likely to be small and would not materially affect the basic system proposed in this report. The important thing from the standpoint of Lower Manhattan is that a satisfactory means be developed for handling traffic across the Island to improve access from the north and from the East River Bridges.

Computer Analysis

To test the adequacy of different street systems, it was necessary to forecast the volumes of traffic which would use each street in the future. To do this, a computer assignment was developed. This consisted of two basic elements: a network and a trip table. The network was simply a description of the street system and the parking areas. It consisted of a series of nodes connected by links. Each street at the periphery of the study area was described as an external zone with the ability to produce and/or attract trips. Each curb face and each parking garage or lot was described as an internal zone with a similar ability.

SCALE: 0 200 400 800

Street System Study Map

Legend:

▭ Traffic Street

▥ Service Emphasis

▦ Pedestrian Emphasis

▬ Complete Closure

▨ Special Projects

LOWER MANHATTAN PLAN **2-11**

The first network described the existing street system; succeeding networks were modifications of the original that reflected proposed changes in the system. Thus, streets to be closed were deleted, and streets to be opened were added, to the network. Similarly, streets could be changed from one-way to two-way operation or their directions reversed.

The trip table was simply a tabulation of trips among all zones. It utilized one-way trips only and was developed by using a simplified model which ignored travel time and distance. In effect, it assumed that trips to or from internal zones were distributed to external zones in proportion to the percentage of total trip productions and attractions for each external zone. Review of previous origin and destination studies revealed that this varied by sub-area in Lower Manhattan, so the distribution of trips was actually done on a sub-area basis and then totaled.

Through trips, for example, trips between external stations, were estimated separately and then deducted from external productions and attractions before distributions of internal trips were calculated.

The productions and attractions of each internal zone were calculated by adding parking, taxi trips, truck deliveries, and bus schedules. A taxi trip would equal one attraction and one production. The same was true for buses and most truck deliveries. Similarly, trips parking at the curb in high turnover space, and private auto trips to fronts of major buildings were nearly equal in productions and attractions. On the other hand, trips to off-street spaces were heavily weighted toward attractions. A special study of off-street parking usage is described in Appendix A.

Trip tables were thus devised for each alternative for which an assignment was made. In the case of proposed new development, estimates of trip productions and attractions were based on the values in Table 1.

These two basic elements, the network and trip table, were stored in a computer and the trip table was the "assigned" to the network. To do this, the computer calculated the shortest path from each zone to every other zone and assigned the trips to that path. Repeating this process for every zone indicated the total number of trips on each link. The purpose of going through this entire process for the existing system was to obtain a check on the accuracy of the method and assumptions. After the first such assignment, several changes were made in the the network, such were, notably, changes in travel times and the insertion of turn penalties at critical intersections. The trip table was also adjusted to give each area its proper number of trips. These changes were very small, but they helped produce an assignment of existing trips to the existing street system which is in remarkable agreement with actual volume counts.

The network, as developed, actually consisted of two parts: one for the area immediately surrounding the Civic Center, the other for the remainder of the study area south of Canal Street. The two can be used individually or, together, as a single network. In evaluating the traffic problems around the Civic Center, the smaller network was used. For forecasts of future trips in the later stages of the study, the entire network was used.

Obviously, the forecasts of future trips are only estimates. However, they are highly accurate for the conditions assumed in each assignment. One reason for this is the preciseness of the exercise, in that each zone has to be analyzed individually, and each must be completed. This forces the estimator to recognize each individual element of the system and to make rational estimates for each one. In addition to this attention to detail, the computer, itself, brings a high degree of accuracy to the thousands of individual calculations required for the process.

Traffic Forecasts

The recommended street system was tested by the assignment to it of two vehicular traffic forecasts, representing: 1) the interim and 2) the final developmental conditions in Lower Manhattan. The former was for the time when committed and proposed projects would be in operation, and the latter represented the ultimate development, as proposed by the planning consultants.

In each case, the network was modified to reflect the actual planned changes in the street system. Trip generation was determined by applying the parameters, developed by this study, to the projected land-use locations and densities.

The intermediate-range forecast — Network 51 — reflects the expected 1970 - 1975 conditions. The following list gives the major new developments upon which the forecast was predicated. Additional private buildings under construction or planned for completion before 1975 were included.

Civic Center completed
Chatham Towers completed
Brooklyn Bridge Southwest Housing
    project completed
Stock Exchange (at South Ferry) completed
World Trade Center completed
Parking garage in the general vicinity of
    Hanover Square — 500 cars — completed
Parking garage Battery Park Addition —
    1,000 cars — completed
Garage east of Police Headquarters — 1,000
    cars — completed
No changes in Washington Market area.
    However, construction of Worth-Harrison
    crosstown arterial completed
No changes in Fulton Fishmarket
Close Cedar Street: Nassau-Greenwich
Close John Street: Broadway-Dutch
Close Nassau: Wall-Beekman
Close Wall: New Street-Pearl Street
Close Pearl: State-Whitehall
Close Coenties Slip West completely
Close Moore Street completely
Close Front Street: Fulton-Maiden Lane and
    Wall-Coenties Slip East

Close Stone Street: Broad Street-
    Hanover Square
Close Broad Street: South Street-Water
    Street and Beaver Street-Wall Street
Reversed Warren and Murray Street (Warren
    West: Murray East bound)
Reverse Thames Street between Broadway-
    Church: Westbound
Reverse Bridge Street: Between State and
    Broad Street, westbound
Reverse Pearl Street: Between State and
    Broad Street eastbound
Reverse William Street: South William-
    Liberty northbound
Reverse Gold Street: Fulton-Liberty
    southbound
Reverse Cliff Street: Fulton-John southbound
Chatham Square with new configuration
Brooklyn Bridge approaches completed
FDR interchange (east of Pearl Street)
    completed
Widened Worth Street (s = 10) between Church
    and Chatham Square
Baxter Street Extension (between Worth and
    Park Row) completed
Lower Manhattan Expressway w/Holland
    Tunnel Exits etc. in service
Greenwich St. 2-way to WTC: dead end at
    Barclay St. (s = 12)
Worth-Harrison widened (s = 10; 2-way)
Hudson Street reduced speed: s = 12
Barclay St. Ferry (674) and Liberty St. Ferry
    (External 669) deleted
City Hall Park Under-pass according DPW
    built and in service
Maiden Lane widened
Coenties Slip east two-way
Water Street widened and two 2-way;
    Coenties Slip-State Street
Williams Street 2-way: Pine-Beekman
Vesey Street one-way eastbound

For the 1970-1975 a.m. peak hour, the total number of trips into the Study area increased over 3,000 (from

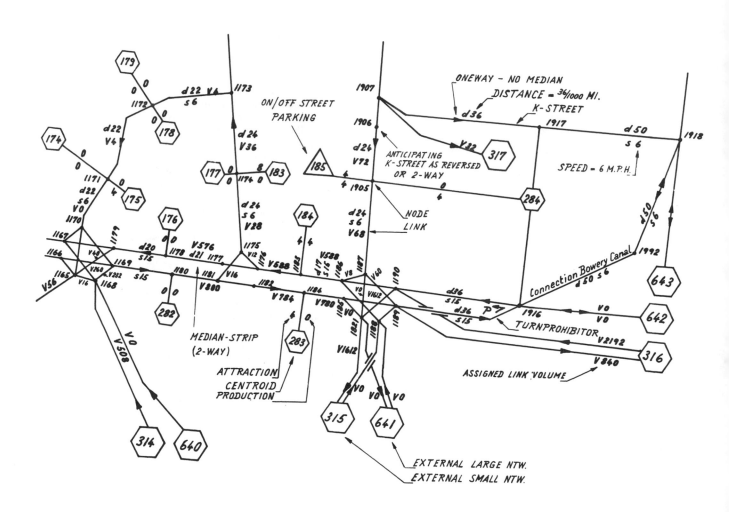

CIVIC CENTER – BROOKLYN BRIDGE
STREET NETWORK

**Street Network
Key Map**

LOWER MANHATTAN PLAN **2-13**

**Traffic
Forecast —
Intermediate Development
1970-1975
8:00-9:00 AM**

LOWER MANHATTAN PLAN **2-14**

12,254 to 15,531), while outbound trips increased by nearly 2,000 (from 6,378 to 8,348). It was assumed that through trips would decline slightly (from 11,990 to 9,779) due to the completion of the Lower Manhattan Expressway or some similar facility. Numbers of trips and vehicle miles for the assignments are shown in Tables 2 and 3.

The effect of such ultimate development (by the year 2010) as is proposed by the planning consultants was tested on Network 61. This assignment assumed the completion of a new peripheral expressway with parallel service roads and full development at maximum allowable densities. New residential construction outbound of the existing bulkhead line was anticipated to mitigate the inbound travel demand that would otherwise be associated with the proposed higher employment.

A partial listing of new major projects includes:

> Full implementation of proposed street system.
> Redevelopment of Washington Street Market area.
> Redevelopment of Fulton Fishmarket area.
> Redevelopment of Industrial area at Holland
>   Tunnel exits.
> New Police Headquarters completed.
> United States Steel Building completed.

Inbound trips again increased by more than 3,000 and outbound by roughly 1,000. Through trips, however, remained basically at the 1970-75 level, showing an increase of only 200 trips during the a.m. peak hour. Figure 15 shows the resultant traffic volumes.

Evaluation of Vehicle System

The vehicle volume forecasts were assigned to the recommended street systems and the resultant volumes were analyzed, by comparison with the capacity curves developed early in this study, to determine how well the systems would perform.

It was evident that the proposed system has sufficient capacity for expected travel demands without wholesale modification. Some improved channelization and integration of control devices would, however, be extremely helpful. In addition, more rigorous enforcement of parking restrictions would allow streets to be utilized fully in their suggested classification.

Only one problem did come to light during this process, however. Increases in both vehicular and pedestrian traffic might create critical obstructions at certain intersections, particularly if provisions for the increased pedestrian volumes are not made. Arcading and street closure for pedestrians use only would definitely limit the number of conflict points.

Therefore, although the proposed increases in Lower Manhattan's employment, floor space, and residential usage are large, the recommended street system, with its classification and control by function, will be able to meet the vehicle movement demands posed by this development.

TABLE 2

COMPARISON OF AM PEAK HOUR TRAFFIC FLOWS AT DIFFERENT
STAGES FOR LOWER MANHATTAN STUDY AREA

	Existing	diff.	1970/75	diff.	1990/2010
Total Tripends	61,544	+5871	67,415	+8019	75,434
External Productions	24,244		25,310		28,425
External Attractions	18,368		18,127		19,221
Accumulation	5,876	+1307	7,183	+2021	9,204
Internal Attractions	12,254		15,531		18,446
Internal Productions	6,378		8,348		9,242
Accumulation	5,876	+1307	7,183	+2021	9,204
External to External Trips	11,990	-2211*	9,779	+ 200	9,979

*Influence LMX-way & other changes.

Check Totals

Zone Att.	12,254	15,531	18,446
+ Ext.-Ext.	11,990	9,779	9,979
= Ext. Prod.	24,244	25,310	28,425
Zone Prod.	6,378	8,348	9,242
+ Ext.-Ext.	11,990	9,779	9,979
= Ext. Att.	18,368	18,127	19,221

TABLE 3

COMPARISON OF AM PEAK HOUR VEHICLE MILES AND VEHICLE HOURS
FOR LOWER MANHATTAN STUDY

	Existing	1970/75	1990/2010
Vehicle miles	30,317	31,535	35,803
Avg. trip length (miles)	0.99	0.94	0.95
Vehicle Hours	1,927	2,014	2,297
Avg. trip length-in hours	0.063	0.060	0.061
-in minutes	3.77	3.60	3.65
Total vehicles	30,622	33,658	37,667

**Traffic
Forecast —
Ultimate Development
1990-2010
8:00-9:00 AM**

Legend:

4000 3000 2000 1500 1000

SCALE: 0 200 400 800

LOWER MANHATTAN PLAN **2-15**

CHAPTER XII

RECOMMENDATIONS

CORE AREA

Proposals for the future street system call for treating the streets according to the following functional definitions: 1) arterial streets, for major movement of traffic; 2) service streets, for access to buildings and delivery of goods; and 3) pedestrian streets, for the free movement of people over short distances.

These three systems are shown in Figure 16 ; their respective designations follow an intensive study of street widths, traffic and pedestrian volumes, parking, loading facilities, truck movements, and transit station capacities and usage. (Additional service roadways within superblocks created by this system are not shown.)

Vehicular System

The major vehicular streets within the core area include Church, Broadway, and Water-Pearl Streets for north-south movement. Worth Street and the Warren-Murray couplet will provide east-west access in the vicinity of the Civic Center. Barclay and Vesey Streets would be major crosstown streets north of the World Trade Center, and the Maiden Lane-Liberty Street couplet will furnish east-west access south of the World Trade Center.

Pedestrian System

The pedestrian system consists of Nassau, Broad, Fulton, Dey, John, and Chambers Streets. This system is an adaptation of existing streets to a new design concept specially tailored to the needs of pedestrians. It will connect directly to points of pedestrian concentration in the new waterfront developments and take advantage of major pedestrian areas either in existence or proposed for the area, e.g., the World Trade Center Plaza, City Hall Park, the Civic Center Plaza, and the Stock Exchange Plaza, as well as many smaller spaces along Nassau, Broadway, William and John Streets. The Chambers Street route will connect the Brooklyn Bridge walkway, Civic Center, and the Police Headquarters with the Washington Street Redevelopment Area.

Where existing street widths are insufficient to accommodate pedestrian loads and the proposed two-way surface transit system, Arcades are proposed in lieu of widening.

Transit Stations

Transit station improvements designed integrally with the pedestrian system are recommended to bring passengers out of the stations to street level with greater speed and with less congestion at the stairways. A special feature of the recommended design is an attempt to open the streets above selected station mezzanines to provide daylight to those areas, enhancing both utility and appearance.

A current proposal for the improvement of transit in the area includes the operation of Long Island trains from Brooklyn into Lower Manhattan. If this proposal is adopted, those station improvements required may be combined with proposals of this type. An example of how these station improvements could be accomplished is shown in Figure 17.

Alternative concepts for the pedestrian system were studied, including underground and overhead arrangements, neither of which seemed suitable or practical for this area. A number of excellent at-grade solutions can be worked out, and have been studied.

Intra-Area Transit

To serve the unique needs of Lower Manhattan, particularly as the core expands and distances between major concentrations of workers and residents become greater, a small, low, moderate-speed vehicle is recommended for selected routes of the pedestrian system. This unique conveyance would provide frequent service for people moving distances of four to ten blocks—too short for subway or taxi, too long for easy walking. Examples are trips from the Staten Island Ferry Terminal to Broad and Wall Streets, or from the new Stock Exchange to the World Trade Center, or from the East to Hudson Rivers. Such service could be initiated in the near future.

There is no vehicle presently in use which is appropriate to Lower Manhattan's special demands. Expressly for the purpose, a new vehicle should be designed with a low floor and relatively open sides that facilitate boarding even at low speeds. Actual stopping time would thus be kept to a minimum.

Specific Actions

The completion of street improvements around the Civic Center and the Brooklyn Bridge ramps should coincide with that of the Civic Center itself. Similarly, the street improvements planned in conjunction with the World Trade Center should be coordinated with the overall construction of the Center.

Around the World Trade Center, Liberty Street-Maiden Lane should be widened across the Island. Widenings of most blocks are either planned or in various stages of completion. This widening will require the demolition of the buildings in the small triangle east of William Street. Because this street is proposed as a major connection to the expressway, the portion of it lying east of Water Street should be widened to at least 60 feet between curbs, with sidewalks at least 10 feet wide and preferably more.

The Trade Center Plan calls for one-way operation on Maiden Lane and Liberty Street west of their junction near Gold Street. It may be possible, however, to operate Liberty Street as a two-way street for its entire length and, thereby, eliminate the necessity for westbound traffic to negotiate two turns at Church Street. This type of operation should be tested at the outset; and, if it proves impractical, one-way operation instituted.

Broadway

To develop additional capacity on Broadway, gradual widenings have been made, particularly in the vicinity of City Hall and the Civic Center. These widenings should be continued north to Canal Street as redevelopment occurs.

Worth Street

Widening of Worth to a two-way crosstown arterial has been planned for some time. The widening to 45 feet east of Broadway should soon be completed and the widening west of Broadway should be given as high a priority as is consistent with the city's ability to develop financing and with any redevelopment of the area.

Water Street

Water Street has recently been widened as far south as Coenties Slip, and the extension of this widening has been mapped to Whitehall Street. This project should be completed in conjunction with clearance and construction on the proposed Stock Exchange site.

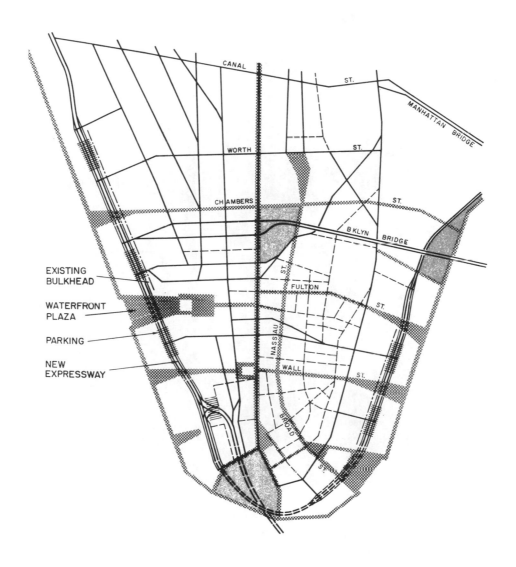

**Proposed
Circulation
System**

Legend:

——————— Traffic

— — — — — Service

▓▓▓▓▓▓ Pedestrian

||||||||||| Parking

LOWER MANHATTAN PLAN **2-16**

**Proposed
Open-Sky
Subway Station—**

Broad and Wall Streets

Nassau Street

This street is proposed for conversion to a pedestrian-emphasis street. A view of the street as it might look following its conversion is shown in Figure 18. The street should be repaved and the sidewalks and crosswalks be delineated by special pavement texture. As the buildings along the street are redeveloped, arcades should be provided. The cost to the city of this improvement should be reasonably small since bonuses for arcades are provided for under the new zoning ordinance. The arcading should be mapped to assure that all new developments on the east side of Nassau Street will include arcading. Deliveries now made over the sidewalk should be prohibited during the mid-day hours--beginning, possibly, with those from 10:00 a.m. to 4:00 p.m. This would permit the prohibition of traffic in the street between Wall and Fulton during those hours. Traffic could continue to use Nassau Street in the morning and evening. At the same time, controls on site plans should be used to require all new buildings to construct loading facilities on the cross streets or to expect limitation of deliveries to early morning or late evening hours.

Intra-Bus System

Within the area, it is proposed to serve trips of about 4 - 10 blocks in length with a system of low, slow, and, in warm weather, open buses. Running on 2 - 3 minute headways, these vehicles would serve those trips which are too long for comfortable walking and too short for the subway. Fares would be nominal, and their collection on an "honor system" would eliminate the need for elaborate door- and fare-control systems.

No vehicle now exists which meets the special requirements of this system, but there are several which approach them. A proposed vehicle, somewhat approximating a San Francisco cable car, while eliminating its noise and inflexibility, is shown in Figure 18. The Washington, D. C. "Minibus" experience has been used to estimate a vehicle cost of $15,000 each and the operating costs are shown in Table 4.

The first route of this system (dumbell-shaped, with loops at either end connected by a central straight) should be opened about the time that a significant portion of the World Trade Center is completed. This route is proposed to run up Broad Street from the Staten Island Ferry to Fulton Street, across Fulton Street to Church Street, down Church Street to the front of the World Trade Center, east on John Street to Nassau Street, and down Nassau Street and Broad Street to the point of origin. It is estimated that ten buses, with two in reserve, would be required to maintain three-minute headways on this route.

Pedestrian volumes in the area are quite large (see Figure 9), and the proposed system would need to capture only a small percentage of them to pay its own way.

The different types of trips which are made by pedestrians in the area help indicate the type of service needed.

Parking employees	- Trips of employees to and from parking.
Transit riding employees	- Trips by employees to and from transit stations.
Employee lunch trips	- Trips by employees to eat lunch.
Business trips	- Trips between buildings, or between parking or transit stations and buildings.
Employee shopping trips	- These are frequently combined with lunch trips in Lower Manhattan.

Although these trips are usually quite short (50 percent are less than 500 feet), they are growing longer as the financial district expands. For example, the World Trade Center and the Stock Exchange are both proposed for construction on the fringe of the existing district. With this expansion and with the latent demand for transit by workers now coming in by ferry and by PATH (and with the unusually high volume of visitors to the stock exchanges, the Trade Center, the Battery, and other tourist attractions), ample demand exists for convenient, middle-distance transit service. Moreover, the proposed system would bridge the cost-gap between taxi and walk by providing a modest-price alternative and one which is readily available.

Operation of the bus system as a free service to the area, while desirable, is ruled out by the question of financing. The overall transit system is currently subsidized from city funds, and it is clear that any additional funds should go to improvement of that system. On the other hand, it seems equally unlikely that since a quarter of a million dollars a year is at stake, private enterprise would underwrite the venture. Use of a special real estate levy would raise complex questions of benefits versus assessments. After considering the many ways in which service could be instituted without prolonged financial exploration, it was decided to recommend fare collection. Normally, this would mean fare control at a single entrance or exit. Since this would destroy the basic concept of the system, that of an easily-boarded vehicle with reduced boarding time and station stops, it was decided to recommend an honor system for the collection of a nominal fare.

Actually, this recommended system is only one of many considered as means to provide the improved circulation within the financial district that was clearly desirable. All such other systems as moving sidewalks, elevated or underground passageways, or elevated rail systems had serious drawbacks. The bus operating on the surface seemed best suited to the needs of most potential users. It also has the virtues of being capable of expansion as the area continues to grow over time and that of being testable. Initial tests on Broad-Nassau Street will provide an opportunity to evaluate different bus designs, fare collection

systems, scheduling, and other operating and service problems.

Fulton Street

Funds for the widening of Fulton Street have been appropriated, and the street has been mapped for widening. Widening the right-of-way to 90 feet, as proposed would require the acquisition of all properties on the south side of the street. The plan was advanced during the period when it was assumed that the World Trade Center would be constructed on the East Side and that Fulton Street would carry crosstown traffic to and from the Miller Highway. With the decision to locate the Trade Center astride Fulton Street on the West Side, the proposal lost some of its urgency.

Assignments of traffic for future conditions show that the principle use of Fulton Street will be for local circulation and that most traffic between the East Side and the World Trade Center would use Barclay-Vesey or Liberty Street with only a few trips using Fulton

In addition, as the location of a transit complex, Fulton Street is now, and will be in the future, heavily used by pedestrians. To provide increased capacity for both pedestrians and vehicles on this important artery, it is proposed that the street be widened and that the improvement include widened openings into the transit stations. Because some of the buildings between Gold Street and Broadway may prove suitable for arcading, it is proposed that the street be widened up to the building fronts on the south side and that the sidewalk on the south side be within an arcade.

The widening between Gold and Water Streets should be completed in conjunction with the Brooklyn Bridge Southwest project. West of Gold, the project could follow one of two possible courses. The first course would be for the city to proceed with property acquisition and widening and re-sell the property for redevelopment. The later course has the virtue of providing the city a means of specifying land use

**Proposed
Pedestrian
Street
With Arcade and Intra-Bus —**

Nassau Street, North of Fulton

TABLE 4

ESTIMATED DAILY COSTS — INTRA-BUS SYSTEM

AMORTIZATION = $15.00 per vehicle, per day – (5-year)

OPERATION   = $7.00 per hour, per vehicle

12 vehicles x $15.00 = $180.00

10 vehicles (operating) x $7.00 x 12-hour day = $840.00

$840.00 (operating costs) + $180.00 (amortization costs)

                              = $1020 per day total daily costs

                    $1020 = 10,200 ten-cent fares*

                              or

                              = 20,400 five-cent fares*

* 10,200 fares per 12 hour day = 850 per hour

  20,400 fares per 12 hour day = 1700 per hour

controls at the time of sale and assisting in the assembly of property. The second course would be to widen the street as buildings on its south side are redeveloped.

John Street

As a part of the total pedestrian system, John Street between Nassau and Church Streets is proposed for conversion to a predominantly pedestrian street. The proposed Intra-bus will operate on this section as part of the Trade Center-Staten Island Ferry Loop. This section is almost ideally located for the pedestrian system on the West Side because it connects directly to the Trade Center Plaza which could ultimately be extended outward to any development in the pier area. This street should be designed with flush pavement, leaving the entire width available for pedestrian movement. All new development in the area should be required to locate access on other streets to the extent possible, and deliveries should only be allowed during early morning and late afternoon hours. During the morning and evening rush hours and mid-day, all vehicles should be excluded.

William Street

To offset the loss of capacity caused by the conversion of Nassau Street to predominantly pedestrian uses, it is recommended that William Street be widened to accommodate two parking lanes and two lanes of moving traffic. William Street is to be used primarily for service to buildings; but, with increased land use intensity in the core, movements of this kind are expected to increase. Accordingly, new buildings should be strongly encouraged to include arcades similar to that constructed on the West Side north of Maiden Lane. This improvement need not predate the conversion of Nassau Street, but it should be carried out as rapidly as redevelopment of the area will permit. Recent new developments in the section have already provided setbacks and arcades. As redevelopment continues, it should not be difficult to obtain similar improvements.

Chambers Street or Reade Street

With the completion of the Civic Center and the diversion of traffic to Warren and Murray Streets, Chambers Street should become very lightly used for vehicular movement. The complex of subway stations and the heavy movement of pedestrians along Chambers now give the street a predominantly pedestrian function. One factor which will further encourage pedestrian use of this street is the possibility of new uses for the land in the Washington Street Redevelopment Area. The subway entrances along Chambers are generally narrow, dark, and congested. To provide a more pleasant atmosphere and greater capacity for pedestrian movement, it is recommended that this street also be redesigned and paved and that subway entrances be enlarged. At such time as new uses occur in the West End, the street should become an Intra-bus route serving those uses and the Civic Center. The route could terminate in the Civic Center Plaza. Through the Plaza, connections could be made to the Brooklyn Bridge-Worth subway station, and further east, to the new Police Headquarters and the housing areas along the East Side. The Brooklyn Bridge walkway can be brought into the Plaza very naturally with the proposed roadway design, and this small pedestrian flow could be served by the Intra-bus. Chambers is already a significant shopping street; and, if housing develops on the West Side, it would be a natural location for additional retail uses. The pedestrian design of the street, together with Intra-bus service and the excellent subway service, would make it readily accessible to workers and residents alike.

Reade Street is an alternate to Chambers Street in the event that the Chambers-Warren couplet is chosen as the connection for the Brooklyn Bridge. The final decision on which of the two streets (Chambers or Reade) to use for the pedestrian connection can be made when it is clear which of the two will best fit the detailed design selected for the Civic Center.

Wall Street

The southernmost crosstown pedestrian facility is proposed for Wall Street. This location interconnects very
well with the peripheral system and with the service
streets. This would be the last element of the system
to be put into effect. Intra-bus service could be provided in a loop composed of the esplanade along the
East River, Fulton, Nassau and Wall Streets.

Madison Street

As presently planned, Madison Street would be closed
between Pearl Street and Robert F. Wagner Street,
through the Police Headquarters' site. This street, although not heavily used for arterial movement, does
provide a means of movement from the Brooklyn Bridge
Southwest Renewal Area to the north that bypasses
Water Street and the complex of intersections created
by the bridge ramp system. In addition, it serves circulation around both the proposed Police Headquarters
and the proposed parking garage. For these reasons, it
is strongly recommended that it be retained in the street
system and that it be connected under the bridge to
Gold Street.

WATERFRONT AREA

The basic purpose of the proposed waterfront circulation plan is to facilitate future residential, commercial,
and recreational development along the East and
Hudson waterfronts—a wide strip of land composed of
the rights-of-way of South and West Streets, plus a
new land fill extending out into the water several
hundred feet, and with a land area (depending on future demand) of between one and two hundred acres.
Earlier engineering studies have indicated the feasibility of such construction along the downtown waterfront.

Insofar as they now hamper access to the waterfront
area, the elevated highways were the subject of study.
After examining a number of alternative solutions—

on-grade, elevated, and depressed—it was concluded
that the solution offering the most harmonious and integrated development was a depressed highway one level
below existing grade, offshore of the existing bulkhead.
It could be built while the existing highway is in operation, would be on city-owned land, and would be free
of utilities and other encumbrances.

To provide for the servicing of adjacent development
areas on both sides of the below-grade expressway,
parallel service roads will connect with inland streets
and with parking garages constructed over, or adjacent
to, the highway. Most new downtown parking facilities
will be located in this peripheral system—within easy
walking distance of the inner core and out of the way
of local service traffic.

The new waterfront will be organized around a series
of community plazas (or nodes), located at the termination of major downtown pedestrian streets (such as Wall,
Fulton, Broad, Nassau, and Chambers). These plazas
would form broad openings into the heart of the city.
They can become the focus of major retail and community services and a meeting place for neighboring
residential and office functions. Direct pedestrian
movement from the core, along pedestrian streets and
across these plazas and onto the waterfront "esplanades",
is thus made possible.

At points midway between these plaza "nodes", the
proposed service roads rise to grade, thus permitting
the necessary connections to the inland access streets
and parking facilities, along with vertical transportation into the buildings above.

This "peripheral" system has been planned for compati-
bility with that of the core. The core system is not,
however, dependent on the peripheral system, and the
first stages of its construction can be implemented immediately. The ultimate development of the waterfront
will require many years and, no doubt several phases
for its accomplishment. The interior system can extend
to meet it over time.

CHAPTER XIII

SUBWAYS

Subway Usage and Capacity

The subway system is the transportation backbone of Lower Manhattan, which area has the heaviest concentration of lines and stations in the Metropolitan Region and serves as the origin or destination for roughly 10 percent of the 4.5 million daily trips on the system. Because of the concentrations of workers, lines and stations, the subway is an efficient carrier; and its importance for the future cannot be overemphasized.

To better understand the role of this system in the overall fabric of the area, its components were examined individually and as parts of the whole. Usage and capacity were compared to determine what deficiencies exist and where there is excess capacity.

This examination showed that access to Lower Manhattan is controlled more by lack of capacity outside the area than by any lack of capacity within it. To see why this is the case, it is necessary to note the origins of subway riders destined for Lower Manhattan. These are shown in Figure 19.

Of the nearly 200,000 people who come to Lower Manhattan by subway every morning, about 80,000 come from Brooklyn, 60,000 from Manhattan, 20,000 from the Bronx, and 40,000 from Queens. Those coming from the Bronx, must first pass through Midtown where congestion is the greatest and those from Queens must traverse two bottlenecks, Midtown and the East River. In the case of those coming from Brooklyn, the capacity bottleneck is not as easily defined but it does occur in Brooklyn and not in Lower Manhattan itself.

With respect to station capacities, Lower Manhattan does not suffer from any appreciable shortage. It is true that some entrances and exits are crowded at peak hours but in general there is enough capacity to handle twice as many people as are now accommodated. Capacities of stations and lines are shown in Tables 5 and 6 and Figures 20 and 21. From these it can be seen that even with allowance for transfers the stations have adequate capacity for additional usage.

Certainly transit service within Lower Manhattan is better than it has been in the past. Patronage has declined on all lines and at all but three stations. This is apparently due to a shift in worker hours as well as a decline in total employment. It was found that although turnstile registrations declined during daylight hours they actually increased slightly during the evening and very early morning hours.

The stations in Lower Manhattan provide excellent service to the entire area. Figures 22 and 23 show the areas within three minute and five minute walks of the stations. It can be seen that Lower Manhattan enjoys much better service in this respect than does any other section of Manhattan.

In addition to the subway system, Lower Manhattan is well served by surface buses and enjoys a favored position with respect to the Staten Island Ferry and the Port Authority Trans-Hudson System (PATH). The latter is rapidly being improved in service and will have a new station in the World Trade Center. There is the additional possibility of obtaining direct service for the Long Island trains which now terminate in Brooklyn, thereby requiring a transfer for workers coming in from Nassau and Suffolk Counties.

Thus, considering growing areas from which new workers might come, Lower Manhattan enjoys a good competitive position with respect to Staten Island, New Jersey, and Long Island. It has a less favorable position with respect to areas to the north. Improved service from the north will require major improvements which will not change Lower Manhattan's competitive position with respect to Midtown for the simple reason that people coming from the north will always come through Midtown. Even so, it is quite clear that the most pressing needs for the city as a whole are relief of the congestion in the East River Crossings and the lines running north to the Bronx.

The Transit Authority has improved service considerably in recent years by the extension of station platforms to provide for longer trains. Two important improvements which are currently underway and several proposals for improved service by both physical and operational improvements are described in the following section.

Subway Improvements Under Construction

The Transit Authority has several projects under construction, which, though not in the Study Area, effect subway service to Lower Manhattan. They are part of a continuous program to improve service and capacity throughout the system.

The most important of these is the Chrystie Street interconnection, which will allow trains from the BMT Jamaica and Brighton Lines to be switched onto the IND Sixth Avenue Line, thus providing more direct express service to Midtown Manhattan from Brooklyn and South Queens. This will mean the closing of the Nassau Loop which presently serves Lower Manhattan. The new routing should, however, reduce the transfers made within the Study Area by those passengers bound ultimately for Midtown, thus reducing congestion and crowding in Lower Manhattan and on those lines passing through it. This new connection also means new and more efficient utilization of the BMT Nassau-Centre Street can be made. See Figure 24.

A project closely tied with Chrystie Street is the new deep-rock tunnel being constructed under Sixth Avenue between the West Fourth and Thirty-fourth Street stations. This will double existing capacity on the line and allow efficient usage of Chrystie Street. With fewer station stops than the existing IND, the new service should have a shorter running time to Midtown.

Another project in this series is the stub-end extension under Sixth Avenue from Fiftieth to Fifty-eighth Streets. This will provide turn-around and storage track for the new trains from Brooklyn, as well as possible connection for a new line from Queens or the Bronx.

Two new stations are being constructed as part of this series, Grand Street on the Chrystie Interconnection and Fifty-seventh Street on the Sixth Avenue stub. Grand Street will provide more access to the residential section north of the Study Area, while Fifty-seventh Street adds service to the East Midtown office district.

The only presently-scheduled improvement which is physically in Lower Manhattan is the Platform Extension Program. Upon completion of this, the IRT Seventh Avenue Line will be able to run ten-car trains,

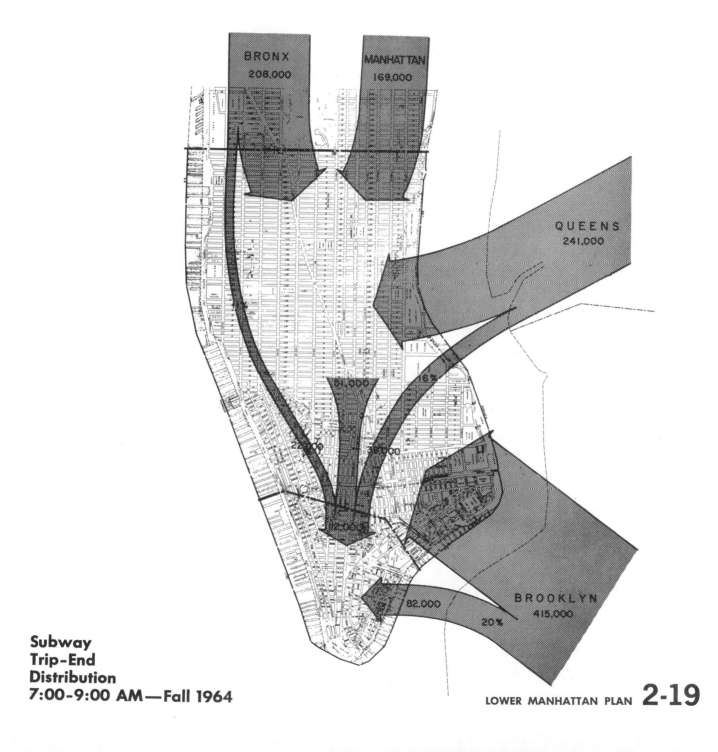

BRONX
206,000

MANHATTAN
169,000

QUEENS
241,000

16%

81,000

22,000   39,000

112,000

BROOKLYN
415,000

82,000   20%

**Subway
Trip-End
Distribution
7:00-9:00 AM—Fall 1964**

LOWER MANHATTAN PLAN **2-19**

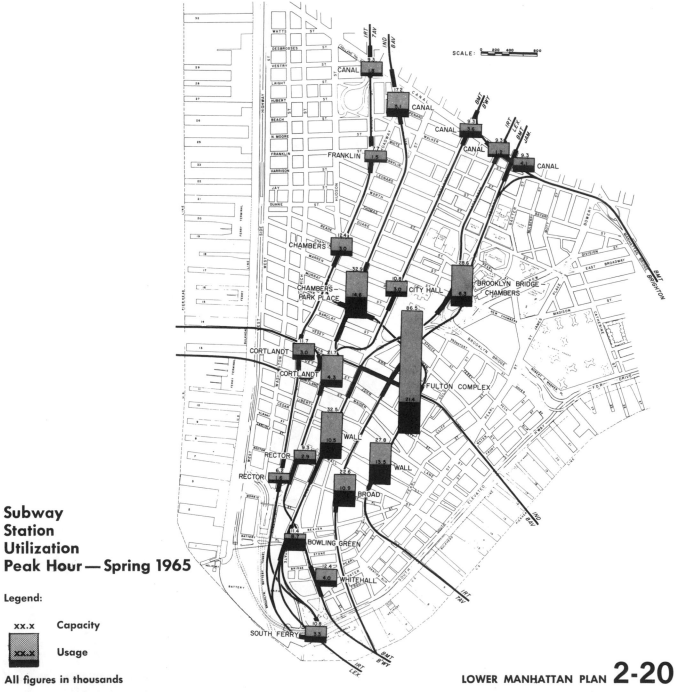

SCALE: 0   200   400   800

**Subway
Station
Utilization
Peak Hour — Spring 1965**

Legend:

xx.x   Capacity

xx.x   Usage

All figures in thousands

LOWER MANHATTAN PLAN 2-20

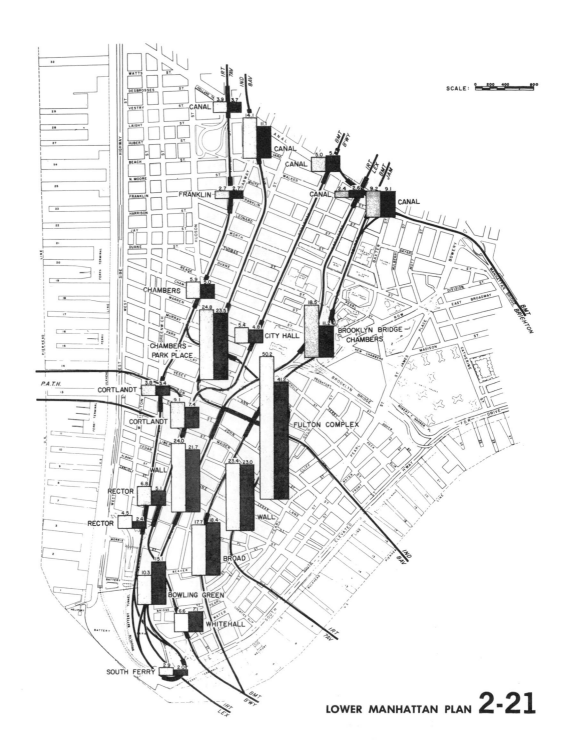

**Subway
Station
Usage
4:00-7:00 PM
1960 vs. 1965**

Legend:

1960   1965

Source: NYCTA

All figures in thousands

LOWER MANHATTAN PLAN **2-21**

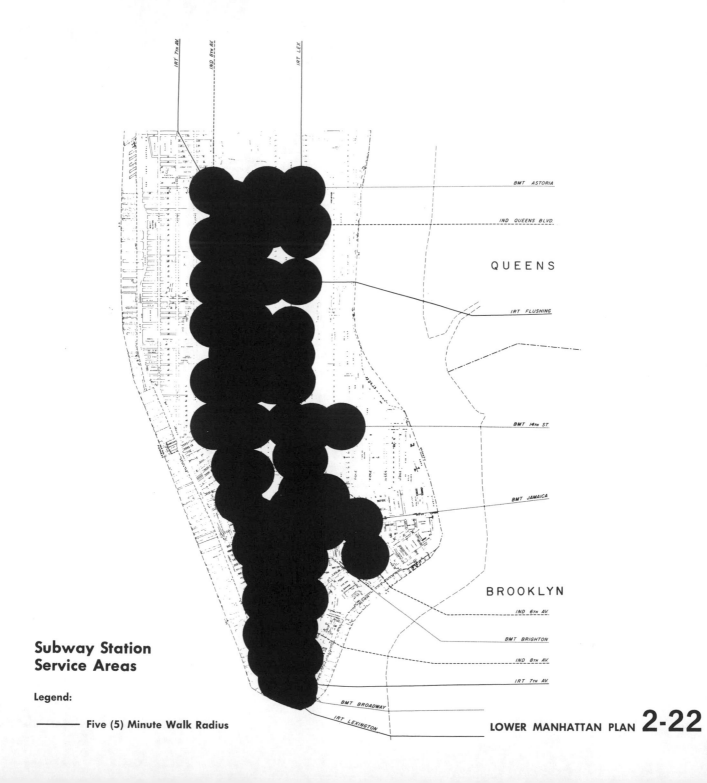

IRT 7TH AV

IND 8TH AV

IRT LEX

BMT ASTORIA

IND QUEENS BLVD.

QUEENS

IRT FLUSHING

BMT 14TH ST.

BMT JAMAICA

BROOKLYN

IND 6TH AV.

BMT BRIGHTON

IND 8TH AV.

IRT 7TH AV.

BMT BROADWAY

IRT LEXINGTON

**Subway Station
Service Areas**

Legend:

———— Five (5) Minute Walk Radius

LOWER MANHATTAN PLAN **2-22**

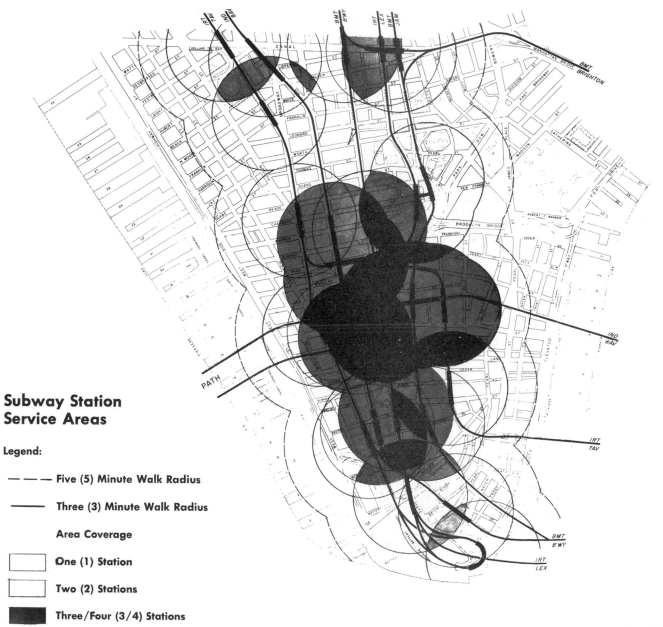

SCALE: 0 200 400 80[0]

Subway Station Service Areas

Legend:

— — — Five (5) Minute Walk Radius

———— Three (3) Minute Walk Radius

Area Coverage

One (1) Station

Two (2) Stations

Three/Four (3/4) Stations

Five (5) or more Stations

LOWER MANHATTAN PLAN **2-23**

TABLE 5

STATION LOAD/CAPACITY — PEAK HOUR — SPRING 1965

Station	Cap.	Load		Excess
Bowling Green-IRT	11.4	8.7		2.7
Broad St.-BMT	22.6	10.9		11.7
Canal St.-IRT 7Av	9.3	1.8		7.4
Canal St.-IND 8Av	28.2	5.1		23.1
Canal St.-BMT Bwy	9.3	3.6		5.7
Canal St.-IRT Lex	9.3	1.2		8.1
Canal St.-BMT Nas	9.3	4.1		5.2
Chambers St.-IRT	12.4	3.0		9.4
City Hall-BMT Bwy	10.8	3.0		7.8
Cortlandt St.-BMT	21.7	1.9		19.8
Cortlandt St.-IRT	11.7	4.3		7.4
Franklin St.-IRT	7.8	1.5		6.3
Rector St.-BMT	9.3	1.6		7.7
Rector St.-IRT	6.2	2.9		3.3
South Ferry-IRT	10.8	3.3		7.5
Wall St.-IRT Lex	32.5	10.4		22.1
Wall St.-IRT 7Av	27.8	13.5		14.3
Whitehall St.-BMT	12.4	4.0		8.4
TRANSFER STATIONS				
Brooklyn Bridge	28.6	12.6	(6.3)	16.0
Chambers St/Park Place	32.9	26.6	(13.3)	6.3
Fulton Complex	86.5	42.8	(21.4)	43.7
TOTALS	410.8	166.8		244.0

(xx.x) Actual turnstile counts at inter-divisional stations.

Data (LOAD) from NYCTA

All figures in thousands.

TABLE 6

Line/Cordon	Peak 20-min. load	Functional Capacity			Operational Capacity			Comfort Capacity			Defi-ciency
			Excess			Excess			Excess		
		Cap.	20 min.	1 hour	Cap.	20 min.	1 hour	Cap.	20 min.	1 hour	
East River from Brooklyn											
IRT Lex X	9.3	16.8	7.5	19.5	13.9	4.6	12.0	11.8	2.5	6.5	
7Av X	9.6	15.1	5.5	14.3	12.5	2.9	7.5	10.6	1.0	2.6	
IND 8Av X	17.4	24.0	6.6	17.1	19.7	2.3	6.0	16.7	-0.7	-0.7	*
6Av X	5.7	24.0	18.3	47.6	19.7	14.0	36.4	16.7	11.0	24.8	
BMT Bwy X	20.0	19.2	-0.8	-0.8	15.8	-4.2	-4.2	13.4	-6.6	-6.6	***
Bwy L	9.0	13.4	4.4	11.4	11.1	2.1	5.5	9.4	0.4	1.0	
Nassau Loop	5.3	5.8	0.5	1.3	4.8	-0.5	-0.5	4.1	-1.2	-1.2	**
Jamaica X/L	10.7	19.2	8.5	22.1	15.8	5.1	13.2	13.4	2.7	7.0	
14th St. L	7.3	19.2	11.9	31.2	15.8	8.5	22.1	13.4	6.1	15.8	
East River from Queens											
IRT Flushing X/L	17.0	18.5	1.5	3.9	15.3	-1.7	-1.7	13.0	-4.0	-4.0	**
IND Queens Blvd. X	23.7	24.0	0.3	0.8	19.7	-4.0	-4.0	16.7	-7.0	-7.0	**
BMT Astoria X/L	8.7	11.5	2.8	7.3	9.5	0.8	2.1	8.1	-0.6	-0.6	*
4th Av L	7.7	7.7	-0-	-0-	6.3	-1.4	-1.4	5.6	-2.1	-2.1	**
60th Street from North											
IRT Lex X	19.0	16.8	-2.2	-2.2	13.9	-5.1	-5.1	11.8	-7.3	-7.2	***
Lex L	13.7	16.8	3.1	8.1	13.9	0.2	0.5	11.8	-1.9	-1.9	*
7Av X	10.8	15.1	4.3	11.2	12.5	1.7	4.4	10.6	-0.2	-0.2	*
7Av L	10.9	13.4	2.5	6.5	11.1	0.2	0.5	9.4	-1.5	-1.5	*
IND 8Av X	23.8	24.0	0.2	0.5	19.7	-4.1	-4.1	16.7	-7.1	-7.1	**
8Av L	9.4	24.0	14.6	37.9	19.7	10.3	26.8	16.7	7.3	7.3	
Canal Street from North											
IRT Lex X	10.9	16.8	5.1	13.3	13.9	3.0	7.8	11.8	0.9	2.3	
Lex L	0.7	16.8	16.1	42.0	13.9	13.2	34.4	11.8	11.1	28.9	
7Av X	8.7	15.1	6.4	16.7	12.5	3.8	9.9	10.6	1.9	4.9	
7Av L	0.6	13.4	12.8	33.4	11.1	10.5	27.4	9.4	8.8	23.0	
IND 8Av X	8.9	24.0	15.1	39.4	19.7	10.8	28.2	16.7	7.8	20.3	
8Av L	1.0	24.0	23.0	60.0	19.7	18.7	48.7	16.7	15.7	41.0	
BMT Bwy L	2.8	13.4	10.6	27.6	11.1	8.3	21.0	9.4	6.6	17.2	
Jamaica	9.9	19.2	9.3	24.2	15.8	5.9	15.4	13.4	3.5	9.1	
Canal Street from South											
IRT Lex X	9.1	16.8	7.7	20.0	13.9	4.8	12.5	11.8	2.7	7.0	
Lex L	2.4	16.8	14.4	37.5	13.9	11.5	30.0	11.8	9.4	24.5	
7Av X	5.3	15.1	9.8	25.5	12.5	7.2	18.7	10.6	5.3	13.8	
7Av L	1.5	13.4	11.9	31.0	11.1	9.6	25.0	9.4	7.9	20.6	
IND 8Av X	7.8	24.0	16.2	42.0	19.7	12.9	33.5	16.7	8.9	23.1	
8Av L	0.7	24.0	23.3	60.5	19.7	19.0	49.4	16.7	16.0	41.6	
BMT Bwy L	5.0	13.4	8.4	21.8	11.1	6.1	15.8	9.4	4.4	11.4	
Jamaica	0.4	19.2	18.8	48.8	15.8	15.4	40.0	13.4	13.0	33.8	

* Deficiency at Comfort Capacity only.

** Deficiencies at Operational and Comfort Capacities.

*** Deficiencies at all capacities.

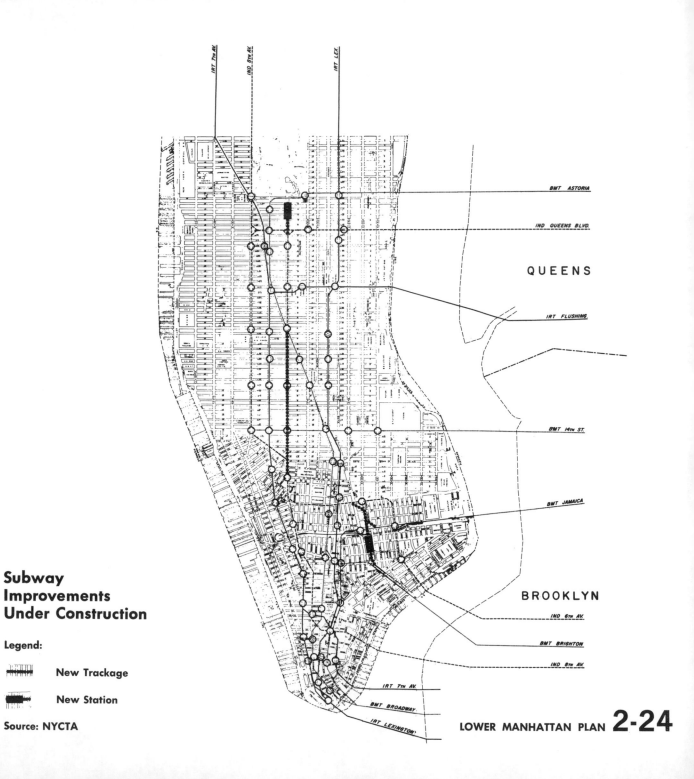

IRT 7th AV.
IND. 8th AV.
IRT LEX.

BMT ASTORIA

IND. QUEENS BLVD.

QUEENS

IRT FLUSHING

BMT 14th ST.

BMT JAMAICA

BROOKLYN

IND. 6th AV.

BMT BRIGHTON

IND. 8th AV.

IRT 7th AV.

BMT BROADWAY

IRT LEXINGTON

**Subway
Improvements
Under Construction**

Legend:

New Trackage

New Station

Source: NYCTA

LOWER MANHATTAN PLAN **2-24**

instead of eight and nine, as at present. Following the modification of the IRT Stations, BMT Lines will get the same treatment, also providing for ten-car trains in place of the existing eight. Capacity on these lines will increase by 11 to 25 percent as a result of these platform modifications.

Proposed Subway Construction

There are, at present, many proposals for new subway lines and stations in the Metropolitan Area (Figure 25.) Like the projects now under construction, they will be mainly outside of Lower Manhattan, but would effect the level of service to it.

The two problems demanding immediate solution, congestion at the East River from Queens and into Midtown from the north, have been studied from many points of view. A new tunnel under the River seems to be the only solution for the former, while a new line from the Bronx, which could run under Second Avenue or through Central Park, is the logical answer to the latter.

There are several alternative means of connecting these proposed lines with the existing system and with other new lines. The new IND Sixth Avenue trackage, which has extra capacity into the CBD and Brooklyn, and the Broadway BMT, which is 4-track from 57th Street south, are capable of handling the 30 express trains per hour which would be brought into Midtown by either of these new lines. Two other possibilities require new construction. One is a line under Madison Avenue, running south to Madison Square, joining the BMT there for eventual distribution in Brooklyn. The other is a new line under Second Avenue and Water Street. Presently proposed as a stub-end in Lower Manhattan, it could be extended to Brooklyn or Staten Island at a later date if such is warranted.

Another proposal is a connection between the subway system and the Long Island Railroad. Since this could be done in either Brooklyn or Queens and would provide a great extension of service at minimal cost, the project would appear to have distinct merit. From Brooklyn, trains would cross the River on the Manhattan Bridge, turn into Lower Manhattan on the BMT Nassau-Centre Street tracks, and dead-end at a terminal under Broad Street at either Wall or Water Streets. A continuous-loop arrangement exiting through the Montague Street tunnel has also been considered, but this would restrict the capacity of the BMT Broadway Local Line to carry the heavier share of the Brooklyn-Lower Manhattan traffic placed on it by the closing of the Nassau Loop.

The Queens Connection is much less definite, since it would involve a connection under the East River. If construction of a subway tunnel were to greatly precede the completion of a new line into Northern Queens, this connection would provide good interim service, offering, as it does, all of the alternative connections in Manhattan that the tunnel would provide.

Any of these proposals would drastically change the transit picture for Lower Manhattan. The excess capacity presently available from Midtown to Downtown could be used by a portion of the additional riders coming into Midtown from the North and Queens. This would effectively increase the accessibility of Lower Manhattan to prospective employees.

Subway Recommendations

Improvements to the subway system in New York City can only be made as part of an overall strategy for meeting the needs of all users in all sections of the city. Clearly, this is, and will continue to be, a difficult, costly and complex process. It should take into account the origins and destinations of people, their desires for service, potential shifts in residence and employment, and the possibilities of new technology in construction methods, equipment and operations. It also will be governed by the availability of funds. While State and Federal funds may become more plentiful, it is obvious that the limited financing available now permits only selected improvements in the immediate future.

Although this study could not go into broad transportation planning, it is clear from the findings that there are urgent needs outside Lower Manhattan. It is equally clear that Lower Manhattan enjoys relatively good service now and that it would benefit from improvements which would cut congestion into Midtown from Queens and from the north. Therefore, no new line construction in Lower Manhattan can be recommended at this time. (See Appendix B.)

However, the quality of service at many stations in Lower Manhattan could be materially improved at modest cost. Opportunities for these improvements exist where street improvements, station changes and new construction are proposed. Station entrances and exits on Fulton Street, Nassau and Broad Streets could be made in conjunction with conversion of those streets to pedestrain ways and as part of overall improvements to the Nassau Loop if Long Island trains are brought into downtown.

While it is not possible to recommend a new subway line for the near future, it is entirely possible that a new line will become practical and desirable in the long range. The most probable location for this line would be Water Street. In planning for development of the east side, care was taken to accommodate that route. The precise form such a subway might take would depend on many factors, including its connections to the system, and the state of technology at the time of construction.

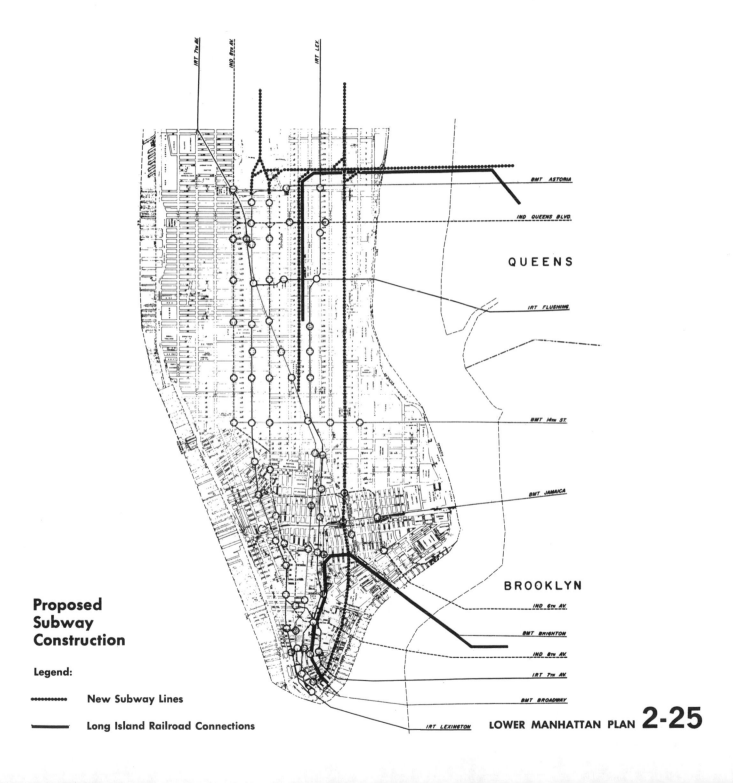

**Proposed
Subway
Construction**

Legend:

••••••••••• New Subway Lines

——— Long Island Railroad Connections

QUEENS

BROOKLYN

IRT 7TH AK
IND 8TH AK
IRT LEX

BMT ASTORIA
IND QUEENS BLVD.
IRT FLUSHING
BMT 14TH ST.
BMT JAMAICA
IND 6TH AV.
BMT BRIGHTON
IND 8TH AV.
IRT 7TH AV.
BMT BROADWAY
IRT LEXINGTON

LOWER MANHATTAN PLAN **2-25**

APPENDICES

APPENDIX A

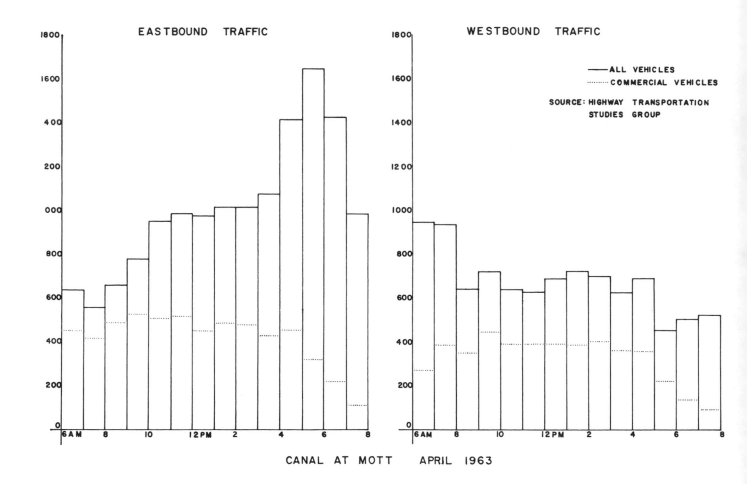

EASTBOUND TRAFFIC

WESTBOUND TRAFFIC

——ALL VEHICLES
·········COMMERCIAL VEHICLES

SOURCE: HIGHWAY TRANSPORTATION
STUDIES GROUP

CANAL AT MOTT   APRIL 1963

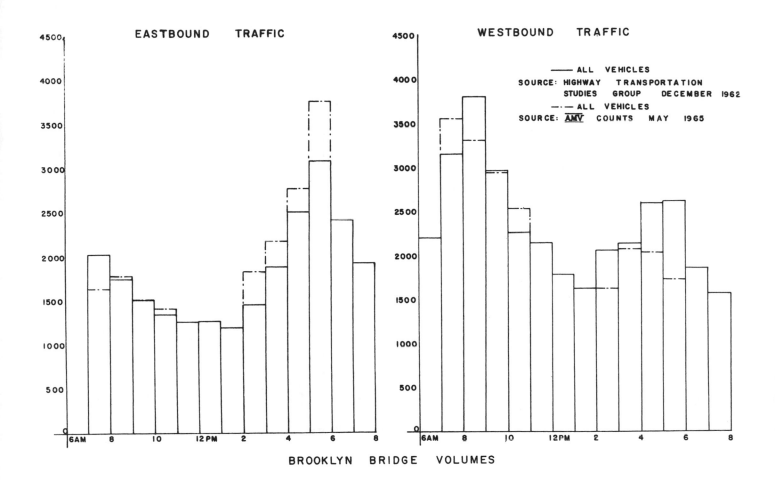

EASTBOUND   TRAFFIC

WESTBOUND   TRAFFIC

— ALL VEHICLES
SOURCE: HIGHWAY   TRANSPORTATION
STUDIES   GROUP   DECEMBER 1962
— ALL VEHICLES
SOURCE: AMV   COUNTS   MAY   1965

BROOKLYN   BRIDGE   VOLUMES

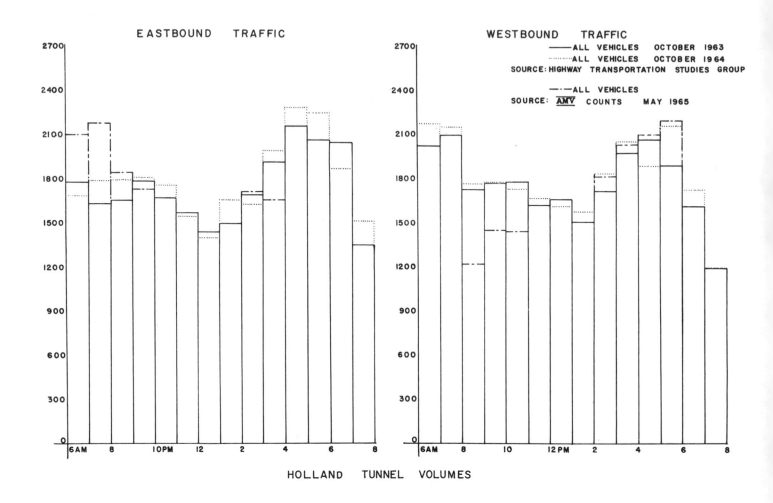

EASTBOUND   TRAFFIC

WESTBOUND   TRAFFIC

ALL VEHICLES   OCTOBER 1963
ALL VEHICLES   OCTOBER 1964
SOURCE: HIGHWAY TRANSPORTATION STUDIES GROUP

ALL VEHICLES
SOURCE: AMV COUNTS   MAY 1965

HOLLAND   TUNNEL   VOLUMES

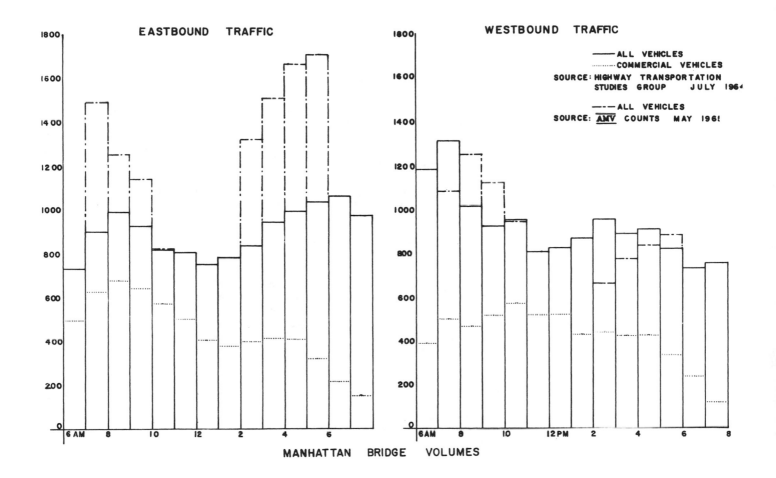

EASTBOUND TRAFFIC

WESTBOUND TRAFFIC

ALL VEHICLES
COMMERCIAL VEHICLES
SOURCE: HIGHWAY TRANSPORTATION
STUDIES GROUP JULY 1964

ALL VEHICLES
SOURCE: AMV COUNTS MAY 196!

MANHATTAN BRIDGE VOLUMES

CAPACITY STUDY

To measure the capacity of the streets in Lower Manhattan, nineteen (19) critical signalized intersections were selected to make complete studies of in order to determine the amount of vehicles
that can pass through the intersection during the peak requirements for the area. These 19 critical
intersections represent the major and minor streets of the system and therefore the system's capacity
can be determined by looking at the capacity of the critical intersections.

Capacity was calculated using procedures outlined in the new Highway Research Board Capacity
Manual. This manual has not been published but the draft was available to the consultants.

The methods and techniques in this new capacity manual have been tested in other cities and found
to give results that compared with the actual conditions of the area.

However, New York City is unique with its traffic patterns. It was, therefore, decided to make
a study to test the applicability of the curves and factors as outlined in the capacity manual.

To make this test, actual conditions were observed at the 19 selected intersections to measure the
level of service that each approach was operating under. This level of service is measured quanti-
tatively by observing how many signal cycles within the peak hour of the approach are fully utilized. The signal cycle was defined as being fully utilized if there were vehicles waiting at the
start of the green phase, and if there were no appreciable gaps between the vehicles in all lanes
of the approach during the entire green phase. The ratio of fully utilized green phases to the
total number of green phases is termed the "load factor." In addition to the load factor measure-
ment, parking practices within the blocks leading to the approach were recorded during the peak
hour.

Using the observed conditions, the capacity of each approach was calculated using the techniques
outlined in the new capacity manual. The capacities were compared to the actual volumes
measured and were found to compare favorably. It was thus decided that these techniques could
be used in New York City.

The actual practical capacity of each approach is a function of the level of service desired which
is indicated by the load factor. This load factor can vary from 0.0 to 1.0 where 0.0 is the ideal
with no fully utilized signal cycles and 1.0 indicates that the maximum number of vehicles are
getting through the intersection but that heavy queuing is the probable result.

It has been found that a tolerable level of service on approaches of isolated intersections is a load
factor of 0.20. At an intersection that is a part of a suitable progressive signal system with pla-
tooning of vehicles created by the previous signal, the result is a tolerable load factor of 0.80.

These two load factors were used in Lower Manhattan to calculate the capacity of the approaches. The factor of 0.20 was used for all minor street approaches into major streets and for most non-progressive streets. The factor of 0.80 was used for all major one-way streets with progressive signal systems.

Canal Street was considered an exception since there are plans for relieving it with the Lower Manhattan Expressway. A load factor of 0.40 was used here.

These load factors were used in calculating practical capacity if the volumes equaled or approached theoretical capacity, resulting in considerable delay to vehicles. These reflect the best operating conditions obtainable on the street. Figure 30 shows the curves used to obtain capacity per hour of green time on the different types of streets. Graph 1 is with a load factor of 0.20 and Graph 2 is with a load factor of 0.80.

Parking along approaches reduces capacity and there is an apparent problem of illegal parking during the peak hours in this area. This has the effect of reducing the capacity of the approach below what it is intended to be. Thus two capacities for each approach were calculated, one with observed parking practices and one with parking conditions as reflected by the signs along the approach. These are shown in Figures 4 and 5.

Table 1 lists the intersections and the approaches where capacity was calculated. It compares the two capacity figures with the measured peak hour volume and all deficiencies are marked with an X.

It can be seen from Table 1 that the following streets have capacity deficiencies even with parking strictly enforced.

> Canal Street
> Church Street, south of Fulton
> The Bowery at Canal
> Chambers Street
> Fulton Street
> Worth Street at Centre Street
> Park Row at New Chambers
> New Chambers Street

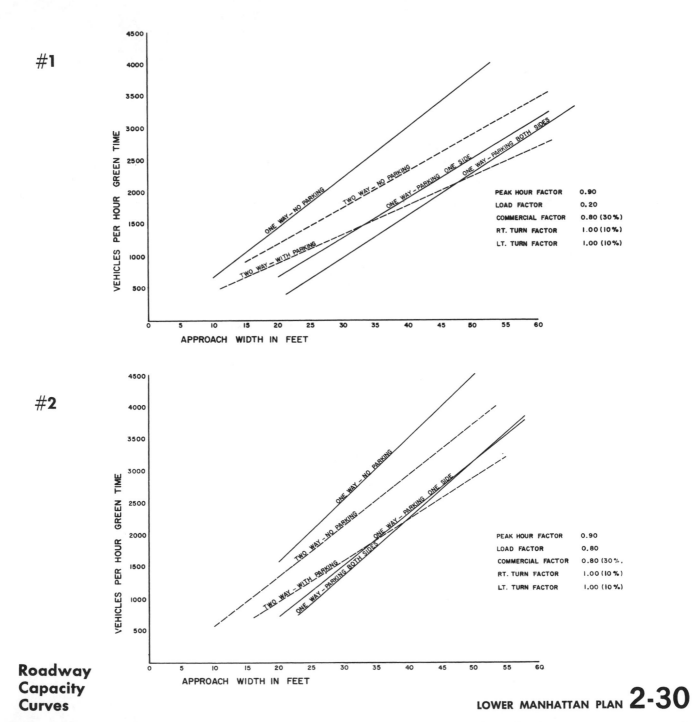

#1

VEHICLES PER HOUR GREEN TIME

ONE WAY - NO PARKING

TWO WAY - NO PARKING

ONE WAY - PARKING ONE SIDE

ONE WAY - PARKING BOTH SIDES

TWO WAY - WITH PARKING

PEAK HOUR FACTOR	0.90
LOAD FACTOR	0.20
COMMERCIAL FACTOR	0.80 (30%)
RT. TURN FACTOR	1.00 (10%)
LT. TURN FACTOR	1.00 (10%)

APPROACH WIDTH IN FEET

#2

VEHICLES PER HOUR GREEN TIME

ONE WAY - NO PARKING

TWO WAY - NO PARKING

ONE WAY - PARKING ONE SIDE

TWO WAY - WITH PARKING

ONE WAY - PARKING BOTH SIDES

PEAK HOUR FACTOR	0.90
LOAD FACTOR	0.80
COMMERCIAL FACTOR	0.80 (30%)
RT. TURN FACTOR	1.00 (10%)
LT. TURN FACTOR	1.00 (10%)

APPROACH WIDTH IN FEET

**Roadway
Capacity
Curves**

LOWER MANHATTAN PLAN **2-30**

TABLE I

Intersection	Approach	Capacity Per Hour in Vehicles		Present Peak Hr. Volume	Capacity Deficiencies	
		Parking Practices	Legal Parking		Parking Practices	Legal Parking
Canal & Broadway	North	1,020	1,480	833		
	East	760	1,030	668		
	West	450	800	759	X	
Chambers & Broadway	North	1,020	1,060	859		
	East	600	600	571		
	West	420	585	453	X	
Broadway & Barclay	North	1,630	1,650	1,156		
	East	1,800	1,800	1,192		
Broadway & Vesey	North	1,610	1,610	1,383		
	West	580	1,160	526		
Fulton & Church	South	750	750	1,077	X	X
	East	220	220	400	X	X
	West	210	210	259	X	X
Church & Warren	South	1,930	1,930	1,260		
	West	530	850	467		
Church & Chambers	South	1,610	1,610	1,564		
	East	530	530	628	X	X
	West	330	440	323	X	
Chambers & West Broadway	North	1,420	1,420	869		
	East	460	460	449		
	West	300	300	114		
Greenwich, Vesey & W. Broadway	North	960	1,400	241		
	Northeast	1,460	1,460	657		
	West	570	570	171		
Greenwich & Liberty	North	450	1,550	455		
	West	450	770	134		
Barclay & West	East	390	390	246		
Chambers & West	West	280	280	306	X	X
Canal & Hudson	South	980	1,330	972	X	X
	East	820	820	973		
	West	650	650	853	X	X
Lafayette & Leonard	North	1,500	1,500	252		
	East	360	360	109		
Centre & Worth	South	1,630	1,630	834		
	East	310	310	479	X	X
	West	420	420	336		
Centre & Chambers	North	1,790	1,790	1,176		
	East	530	530	508		
	West	730	730	487		
Park Row & New Chambers	North	450	450	572	X	X
	South	300	300	616	X	X
	East	740	740	1,057	X	X
	West	3,900	3,900	925		
Fulton & Water	North	1,130	1,130	493		
	South	1,130	1,130	906		
	East	430	430	143		
	West	270	270	56		
Canal & Bowery	North	300	300	334	X	X
	South	430	430	646	X	X
	East	1,440	1,440	727		
	West	1,060	1,060	1,067	X	X

**Parking Facility
Study Map**

Legend:

M   Metered Curb

L   Lot

G   Garage Structure

LOWER MANHATTAN PLAN **2-31**

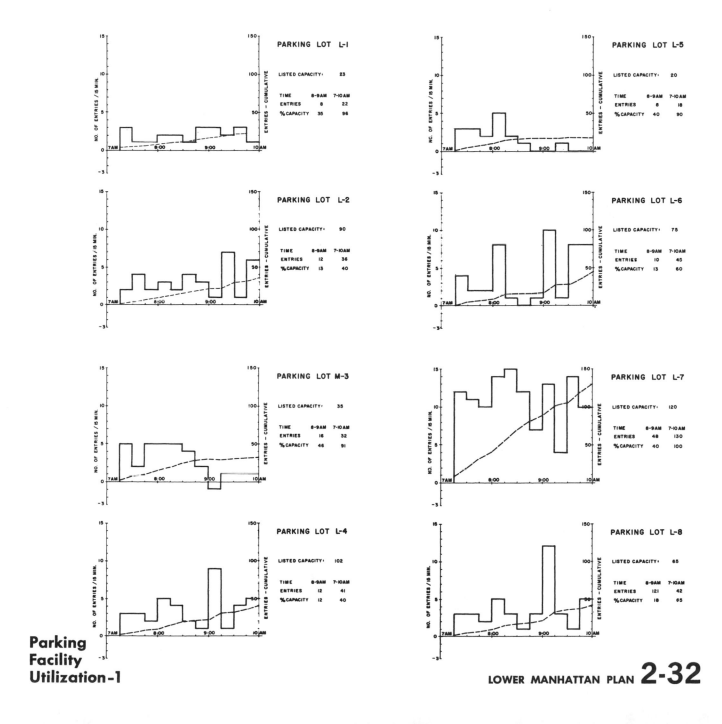

PARKING LOT L-1

LISTED CAPACITY: 23

TIME	8-9AM	7-10AM
ENTRIES	8	22
%CAPACITY	35	96

PARKING LOT L-5

LISTED CAPACITY: 20

TIME	8-9AM	7-10AM
ENTRIES	8	18
%CAPACITY	40	90

PARKING LOT L-2

LISTED CAPACITY: 90

TIME	8-9AM	7-10AM
ENTRIES	12	36
%CAPACITY	13	40

PARKING LOT L-6

LISTED CAPACITY: 75

TIME	8-9AM	7-10AM
ENTRIES	10	45
%CAPACITY	13	60

PARKING LOT M-3

LISTED CAPACITY: 35

TIME	8-9AM	7-10AM
ENTRIES	16	32
%CAPACITY	46	91

PARKING LOT L-7

LISTED CAPACITY: 120

TIME	8-9AM	7-10AM
ENTRIES	48	130
%CAPACITY	40	100

PARKING LOT L-4

LISTED CAPACITY: 102

TIME	8-9AM	7-10AM
ENTRIES	12	41
%CAPACITY	12	40

PARKING LOT L-8

LISTED CAPACITY: 65

TIME	8-9AM	7-10AM
ENTRIES	121	42
%CAPACITY	18	65

**Parking
Facility
Utilization-1**

LOWER MANHATTAN PLAN **2-32**

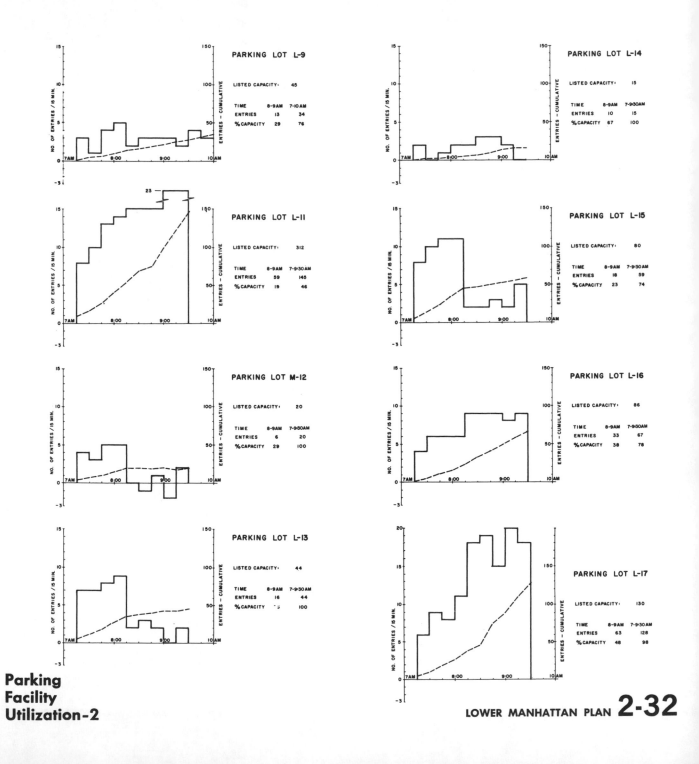

**Parking
Facility
Utilization-2**

LOWER MANHATTAN PLAN **2-32**

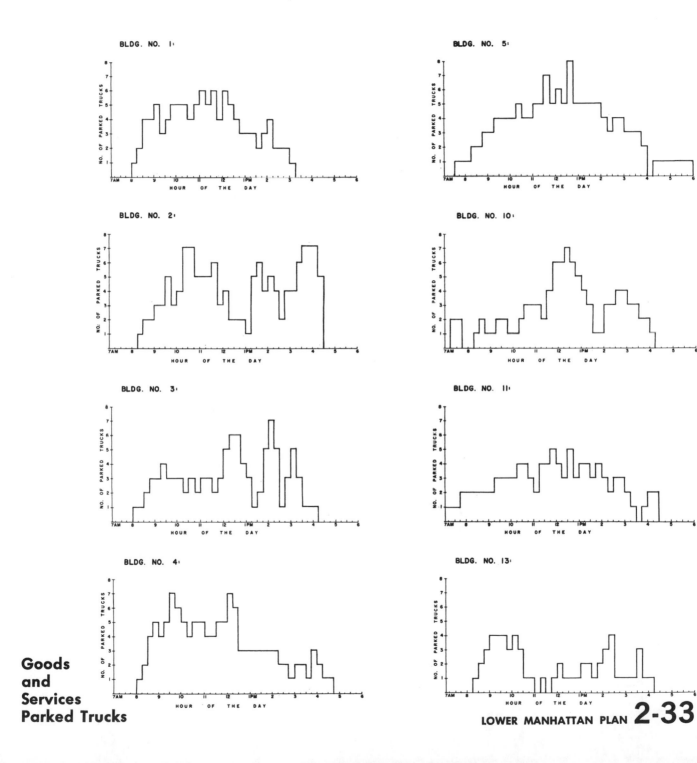

**Goods
and
Services
Parked Trucks**

LOWER MANHATTAN PLAN **2-33**

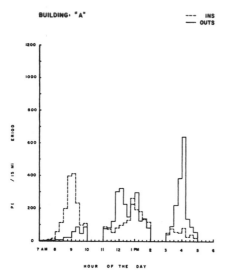

BUILDING: "A"

- - - INS
——— OUTS

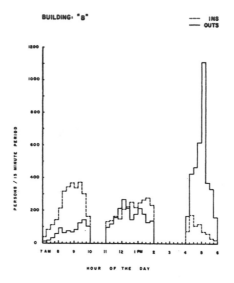

BUILDING: "B"

- - - INS
——— OUTS

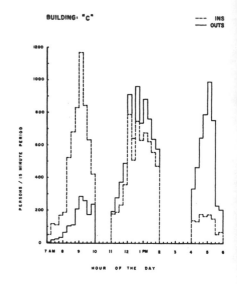

BUILDING: "C"

- - - INS
——— OUTS

**Pedestrian
Door
Counts**

APPENDIX B

TURNSTILE REGISTRATIONS

The following are the actual entering registrations at each of the stations within the Study Area. Taken twice a year, they are usually in March and October and are tabulated on an hourly basis for a twenty-four (24) hour period. They were used in this Project to show ridership trends and for comparison against the accretions and drops of the Cordon Counts.

The only real problem with Turnstile Counts is that they do not include school children, Transit Authority employees, and other pass-using groups. In Lower Manhattan, this is not a significant total and, therefore, these counts are considered the most accurate bases available.

Each of the twenty-one (21) stations within the Study Area is shown for the P.M. Peak Period, 4-7 p.m., and for the twenty-four (24) hours. The counts for spring 1960 and 1965 are shown on the following table and graphically on Figure 21. The same data for Midtown and the Valley are compared also with Lower Manhattan in Table 2.

The trend in Lower Manhattan is a slow, steady decline. This shows that there is a decrease in the number of people employed in the area, and/or that there is a definite mode shift for the journey to work, particularly during the normal work day. There is an absolute increase of some 8,000 registrations for the hours of 7 p.m. to 7 a.m., which shows an increase in the nighttime population. This does not make up the entire daytime drop, but may explain part of it. Privately-owned automobiles should be more popular at night due to the lifting of curb parking restrictions and lack of congestion.

In general, there is real growth in Eastern Midtown and general decline in Lower Manhattan. The three stations which show gains of 500 or more during the Peak Period are grouped in the southern part of the Study Area, where most of the new construction is taking place and where the most definite plans have been formulated.

Figure 37 shows the hourly distribution, expressed as a percentage of the daily total. This is an average of ten stations in Lower Manhattan.

TABLE 1

TURNSTILE REGISTRATION COMPARISON – DAILY TOTAL 1960/1965

Station	1960	1965	✓/-
Bowling Green IRT	25.3	25.8	✓0.5
Broad St. BMT	23.5	22.5	-1.0
Canal St. IRT 7Av	7.8	6.6	-1.2
Canal St. IND 8Av	20.7	19.8	-0.9
Canal St. BMT Bwy	9.7	9.5	-0.2
Canal St. IRT Lex	3.8	3.8	0.0
Canal St. BMT Nas	19.3	21.0	✓1.7
Chambers St. IRT	12.6	10.8	-1.8
City Hall BMT	9.8	9.8	0.0
Cortlandt St. BMT	17.1	14.2	-2.9
Cortlandt St. IRT	9.5	8.2	-1.3
Franklin St. IRT	4.8	4.6	-0.2
Rector St. BMT	11.1	10.7	-0.4
Rector St. IRT	7.7	7.9	✓0.2
South Ferry IRT	14.4	13.4	-1.0
Wall St. IRT Lex	36.5	34.1	-2.4
Wall St. IRT 7Av	34.3	33.8	-0.5
Whitehall St. BMT	13.7	13.7	0.0
TRANSFER STATIONS			
Brooklyn Bridge	35.5	28.3	-7.2
Chambers St-Park Pl	47.7	44.9	-2.8
Fulton Complex	79.7	70.8	-8.9
TOTAL	444.5	414.2	-30.3

Data from NYCTA Turnstile Counts

All figures in thousands

TABLE 2

TURNSTILE REGISTRATION COMPARISON – MIDTOWN 1960/1965

Station	1960	1965	⟋/–
Astor Place IRT Lex	7.3	7.4	⟋0.1
Bleeker St. IRT Lex	5.6	5.4	–0.2
Bowery BMT Nassau	1.3	.6	–0.7
Broadway IND 6Av	8.0	7.4	–0.6
Christopher St. IRT 7Av	1.9	1.9	0.0
E. Broadway IND 6Av	3.2	3.1	–0.1
Grand Central IRT	72.0	79.3	⟋7.3
Houston St. IRT 7Av	8.0	7.9	–0.1
Lexington Av IND QB	11.6	17.3	⟋5.7
Prince St. BMT Bwy	5.3	5.6	⟋0.3
Spring St. IND 8Av	6.4	4.8	–1.6
Spring St. IRT Lex	4.7	3.5	–1.2
1st Av BMT 14th	2.4	2.2	–0.2
3rd Av BMT 14th	1.6	1.4	–0.2
2nd Av IND 6Av	2.1	1.7	–0.4
5th Av IND QB	18.9	22.7	⟋3.8
5th Av IRT Flushing	11.1	11.8	⟋0.7
5th Av BMT Bwy	7.7	11.6	⟋3.9
7th Av IND Queens Bl.	3.6	5.5	⟋1.9
W 4th St. IND 8Av	8.1	7.9	–0.2
8th St. BMT Bwy	7.5	7.4	–0.1
14th St. IRT 7Av	7.8	7.8	0.0
14th St. IND 6Av	11.2	10.2	–1.0
18th St. IRT 7Av	4.4	4.2	–0.2
23rd St. IND 8Av	7.7	7.2	–0.5
23rd St. IND 6Av	18.7	15.1	–3.6
23rd St. IRT 7Av	7.7	8.1	⟋0.4
23rd St. IRT Lex	20.0	18.9	–1.1
23rd St. BMT Bwy	14.6	15.6	⟋1.0
28th St. IRT 7Av	10.5	7.3	–3.2
28th St. IRT Lex	14.5	14.7	⟋0.2
28th St. BMT Bwy	7.6	8.0	⟋0.4
33rd St. IRT Lex	15.1	15.3	⟋0.2
34th St. IND 8Av	28.5	23.1	–5.4
34th St. IRT 7Av	31.7	27.6	–4.1
42nd St. IND 8Av	24.5	21.8	–2.7

TABLE 2 (Cont.)

Station	1960	1965	+/-
42nd St. IND 6Av	27.9	22.7	-5.2
49th St. BMT Bwy	8.6	11.0	+2.4
50th St. IND 8Av	5.7	5.0	-0.7
50th St. IND 6Av	29.9	35.1	+5.2
50th St. IRT 7Av	7.0	13.3	+6.3
51st St. IRT Lex	12.3	14.4	+2.1
57th St. BMT Bwy	9.8	12.9	+3.1
TRANSFER STATIONS			
Delancy-Essex	4.8	2.9	-1.9
Columbus Circle	19.1	20.4	+1.3
Lexington Av-59th St.	15.5	18.6	+3.1
Times Square-42nd St.	65.3	59.4	-5.9
Union Square-14th St.	41.3	36.1	-5.2
14th St-8th Av	12.2	12.1	-0.1
34th St.	65.4	57.0	-8.4
TOTAL	747.6	742.2	-5.4

Data from NYCTA Turnstile Counts

All figures in thousands

CORDON COUNTS

Taken each fall at major crossings, cordon counts are used by the Transit Authority as a check on scheduling and service. For a 24-hour period, in twenty-minute increments, counts are made of the number of cars and trains passing the cordon line. Estimates are made of the number of passengers on the basis of loading parameters.

These visual interpretations do have some built-in error; and the parameters are not constant, but vary from individual to individual. During this study, it was found that the counts on lines using cars of types R-16, 27, and 30 (IND and BMT) were low by approximately 10 percent. For this reason, each such count was factored by that amount for comparison with the capacity figures.

The following are the actual counts for the a.m. peak period, 8-9 a.m. at each of the major cordons for fall, 1964. The Canal Street cordon, originally taken in 1958, was updated on the basis of line differentials at the East River and 60th Street cordons.

Figure 35 shows the totals for the hour 8-9 a.m. at the river crossings. On a larger scale, Figure 36 shows the Study Area cordons for the same time period.

Cordon Counts — Fall 1964   A.M. Inbound

Line	7:00	20	40	8:00	20	40	9:00	20
60th Street from North								
IRT Lex X	10.3	15.8	15.0	19.0	17.7	14.0	7.7	4.1
Lex L	4.6	7.2	8.8	12.3	10.6	13.7	7.5	4.2
7Av X	4.7	5.9	8.9	10.8	9.1	8.1	5.6	3.2
7Av L	2.5	5.0	5.2	10.9	10.0	10.3	4.1	2.0
IND 8Av X	10.7	13.1	19.7	20.2	23.8	11.9	6.9	6.1
8Av L	2.1	4.4	5.8	7.5	9.4	7.2	2.9	1.4
East River from Queens								
IND QB X	6.9	13.2	17.8	19.1	23.7	23.4	17.1	6.5
IRT Flush.	3.4	5.5	10.2	14.4	17.0	13.0	7.2	6.0
BMT BL/WEX	3.4	5.1	7.3	8.7	8.9	6.9	3.3	2.9
4Av L	2.1	3.1	6.5	7.7	7.6	6.5	3.5	1.7
East River from Brooklyn								
IRT Lex X	3.6	5.5	7.8	9.3	6.9	5.3	8.0	3.8
7Av X	2.1	3.5	4.3	6.6	9.6	8.4	3.4	2.5
IND 8Av X	5.8	7.8	14.2	16.0	17.4	13.2	5.8	3.3
6Av X	2.5	3.5	5.0	5.6	5.7	.4.4	2.0	1.4
BMT Bwy X	6.2	8.9	14.2	15.8	17.3	20.0	8.7	5.5
Bwy L	2.9	3.4	4.3	7.9	8.6	9.0	3.2	1.7

Cordon Counts — Fall 1964   A.M. Outbound

Line	7:00	20	40	8:00	20	40	9:00	20
60th Street from North								
IRT Lex X	2.2	2.3	2.0	2.0	2.1	1.0	0.7	0.6
Lex L	1.5	2.8	2.7	3.0	2.6	3.3	1.7	1.4
7Av X	0.6	0.7	0.7	0.6	0.7	0.6	0.5	0.5
7Av L	0.9	1.1	1.4	1.4	1.4	1.4	0.9	1.0
IND 8Av X	1.2	1.5	1.3	1.2	1.9	1.3	1.0	0.9
8Av L	0.1	0.6	0.4	0.4	0.3	0.4	0.4	0.4
East River to Queens								
IND QBv X	1.3	2.1	1.7	2.2	0.7	1.2	0.8	0.6
IRT Flush.	2.1	3.4	2.1	1.5	1.0	0.8	0.4	0.3
BMT BL/WEX	1.3	1.8	1.8	0.9	0.7	0.4	0.3	0.2
4Av L	0.7	1.3	0.8	0.6	0.2	0.3	0.1	0.1
East River to Brooklyn								
IRT Lex X	0.6	0.7	0.4	0.6	0.9	1.3	0.7	0.6
7Av X	0.4	0.4	0.4	0.5	0.6	0.5	0.4	0.4
IND 8Av X	1.1	2.6	1.3	1.3	1.5	0.9	0.9	0.7
6Av X	1.4	1.5	0.8	1.4	0.7	0.7	0.4	0.3
BMT Bwy X	3.1	1.9	2.3	1.8	1.0	0.8	0.6	0.4
Bwy L	0.4	0.3	0.3	0.6	0.7	0.6	0.3	0.2
NL TX	Total of 100 passengers							
NL BX	No service scheduled							
J/M	1.0	1.1	0.6	1.1	0.4	0.4	0.3	0.3

All figures in thousands.

Data from NYCTA Cordon Counts

East River from Brooklyn - (Cont'd.)

NL TX	0.4	0.7	1.1	2.1	3.6	5.3	1.4	0.6
NL BX				2.6	2.2	3.3		
14/Can.	2.2	5.5	5.4	6.5	7.3	3.9	2.2	1.5
J/M	4.9	5.9	7.7	8.4	10.7	8.3	3.2	1.8

All figures in thousands.

Data from NYCTA Cordon Counts.

Cordon Counts — Fall 1964   **A.M.** Northbound

Line	7:00	20	40	8:00	20	40	9:00	20
Canal/Chambers								
IRT Lex X	2.5	4.0	4.3	8.7	8.0	9.1	3.4	2.6
Lex L	0.8	0.9	1.5	2.2	2.4	2.0	0.8	0.6
7Av X	1.9	2.5	3.3	4.8	5.3	4.6	2.9	1.6
7Av L	0.5	0.7	1.3	1.5	1.1	1.1	0.8	0.4
IND 8Av X	3.0	3.1	5.1	7.8	1.6	6.8	4.5	0.9
8Av L	0.1	0.1	0.1	0.2	0.4	0.7	0.4	0.2
BMT Bwy L	1.2	2.2	2.3	3.6	5.0	3.2	1.7	0.7
J/M	0.4	0.4	0.3	0.4	0.3	0.2	0.2	0.2

A.M. Southbound

Line	7:00	20	40	8:00	20	40	9:00	20
Canal/Chambers								
IRT Lex X	2.7	3.5	4.2	6.2	10.9	10.9	5.2	4.2
Lex L	0.1	0.1	0.3	0.5	0.6	0.7	0.6	1.1
7Av X	1.3	1.9	3.0	3.6	5.7	8.7	4.5	2.7
7Av L	0.1	0.1	0.1	0.1	0.5	0.6	0.1	0.2
IND 8Av X	2.0	2.8	4.6	6.4	8.5	8.9	7.3	4.8
8Av L	0.2	0.4	0.2	0.8	0.9	1.0	0.8	0.8
BMT Bwy L	0.6	0.6	0.9	1.2	1.8	2.8	1.0	1.0
J/M	1.3	2.0	2.0	3.4	9.9	5.2	2.9	1.7

All Figures in thousands.

Data from NYCTA Cordon Counts.

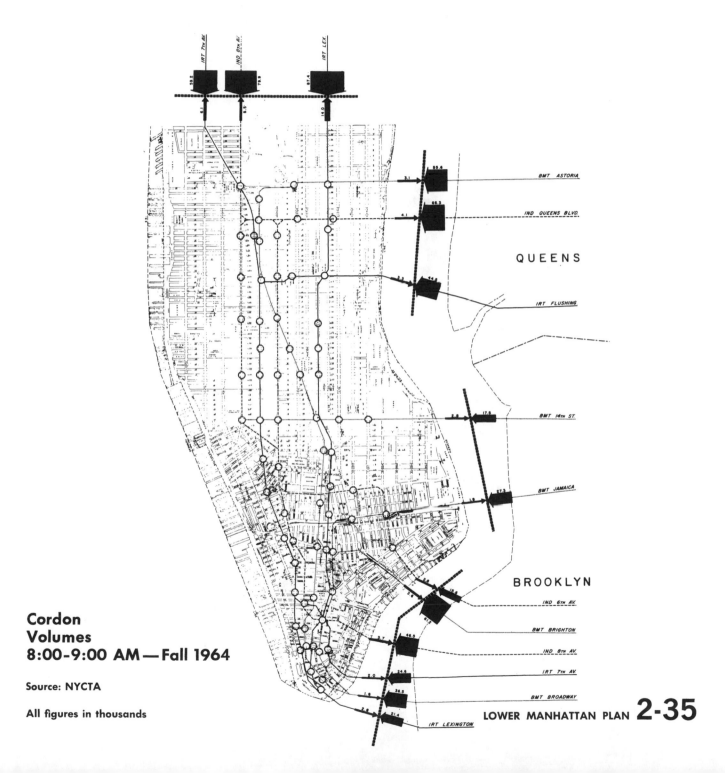

**Cordon
Volumes
8:00-9:00 AM — Fall 1964**

Source: NYCTA

All figures in thousands

LOWER MANHATTAN PLAN **2-35**

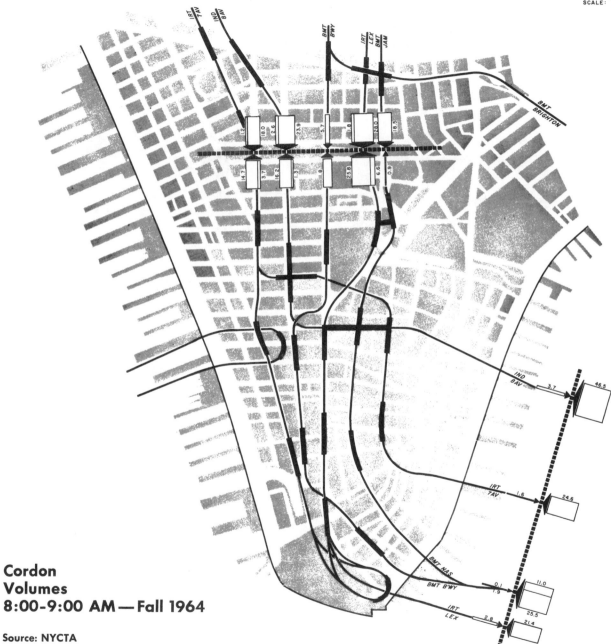

SCALE: 0 200 400 800

**Cordon
Volumes
8:00-9:00 AM — Fall 1964**

Source: NYCTA

All figures in thousands

LOWER MANHATTAN PLAN **2-36**

STATIONS CAPACITIES

While the number of cars which can be moved past a certain point in a given time determines overall capacity, the stations control whether this capacity can be used. There may be excess capacity on a line, but it means very little if the stations, which channel the people from the street into the cars, cannot process the requisite number of passengers. To determine existing utilization and possible future loading patterns, counts were made to develop means for quantifying station capacities.

These parameters were then checked in test stations and compared with those used by the Transit Authority. Based on the two minute scheduling of the Peak Period, each station was then calculated on the basis of the longest allowable headway. In all cases except the IRT Lexington Avenue Line, six (6) minutes was an acceptable maximum. On the Lexington Avenue Line, it was four (4) minutes due to small stations with balanced components.

For the initial capacities, each item was factored for two minutes. The lowest component at each station was then taken as the actual limit. In most cases, it was the turnstiles which limited the movements of potential riders.

Extending these for twenty (20) minute periods, a functioned factor of 85 percent was applied to allow for congestion at certain points within the station and actual differences in the headways.

The hourly capacities, against which the turnstile registrations were compared, were modified on the basis of line surge during the peak hour. In the Study Area, the total hourly line load is approximately 2.6 times the load for the Peak 20-Minute period. Applying this to the capacity figure for twenty (20) minutes gives the hourly capability, which is a better measure of probable limitations than a strict capacity figure.

The results are shown in Table 3.

STATION CAPACITY CRITERIA

Corridors and Passageways:

    0.33 persons/ft. width/second, or 1200 persons/hour.

Ramps:

    0.25 persons/ft. width/second, or 900 persons/hour.

Stairs:

    0.22 persons/ft. width/second, or 800 persons/hour.

Escalators:

	@90 fpm	@ 120 fpm
2'8"	4,000 persons	5,400 persons
4'0"	7,500 persons	10,000 persons

Turnstiles:

    Standard Bar Type - 35 persons per minute

    Revolving Gate   - 10 persons per minute

Platforms:

    Based on Net Area, 1.5 feet from platform edge, minus

        all stairways, stanchions, kiosks, etc.

    1 Line, Local or Express   -   0.30 persons/sq. ft.

    1 Line, Local and Express   -   0.25 persons/sq. ft.

    2 Lines or Directions   -   0.20 persons/sq. ft.

TABLE 3

STATION CAPACITIES

Name and Line	2Min	20Min	1Hour
Bowling Green IRT Lex	520	4,420	11,400
Broad Street BMT Nassau	1,020	8,670	22,600
Canal Street IRT 7Av	420	3,650	9,300
Canal Street IND 8Av	1,280	10,870	28,200
Canal Street BMT Bwy	420	3,650	9,300
Canal Street IRT Lex	420	3,650	9,300
Canal Street BMT Nassau	420	3,650	9,300
Chambers Street IRT 7Av	560	4,760	12,400
City Hall BMT Bwy	490	4,160	10,800
Cortlandt Street BMT Bwy	980	8,320	21,700
Cortlandt Street IRT 7Av	530	4,500	11,700
Franklin Street IRT 7Av	350	2,980	7,800
Rector Street BMT Bwy	420	3,650	9,300
Rector Street IRT 7Av NB	280	2,370	6,200
South Ferry IRT Lex/7Av	490	4,160	10,800
Wall Street IRT Lex	1,470	12,500	32,500
Wall Street IRT 7Av	1,260	10,700	27,800
Whitehall Street BMT Bwy	560	4,760	12,400

Interdivisional Transfer Stations

	2Min	20Min	1Hour
Brooklyn Bridge	1,290	11,000	28,600
Chambers/Park Place	1,490	12,700	32,900
Fulton Complex	3,900	33,200	86,500

STATION SERVICE AREAS

In an analysis of the subway system, the service area of each station is important because it is one of the determining factors of the level of service and, thus, has particular implications for the future that concern the amount and distribution of increased patronage should land use within the area be intensified.

Nationally, the standards are a five-minute walk at 300 feet per minute, or a straight-line distance of 1,500 feet. Conversion to airline distance on an attenuated grid street system gives a radius of 1,200 feet. This airline distance is a compromise, since it is possible to walk 1,500 feet in a straight line from a station and thus exceed the radius. On Figure 23, the five-minute walk is shown as a dashed line, the sum function of all of the stations in Lower Manhattan.

Because the Study Area has a heavy concentration of lines and stations, allowing wide latitude of choice, and because of the surface congestion during the peak periods, it was thought more realistic to examine each station on a more restricted basis.

Therefore, an airline distance of 800 feet was chosen as the standard. This is equivalent to a three-minute walk at 270 feet per minute. The inner, solid circles on Figure 23 show the coverage of each station under these conditions.

The map also shows the station choice available to the rider within the restricted walking distance. Measured from platform center, not the exits, these radii include the time spent negotiating the internal structure of the station. This tends to limit rather than extend the actual service areas.

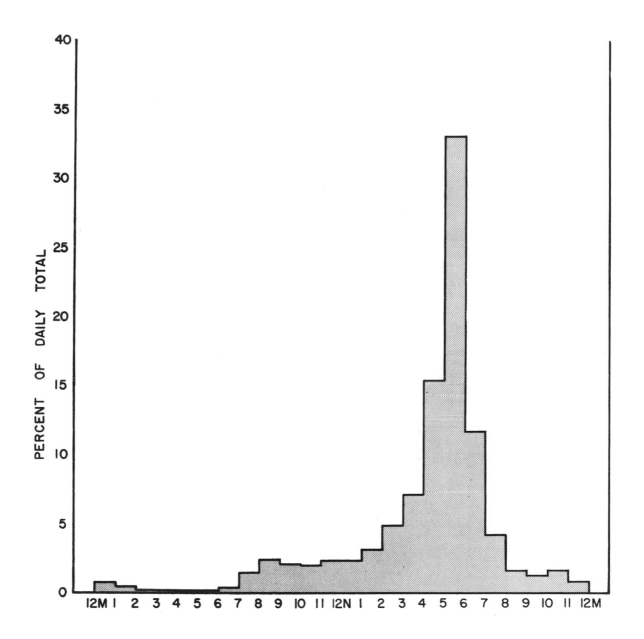

**Hourly Distribution
of
Turnstile Registrations**

CAR CAPACITIES

Since the psychological aspects of transit ridership are as important as the size of the cars in determining capacities, three (3) levels were developed and used in this study.

The first, the Theoretical Capacity, was based on the seating capacity and the free floor area of each type. To allocate the free area, a factor of 1.4 was applied, giving:

$$\text{Theoretical Capacity} = \text{No. of Seats} + (\text{Free Area}/1.4)$$

Type 28 (IRT)	44 Seated
	154 Standees
	198 Total Passengers

Type 16 (IND/BMT)	54 Seated
	233 Standees
	287 Total Passengers

Type 27/30	50 Seated
	232 Standees
	282 Total Passengers

This loading assumes sufficient time to pack the vehicle, a minimum of packages, etc., and the willingness of the riders to stand packed together, without any extra space. This capacity forms the upper limit, which can be approached but not exceeded.

Functional Capacity is the realistic limit of the system. It takes into consideration the variety of passenger size and shape, the many, hand-carried packages, and, particularly, the tendency for people to stand near the car doors in preparation for off-loading. A study of these factors produced a parameter of 0.85, which translates the Theoretical Capacity to the Functional level.

Functional Capacities are:

Type 28	$198 \times 0.85 = 168$ Passengers
Type 16	$287 \times 0.85 = 244$ Passengers
Type 27/30	$282 \times 0.85 = 240$ Passengers

At this level, it is barely possible to read a newspaper, but the maximum fifty (50) second station stop can be maintained and a certain amount of shifting in preparation for unloading tolerated.

Finally, in an attempt to equate some level of comfort, a third level of capacity was developed. This Comfort Loading accepts the psychological aspects of crowding and comfort which contribute to the decision-making process of whether to take a particular train, wait for another, or, perhaps, switch modes.

On the basis of actual car counts, it was found that at 70 percent of the Theoretical Capacity, or:

Type 28	$198 \times 0.70 = 139$ Passengers
Type 16	$287 \times 0.70 = 200$ Passengers
Type 27/30	$282 \times 0.70 = 197$ Passengers

there was a reasonable amount of space available for reading, moving, or preparing to get off.

These three capacities give a wide range of possible loadings. The Theoretical Load is primarily a design limit, while the Functional is an operational one. Any time that the Functional limit is exceeded, the system is being overloaded, and will tend to break down (slower speed, longer station stop, etc.). The Comfort Load is the practical maximum, the ideal level of service which should be the target of any program. When this loading is exceeded, it is an indication of definite problems, and a signal for long-range planning.

LINE CAPACITIES

The capacity of a line is determined by three factors: the capacities of the cars, the ability of the system to move cars, and the car-loading patterns within the trains. From the functional and comfort car capacities, the design limitations of the system, and loading patterns as reflected by station usage, three capacities were developed for each line.

The ability to move cars depends upon such operating characteristics as the signal system, switches, curvature and grade of track, and acceleration and deceleration rates of the vehicles. All lines in the system are mechanically capable of 90-second headways, but manual operation, extended station stops, and other factors necessitate the scheduling of 120-second headways during the peak periods. After discussion with the Transit Authority, this figure was chosen for use in this evaluation. It gives a capacity of 30 trains per track per hour, each of which was assumed to be composed of the maximum number of cars which the station platforms were capable of handling.

Development of capacity levels must take into consideration both possible and probable distributions of passengers. Due to stairway locations on the platforms and the tendency of people to move toward the center of the train, there is unused, undesirable space on every train, primarily in the first and last cars. Allowing for this, a factor of 0.85 was applied to the operational capacity to get a comfort loading, which, although somewhat arbitrary, reflects the actual amount of space utilization under present psychological conditions.

There are, therefore, three capacities for each line: a functional capacity which is an upper limit, exceeded only under peak-hour conditions when the need for transportation outweighs any comfort consideration; a comfort capacity which forms an optimal utilization level, embodying certain criteria of humaneness; and an operational loading which considers the comfort capacity in light of unequal car loadings.

The following are the line capacity figures developed to represent maximum utilization under the different loading criteria, and for use as measures of overcrowding.

Division/Line	20 minutes	1 hour
IRT Flushing/Queensboro Express/Local		
F/11	18.5	55.4
O/	15.3	45.8
C/	13.0	38.9
Lexington Avenue Express and Local		
F/10	16.8	50.4
O/10	13.9	41.7
C/10	11.8	35.4
7th Avenue Express		
F/9	15.1	45.4
O/9	12.5	37.5
C/9	10.6	31.9
7th Avenue Local		
F/8	13.4	40.3
O/8	11.1	33.3
C/8	9.4	28.3
IND – All Lines – Express and Local		
F/10	24.0	72.0
O/10	19.7	59.1
C/10	16.7	50.3
BMT 14th Street/Canarsie – Local		
Jamaica/Myrtle – Express/Local		
Broadway – Express		
F/8	19.2	57.6
O/8	15.8	47.4
C/8	13.4	40.3
4th Avenue – Local		
F/8	4/ 7.7	12/ 23.01
O/8	6.6	19.7
C/8	5.6	16.7

Division/Line		20 minutes		1 hour
BMT Astoria – Express/Local				
F/8	6/	11.5	18/	34.6
O/8		9.5		28.4
C/8		8.1		24.2
Broadway – Local				
F/8	7/	13.4	21/	38.4
O/8		11.1		33.3
C/8		9.4		28.3
Nassau Loop – via Bridge or Tunnel				
F/8	3/	5.8	9/	17.3
O/8		4.8		14.4
C/8		4.1		12.3

F/ – Functional Capacity
O/ – Operational Capacity
C/ – Comfort Capacity

/8 – Eight cars per Train
/9 – Nine cars per Train
/10 – Ten cars per Train
/11 – Eleven cars per Train

Normal loads are ten (10) trains per 20 min., 30 per hour.
   Any other case is noted: X/
Local/Express – Both utilize same track at cordon.
All passenger figures in thousands.

OTHER MASS TRANSIT FACILITIES

In addition to the subway system, Lower Manhattan may be reached via the PATH System, the surface bus system and the Staten Island Ferry. These contribute significantly to the total number of employees transported to the Study Area every day. While this study did not attempt to analyze them in depth, some data collection and evaluation did take place within the context of examining the overall transportation pattern.

The PATH System, operated by the Port of New York Authority, brings some 30,000 persons into the Hudson Terminal every day. Of these, about 18,000 arrive during the A.M. Peak Period. Since a separate PATH line runs up into Midtown, it can be assumed that the majority of these passengers are destined for jobs located in Lower Manhattan.

During the short period since its acquisition by the Port Authority, PATH service has been improved through the addition of new cars and improved scheduling. Plans call for a continuing increase in trains from New Jersey; and, with a new station in the World Trade Center, PATH will reach new levels of comfort and convenience, particularly at the Downtown terminal. Therefore, with the additional capacity provided by these improvements and the continued growth of the New Jersey sector, PATH can be expected to contribute significantly to the healthy growth of Lower Manhattan.

Surface bus service to the Downtown area is light. It provides an alternate mode for those who dislike the subway and is the only public facility available to those living inconveniently far from the subway. The Bronx and Manhattan Surface Operating Authority plans to increase service to Lower Manhattan if ridership should increase significantly above the present 15,000 passengers. Transit congestion makes surface relatively slow, but it is still more effective as a means of moving numbers of people than the private automobile. Figure 38 shows the routes presently served.

Staten Island is now connected to the other boroughs by the Verrazano Narrows Bridge, yet ridership on the ferries operated by the New York City Department of Marine and Aviation continues to increase. About 40,000 people are thus transported across the harbor each way during the average day, some 23,000 during the Peak Periods. Although the provision of a highway connection has increased usage of the Island as a residential area for those employed in Manhattan, the ferry is evidently necessary to meet the commutation needs of Island residents.

In comparison to the daily total ridership on the subway system, the 60,000 employees transported daily by the above facilities may seem insignificant. If one considers, however, that these 60,000 represent the average total employment of a city of 200,000 people, the importance of these ancillary facilities becomes clear.

SCALE: 0 200 400 800

Bus Routes

APPENDIX I

STRUCTURES OF PERMANENT VALUE

No part of New York City contains so complete a record of past urban achievement as Lower Manhattan. The City's historic and cultural heritage, as embodied in these many structures, should not only be safeguarded against further encroachment, but incorporated into the future downtown development, wherever possible.

For this reason an inventory of downtown's architectural and historic building stock was taken early in the study. Map 18 summarizes the result of this inventory, and was subsequently used in the development of the plan for the area. Particular attention was paid to those older buildings which, forming part of a group, create significant urban spaces and which stand together, on their own. An example is the group of buildings standing on the southern side of Fulton Street, between Front and South Streets.

The basis for this Map is shown in this Appendix. The buildings cited are taken from several sources: the Municipal Art Society, the Landmarks Preservation Commission, and the noted architectural historian, Ada Louise Huxtable. Still other buildings have been deemed worthy of preservation in the opinion of Consultants on the basis of extensive field observation.

Several of the buildings have been selected because they form part of an aesthetic and historic district. The very distinctiveness of these areas would be significantly impaired by their absence, although the buildings have little historical or architectural merit of themselves. Similarly, several buildings have been included because they are among the skyscraper structures which define the traditional lower Manhattan skyline.

Coherent areas and spaces are also shown on the map in two general categories:

a. The darker areas are those that are enclosed or semi-enclosed; they generally form "nodal" spatial units, pivotal points in the progression of downtown space.

b. The lighter areas are open-ended spaces between the "nodal" spaces; they are usually streets.

STRUCTURES OF PERMANENT VALUE

NO.	NAME OR ADDRESS	LMP	MUNICIPAL ART SOCIETY	LANDMARKS PRESERVATION COMMISSION	ADA LOUISE HUXTABLE	FORMS PART OF COHERENT AREA
1	Manhattan Savings Bank			x		
2	5th Pct. Police Station	x				x
3	Ch. of the Transfig.				x	
4	18 Bowery			x		x
5	Chatham Towers	x				
6	Chatham Green	x				
7	Mariners Temple			x	x	
8	Graveyard			x		
9	St. James Church		x		x	
10	St. James School			x		
11	Bklyn Br SW (proposed)	x				
12	181 Front Street			x	x	x
13	182-98 Front Street			x	x	x
14	171 John Street			x	x	x
15	2-18 Fulton Street			x	x	x
16	170 John Street			x	x	x
17	161-65 Front Street			x	x	x
18	156 Front Street			x	x	
19	Metal Exchange Bldg.		x		x	
20	139-51 Front Street			x	x	x
21	142-54 Front Street			x	x	x
22	136 Front Street			x	x	x
23	133 Front Street			x	x	x
24	130-134 Front Street			x	x	x
25	129 Front Street			x	x	x
26	96-110 Front Street			x	x	x
27	101 Front Street			x	x	x
28	94 Front Street			x	x	x
29	91-93 Front Street			x	x	x
30	1st Pct. Police Station			x		
31	76 Front Street			x	x	x
32	62-4 Front Street			x	x	x
33	55-61 Front Street			x	x	x
34	65-75 Front Street			x	x	x
35	44-54 Front Street			x	x	x
36	10 Hanover Square	x				x
37	Grace National Bank	x				x

STRUCTURES OF PERMANENT VALUE (Continued)

NO.	NAME OR ADDRESS	LMP	MUNICIPAL ART SOCIETY	LANDMARKS PRESERVATION COMMISSION	ADA LOUISE HUXTABLE	FORMS PART OF COHERENT AREA
38	2 Coenties Slip				x	x
39	62 Pearl Street				x	x
40	Fraunces Tavern		x	x	x	x
41	Furness House			x		x
42	32 Whitehall Street	x				x
43	Our Lady of the Rosary		x	x	x	x
44	Castle Clinton Man.		x	x	x	
45	U.S. Custom House		x	x	x	x
46	I Broadway			x		x
47	Cunard Building			x		x
48	22 West Street	x				x
49	26 Broadway	x				x
50	67-97 Pearl Street				x	x
51	India House		x	x		x
52	Lehman Building	x				x
53	Chemical Corn Exchange Bank	x				x
54	1st National City Bank	x				x
55	1st National City Bank		x	x	x	
56	J.P. Morgan & Co.		x			
57	N.Y. Stock Exchange		x	x		
58	71 Broadway	x				x
59	67 Greenwich Street			x	x	
60	94-96 Greenwich Street			x	x	
61	Trinity Church		x	x	x	x
62	Irving Trust Company	x				x
63	American Surety Co.		x			x
64	Bankers Trust Co.			x		x
65	U.S. Sub-Treasury Building		x	x	x	x
66	40 Wall Street	x		x		x
67	60 Wall Street	x				x
68	Chase Manhattan Bank	x				x
69	Equitable Building	x				x
70	Trinity Building	x				x
71	U.S. Realty Building	x				x
72	N.Y.U. Grd. Bus. Schl.	x				x
73	Thames Building	x				
74	134 Greenwich Street	x				
75	World Trade Center	x				x

STRUCTURES OF PERMANENT VALUE (Continued)

NO.	NAME OR ADDRESS	LMP	MUNICIPAL ART SOCIETY	LANDMARKS PRESERVATION COMMISSION	ADA LOUISE HUXTABLE	FORMS PART OF COHERENT AREA
76	Singer Building		x			x
77	140 Broadway	x				x
78	Chamber of Commerce		x	x		x
79	Federal Reserve Bank		x	x		x
80	John St. Meth. Ch.		x	x	x	x
81	Am. Tel. & Tel. Co.		x	x		x
82	St. Pauls Chapel		x	x	x	x
83	Bennet Building	x				
84	NY County Law Assn.		x	x		
85	Garrison Bldg.			x		
86	St. Peters Ch.		x	x	x	
87	N.Y. Telephone Co.		x			
88	Woolworth Building		x	x		x
89	City Hall		x	x	x	x
90	Surrogates Court			x		x
91	Municipal Building			x		x
92	U.S. Court House			x		x
93	N.Y. City Ct. House			x		
94	317 Broadway	x				x
95	319 Broadway	x				x
96	925-31 Broadway	x				x
97	217-27 Church Street	x				
98	151 W Broadway	x				
99	39-47 Worth Street	x				
100	65-85 Worth Street	x				
101	65-94 Leonard Street	x				x
102	Fire Batt. No. 2 Sta.			x		
103	363 Broadway	x				x
104	40-48 Leonard Street	x				
105	18-20 Leonard Street	x				
106	US Public Hlth Ser.	x				
107	Mercantile Exchange	x				
108	180 Franklin Street	x				
109	Powell Building	x				
110	158 Franklin St.	x				
111	154 Franklin St.	x				
112	3 N. Moore St.				x	
113	242 W. Broadway				x	
114	79-101 Laight Street	x				
115	63 Vestry Street	x				
116	34 White Street				x	x

STRUCTURES OF PERMANENT VALUE (Continued)

NO.	NAME OR ADDRESS	LMP	MUNICIPAL ART SOCIETY	LANDMARKS PRESERVATION COMMISSION	ADA LOUISE HUXTABLE	FORMS PART OF COHERENT AREA
117	31-65 Walker Street	x				x
118	382 Broadway	x				x
119	80 White Street	x				x
120	116-20 White Street				x	

3000-9999	5
10,000-11,999	6
12,000-13,999	7

APPENDIX II

COMPOSITE BLOCK EVALUATION

Deteremining the "quality" of each block can provide a relatively simple, objective method of determining the "soft" blocks in the area, which by nature of their location may be expected to develop shortly, or for which some development should be proposed. In either case, development might be expected to proceed more readily in blocks with a lower rating than those with a higher one.

A similar process, described in detail at the beginning of Chapter III, was used in the development (on a building-by-building basis) of the Life Expectancy Maps.

Ratings for each of the blocks are listed below. These ratings are a composite of the ratings for each of six individual criterion. Each of these criterion and their point value follow below.

1. Working Population   Point Value

0-1999	1
2000-3999	2
4000-5999	3
6000-7999	4

2. Building Height   Point Value

Majority of Structures less than 1-3 stories in height	1
3-6	2
6-9	3
9-12	4
12-15	5
15 and over	6

3. Building Age and Condition   Point Value

Majority of structures built prior to 1885, not fireproofed, not modernized	1
Majority of structures built prior to 1915, fireproofed not modernized.	2
Majority of structures built prior to 1915, fireproofed not modernized	3
Majority of structures built between 1915-45, not modernized	4
" " modernized since 1945	5
" " constructed since 1945	6

4. Those blocks which contain buildings of historical cultural or aesthetic significance as noted in Table have been assigned a point value of 4.

5. Those blocks whose structures regardless form part of a coherent area have been assigned a point value of 4.

6. <u>Assessed Valuation</u>   <u>Point Value</u>

Assessed Valuation	Point Value
0-99	1
100-199	2
200-299	3
300-399	4
400-499	5
500-599	6
600-699	7
700-799	8
800-899	9
900-	10

APPENDIX II

COMPOSITE BLOCK EVALUATION

BLOCK NO.	EMPLOYMENT	BLDG. HEIGHT	BUILDING AGE AND CONDITION	ARCH. SIGNIF-ICANCE	COHERENT AREA	ASSESSED VALUATION	COMPOSITE RATING
1	1	3	1			1	6
2	1	4	2			1	8
3	1	2	2			1	9
4	1	2	2			1	6
5	1	4	3			1	9
6	1	2	3			1	7
7	1	2	3			1	7
8	1	4	3			1	9
9	1	4	5			1	11
10	1	2	3			1	11
11	1	3	2	4		1	7
12	1	3	2			1	7
13	1	3	2			1	7
14	1	4	4	4		1	14
15	1	2	4			1	8
16	1	3	3			1	8
17	1						
18	1	4	6			1	12
19	1	2	2			1	6
20	1	3	6			1	11
21	1	2	3			1	7
22	1	2	3			1	7
23	1	4	4			1	10
24	1	2	1	4		1	9
25	1	2	3	4		1	11
26	1	3	2	4		1	11
27	1	3	3			1	8
28	1	4	2	4		1	12
29	1	3	3			1	8
30	1	2	3			1	7
31	1	2	2	4		1	10
32	1	3	2	4		1	11
33	1	2	3	4		1	11
34	1	4	6		4	1	16

APPENDIX II

COMPOSITE BLOCK EVALUATION

BLOCK NO.	EMPLOYMENT	BLDG. HEIGHT	BUILDING AGE AND CONDITION	ARCH. SIGNIF- ICANCE	COHERENT AREA	ASSESSED VALUATION	COMPOSITE RATING
35	3	6	6			2	17
36	1	3	3		4	1	12
37	1	2	2		4	1	10
38	1	2	2			1	6
39	1	2	2			1	6
40	1	2	3			1	7
41	1	2	8			1	12
42	1	4	8			3	16
43	1	4	5			1	11
44	3	6	5			8	22
45	1	2	3			1	7
46	1	2	2		4	1	10
47	3	6	5			10	24
48	2	3	3	4	4	1	17
49	1	2	3			1	7
50	1	2	4			1	8
51	1	2	2	4	4	1	14
52	1	2	2			1	6
53	1	3	2		4	1	11
54	1	3	3		4	1	12
55	1	3	5			2	11
56	1	2	4	4	4	1	16
57	1	2	3	4		1	11
58	2	3	3	4	4	1	17
59	2	5	4	4		2	17
60	1	2	1	4	4	1	13
61	1	2	3			1	7
62	1	4	8			4	17
63	1	2	3	4	4	1	15
64	1	2	3			1	7
65	2	3	4		4	1	14
66	1	2	3			1	7
67	1	3	4		4	1	13
68	1	2	3		4	1	11
69	2	3	4		4	1	14

APPENDIX II

COMPOSITE BLOCK EVALUATION

BLOCK NO.	EMPLOYMENT	BLDG. HEIGHT	BUILDING AGE AND CONDITION	ARCH. SIGNIFI-CANCE	COHERENT AREA	ASSESSED VALUATION	COMPOSITE RATING
70	1	2	3			1	7
71	1	3	4		4	1	13
72	2	5	6			3	16
73	1	3	6		4	1	15
74	3	6	8			4	21
75	6	5	7	4	4	3	27
76	3	4	6			2	15
77	3	3	5	4	4	2	21
78	St. Paul's Church						
79	2	6	7	4	4	4	27
80	1	2	4			2	9
81	3	5	5			3	16
82	1	2	3			1	7
83	1	3	2			1	7
84	1	3	3			1	8
85	1	5	4		4	2	16
86	2	5	5			2	14
87	1	2	1	4		1	9
88	1	3	6	4	4	2	20
89	2	6	7	4	4	3	26
90	0	2	1			1	5
91	1	4	2			1	8
92	3	5	7		4	2	21
93	2	6	7	4	4	2	25
94	3	5	5			1	14
95	1	2	5			1	9
96	1	3	1			1	6
97	2	6	7			2	17
98	1	3	3	4		1	12
99	3	6	6	4	4	4	27
100	3	4	5		4	2	18
101	4	5	5		4	2	24
102	5	6	7	4	4	2	28
103	1	2	5			1	9
104	1	2	4			1	8
105	1	2	2			1	6

APPENDIX II

COMPOSITE   BLOCK   EVALUATION

BLOCK NO.	EMPLOYMENT	BLDG. HEIGHT	BUILDING AGE AND CONDITION	ARCH. SIGNIF- ICANCE	COHERENT AREA	ASSESSED VALUATION	COMPOSITE RATING
106	1	2	3			1	7
107	1	2	2			1	6
108	1	2	3			1	7
109	1	3	2			1	7
110	1	2	2			1	6
111	1	2	6			1	10
112	2	5	7		4	2	20
113	2	3	3		4	1	13
114	1	3	3			1	8
115	2	4	4			1	11
116	1	3	6			2	12
117	3	5	7	4	4	4	27
118	1	3	6		4	1	15
119	2	6	7		4	2	21
120	1	4	3		4	1	13
121	1	3	4		4	1	13
122	3	5	7		4	3	22
123	3	4	7		4	3	21
124	2	3	6		4	2	17
125	2	4	5		4	1	16
126	1	2	2			1	6
127	1	2	3	4	4	1	15
128	1	2	2	4	4	1	14
129	2	4	4		4	2	16
130	3	4	6	4	4	2	23
131	2	6	6		4	2	20
132	3	5	5		4	3	20
133	1	2	2	4		1	10
134	1	2	3	4	4	1	15
135	1	3	2	4	4	1	15
136	1	4	4		4	2	15
137	1	3	3		4	1	12
138	1	6	8			3	18
139	1	3	4	4	4	1	17
140	1	2	4			1	8

APPENDIX II

COMPOSITE BLOCK EVALUATION

BLOCK NO.	EMPLOYMENT	BLDG. HEIGHT	BUILDING AGE AND CONDITION	ARCH. SIGNIFI- CANCE	COHERENT AREA	ASSESSED VALUATION	COMPOSITE RATING
141	3	5	4	4	4	2	22
142	2	4	5	4	4	4	23
143	1	6	5		4	3	19
144	3	5	8	4	4	4	28
145	7	2	5	4	4	7	29
146	7	6	8	4	4	8	37
147	3	4	6		4	3	20
148	5	6	5	4	4	3	27
149	6	6	8		4	5	29
150	1	2	2	4	4	1	14
151	1	2	1	4	4	1	13
152	1	2	2	4	4	1	14
153	1	3	1	4	4	1	14
154	4	6	7	4	4	6	31
155	7	4	7	4	4	6	32
156	5	5	6		4	3	23
157	1	4	4		4	2	15
158	1	2	5	4	4	1	17
159	2	6	7	4	4	2	25
160	3	5	7	4	4	6	29
161	4	5	6	4	4	6	29
162	4	6	7	4	4	6	31
163	1	4	7	4	4	3	23
164	2	4	6		4	5	21
165	8	6	6	4	4	3	31
166	3	5	6	4	4	3	25
167	3	5	5		4	2	19
168	2	6	7	4	4	7	30
169	7	5	7		4	3	26
170	3	5	7		4	3	22
171	2	6	3		4	4	19
172	1	5	4		4	2	16
173	2	4	4	4	4	2	20

APPENDIX II

COMPOSITE BLOCK EVALUATION

BLOCK NO.	EMPLOYMENT	BLDG. HEIGHT	BUILDING AGE AND CONDITION	ARCH. SIGNIFI- CANCE	COHERENT AREA	ASSESSED VALUATION	COMPO- SITE RATING
174	3	6	6		4	2	21
175	1	3	4		4	4	16
176	1	3	3		4	2	13
177	3	3	4	4	4	1	19
178	1	3	5		4	1	14
179	1	3	3		4	1	12
180	1	2	2		4	1	10
181	1	3	3	4	4	1	16
182	1	5	4		4	7	21
183	1	2	2	4	4	1	14
184	1	3	4	4	4	1	17
185	1	3	5		4	1	14
186	1	4	2	4	4	1	16
187	1	3	2		4	1	11
188	1	2	2	4	4	1	14
189	1	2	3	4	4	1	15
190	1	2	4	4	4	1	16
191	0	2	4			1	7
192	0	2	4	4	4	1	15
193	1	2	2	4	4	1	14
194	1	2	1	4	4	1	13
195	1	2	2	4	4	1	14
196	1	3	4		4	1	13
197	1	3	2		4	1	11
198	1	3	2		4	1	11
199	1	3	2			1	7
200	1	3	1			1	6
201	1	3	2	4	4	1	15
202	1	3	1	4	4	1	14
203	1	3	2	4		1	11
204	1	3	3	4		1	12
205	2	3	3		4	1	13
206	1	3	3		4	1	12
207	1	4	8			4*	17
208	1	5	5		4	4*	19

- 15 -

APPENDIX II

COMPOSITE BLOCK EVALUATION

BLOCK NO.	EMPLOYMENT	BLDG. HEIGHT	BUILDING AGE AND CONDITION	ARCH. SIGNIFI-CANCE	COHERENT AREA	ASSESSED VALUATION	COMPO-SITE RATING
209	2	3	3		4	1	13
210	1	4	5		4	2	16
211	2	4	5		4	4*	19
212	8	6	8	4	4	9*	38
213	1	6	5		4	4*	20
214	2	6	6		4	2	20
215	1	6	5		4	4*	20
216	3	6	7		4	4*	24

APPENDIX III

NEIGHBORHOOD DEVELOPMENT AREAS

(see Graphic 63)

The characteristics of the proposed waterfront development communities are shown in Graphic 63, Neighborhood Development Areas.

There are six Neighborhood Development Areas. Areas I- III are on the west side of the island. Areas IV-VI are on the east side.

The upland boundary of each Neighborhood Development Area is generally the line separating the "hard" Core area containing buildings with a long life expectancy from the low-intensity areas occupied by buildings with a shorter life expectancy which lie between the Core and the waterfront. This low-intensity area includes the Washington Street Renewal Area and other current redevelopment projects.

The basis for these development divisions are discussed elsewhere.

Inner and Outer Area

For purposes of analysis the Neighborhood Development Districts were divided into inner and outer areas. The inner area extends from the line of the "hard" core to the property line of South and West Streets. This land is predominantly in private ownership.

The Outer Areas extend from the South and West Street property lines to the outermost line of new development. They are now predominantly in public ownership.

Identity

Each Neighborhood Development Area is identified by the name of the street which terminates in its waterfront community plaza or the major new development adjacent to the plaza. The Chambers Street, World Trade Center and Rector Street Neighborhood Development Areas are on the West Side. The Stock Exchange, Wall Street and Fulton Street Neighborhood Development Areas are on the East Side.

Total Area

The total area of a Neighborhood Development Area is the inclusive area within its boundaries, including all public and private property, streets and wet areas.

Area of Sites to be Developed

The area of sites to be developed is the inclusive area of all land within each Neighborhood Development Area which can be reasonably expected to be redeveloped in the future, as indicated by Building Life Expectancy Map. They are the sum of all buildable sites within the Land Use Units in that Neighborhood Development Area.

New Uses

Basically, there were two categories of use proposed for the redeveloped land: office and residential. The third category -- "other uses" -- was a catch-all to account for both open space requirements and miscellaneous uses.

Under open space was included both passive and active reaction space, including parks, esplanades, pedestrian plazas, private play areas.

Miscellaneous uses include retail space, theatres, institutions, community facilities (schools, libraries, clinics, fire and police stations), and parking garages.

These uses are predominantly concentrated in the "outer areas", and occupy between 25 to 50 per cent of the area of the Land Use Units. By far the largest single element, in terms of land coverage, is open space.

In each Land Use Unit (see Graphic 62) a ratio of the three component elements was determined on a trial basis: for, example, in L.U.U. "A" in Zone VI, the ratio of office space to residential space was fixed at 3:1. This meant that three times as much area was given to office usage as was given to residential usage. After a complete "cycle" of figures, representing the entire downtown community, was assembled and appraised, many of these initial ratios were revised in light of various over-all feasability factors. In this particular case, the ratio was altered to 4:1, residential to office.

Space

Space calculations were made for future residential and office use.

Space was calculated for residential and office use on the basis of the land assigned to each of these uses in the initial programming procedure within each Land Use Unit as follows:

Gross Residential Space. The maximum allowable gross square feet for this use on every parcel assigned to residential use was determined by multiplying the land area available by an FAR of 12. This represents on FAR 10, the maximum allowable under the New York City Zoning Ordinance for residential use, plus the maximum allowable plaza bonus of 20%.

Gross Office Space. The same method was employed, using F.A.R. maximums of 12 and 18 (see Graphic 46) for the two office zoning categories designated. These represent the maximum allowable plaza bonus of 20%.

In cases where site area was restricted, and plazas were unfeasible, no bonus was included.

In the case of planned projects, such as the World Trade Center, Brooklyn Bridge Southwest, the New York Stock Exchange, the actual planned space figures were included. In many cases this represented floor area smaller than the allowable development.

Population

Present Employment

Existing population figures come from New York State Department of Labor survey of CBD employment, as modified and published in the 1963 Downtown Lower Manhattan Association report, Lower Manhattan. These figures were subsequently modified to account for recent trends (see Table V).

Future Employment

This figure is composed of two elements. First, that part of existing employment which is still presumed to work in the Land Use Unit -- consisting primarily of employees in buildings with a long "life expectancy." Second, the anticipated employment in new buildings.

This latter figure was arrived at by dividing the net office space (assumed to be 80% of gross space) by an assumed future average space-per-worker. Today this is believed to be around 150 square feet per worker; for purposes of this analysis (and based on current rates of change), the future figure is assumed to be 170 square feet per office worker.

Existing Residents

No significant residential population now lives in the future Neighborhood Development Areas.

Future Residents

The gross floor area figures arrived at earlier were converted into net floor area, assuming that the latter is roughly 80 per cent of the former, a commonly accepted ratio. This figure was divided by 350 square feet to determine the number of new residents. The city-wide average for middle-income housing is around 325 square feet per person; for luxury housing, 375 square feet per person.

Parking

The number of parking spaces was calculated on the basis of certain assumptions concerning planned residential and office usage. For a more detailed discussion, see Part II of this report.

The number of residential parking spaces is based on the New York City Zoning Ordinance which, for the R-10 class-ification, requires space for 40 per cent of the dwelling units.

Parking for new office space was based on the principle of providing off-street space for 3% of the working population in each Neighborhood Development Area. This represents the difference between the 2% of the employment popula-tion now being provided with parking space, and the World Trade Center's plan to provide space for 4% of its employees.

DWELLING UNIT CHARACTERISTICS

Dwelling Unit Size

An average dwelling unit size of 2.0 and 3.0 persons reflects existing dwelling unit size in Manhattan today, for high income and middle income families respectively. These figures have been adjusted upward to account for the attempt to provide a range of housing choices for different incomes within each Neighborhood Development Area.

Number of Dwelling Units

The total number of dwelling units was determined by dividing the total number of future residents in each Neighborhood Development Area, as determined above, by the average dwelling unit size.

Ratio of Children Per Dwelling Unit

The ratio of children per dwelling unit was based on data gathered by the School Section of the New York City Planning

Commission. This ratio is 0.1 child per upper income dwell-ing unit and 0.3 children in middle income dwelling units. For the purposes of calculation, each Neighborhood Develop-ment Area was assumed to consist of one predominant income group.

Number of Children

The number of children in each Neighborhood Development Area represents the number of dwelling units in that Area multiplied by the appropriate ratio of children per dwelling unit.

Active Recreation Areas

Standards vary so widely in this field that no single figure could be accepted to cover so complex a problem. One stand-ard used for urban situations by the National Recreation Asso-ciation calls for 2.5 acres of open space per thousand resi-dents, of which 1.25 acres is to be specifically devoted to act-ive recreation. This column lists the results of this equation. While the overall downtown total roughly corresponds to this requirement, there are of course substantial variations within each development unit. The stress, however, is on small units serving each local cluster of residential buildings (see Optimum Site Plan, Graphic 77).

Schools

To determine the number and type of schools, it was first neces-sary to determine the age distribution of prospective students. The following table, based on information supplied by the New York City Planning Department, gives the currently accepted breakdown distribution of prospective students for different income levels.

	Children/D.U.		
	High	Middle	Low
Primary School K-4	.07	.20	.55
Intermediate School 5-8	.07	.20	.55
High School 9-12	.06	.20	.55

For each Neighborhood Development Area, the number of probable students was calculated by multiplying the total number of dwelling units in that area by the factor assumed to represent the predominant income level in that Area.

To determine the number of schools necessary to house these students, it was necessary to determine the optimum size of each of these schools. For planning purposes, the School Section of the New York City Planning Department uses the figures below, which were adopted for our purposes.

Type	Optimum Size
Primary	1200 students
Intermediate	1800 students
High	4000 students

By these standards, a high school for the exclusive use of the new downtown residential community would not be required. However, if the new downtown demand is taken in conjunction with the need for new service for overcrowded schools in the area to the northeast, a downtown high school could well be justified.

Libraries

Standards used by the New York Public Library for planning new facilities was adopted. Two libraries are called for within the Neighborhood Development Areas, each serving a population of 35,000 - 50,000 persons, who live within a 1/2- 1 mile radius.

Commercial Space

Based on current experience in major U.S. cities, approximately 4,000 square feet of retail space has been provided for each 1,000 residents. It is assumed that each Neighborhood Development Area would contain its own retail facilities, located in large part on or adjoining the waterfront community plaza.

Residential Density

As shown in the Table (Graphic 63), the net residential density is defined as the density per acre of all land used exclu-

sively for residential use. Gross residential density (or "neighborhood density") is the density per acre of all newly developed land within each Neighborhood Development Area.

Subsequent detailed analysis of one prototype development district (the East Side Case Study) indicated that the de facto zoning resulting from these calculations would be better expressed as R-9 rather than R-10. That is to say, instead of analyzing each separate building parcel as a discrete unit (for which R-10 is an appropriate zoning category), the entire residential portion of the district should be treated as a single zoning entity, including open space, recreation area, etc. much of which has a public character. This would allow for a far more flexible program within the planning district.

The East Side development district (between Fulton and Wall Streets) is 1,060,000 square feet or 24.5 acres, of which the residential portion is calculated to be 19.5 acres. [1]

This means a residential density, for this portion, of 615 persons per acre (12,000 by 19.5).

The gross overall residential density (including the office area) is 490 persons per acre.

The residential density in the built-up residential area (excluding waterfront plaza and esplanade) is 830 persons per acre.

In calculating zoning density it is the first of these definitions -- the residential area of 19.5 acres -- that is the most appropriate. In this situation, assuming medium-to-luxury apartments averaging three rooms and around 900 sq. ft. per dwelling unit -- the most suitable category would be R-9. That is, dividing the total square footage required -- 5.5 million -- by the land available -- 850,000 square feet results in an FAR of 6.5, which is at the bottom of the range provided for in the R-9 Category.

[1] Since the office and residential portions of the district are no geographically exclusive of each other, this figure has only abstract significance. It was arrived at by dividing the designated residential and office floor areas (5.5 million and 2.2 million sq. ft.) by the respective FARs (12 and 18) to obtain a proportion of the "land" covered by each usage. 80% of 24.5 acres would thus be residential, that is, 19.5 acres.

APPENDIX IV

COST ESTIMATES: DEPRESSED HIGHWAY AND NEW LAND FILL

Highway

Fundamentally, the proposed highway solution is what is termed a "one basement" solution, which is to say, one level below grade.

The top of the proposed fill is at plus 7 (Borough Works Datum, Mean High Tide at Battery – 0), which is two – to – three feet above existing grade at the edge of the island. The new roadway, which requires 14 feet clearance and at least two feet of construction, will then be at elevation minus 9.

Good engineering practice requires that, in designing for hydrostatic pressure, water level is assumed at four feet above mean high tide -- to allow for exceptional high tides. Assuming roughly three feet of construction beneath the roadway, this would mean approximately 16 feet of construction below this maximum theoretical water level (around 1000 lbs. of uplift per square foot).

Since costs of such construction increase at a geometrical rate with each additional foot of depth below water-line, closer analysis may suggest a modification of the height of the fill as one of the variables in fixing the final highway-and-fill cost equation.

Placement of the highway past the bulkhead line should minimize its cost. No existing services need be interrupted, no relocation of utility lines is involved. Fill would be placed in the future highway location to assist in the compaction of the materials below. This fill would then be easily removed.

It is assumed that the highway will be built prior to the construction of the structures overhead. If, however, they are built simultaneously, the weight of the overhead structures would assist in overcoming the hydrostatic uplift, and reduce highway costs accordingly.

For purposes of approximation, the cost of the depressed highway has been assumed at $75 a square foot. This is based on the updated cost of the nearby Battery Underpass (a similar "one-basement" project), which checks out with projected costs for another comparable project, the Delaware Expressway in Philadelphia (around $45,000,000 per mile).

East Side

The new East Side Highway, which will be comprised of four depressed express lanes and four partially depressed service lanes, will thus cost around $7,000 per linear foot of waterfront development. Assuming a cost of $15 per square foot for land fill (including site preparation), the cost per linear foot of fill will be $5,000.

Thus, the cost of both highway and fill for the East Side will be around $12,000 per linear foot. Altogether, including the bed of South Street, some 530 square feet of land are now available for each linear foot, making the overall cost of the "created" land $22.50 per square foot.

The highway and fill for the East Side should therefore come to around $57,000,000.

West Side

The West Side highway will be comprised of six completely depressed lanes and four partially depressed lanes, costing $9,000 per linear foot of waterfront development. New fill will extend 560 feet into the river, costing $8,400 per linear foot of development. The cost of the highway and fill will thus be around $17,400 per linear foot.

Including West Street, some 790 feet of land will thus be available for each linear foot, and the cost will be roughly $22.00 per square foot. Highway and fill on the West Side should therefore cost around $132,000,000.

APPENDIX V

INTERVIEW SOURCES

In the course of this Study, a wide variety of people were interviewed, as a source of both experienced opinion and broader understanding.

Their contribution to this study has been substantial. The Downtown-Lower Manhattan Association, through its Executive Director, John Goodman, was helpful in arranging for many of the interviews.

Clark T. Abbott, Senior Engineer, Coverdale and Colpitts; John Quincy Adams, President, Manhattan Refrigerating Co.; Charles A. Agemian, General Comptroller, Chase Manhattan Bank; Edward Alcott, Chief, Planning Division, Port of New York Authority.

John R. Bermingham, Vice President, New York Stock Exchange; Gordon S. Braislin, Chairman, Braislin, Porter and Wheelock; William H. Braun, Assistant Vice-President, Federal Reserve Bank of New York; George F. Brunner, Vice President, Chicago Title Insurance Company; John D. Butt, former President, Downtown Lower Manhattan Association; Martin Beck, Director of Planning and Supervising Architect, New York University; A. W. J. Beeney, Director, Beekman-Downtown Hospital; Henry Birnbaum, Chief Librarian, Pace College; Murray H. Block, President, Borough of Manhattan Community College; Alan Burnham, Executive Director, Landmarks Preservation Commission of New York; Gordon Bunshaft, Partner, Skidmore, Owings and Merrill.

John L. Cataletto, Vice-President, Irving Trust; Howard O. Colgan, Jr., Partner, Milbank, Tweed, Hadly and McCloy; Halsey Cook, Executive Vice-President, First National City Bank; Robert Cronin, Charles Noyes Associates; Robert S. Curtiss, President, Horace S. Ely & Company.

Richard De Turk, Regional Plan Adjustment Section, Tri-State Transportation Commission; Edward DuMoulin, Vice President, Bache and Company; Ernest Durham, Associate, Skidmore, Owings and Merrill.

L. A. Erickson, V. President, First National City Bank.

Nicholas Farkas, Partner, Farkas and Barron; Lawrence Fitzpatrick, Vice-President, Cushman & Wakefield, Inc.; Paul H. Folwell, Partner, Millbank, Tweed, Hadley and McCloy; Edward Forrest, Data Processing Consultant, First National City Bank; Abraham Frank, N. Y. City Department of Markets; Dr. Carl Franzman, Port of New York Authority; Elbert K. Fretwell, Jr., Dean, Academic Development, City University of New York; Alan Friedberg, Vice President, Charles J. Greenthal & Co.; Jack Friedgut, Assistant Cashier, First National City Bank; Betty Friedman, Manager, Gov. Alfred E. Smith Houses; Vincent Furno, office of Edward Durell Stone.

B. Everett Gray, Consultant to National Shoe Manufacturers Association; James Green, Vice-President, American Telephone and Telegraph Corporation; Jordan Gruzen, Partner, Kelly & Gruzen.

William Harless, Security Analyst, Value Line Securities Service.

Robert Johnston, Partner, Mueser, Rutledge, Wentworth & Johnston.

Leon Kendall, Vice President, New York Stock Exchange; Kevin Kinney, New York Stock Exchange; Charles Kane, Consultant to Kidder, Peabody Company; Paul Kurzman, Staff Associate, Two Bridges Neighborhood Council.

William Lescaze, William Lescaze & Associates; Warren Lindquist, Associate of David Rockefeller; Chester S. Liptock, Second Vice-President, Chase Manhattan Bank; Malcolm P. Levy, Chief, Planning Division, The World Trade Center, Port of New York Authority; Warren Lovejoy, Port of New York Authority.

Philip J. Miller, Realtor; Harold M. Mills, Vice President, First National City Bank; Henry J. Muller, Vice President, First National City Bank; J.D. Massoletti, Sr., Vice-President Massoletti's Restaurant; Robert B. Mitchell, Consultant; Dr. Edward J. Mortola, President, Pace College.

John Nordlen, Vice-President, Director, Personnel, Continental Insurance Company.

Paul O'Keefe, Charles Noyes Associates; Ray. T. O'Keefe, Senior Vice President, Chase Manhattan Bank; Paul O'Brien, Executive Director of Printing Industries of Metropolitan New York.

Sanford Parker, Chief Economist, Fortune Magazine; Everett Post, Planning Manager, Federal Reserve Bank of New York; Anthony J. Peters, Executive Vice-President, Cushman & Wakefield, Inc.

Bernard Ramsay, Director of General Services, Merrill, Lynch, Pierce, Fenner and Smith; Chester Rapkin, Economic Consultant; John Reid, Director of Public Relations, Beekman-Downtown Hospital; William Reid; Murray Rossant, Editorial Department, The New York Times; Lewis Rudin, Rudin Management Company; Samuel Rudin, President, Rudin Management Company, Inc.

Peter Samton, Architect, Kelly and Gruzen; J. Walter Severinghaus, Partner, Skidmore, Owings & Merrill; Ted Simmis, Vice President, New York Telephone Company; Edgar J. Smith, President, Sixty Wall Tower, Inc.; Mrs. Nathan Strauss III, Executive Assistant to the Dean of Academic Development, City University of New York; Julien J. Studley, President, Julien J. Studley, Inc.; Arthur Sweeny, Consultant to Downtown Lower Manhattan Association, Vice-President, Braislin, Porter & Wheelock.

Stanley Tankel, Director, Planning Division, Regional Plan Association; Emanuel Tobier, Chief Economist, Regional Plan Association; Guy Tozzolli, Director, World Trade Department, Port of New York Authority.

Charles H. Upham, General Manager, John Wanamaker Department Store.

William Walker, Comptroller, U.S. Steel Corporation; Max Wechsler, Partner, Wechsler & Schimenti; Admiral John M. Will, President, American Export Lines- Isbrandtsen; John Wilson, Director of Marine Terminal Design, Port of New York Authority; Edward Wagner, President, Seaman's Savings Bank; Crawford Wheeler, Vice-President (retired), Chase Manhattan Bank; Grant W. Van Saun, Vice President, Irving Trust.

LIST OF GRAPHICS

A. LAND USE

No.	Title	No.	Title	No.	Title
1.	Existing Conditions Problems	15.	Subway Lines	30.	Generalized Land Acquisition Costs.
2.	Future Development: Opportunity Areas	16.	Employment Inventory:- 1965 (With Selected Future Developments)	31.	Maximum Land Cost Allowable for Specified Rates of Return for Selected Building Types
3.	Manhattan CBD: Functional Areas - 1950	17.	Functional Areas: Distribution of Chinese-American Population.	32.	Section Through World Trade Center: Looking North
4.	Manhattan CBD: Functional Areas - 1965	18.	Areas and Structures of Permanent Value.	33.	Waterfront Development: World Trade Center
5.	Growth of Office Space in Manhattan CBD	19.	Pier Use and Condition	34.	Civic Center: Problems and Prospects
6.	Gross National Product and N.Y. Stock Exchange Volume (Projected to 1975)	20.	Building Age and Condition	35.	Civic Center: Brooklyn Bridge Traffic Distribution (3-9 AM)
7.	Generalized Functional Areas: Present	21.	Area Evaluation (by block)	36.	Civic Center:(Network Area)
8.	Functional Areas	22.	Building Life Expectancy	37.	Civic Center:(Network Area)
9.	Financial Community	23.	Building Life Expectancy (Long Term)	38.	Civic Center: Traffic Assignments
10.	Functional Areas: "Northwest" Goods Handling Area	24.	Construction and Modernization Since 1946	39.	Civic Center: Underpass Alternates
11.	Commuter Travel Patterns: East Midtown and Lower Manhattan	25.	Topography	40.	Civic Center: Section thru Underpass.
12.	Place of Residence: East Midtown and Lower Manhattan.	26.	Waterfront: Historical Development 1650-1980	41.	Land Use: Basic Concepts
13.	Place of Employment.	27.	Growth of Manhattan Island, 1650-1980.	42.	Future Land Use
14.	Downtown Employment: Classification by Place of Residence.	28.	Cross-Island Sections: Looking North at Wall Street 1950-1980	43.	Generalized Functional Areas: Future.
		29.	Offshore Subsurface Conditions		

LIST OF GRAPHICS (Continued)

No. Title

44. Circulation System I

45. Distribution of Employees and Residents- East Mid-town Manhattan

46. Present Zoning

47. Pedestrian System

48. Pedestrian System: Broad-Nassau Route

49. Waterfront Development: Highway Alternatives.

50. Proposed Highway Relocation

51. Waterfront Development: New Highway Alignment

52. Waterfront Development: New Highway and Proposed Land Fill

53. Waterfront Development: New Highway and Service Areas

54. Circulation System II

55. Waterfront Development: Circulation System

56. Waterfront Development: Cutaway Section of Typical Unit

57. Waterfront Development

58. Plan Development: Immediate action

59. Plan Development: First Stage

No. Title

60. Plan Development: Second Stage

61. Plan Development: Third Stage

62. Land Use Zones and Units

63. Waterfront Development Districts: Program Estimates

64. Waterfront Development: Population and Dwelling Units

65. Prototype Development Sequence: I - Planned Development District.

66. Prototype Development Sequence: II - Existing Conditions

67. Prototype Development Sequence: III - Inland Site Organization

68. Prototype Development Sequence: IV - Public Construction (1)

69. Prototype Development Sequence: V- Public Construction (2)

70. Prototype Development Sequence: VI - Private Construction

71. Prototype Development Sequence: VII- Costs and Figures

72. Prototype Development Sequence: VIII - Program and Controls

No. Title

73. Prototype Development Sequence: IX Optimum Development

74. Rates of Change: Goal Achievement Levels

75. Action Choices Over Time

76. Site Development: Stage I

77. Optimum Site Plan

78. Special Functions and Services

79. Pedestrian System - Wall Street

LIST OF GRAPHICS (Continued)

B. TRANSPORTATION

Facing   Regional Highway System

Facing   Regional Rail System

2-1   Existing Street System

2-2   Existing Traffic Flow – 8:00 – 9:00 A.M.

2-3   Existing Traffic Flow – 4:30 – 5:30 P.M.

2-4   Peak Hour Intersection Approach Volumes and Capacities with Existing Parking Practice

2-5   Peak Hour Intersection Approach Volumes and Capacities and Existing Parking Restrictions

2-6   Travel Speed and Delay

2-7   Loading Docks and Side- walk Elevators

2-8   Traffic Volumes with Parked Trucks

2-9   Pedestrian Volumes with Parked Trucks

2-10   Pedestrian Densities with Parked Trucks

2-11   Street System Study Map

2-12   Network Coding Key

2-13   Network Key Map

2-14   Projected Traffic Flow-8:00- 9:00 A.M. 1970-1975

2-15   Projected Traffic Flow – 8:00 - 9:00 A.M. 1990-2010

2-16   Proposed Circulation System

2-17   Rendering of Broad and Wall Streets – Open-Sky Subway Station

2-18   Rendering of Nassau Street Arcading and Intra-bus

2-19   Subway Trip End Distribution

2-20   Subway Station Utilization – 1965

2-21   Subway Station Utilization – 1960- 1965

2-22   Station Service Areas – Man- hattan

2-23   Station Service Areas – Lower Manhattan

2-24   Subway Improvements Under Construction

2-25   Proposed Subway Construction

APPENDIX A

2-26

2-27

2-28   Traffic Volume Counts

2-29

2-30   Street Capacity Curves

2-31   Parking Study Key Map

2-32   Parking Lot Utilization (Part I) Parking Lot Utilization (Part II)

2-33   Goods and Services Study – Parked Trucks

2-34   Pedestrian Door Counts

APPENDIX B

2-35   Subway Cordons – Manhattan

2-36   Subway Cordons – Lower Manhattan

2-37   Hourly Distribution of Turnstile Regis- trations

2-38   Bus Routes

LIST OF TABLES

A. LAND USE

TABLE I   Northwest Lower Manhattan: Summary Tabulation of Estimated Employment by Function .

TABLE II   Estimates of Employment in the Lower Manhattan Financial District, 1965-1985.

TABLE III   Percentages of Persons Employed in Selected Areas of CBD by Residential Area.

TABLE IV   Percentages of Persons Living in Counties of Metropolitan Region Employed in Selected Areas of CBD.

TABLE V   Working Population- Estimates and Projections

TABLE VI   Population Estimates by Function

TABLE VII   Future Office Space-Estimates

TABLE VIII   East Side Case Study: Estimated Property Acquisition and Site Preparation Costs

TABLE IX   East Side Case Study: Estimated Land Values Generated by Proposed Uses (I)

TABLE X   East Side Case Study: Estimated Land Values Generated by Proposed Uses (II)

TABLE XI   East Side Case Study: Estimated Cost, Value and Real Property Tax Return.

B. TRANSPORTATION

TABLE I   Trip Attraction and Production for Lower Manhattan

TABLE 2   Comparison of A.M. Peak Hour Traffic Flows at Different Stages for Lower Manhattan Study Area

TABLE 3   Comparison of A.M. Peak Hour Vehicle Miles and Vehicle Hours for Lower Manhattan Study

TABLE 4   Estimated Daily Costs -- Intra-Bus System

TABLE 5   Subway Station Load/Capacity -- Peak Hour -- Spring, 1965

TABLE 6   Subway Load/Capacity at Major Cordons

APPENDIX A

TABLE I   Intersection Approach Volumes and Capacities

APPENDIX B

TABLE I   Turnstile Registration, 1960-65 , Lower Manhattan

TABLE 2   Turnstile Registration, 1960-65, Midtown

TABLE 3   Station Capacities

ORGANIZATION OF THE STUDY

This study was conducted by three firms, serving as Consultants to the Department of City Planning. It was begun in March 1965 and completed in May, 1966.

The work was done within the context of the full participation and assistance of the staff of the Department of City Planning. Its director, William F. R. Ballard, personally guided the study throughout its length, providing both ideas and leadership.

Mr. Richard K. Bernstein, the Department's Executive Director, and Mr. Alan K. Sloan, the Assistant Executive Director, assisted in the overall development of the study.

Mr. Jack C. Smith, Special Consultant to the Department of City Planning, had special supervisory responsibility for the Lower Manhattan Plan.

Mr. Joseph Leiper, Director of Transportation Planning, supervised the development of the transportation side of the study.

The first series of analytical maps of Lower Manhattan were prepared by the Department of City Planning under the direction of Mr. Arthur Wrubel, who served as coordinator with related city agencies, and, as the Department's Project Manager, worked closely with the Consultants.

Among other members of the Department's staff who were particularly helpful at various critical points were Irving Ashworth, Ralph Field, Edwin Friedman, Harvey Gordon, Millard Humstone, Lebyl Kahn and Adolph Oppenheim.

In a still larger context, the Report is based on the substantial contribution and support of many City departments and agencies, in particular the Departments of Traffic, Parks, Highways, and Public Works and the Transit Authority. The help given by the Housing and Redevelopment Board, an agency heavily involved in the downtown area, was also very important to the study, as was the help of the office of the Borough President.

The transportation phase of the study benefited from the guidance of a special group established for this study -- the Street System Technical Committee for Lower Manhattan -- composed of representatives of the Departments of Traffic, Public Works, Highways, the Borough President's Office and the New York City Transit Authority.

Among civic and business organizations, the cooperation of the Regional Plan Association and the Downtown - Lower Manhattan Association was of particular importance -- the former for helping pinpoint significant regional trends, and the latter for having prepared the basic groundwork for this Report in its two earlier studies of 1957 and 1963. Discussions with the DLMA were also helpful throughout the length of the study.

The Port of New York Authority and the Tri - State Transportation Commission also lent their great technical and professional support.

PARTICIPATING   GROUPS

Wallace, McHarg, Roberts & Todd,
                Architects & Planners
Whittlesey, Conklin & Rossant,
                Architects & Planners

Paul Willen, Project Director
Marvin Richman, Senior Planner

Richard Dybvig
Theodore Lundy
Michael John Pittas

Charles D. Laidlow
Scott Killinger
Margaret Porter

Donald Kvares

Alan M. Voorhees and Associates,
                Transportation & Planning Consultants

David W. Schoppert, Partner-in-Charge.

Erich Ch. Boppart
John F. Callow
William J. Tierney, III

Jerry Currier
Keith Graham
Thomas Wagner

New York City Department of City Planning

William F. R. Ballard, Director
Richard K. Bernstein, Executive Director
Alan K. Sloan, Assistant Executive Director, Program Coordinator

Jack C . Smith, Special Consultant to the Department of City Planning
Samuel Joroff,   Director of Special Area Planning
Joseph Leiper,   Director of Transportation Planning
Arthur Wrubel, Project Manager